On the
way to
Fuller
Koinonia

On the way to Fuller Koinonia

EDITED BY
THOMAS F BEST AND
GÜNTHER GASSMANN

Faith and Order Paper no. 166
WCC Publications, Geneva

Cover design: Edwin Hassink

ISBN 2-8254-1127-2

© 1994 WCC Publications, World Council of Churches,
150 route de Ferney, 1211 Geneva 2, Switzerland

Printed in Switzerland

TABLE OF CONTENTS

PREFACE

A call, a vision, and a hope were expressed by the theme of the fifth world conference on Faith and Order: "Towards Koinonia in Faith, Life and Witness". Thirty years after the last Faith and Order world conference at Montreal in 1963 participants from all parts of the world and all Christian traditions met from 3 to 14 August 1993 to evaluate the achievements of the last decades, discuss the still-existing barriers to the visible unity and full koinonia of the church of Jesus Christ, and indicate directions and themes for the future work of the Commission on Faith and Order within the World Council of Churches and the wider ecumenical movement.

The Message and four section reports from the world conference were already published in September 1993, four weeks after the closing of the world conference (see *Fifth World Conference on Faith and Order, Santiago de Compostela 1993: Message, Section Reports, Discussion Paper*, Faith and Order paper no. 164, Geneva, WCC, 1993). The preparation of the present comprehensive report needed more time, especially since some of the texts were received only in November 1993. I am very grateful to my colleague, the Rev. Dr Thomas F. Best, who untiringly struggled — and succeeded — with the difficult task of editing such an extensive volume.

The publication of this full report gives us again occasion to thank all who have contributed to the preparation, implementation and follow-up of the world conference. To single out only one person, it is certainly Dr Mary Tanner, moderator of the Faith and Order Commission, who deserves great praise and thanks. With immense spiritual and physical energy she kept the preparations for the world conference moving forward, and acted as gracious, determined and fully-engaged leader during the conference itself. She was supported by her co-moderators, the other members of the Faith and Order Standing Commission, and my colleagues in the relatively small Geneva Faith and Order staff. For over two years this staff had to carry an extremely heavy work-load — a load which has now become considerably lighter with the publication of the reports of the world conference in different languages. We would also like to thank especially the many churches without whose encouragement, and generous financial contributions, the world conference would not have been possible.

It is our wish and expectation that also through this report the experiences, insights and hopes of the fifth world conference on Faith and Order will encourage and sustain us in our growing koinonia in the ecumenical movement, and strengthen our commitment to continue faithfully on our ecumenical pilgrimage.

> Günther Gassmann
> (North Elbian Evangelical Lutheran Church, Germany)
> Director of the Secretariat
> Faith and Order Commission

EDITORIAL INTRODUCTION

This book is the official record of the fifth world conference on Faith and Order held at Santiago de Compostela, Spain, in August 1993. Its aim is to document, as clearly as is possible for such a complex event, both the life and work of the meeting itself and the results which it achieved.

This report now joins those from the first four world conferences on Faith and Order[1] as a summary, unique for its own time, of the churches' search for visible unity and their vision of the next necessary steps on the ecumenical pilgrimage. The purpose of this brief editorial introduction is to indicate how this report is organized, and the nature of the texts which are included within it.

The first major division of the volume documents the speeches, papers and sermons presented at the world conference and, where appropriate, records the reactions of the conference in plenary session. All the speeches and papers given in plenary are included, except for a very few for which no written texts were available. In presenting this material we have followed a topical arrangement, grouping together the plenary papers and discussion on each area, for example on "The Biblical Witness to Koinonia" or on the conference theme, "Towards Koinonia in Faith, Life and Witness", and its sub-themes. Each area begins with an introductory statement indicating the plenaries which were devoted to this subject, their moderators, the names of all persons who made presentations, and any events of special note which occurred. The relevant papers are then printed, followed by an account of any plenary discussion which they enjoyed. Readers will note that such discussion had occasionally to be postponed to a later plenary and that, due to limitations of time, it was not possible to discuss in plenary all the papers which were presented.

Given the importance which worship assumed within the life of the world conference, it is only appropriate that we should include the sermons preached at the opening and closing services, as well as at the eucharistic service brought by the Spanish WCC (Protestant) member churches and at the Orthodox and the Roman Catholic vespers. The biblical expositions for the world conference have already been published[2] and are available directly from the Faith and Order secretariat. Another important element in the experience of the world conference, our interaction with the complex heritage from the Spanish context in which we met, is reflected in the record of the plenary on "Spain: Its Faith, People and Life".

Since the meeting several authors have suggested corrections or slight revisions to their papers, generally reflecting their actual delivery of the text, and these changes have been incorporated into the versions printed here. Apart from this, in preparing the texts for publication editorial work has been kept to a minimum. In particular there has been no attempt to introduce an artificial evenness of tone. Indeed, we hope that the rich variety of backgrounds and perspectives within the Faith and Order Commission itself, and in the world conference as a whole, can become visible in the pages of this book.

The second major division of the volume documents the written results produced in Santiago de Compostela and the reactions of the conference in plenary session, including formal actions. An introduction, account of plenary discussion, and record of motion and vote document the process by which the world conference formally adopted the Message. A similar sequence records the process by which the four section reports, each having been adopted by the section which produced it, were "commended to the churches for their study and action and to the Plenary Commission of Faith and Order for its future work". We have also printed the discussion paper once again, as it formed the central preparatory document for the world conference and is complementary to the section reports.

The volume concludes with several appendices. The first contains some of the messages which were received by the world conference. The messages of congratulations and of hope for our work in Santiago de Compostela came from the Archbishop of Canterbury, the Ecumenical Patriarch, the Pope, the Moscow Patriarch, the World Alliance of Reformed Churches, the Conference of European Churches, the Religious Society of Friends, London Yearly Meeting, and the Ecumenical Women's Synod of the Netherlands. They were presented at various points throughout the world conference, in plenaries VII, VIII, IX, X, and XV. Regrettably it has not been possible to print all of these messages; those which have been included come from larger, worldwide Christian bodies. They are printed in the order in which they were presented in plenary.

Other appendices summarize in convenient form the major elements of the world conference (the sequence of plenaries and their content, the worship and Bible study events, and the documents and materials which were produced for the meeting). Still others record the membership of the Faith and Order Commission, and the by-laws under which Faith and Order was operating at the time of the fifth world conference.

The introductions to the various plenaries, together with the accounts of plenary discussions and the records of formal actions taken, form the minutes of the fifth world conference on Faith and Order. These minutes are based upon the records kept by the official conference minuters, Stephen Cranford and Colin Davey, to whose detailed and careful work we are deeply indebted. As it has not been practicable to print their record in its entirety, I have summarized and ordered the material to form the present accounts of the plenary discussions (the occasional quotations are taken directly from their record). These summaries, while not exhaustive, do intend to give an accurate indication of the range of topics addressed in the interventions, and the central points which were made.

It is a pleasant duty to thank all those who have contributed to this volume. This includes first the authors of the speeches, papers, sermons, Message and reports, and the conference minuters. I am grateful also to Mary Tanner and Günther Gassmann for their helpful suggestions about the plenary summaries, though of course the responsibility for their final form rests with me. Lastly, thanks are due to the WCC publications staff for its energy and expertise in dealing with such a complicated manuscript.

These, then, are the *words* of the fifth world conference on Faith and Order – what we said to one another, what we heard from one another, in Santiago de Compostela. In the face of so many weighty words, may I be permitted a parting plea for the *spirit* of Santiago, for a reading of this book which looks beyond the words, to the deeper source and basis of all our ecumenical work? For even as we spoke and reasoned and argued in Santiago de Compostela we were aware that unity will come, finally, not through our own efforts but as God's gracious gift. We knew that there is something which holds us together even when the words run out, or become too difficult to say, or when words have been spoken which were better left unsaid.

This is why this book should finally be read in the spirit of the world conference prayer. This prayer, offered from our Santiago preparations process to the ecumenical movement as a whole, was said often during the world conference and has continued to nourish and sustain many around the world in their work for Christian unity:

O God, holy and eternal Trinity,
we pray for your Church in all the world.
Sanctify its life; renew its worship;
empower its witness; heal its divisions;
make visible its unity.

Lead us, with all our brothers and sisters,
towards communion in faith, life and witness
so that, united in one body by the one Spirit,
we may together witness to the perfect unity
of your love.

Amen.

It is the spirit of this prayer which breathes life into the words of the world conference and it is in this spirit that we offer this volume, trusting that it will serve the churches and Christians well in their continued journey together towards the visible unity of Christ's church.

Thomas F. Best
(Disciples of Christ, USA)
Executive Secretary in the Secretariat
Faith and Order Commission

NOTES

[1] For the reports of previous world conferences see: H.N. Bate ed., *Faith and Order: Proceedings of the World Conference, Lausanne, August 3-21, 1927*, London, SCM, 1927; Leonard Hodgson ed., *The Second World Conference on Faith and Order: Edinburgh 1937*, New York, MacMillan, 1938; Oliver S. Tomkins ed., *The Third World Conference on Faith and Order held at Lund, August 15th to 28th, 1952*, London, SCM, 1953; P.C. Rodger & L. Vischer eds, *The Fourth World Conference on Faith and Order: The Report from Montreal, 1963*, Faith and Order paper no. 42, London, SCM, 1964.
[2] Frances M. Young, *All of You Are One in Christ Jesus*, Geneva, Faith and Order Commission, 1993.

AN EXPERIENCE OF KOINONIA:
IMPRESSIONS OF THE FIFTH WORLD CONFERENCE
ON FAITH AND ORDER

Guests in Santiago de Compostela

The fifth world conference on Faith and Order took place in a famous historical pilgrimage city dedicated to the memory of St James the Apostle. The atmosphere in the city was charged; as the saint's birthday (25 July) fell on a Sunday, 1993 had been declared a "holy year" and the religious and civic life of Santiago de Compostela was even more intense than usual. The Faith and Order world conference met in the midst of the old town and the participants mingled with the crowds of pilgrims and tourists on the narrow streets. Many of the world conference activities, including the section and group meetings and morning and evening worship, and most of the administrative functions, were located in the impressive Seminario Mayor with its wonderful cloisters and grandiose staircases. In stark contrast to this was the sports hall of the Colegio La Salle, a brisk ten-minute walk away, where the conference plenary sessions were held; this offered a plain, but spacious and practical, setting for theological reflection and discussion.

That we could use these buildings for our meetings; that they were also available as accommodations for our participants; that we could celebrate our opening worship in the cathedral of St James, morning and evening services in the large chapel of the Seminario Mayor, and other services in the Franciscan church; that all this was offered practically free of charge — these were only some of the expressions of hospitality extended to Faith and Order by the Roman Catholic Archbishop of Santiago de Compostela, Dr Antonio María Rouco Varela, and other officials in the name of their church. For this church, and for the town and region of Galicia, the world conference constituted an encounter with worldwide and ecumenical Christianity in a city which was exclusively Roman Catholic. It was a historic contact which created much interest among the city's inhabitants and received much attention in the media. For participants as well as inhabitants, for guests as well as hosts, this was a fascinating experience, heightened by the awareness that it would have been quite impossible only thirty years ago.

Seen in this light, the fact that the world conference met at this place was also a powerful sign of a changed ecumenical situation, reflecting a growth of closer relationships also with the worldwide Roman Catholic Church. This new situation also made it possible that some darker aspects of Spanish history connected with Santiago de Compostela could be raised in a plenary session by a Spanish Protestant (Anglican) pastor in an open, critical and yet pastoral way.

The participants

Some four hundred participants had made their way to Santiago de Compostela. They came with a wide variety of functions and assignments: as delegates, official guests, representatives of local churches, speakers, representatives of Christian World Communions, consultants, "younger theologians", stewards and staff. There could of course have been many more participants; and it was a pity that, because of lack of space, the many requests from persons hoping to come to Santiago de Compostela as observers or accredited visitors had to be refused. On the other hand, given the difficulty of communicating the issues and work of a Faith and Order conference to a larger public, it was surprising and encouraging that more than seventy journalists from all over the world were on hand to cover the event.

The changed ecumenical scene found a most positive expression also in the composition of those who took part in this world conference. This was especially clear by comparison with the last world conference on Faith and Order held thirty years ago in Montreal in 1963. In 1993 in Santiago de Compostela a much larger proportion of the participants came from the southern hemisphere. The Orthodox delegates, consultants and younger theologians formed now the largest confessional group, followed by the Presbyterians. Over 30 percent of those in these three official groups of participants were women, compared with the three (!) women at Montreal in 1963. Since the Roman Catholic Church is officially represented on the Faith and Order Commission and in its work since 1968, it was only natural that this church was now for the first time officially involved in a worldwide ecumenical gathering. In order to introduce a new generation into the work and task of Faith and Order, a larger group of younger theologians had been invited to the world conference. This initiative was very much appreciated by all participants and welcomed as an expression of an ongoing strategy to be pursued in the years ahead. In addition we were graced by an energetic group of stewards with many gifts both theological and practical. The thanks extended to them in one plenary session was heartfelt indeed. Finally, a new step was the inclusion also of theologians from Evangelical and Pentecostal churches and movements; this too should be continued and broadened during the coming years.

The programme of the world conference

On the evening of Wednesday, 4 August 1993, the participants — surrounded by a large congregation of pilgrims and residents of Santiago de Compostela — gathered in the cathedral of St James for the opening worship service. The Archbishop of Tarragona, H.E. Ramon Torella Cascante, preached, the Archbishop of Santiago de Compostela presided, and the officers and some Faith and Order commissioners led the various sections of the liturgy, with the congregation singing hymns from many different parts of the world. All this was certainly a "premiere" in this cathedral. The opening plenary session of the world conference started with a brief act of prayer. This included (as did the opening worship) words from the previous world conferences on Faith and Order, recalling us to our identity as a movement of the churches towards visible unity. Five banners were brought forward, recalling the sites of the five world conferences: Lausanne 1927, Edinburgh 1937, Lund 1952, Montreal 1963, and now Santiago de Compostela 1993. The conference was opened by Faith and Order moderator Dr Mary Tanner, and words of welcome were extended by the local archbishop, H.E. Antonio María Rouco Varela, Bishop Arturo Sanchez of the Spanish Reformed Episcopal Church (Anglican), Rev. Julio R. Asensio, synod president of the permanent commission of the Spanish Evangelical Church (Reformed), and by leading representatives of the city and the province of Galicia, including the deputy mayor of Santiago de

Compostela and Don Manuel Fraga Iribome, president of the Xunta of Galicia. At one dramatic and colourful point the proceedings were "interrupted" by a troop of bagpipers, welcoming us with this traditional instrument so typical of the culture of Galicia.

The world conference began its work in several plenary sessions with presentations by the Faith and Order moderator and director, and on the biblical witness to koinonia and the conference theme and sub-themes. There was some chance for response and reaction in plenary to these papers (though more time could certainly have been used for discussion of these and later presentations). The conference then divided into four sections. Of these (1) dealt with the theme, koinonia/communion, and the others with the sub-themes: (2) koinonia in confessing the one apostolic faith, (3) koinonia in sharing a common life with Christ, and (4) koinonia in the calling to common witness for a renewed world. Each of the four sections divided into four or five working groups; after one day of reflection these groups presented their reports to the sections. On the basis of these group texts a report was elaborated which, after discussion and revision, was adopted by the section as a whole. In this process the preparatory paper *Towards Koinonia in Faith, Life and Witness*,[1] which had been developed over the previous two years and reviewed at a series of regional meetings around the world, was regarded as a most helpful tool for the discussions.

Excursions to monasteries in different parts of Galicia on Sunday, 8 August 1993, and a plenary session with presentations by Spanish Protestant and Roman Catholic representatives on Spanish church history and ecumenical relations, helped partici-pants gain a better understanding of the complex religious, cultural and social context in which they were guests for eleven or more days. Another feature of the programme was a set of regional meetings in which participants discussed the implications of the conference theme in light of the distinctive issues and perspectives of various parts of the world. These meetings echoed those held in the various regions as part of the world conference preparatory process in calling for greater involvement of the regions in defining and carrying out the work of Faith and Order.

The concluding plenary sessions on Friday, 13 August, dealt with the future of the ecumenical movement and with the role and calling of Faith and Order in serving this movement. During these sessions the reports of the sections were presented and received and the world conference Message was discussed and, after two revisions, adopted. Having concluded their work, and thanks having been expressed to all who had helped to bring this world conference safely and efficiently to its conclusion, the participants assembled in the large Franciscan church for the closing worship service. The sermon was preached by the Rev. Nélida Ritchie, a Methodist pastor from Uruguay and one of the two vice-moderators of the WCC central committee. After the blessing the participants, preceeded by the conference banners, marched in a joyful procession through the streets of Santiago de Compostela witnessing, in this city so marked over the centuries by pilgrimage, to that wider ecumenical pilgrimage of the churches towards visible unity. Returning to the Seminario Mayor, with its spacious cloisters surrounding a central fountain, they enjoyed on a mild summer evening a final social gathering to which they had been invited by the stewards.

The worship life of the world conference

The programme and spirit of the world conference were marked by an intense worship life which had been carefully prepared and which met with much appreciation and participation among members of the conference. Faith and Order has always understood that its work must be related to issues of worship (though the connection has not always been actively developed, particularly in recent years); but no Faith and Order meeting so far had given so much attention to the actual life of worship and its impact on the meeting. In addition to opening and closing services mentioned above, special events included Orthodox and Roman Catholic vespers. For the Orthodox vespers on the eve of the Feast of Transfiguration the sermon was preached by Archbishop Stylianos of Australia; at the Roman Catholic vespers Bishop Dr Paul-Werner Scheele preached — to a congregation which included members of his own diocese in Germany who had walked as pilgrims to Santiago de Compostela, arriving that very day.

The issues involved in offering a service of holy communion at such a gathering are complex; we chose to return to an earlier Faith and Order practice according to which a local member church of the WCC should act as the host for the service. Accordingly, the two Spanish Reformed and Anglican member churches of the WCC were responsible for a eucharistic service presided over by the Rev. Rogelio Prieto, with the Rev. Alberto Araujo preaching. This service made visible the positive results of the numerous official agreements which have brought many Anglican, Old Catholic and Protestant churches together at the Lord's table — and reminded us of the divisions there which are yet to be overcome.

The daily morning worship followed a basic order of prayer, biblical reading and song common to many Christian traditions; within this pattern a rich variety of languages and cultural and confessional forms were used. Evening worship, quieter in tone, followed the pattern used in many religious communities. In both morning and evening services free prayer and silence had a greater role than in most ecumenical gatherings. In response to the plenary presentation by Bishop Tutu, a silent meal and evening vigil were organized on behalf of victims of violence in all parts of the world.

The morning worship included biblical expositions treating systematically the whole of St Paul's Letter to the Galatians. These stressed the ecumenical implications of Paul's picture of this particular Christian community as it struggled to realize koinonia within its life. These presentations by Prof. Frances M. Young were published for the conference under the title *All of You Are One in Christ Jesus*[2] and are available directly from the Faith and Order secretariat in Geneva. These Bible studies, together with the four biblical papers in plenary, were intended to be discussed in the working groups within the four sections and were part of our attempt to ground the work of the conference in the biblical witness to koinonia.

The impact of the world conference

An evaluation of the results and impact of the fifth world conference on Faith and Order is not our task here. This has been undertaken by participants and within both the churches and the broader ecumenical community. This process of evaluation and "reception" will have to continue, also with the help of this report. But the most fundamental result seems already to be quite obvious: the world conference has confirmed and affirmed the significant progress made during the last three decades in the theological struggle for the manifestation of the unity of the church of Jesus Christ. As a consequence, the world conference has called and encouraged the churches *really to receive these achievements into their thinking and life as elements of enrichment and renewal.*

To facilitate this process in the future and to overcome barriers which remain, the world conference has presented perspectives and recommendations for the future work of the Commission on Faith and Order. In this framework the world conference, finally, has stated clearly that the theological mandate and contribution of this Commission remains indispensable for the future way and work of the World Council of Churches and of the ecumenical movement. This conviction and commitment was underlined by the presence and active participation in Santiago de Compostela of the present leadership team of the WCC: the moderator of its central committee, Archbishop Aram Keshishian, its two vice-moderators, Ephorus Dr Soritua Nababan and the Rev. Nélida Ritchie, WCC general secretary the Rev. Dr Konrad Raiser, as well as Prof. Anna Marie Aagaard, a president of the WCC.

The ecumenical movement has often been interpreted as a pilgrimage of the churches together towards visible unity, and so it was natural that the world conference, meeting in the historic pilgrimage city of Santiago de Compostela, should be linked to this idea. But it was clear that this "pilgrimage" would not reach — and could not reach — its goal in Santiago de Compostela. This meeting will be a station on the way, one among many markers on our path together. The true measure of its significance will be the extent to which its insights and impetus are taken up into the life of the churches and the ecumenical movement. May the world conference at Santiago de Compostela, like its forerunners in Lausanne in 1927, Edinburgh 1937, Lund 1952 and Montreal 1963, become an inspiration and a source of renewed energy for continuing the pilgrimage towards the visible unity of the church for the sake of God's saving purpose for all humanity and creation.

Günther Gassmann and Thomas F. Best

NOTES

[1] *Towards Koinonia in Faith, Life and Witness: A Discussion Paper*, Faith and Order paper no. 161, Geneva, WCC, April 1993.

[2] Frances M. Young, *All of You Are One in Christ Jesus: Bible Studies*, Geneva, Faith and Order Commission, 1993.

LIST OF PARTICIPANTS

Delegates

The Rev. Dr Eshetu ABATE (Ethiopian Evangelical Mekane Yesus Church), Ethiopia

**Deaconess Bella ADEMOLA (Methodist Church, Nigeria), Nigeria

The Rev. Dr Dan ANTWI (Presbyterian Church of Ghana), Ghana

**Dr Kamol ARAYAPRATEEP (Church of Christ in Thailand), Thailand

Dean Niels Henrik ARENDT (Evangelical Lutheran Church of Denmark), Denmark

The Rev. Dr Festus A. ASANA (Presbyterian Church in Cameroon), Republic of Cameroon

**Archbishop Mesrob ASHJIAN (Armenian Apostolic Church, Cilicia), USA

Prof. Dr Torleiv AUSTAD (Church of Norway), Norway

Bishop Viken AYKAZIAN (Armenian Apostolic Church — representing Diocese of Armenian Church of America), Switzerland

The Rev. Dr Sebastian BAKARE (Anglican Church), Zimbabwe

**The Rev. Alyson BARNETT-COWAN (Anglican Church of Canada), Canada

The Rev. Eroni BAUTANI (Methodist Church in Fiji), Fiji Islands

Subpriorin Hannelore BENKARD (Evangelical Church in Germany: Evangelical Lutheran Church in Bavaria), Germany

**Prof. Dr Wolfgang BIENERT (Evangelical Church in Germany: Church of Kurhesse-Waldeck), Germany

Prof. Dr André BIRMELE (Church of the Augsburg Confession of Alsace and Lorraine), France

**Metropolitan BISHOY of Damietta (Coptic Orthodox Church), Egypt

The Rev. Merryl BLAIR (Churches of Christ in Australia), Australia

**Prof. Dr Klauspeter BLASER (Swiss Protestant Church Federation), Switzerland

**The Rev. Canon Hugh Blessing BOE (Church of Melanesia, Anglican), Solomon Islands

**Dr Roberta BONDI (United Methodist Church), USA

Protopresbyter Prof. Vitaly BOROVOY (Russian Orthodox Church), CIS

**The Rev. Fr Frans BOUWEN (Roman Catholic Church), Israel

The Rev. Stephen de BRUIN (Lutheran Church), Botswana

VDM Tobias BRANDNER (Swiss Protestant Church Federation), Switzerland

**The Rev. Eva BREBOVSZKY-GERÖFI (Lutheran Church in Hungary), Hungary

**The Rev. Dr Sven-Erik BRODD (Church of Sweden), Sweden

**The Rt Rev. Dr Manas BUTHELEZI (Evangelical Lutheran Church in South Africa), Republic of South Africa

---

* = Faith and Order Standing Commission member
** = Faith and Order Plenary Commission member

*The Rev. Neville CALLAM (Jamaica Baptist Union), Jamaica, West Indies

Dr Blanca CASTILLA y Cortazar (Roman Catholic Church), Spain

**Metropolitan CHRYSANTHOS of Limassol (Church of Cyprus), Cyprus

**The Rev. Keith CLEMENTS (Baptist Union of Great Britain), England

The Rev. Dr Donald G.L. CRAGG (Methodist Church of Southern Africa), South Africa

*The Rev. Janet CRAWFORD (Anglican Church in Aotearoa, New Zealand and Polynesia), New Zealand

*The Rev. Martin CRESSEY (United Reformed Church), England

*The Rev. Dr Paul A. CROW Jr (Disciples of Christ), USA

Prof. Dr Johannes DANTINE (Evangelical Church of the Augsburg Confession), Austria

*Dr Sophie DEICHA (Archdiocese of the Russian Orthodox Parishes in Western Europe/ Ecumenical Patriarchate), France

Mrs Christiane DIETERLE (Reformed Church in France), France

**V. The Rev. Prof. Dr George DRAGAS (Greek Orthodox Archdiocese of Thyatheira/ Ecumenical Patriarchate), England

*The Rt Rev. Sigqibo DWANE (Church of the Province of Southern Africa, Anglican), South Africa

**Mrs Marguerite FASSINOU (Methodist Church), Republic of Benin

The Rev. Dr Fulvio FERRARIO (Waldensian Church), Italy

The Rev. Jean FENOMANANA (Malgasy Lutheran Church), Madagascar

The Rt Rev. Kenneth FERNANDO (Church of Ceylon, Anglican), Sri Lanka

**Prof. Pavel FILIPI (Evangelical Church of the Czech Brethren), Czech Republic

**Prof. Dr Kyriaki FITZGERALD (Greek Orthodox Archdiocese of North and South America/ Ecumenical Patriarchate), USA

*The Rev. Prof. Duncan FORRESTER (Church of Scotland), Scotland

Sister Lorelei F. FUCHS (Roman Catholic Church), USA

The Rev. Dr Gédéon GAKINDI (Presbyterian Church of Rwanda), Rwanda

**Ms Olga GANABA (Russian Orthodox Church), CIS

The Rev. GAO Ying (China Christian Council), China

The Rev. Julia M. GATTA (Episcopal Church), USA

**Sister Dr Donna GEERNAERT, SC (Roman Catholic Church), Canada

Mr António Jorge Gameiro GOMES (Evangelical Presbyterian Church of Portugal), Portugal

**The Rev. Dr J.W. GLADSTONE (Church of South India), India

The Rev. Prof. Adolfo GONZALEZ-MONTES (Roman Catholic Church), Spain

The Rev. Prof. James HAIRE (Uniting Church in Australia), Australia

Dr Susan HARDMAN MOORE (Methodist Church of Great Britain), England

H.E. Archbishop Stylianos HARKIANAKIS of Australia (Ecumenical Patriarchate), Australia

**Dr Salesi T. HAVEA (Methodist Church of Tonga), Tonga

**Prof. Mark S. HEIM (American Baptist Churches USA), USA

**Mrs Justinia HILUKILUAH (Church of the Province of Southern Africa, Anglican), Namibia

**Prof. Dr L.A. HOEDEMAKER (Netherlands Reformed Church), Netherlands

The Rev. Prof. Thomas HOPKO (Orthodox Church in America), USA

*Prof. Dr Thomas HOYT (Christian Methodist Episcopal Church), USA

**Prof. Dr Hristo S. HRISTOV (Bulgarian Orthodox Church), Bulgaria

The Rev. Basa HUTABARAT (Huria Kristen Batak Protestant (Lutheran)), Indonesia

The Rev. Prof. Arthur JAMES (United Presbyterian Church of Pakistan), Pakistan

Bishop B. JAMES (Methodist Church of India), India

The Rev. Paul JANSSEN (Reformed Church in America), USA

The Rev. Fr Nerses JEBEJIAN (Diocese of the Armenian Church of America), USA

**Sister Dr Margaret JENKINS CSB (Roman Catholic Church), Australia

**H.E. Metropolitan JOHN of Pergamon (Zizioulas) (Ecumenical Patriarchate), Greece

The Rev. Dr Cheryl Bridges JOHNS (Church of God), USA

The Rt Rev. Dr Samuel B. JOSHUA (Church of North India), India

The Very Rev. Dean Peeter KALDUR (Estonian Evangelical Lutheran Church), Republic of Estonia

**The Rev. Prof. Kenji KANDA (United Church of Christ of Japan (Kyodan)), Japan

Mrs Sarah KAULULE (United Church of Zambia)

The Rev. Dr Gerard KELLY (Roman Catholic Church), Australia

Metropolitan Georges KHODR (Greek Orthodox Patriarchate of Antioch), Lebanon

The Rev. Baranita KIRATA (Pacific Conference of Churches), Fiji

The V. Rev. Leonid KISHKOVSKY (Orthodox Church in America), USA

**Mgr Prof. Dr Aloys KLEIN (Roman Catholic Church), Germany

Bishop Dr Elemér KOCSIS (Reformed Church in Hungary), Hungary

**Fr Johns A. KONAT (Malankara Syrian Orthodox Church), India

Prof. Dr Ulrich KÜHN (Evangelical Church of Germany: Evangelical Lutheran Church of Saxony), Germany

**The Rev. Dr Abraham KURUVILLA (Mar Thoma Syrian Church of Malabar), Australia

The Rev. Dr Ronald A. KYDD (Pentecostal Assemblies of Canada), Canada

**The Rev. Fr Kwame Joseph LABI (Greek Orthodox Patriarchate of Alexandria), Ghana

Dr Prof. Nadia LAHUTSKY (Disciples of Christ), USA

**Dom Emmanuel LANNE, OSB (Roman Catholic Church), Belgium

Prof. Dr Grigorios LARENTZAKIS (Ecumenical Patriarchate), Austria

**The Rev. Dr Dorothy LEE (Uniting Church in Australia), Australia

*Prof. Kyung Sook LEE (Methodist Church), Korea

Prof. Marilyn LEGGE (United Church of Canada), Canada

The Ven. Howard LEVETT (Episcopal Church in Jerusalem and the Middle East), Egypt

The Rt Rev. Glauco Soares de LIMA (Episcopal Church, Brazil), Brazil

The V. Rev. Prof. Dr Gennadios LIMOURIS (Ecumenical Patriarchate), Turkey

**The Rev. Dr Lars LINDBERG (The Mission Covenant Church of Sweden), Sweden

Sister Maria Josefina LLACH (Roman Catholic Church), Argentina

The Most Rev. Antonio Cañizares LLOVERA (Roman Catholic Church), Spain

The Rt Rev. Robert L.O. LONGID (Episcopal Church in the Philippines), Philippines

*Prof. Nicolas LOSSKY (Russian Orthodox Church), France

**The Rev. Harald MALSCHITZKY (Evangelical Church of Augsburg Confession in Brazil), Brazil

**The Rev. Dr Marcello MAMMARELLA (Roman Catholic Church), Italy

Abbé André MAMPILA MAMBU (Roman Catholic Church), Republic of Zaire

The Rev. Perry Mubita MANGE'LELE (United Church of Zambia), Zambia

The Rev. Taaroanui MARAEA (Evangelical Church of French Polynesia), Tahiti, French Polynesia

The Rev. Dr W.J. MARSHALL (Church of Ireland), Ireland

**The Rev. Dr Frank J. MATERA (Roman Catholic Church), USA

*Dr Melanie A. MAY (Church of the Brethren), USA

The Rev. Dr Everett MENDOZA (United Church of Christ in the Philippines), Philippines

The Rev. Prof. Emilio N. MONTI (Evangelical Methodist Church, Argentina), Argentina

Prof. MUNDUKU Ngamayamu-Dagoga (Church of Christ in Zaire), Republic of Zaire

Mgr John MUTISO-MBINDA (Roman Catholic Church, Nigeria), Vatican

**The Rev. Dr Samuel MWANIKI (Presbyterian Church of East Africa), Kenya

Dr Marian NADZAM (Orthodox Church in Czech Lands), Slovakia

Ms Anoush NAKASHIAN (Armenian Apostolic Church), Israel

**The Rev. Canon James NDYABAHIKA (Anglican Church of Uganda), Uganda

**The Rev. Felix NEEFJES, OFM (Roman Catholic Church), Brazil

The Rt Rev. Dr V. Nerses NERSESSIAN (Armenian Apostolic Church, Etchmiadzin), England

**Ms Kirsten Busch NIELSEN, B.D. (Evangelical Lutheran Church of Denmark), Denmark

**Dr Elizabeth NORDBECK (United Church of Christ), USA

The Most Rev. Alfons NOSSOL (Roman Catholic Church), Poland

Hegoumen Veniamin NOVIK (Russian Orthodox Church), CIS

*Sister Dr Mary O'DRISCOLL (Roman Catholic Church), Italy

**The Rev. Lucretia van OMMEREN (Evangelical Lutheran Church in Surinam), Surinam

*The Most Rev. John ONAIYEKAN (Roman Catholic Church), Nigeria

Dr Donna ORSUTO (Roman Catholic Church), Italy

**Prof. Alexy I. OSIPOV (Russian Orthodox Church), CIS

**The Rev. Prof. Martin F.G. PARMENTIER (Old Catholic Church), Netherlands

The Rev. Carolina PATTIASINA (Protestant Church in the Moluccas (Reformed)), Indonesia

Dr Emmanuel P. PERSELIS (Greek Orthodox Patriarchate of Alexandria), Greece

The Rev. Dr Kenneth L. PETERSON (Evangelical Lutheran Church in Canada), Canada

**Prof. Vlassios PHEIDAS (Church of Greece), Greece

**Dr Juha PIHKALA (Evangelical-Lutheran Church of Finland), Finland

The Rev. Dr Nelson PINTO HORTA (Lusitanian Catholic Apostolic Evangelical Church), Portugal

Ms Jennifer POTTER (Methodist Church), Botswana

The Rev. Rogelio PRIETO DURAN (Spanish Episcopal Reformed Church), Spain

Msgr John A. RADANO (Roman Catholic Church), Vatican City

The Rev. Jean A. RAVALITERA (Church of Jesus Christ in Madagascar), Madagascar

The Rev. Dr Hyung Ki RHEE (Presbyterian Church of Korea), Korea

The Rev. Dr Bruce W. ROBBINS (United Methodist Church), USA

**Dr Cecil M. ROBECK, Jr (Assemblies of God), USA

*The Rev. Araceli ROCCHIETTI (Methodist Church), Uruguay

*The Rev. Raquel RODRIGUEZ (Lutheran Church of El Salvador), USA

*The Rt Rev. Barry ROGERSON (Church of England), England

The Rev. Don Eugenio ROMERO POSE (Roman Catholic Church), Spain

*The Rev. Dr William G. RUSCH (Evangelical Lutheran Church in America), USA

The Rev. Elga SARAPUNG (Indonesian Protestant Church in Gorontalo (Reformed)), Indonesia

The Rev. Dr Ioan SAUCA (Romanian Orthodox Church), Romania

Prof. Dr Zdenek SAZAVA (Czechoslovak Hussite Church), Czech Republic

**The Rev. Jorge SCAMPINI, OP (Roman Catholic Church), Argentina

The Rev. Hermann SCHÄFER (Evangelical Church in Germany: Reformed), Germany

The Most Rev. Paul-Werner SCHEELE (Roman Catholic Church), Germany

Dr Faye E. SCHOTT (Evangelical Lutheran Church in America), USA

Mrs Ninive SEDDOH (Evangelical Church of Togo), Togo

*Prof. Dr Turid Karlsen SEIM (Church of Norway), Norway

The Rev. Tautiago SENARA (Congregational Christian Church of Western Samoa), Western Samoa

**Oberkonsistorialrat Dr Matthias SENS (Evangelical Church in Germany: Church Province of Saxony (United)), Germany

The Rev. Pedro C. SEVILLA, SJ (Roman Catholic Church), Philippines

**Dr David T. SHANNON, President (National Baptist Convention, USA, Inc.), USA

**The Rev. Dr Herman SHASTRI (Methodist Church), Malaysia

The Rev. Prof. Einar SIGURBJOERNSSON (Church of Iceland (Lutheran)), Iceland

The Rev. Ephorus H. SIMANGUNSONG (Indonesian Christian Church (Lutheran)), Indonesia

Prof. Dr Pribislav SIMIC (Serbian Orthodox Church), Yugoslavia

**The Rev. Einar SITOMPUL (Batak Protestant Christian Church (Lutheran)), Indonesia

The Rev. Dr Allan SPENCE (Zimbabwe Council of Churches), Zimbabwe

The Rev. Dr Susie C. STANLEY (Church of God), USA

*Ms Veronica SWAI (Evangelical Lutheran Church in Tanzania), Scotland

The Rev. Iosif SZEKELY (Reformed Church of Romania — Siebenbürger Distrikt), Romania

*Dr Mary TANNER (Church of England), England

**Dr Constance TARASAR (Orthodox Church in America), USA

The Rev. Dr George B. TELFORD (Presbyterian Church (USA)), USA

*Prof. Evangelos THEODOROU (Church of Greece), Greece

**The Rev. Livingstone THOMPSON (Moravian Church), Jamaica, West Indies

*The Rev. Prof. Jean-Marie TILLARD, O.P. (Roman Catholic Church), Canada

The Rev. José Luis TRONCOSO (Spanish Evangelical Church), Spain

The Rev. TSO Man-king (Hong Kong Christian Council), Hong Kong

The Rev. Pirjo TYOERINOJA (Evangelical-Lutheran Church of Finland), Finland

The Rt Rev. Attila VERES-KOVACS (Reformed Church in Romania), Romania

**The Rev. Prof. Dr S. Wismoady WAHONO (East Java Christian Church), Indonesia

The Rev. Terry WALL (Methodist Church of New Zealand), England

Dr Martin WANG (Presbyterian Church in Taiwan), Taiwan

H.G. Bishop Kallistos WARE of Diokleia (Ecumenical Patriarchate), England

*Prof. Dr Dorothea WENDEBOURG (Evangelical Church in Germany: Evangelical Lutheran Church of Hanover), Germany

**Prof. Dr Gunther WENZ (Evangelical Church in Germany: Evangelical Lutheran Church of Bavaria), Germany

**The Rev. Olivia WESLEY (Methodist Church), Sierra Leone

The Rev. Dr Monrelle WILLIAMS (Church in the Province of the West Indies, Anglican), Barbados, West Indies

The Rt Rev. Dr Rowan D. WILLIAMS (Church of Wales, Anglican), Wales

The Rev. William Bryn WILLIAMS (Presbyterian Church of Wales), Wales

**Prof. Antoinette Clark WIRE (Presbyterian Church (USA)), USA

The Rev. Canon Prof. J. Robert WRIGHT (Episcopal Church), USA

The Rev. Dr Trevor John WRIGHT (Anglican Church in Australia), USA

*The Rev. Dr YEMBA Kekumba (Church of Christ in Zaire — Methodist Community), Zimbabwe

*The Rev. Dr YEOW Choo Lak (Presbyterian Church in Singapore), Republic of Singapore

The Rev. Dr A.A. YEWANGOE (Christian Church of Sumba (Reformed)), Indonesia

Fr Georgy ZIABLINTSEV (Russian Orthodox Church), CIS

Official guests

Dr Anna Marie AAGAARD (Evangelical Lutheran Church in Denmark; president, World Council of Churches), Denmark

The Rev. Dr Keith BRIDSTON (Evangelical Lutheran Church in America; former executive secretary, Faith and Order), USA

H.E. Edward Idris Cardinal CASSIDY (Roman Catholic Church; president, Pontifical Council for Promoting Christian Unity), Vatican City

The Rev. Dr Emilio CASTRO (Methodist Church; former general secretary, World Council of Churches), Uruguay

Archbishop Dr Aram KESHISHIAN (Armenian Apostolic Church; moderator of central committee, World Council of Churches), Lebanon

Ephorus the Rev. D. Dr Soritua NABABAN (Huria Kristen Batak Protestan (Lutheran); vice-moderator of central committee, World Council of Churches), Indonesia

Prof. J. Robert NELSON (United Methodist Church; former chairman of Faith and Order working committee and former executive secretary), USA

The Rev. Dr Konrad RAISER (Evangelical Church in Germany; general secretary, World Council of Churches), Switzerland

The Rev. Nélida RITCHIE (Evangelical Methodist Church; vice-moderator of central committee, World Council of Churches), Argentina

Bishop Patrick RODGER (Episcopal Church in Scotland; former executive secretary, Faith and Order), Scotland

The Most Rev. Desmond TUTU (Church of the Province of South Africa; former Faith and Order commissioner), South Africa

The Rev. Prof. Lukas VISCHER (Swiss Protestant Church Federation; former director, Faith and Order), Switzerland

Christian World Communions

The Rev. Dr Donald ANDERSON (Anglican Communion), England

The Rev. Julio R. ASENSIO (World Alliance of Reformed Churches), Spain

Dr Bert B. BEACH (General Conference of Seventh-day Adventists), USA

The Rev. Dr Eugene BRAND (Lutheran World Federation), Switzerland

The Rev. Dr Thomas FINGER (Mennonite Church), USA

Dean FREIDAY (Friends World Committee for Consultation), USA

Colonel David E. GUY (Salvation Army), England

Dr Joe HALE (World Methodist Council), USA

Dr William TABBERNEE (Disciples Ecumenical Consultative Council), Australia

Dr George VANDERVELDE (Reformed Ecumenical Council and World Evangelical Fellowship), Canada

Local host

Archbishop D. Antonio María ROUCO VARELA (Archbishop of Santiago de Compostela), Spain

Local staff

Mgr Julián GARCIA HERNANDO (Secretariat of the Episcopal commission on interconfessional relations), Spain

The Rev. D. Elisardo TEMPERAN (Archbishopric of Santiago de Compostela), Spain

Speakers

Dr Anna Marie AAGAARD (see under official guests)

Dr Simon CHAN (Assembly of God of Singapore), Republic of Singapore

**Metropolitan JOHN of Pergamon (Zizioulas) (see under delegates)

Archbishop Dr Aram KESHISHIAN (see under official guests)

Metropolitan Georges KHODR (see under delegates)

**The Rev. Dr Dorothy A. LEE (see under delegates)

*The Most Rev. John ONAIYEKAN (see under delegates)

Prof. Dr Wolfhart PANNENBERG (Evangelical Church in Germany: Evangelical Lutheran Church in Bavaria), Germany

The Rev. Dr Konrad RAISER (see under official guests)

The Rev. Prof. John REUMANN (Evangelical Lutheran Church in America), USA

Ms Elizabeth TEMPLETON (Church of Scotland), Scotland

Archbishop Ramon TORRELLA CASCANTE (Roman Catholic Church), Spain

The Most Rev. Desmond TUTU (see under official guests)

Dr Frances YOUNG (Methodist Church of Great Britain), England

Consultants

Ms Souraya ABDALLAH (Greek Orthodox Patriarchate of Antioch), Lebanon

**The Rev. Christobella BAGH (Church of North India), India

Dr Athanasios BASDEKIS (Ecumenical Patriarchate), Germany

Prof. Edith BLUMHOFER (United Methodist Church), USA

Ms Gunnel BORGEGAARD (Mission Covenant Church, Sweden), Sweden

Ms Catherine CHIOTELLIS (Church of Greece), Greece

Mr Martin CONWAY (Church of England), England

The Rev. Alan D. FALCONER (Church of Scotland), Ireland

The Rev. Prof. Thomas FITZGERALD (Greek Orthodox Archdiocese of North and South America/Ecumenical Patariarchate), USA

Deaconess Chita R. FRAMO (United Methodist Church), Philippines

The Rev. Dr K.M. GEORGE (Malankara Syrian Orthodox Church), Switzerland

Brother Jeffrey GROS (Roman Catholic Church), USA

The Rev. Yasuo HATAKEYAMA (National Christian Council in Japan), Japan

The Rev. Dr Matthias HAUDEL (Evangelical Church in Germany: Evangelical Church of Westphalia), Germany

The Rev. Prof. William HENN, OFM (Roman Catholic Church), Italy

The Rev. Dr Rena Weller KAREFA-SMART (Episcopal Church), USA

The Rev. Lorna KHOO (Methodist Church), Republic of Singapore

The Rev. Dr Michael KINNAMON (Disciples of Christ), USA

Prof. Dr Jaci MARASCHIN (Episcopal Church, Brazil), Brazil

The Rev. Dr Lauree Hersch MEYER (Church of the Brethren), USA

**Dr Nestor MIGUEZ (Methodist Church), Argentina

Ms Yara N. MONTEIRO (Christian Congregation in Brazil), Brazil

Prof. Mercy Amba ODUYOYE (Methodist Church of Nigeria), Switzerland

Prof. Dr PARK Keun-Won (Presbyterian Church in the Republic of Korea), Korea

The Rev. Dr Constance F. PARVEY (Evangelical Lutheran Church in America), USA

The Rev. Dr Margriet POSTMA-GOSKER (Reformed Churches in the Netherlands), Netherlands

The Rev. Dr Horace O. RUSSELL (Jamaica Baptist Union), USA

Ms Janet SCOTT (London Yearly Meeting of the Religious Society of Friends (Quakers)), England

Prof. Eva SUVARSKA (Orthodox Church of Czech Lands), Czech Republic

Mrs Weddad Abbas TEWFIK (Coptic Orthodox Church), Egypt

The Rev. Prof. Joseph VERCRUYSSE, SJ (Roman Catholic Church), Italy

The Rev. Prof. Geoffrey WAINWRIGHT (Methodist Church), England/USA

The Rev. Dr Sr Teresa J. WHITE (Church of England), England

OKR Klaus WILKENS (Evangelical Church in Germany), Germany

Younger theologians

The Rev. Dr Kajsa AHLSTRAND (Church of Sweden), Sweden

The Rev. Emmanuel BADEJO (Roman Catholic Church), Nigeria

Ms Claudia BRUWELEIT (Evangelical Church in Germany), Germany

Mr Christos CHRISTAKIS (Church of Greece), England

Prof. Dawn DeVRIES (Presbyterian Church (USA)), USA

The Rev. Dr Peter DONALD (Church of Scotland), Scotland

The Rev. Susan DURBER (United Reformed Church), England

The Rev. Mercedes GARCIA BACHMANN (United Evangelical Lutheran Church), Argentina

Ms Ruth GREY-SMITH (Anglican Church of Australia), Australia

Dr Valerie KARRAS (Greek Orthodox Archdiocese of North and South America/Ecumenical Patriarchate), USA

Ms Rita KHATER (Greek Orthodox Patriarchate of Antioch), Lebanon

The Rev. Elizabeth MAILOE-MARANTIKA (Protestant Church in the Moluccas), Indonesia

Fr Reji MATHEW (Malankara Orthodox Syrian Church), Germany

Ms Madalina-Marie MAZILESCU (Romanian Orthodox Church), Romania

The Rev. Marius MEZINCA (Romanian Orthodox Church), Germany

The Rev. Sarah Mwanga MKANZA (Lutheran Evangelical Church of Tanzania), Tanzania

Ms Angela MORGAN (Jamaica Baptist Union), Jamaica, West Indies

Ms Rebecca E. Garcia MORRIS (Presbyterian Church), Cuba

Lic. Dalila C. NAYAP-POT (Nazarene Church, Belize), Scotland

The Rev. Evanson NJOGU WAWERU (Roman Catholic Church, Nigeria), Italy

Ms Elisabeth PARMENTIER (Evangelical Church of the Augsburg Confession of Alsace and Lorraine), France

Ms Teresa Francesca ROSSI (Roman Catholic Church), Italy

The Rev. Sam SAHU (Church of Melanesia), Solomon Islands

Mr José SCOTT Mohring (Evangelical Church of the River Plate), Germany

Mr Sturla STALSETT (Church of Norway), Norway

The Rev. Walter TAYLOR (Disciples of Christ), USA

Mr Stylianos TSOBANIDIS (Church of Greece), Germany

Ms Vuadi VIBILA (Church of Christ in Zaire — Presbyterian Community), Germany

The Rev. Daphne C. WIGGINS (American Baptist Church), USA

The Rev. Flora WINFIELD (Church of England), England

Dr YEO Khiok-Khng (United Methodist Church), Hong Kong

Stewards

Mr Carlos ABEIJON PIÑEIRO (Roman Catholic Church), Spain

Mr Rubén ARAMBURU MOLET (Roman Catholic Church), Spain

Mag. Phil. Christian A.K. AYIVI (Evangelical Church of Togo), Togo

Ms Klaudia BALKE (Roman Catholic Church), Germany

Mr Alvaro BARROS QUIVEN (Roman Catholic Church), Spain

Ms Ana BORRAFAS (Roman Catholic Church), Spain

Mr José Miguel CARNEIRO MOSQUERA (Roman Catholic Church), Spain

Ms Isabel CASANOVA PIN (Roman Catholic Church), Spain

Ms Remedios CASANOVA PIN (Roman Catholic Church), Spain

Mr David E. COBB (Disciples of Christ; head steward), USA

Ms María del Carmen CORREA FOLGAR (Roman Catholic Church), Spain

Ms Donata DOERFEL (Evangelical Lutheran Church of North Elbia; head steward), Germany

Ms Caterina DUPRE (Waldensian Church), Italy

Ms Ana Isabel DURO FERNANDEZ (Roman Catholic Church), Spain

Mr Andrés FERNANDEZ FARTO (Roman Catholic Church), Spain

Ms Azucena FERREIRO BLANCO (Roman Catholic Church), Spain

Mr Joseph FLEMING (Roman Catholic Church), Spain

Ms Loli GONZALEZ CAAMAÑO (Roman Catholic Church), Spain

Mr Luis GULIN IGLESIAS (Roman Catholic Church), Spain

Deacon Aren S. JEBEJIAN (Armenian Apostolic Church in USA), USA

Ms Mariel LARRIVA LEIRA (Roman Catholic Church), Spain

Ms Laura LOJO RODRIGUEZ (Roman Catholic Church), Spain

Ms Faith Kokubelwa LUGAZIA (Evangelical Lutheran Church in Tanzania), Tanzania

Mr Pierre MARCOMBE (Roman Catholic Church), France

Ms Isabel MARTINEZ RODRIGUEZ (Roman Catholic Church), Spain

Ms Ana Belén MONTERO (Roman Catholic Church), Spain

Mr María José MONTERO (Roman Catholic Church), Spain

Ms Elisabeth NAURATH (Evangelical Church in Germany), Germany

Ms Anna G. PATTIASINA (Protestant Church in the Moluccas), Indonesia

Ms María Inés PERNAS DIJON (Roman Catholic Church), Spain

Ms Despina D. PRASSAS (Greek Orthodox Archdiocese of North and South America, Ecumenical Patriarchate), USA

Mr Alejandro RODRIGUEZ VAZQUEZ (Roman Catholic Church), Spain

The Rev. Antti SAARELMA (Evangelical Lutheran Church of Finland), Finland

Ms Myriam M. SINTADO (National Protestant Church of Geneva), Switzerland

Mr Rajan C. THOMAS (Mar Thoma Syrian Church of Malabar), India

Faith and Order staff

Dr Silke-Petra BERGJAN (Evangelical Church in Germany (Reformed)), Germany

The Rev. Dr Thomas F. BEST (Disciples of Christ), USA

Ms Béatrice FLEURY (Roman Catholic Church), France

The Rev. Dr Günther GASSMANN (Evangelical Church in Germany (Lutheran)), Germany

The Rev. Dr Dagmar HELLER (Evangelical Church in Germany (United)), Germany

Mrs Renate SBEGHEN (Evangelical Church in Germany (Lutheran)), Switzerland

Co-opted staff

The Rev. Alain BLANCY (Reformed Church of France), France

Mrs Renate BRAUN-EICHRODT (Swiss Protestant Church Federation), Germany

Mrs Eileen CHAPMAN (Reformed), Australia

Mrs Natalia CHERNYKH (Russian Orthodox Church), CIS

The Rev. Tony COATES (United Reformed Church), England

Mrs Donata COLEMAN (Church of England), England

The Rev. Stephen CRANFORD (Disciples of Christ), USA

Mrs Mary CROW (Disciples of Christ), USA

The Rev. Dr Colin DAVEY (Church of England), England

Mrs Elisabeth DELMONTE (Evangelical Waldensian Church of the River Plate), Uruguay

The Rev. Dr Milton B. EFTHIMIOU (Greek Orthodox Archdiocese of North and South America/Ecumenical Patriarchate), USA

Mrs Tomoko FAERBER-EVDOKIMOV (Ecumenical Patriarchate), Switzerland

Prof. Robert FAERBER (Evangelical Church of the Augsburg Confession of Alsace and Lorraine), Switzerland

Mrs Ursula GASSMANN (Evangelical Church in Germany (Lutheran)), Switzerland

Mrs Roswitha GINGLAS-POULET (Roman Catholic Church), Switzerland

OKR Dr Reinhard GROSCURTH (Evangelical Church of the Union), Germany

Mr Michel HOURST (Roman Catholic Church), France

Prof. Dr Anton HOUTEPEN (Roman Catholic Church), Netherlands

The Rev. Roberto JORDAN (Presbyterian Church), Argentina

The Rev. Dr Irmgard KINDT-SIEGWALT (Evangelical Church of the Augsburg Confession of Alsace and Lorraine), France

The Rev. Dr Hans-Georg LINK (Evangelical Church in Germany: United), Germany

Ms Simei MONTEIRO (Methodist Church), Brazil

Mrs Zinaida NOSOVA (Russian Orthodox Church), Russia

The Rev. William J. NOTTINGHAM (Disciples of Christ), USA

Ms Margaret PATER (Methodist Church of Great Britain), Germany

Ms Madeleine RICHTER, Switzerland

Prof. Dr Michael ROOT (Evangelical Lutheran Church in America), France

The Rev. Dr Eugene STOCKWELL (United Methodist Church), Argentina

The Rev. Christian TAMAELA (Presbyterian Church), Indonesia

Ms Ute THRÄNE (Evangelical Church in Germany), Germany

Ms Pilar TOSAT-DELARAYE (Roman Catholic Church), Switzerland

V.The Rev. Joachim TSOPANOGLOU (Ecumenical Patriarchate), France

The Rev. Fr Milos VESIN (Serbian Orthodox Church), USA
Sister Heidi WAEFLER (Grandchamps Community), Switzerland
Ms Ursula ZIERL (Evangelical Church in Germany), Switzerland

WCC staff

The Rev. Dr Wesley ARIARAJAH (Methodist Church), Sri Lanka
The Rev. Myra BLYTH (Baptist Union of Great Britain), Scotland
The Rev. Prof. Ion BRIA (Orthodox Church in Romania), Romania
Ms Maryse COURVOISIER (Reformed Church of France), France
Ms Rosemarie DÖNCH (Evangelical Church in Germany (Reformed)), Germany
The Rev. Wesley GRANBERG-MICHAELSON (Reformed Church in America), USA
Ms Rosemary GREEN (United Reformed Church in the United Kingdom), England
Ms Helga KAISER (Evangelical Church of Germany), Germany
Ms Ana LANGERAK (Lutheran Church in Costa Rica), Costa Rica
Ms Yasmina LEBOUACHERA (Muslim), France
The Rev. Terry MACARTHUR (United Methodist Church), USA
Mr John MCVIE (Church of Scotland), Scotland
Ms Anne-Lyse NABAFFA (Roman Catholic Church), Switzerland
The Rev. Prof. Jacques NICOLE (Swiss Protestant Church Federation), Switzerland
The Rev. Prof. Ofelia ORTEGA (Reformed Church), Cuba
Ms Joan REILLY (Church of Scotland), Scotland
Prof. Todor SABEV (Bulgarian Orthodox Church), Switzerland
Ms Violaine de SANTA ANA (Swiss Protestant Church Federation), Switzerland
The Rev. Dr Beate STIERLE (Evangelical Lutheran Church of Hanover), Germany
Mrs Daphne TISCHHAUSER (Swiss Protestant Church Federation), England

Communication staff

Mrs Andrée D'ALESSANDRI, Roman Catholic Church (co-opted)
Mr Lino D'ALESSANDRI, Roman Catholic Church (co-opted)
Mr Rafael Arias VILLALTA (co-opted)
Ms Danielle CHAPERON, Roman Catholic Church
Mr Gilbert CUDRÉ-MAUROUX, Roman Catholic Church
Mr Tracy EARLY, American Baptist Churches
Mr Robert EQUEY, Roman Catholic Church (co-opted)
Mr Udo HAHN, Evangelical Church in Germany (co-opted)
Mr Edwin HASSINK, Society of Friends
Mr Jan KOK, Reformed Churches in the Netherlands
Ms Sheila MESA, Church of Scotland
Ms Catherine NERFIN, Roman Catholic Church
Mr John NEWBURY, Methodist Church (UK)

Ms Dafne de PLOU, Evangelical Methodist Church of Argentina (co-opted)
Ms Heather STUNT, Church of England
Mr Geoffroy de TURCKHEIM, Reformed Church of France (co-opted)
Mr Marlin VANELDEREN, Christian Reformed Church in North America
Ms Libby VISINAND, Swiss Protestant Church Federation
Mr Peter WILLIAMS, Evangelical Lutheran Church of Denmark

APOLOGIES

Faith and Order Commission members

**Dr Charles AMJAD-ALI (United Church of Pakistan)

*The V. Rev. Prof. Emmanuel CLAPSIS (Greek Orthodox Archdiocese of North and South America/Ecumenical Patriarchate)

*Metropolitan DANIEL of Moldavia and Bukovina (Romanian Orthodox Church)

**Prof. Dr Beverley GAVENTA (Disciples of Christ)

**Ms Najla Abou Sawan KASSAB (National Evangelical Synod of Syria and Lebanon)

**The Rev. Arthur KO LAY (Myanmar Baptist Convention)

**The Rev. Dr Friederike STOCKMANN-KÖCKERT (Evangelical Church in Germany: United)

**Ms Alina SZRYNSKA (Polish Orthodox Church)

**Ms Catrin WILLIAMS (Presbyterian Church of Wales)

**Rt Rev. Artemio ZABALA (Philippine Episcopal Church)

Appointed delegates

The Rev. JI Tai (China Christian Council)

Archbishop MEKARIOS (Ethiopian Orthodox Tewahido Church)

The Rev. Chris MOSTERT (Uniting Church in Australia)

Dr Samuel NAFZGER (Lutheran Church-Missouri Synod)

Ms Oliula PANAPA (Tuvalu Christian Church)

The Rev. Danko RADOSLAV (Slovak Evangelical Church)

The Rev. TUBAKADI Kuendala Marie-Josée (Church of Jesus Christ on Earth by the Prophet Simon Kimbangu, Zaire)

Mr Guillaume VOUMINA (Evangelical Church of the Congo)

Consultants

The Rev. Paul CHEN (Presbyterian Church in Taiwan)

---

  * = Standing Commission
 ** = Plenary Commission

A

Presentations, Sermons, Minutes

I

Opening the Fifth World Conference

☐ Introduction

Plenary I of the fifth world conference on Faith and Order was held on 4 August at 9h., with Faith and Order moderator Dr Mary Tanner presiding. This and subsequent plenaries were held in the sports hall of the Colegio La Salle in Santiago de Compostela, Spain.

The world conference began with a brief **opening act of worship** which emphasized the urgency of our task: "we remain restless until we grow together according to the wish and prayer of Christ that those who believe in him may be one". Banners were brought forward bearing the names of the venues of the Faith and Order world conferences (Lausanne 1927, Edinburgh 1937, Lund 1952, Montreal 1963 and now Santiago de Compostela 1993), and the scriptural passages John 17:20-23 (used in the opening worship at Lausanne) and John 14:23-26 (used in the opening worship at Montreal) were read. The plenary prayed together, using a phrase taken from the conference prayer, that it accepted its "calling to make visible our unity in Christ". Following these thanks to God for the opportunity now present in Santiago de Compostela to take fresh steps towards visible unity the moderator formally declared: "This meeting is now open."

The moderator then delivered her **Opening Remarks**, expressing thanks to all those (in Geneva, in Santiago de Compostela and other parts of Spain, and elsewhere around the world) who had been involved in planning and preparing for the world conference, and recalling the names of some who had preceded us on our pilgrimage towards unity.

The moderator then introduced a series of dignitaries who extended **greetings** and brought **welcomes** to the conference: the deputy mayor of Santiago de Compostela; Don Manuel Fraga Iriborne, the president of the Xunta of Galicia, the Spanish state within which Santiago is located; Archbishop D. Antonio María Rouco Varela, the Roman Catholic archbishop of Santiago de Compostela, our host; and the Rt Rev. Arturo Sanchez, the bishop of the Spanish Episcopal Reformed Church, and the Rev. Julio R. Asensio, the president of the Spanish Evangelical Church, the two Spanish WCC member churches. Through these greetings the participants experienced already the warmth of the Spanish welcome, and something of the country's cultural and religious vitality and diversity. The conference in its life and work was urged to continue in prayer to the Lord, "that our eyes might be fixed on him whose will is the unity of the church".

The director of Faith and Order the Rev. Dr Günther Gassmann began the roll call of delegates. He indicated that for practical reasons the process of introducing all the participants in the world conference would be extended over several plenaries.

The rest of plenary I was devoted to Dr Gassmann's presentation of his **Director's Report** on Faith and Order activities since the previous Faith and Order world conference at Montreal in 1963. The text begins on p. 12; the brief plenary discussion of the paper is summarized on p. 35.

OPENING REMARKS

MARY TANNER

It is with great joy and in anticipation of what lies ahead that I open this fifth world conference here in Santiago de Compostela. The months of careful planning by the Standing Commission of Faith and Order and the dedicated work of our director and small staff have borne fruit and we are at last gathered in this place. We are grateful to you, your Grace, to the Protestant churches and to the leaders of this community for welcoming us to Spain. You, your Grace, responded warmly to our plans to come to this city. We have received much help and support in the complicated preparations for such an ambitious world conference as this. It is not without significance that the first world conference at which the Roman Catholic Church is a full member of the Faith and Order Commission should be held in Santiago. We see it as a sign of your own commitment and the commitment of the Roman Catholic Church to the ecumenical movement.

Santiago is a place familiar to only a few of us. It is a place assuming greater significance for others of us in Europe of Anglican, Orthodox, Lutheran and Protestant traditions who now travel the pilgrim route to Santiago. For still others, it is a strange place, enigmatic and not without ambiguity. There is no place in our world that does not require of us a costly healing of memories, a reconciliation of the past. These days together will provide time to explore something of what this place has stood for in successive periods of your history and what it stands for today in this holy year — a year of renewal.

In my own preparations I have been impressed by what coming to this place has meant for pilgrims through the centuries, from Picaud who wrote an early pilgrim's guide in the twelfth century, warning of the dangers on the way, to a contemporary evangelical pilgrim from my own church who told of conversion here. Of all of them it was the medieval women pilgrims, foreshadowing today's Christian women's movement, that most moved me: Saint Brigitte of Sweden and, following her example, Margery Kempe from England who travelled the hard route here and each found their life changed.

We share with these faithful pilgrims a deep yearning and longing for greater wholeness, greater holiness. Pilgrims on the way find in searching for God that they have already found him, for God is not an end, nor a beginning, but the beginning without end. Similarly we discover on the pilgrimage to visible unity that unity is not an end which will suddenly be granted to us but that which we already experience by God's grace and in which we grow as long as we travel with constant repentance (metanoia), and the refusal to give up on one another.

As we begin this world conference we are mindful of all who have walked the ecumenical pilgrim way before us, those who since Lausanne in 1927 have contributed to the work of Faith and Order within the wider ecumenical movement, not least of all the moderators, directors and staff of Faith and Order; John Meyendorff, Nikos Nissiotis and the chairman of the Montreal fourth world conference; my own bishop, Oliver Tomkins, who the night before his death shared with me hopes for this world conference; John Deschner and Paul Minear, both sadly prevented at the last moment from being with us.

Dr Mary Tanner is general secretary of the Council for Christian Unity of the General Synod of the Church of England, and moderator of the Faith and Order Commission.

We remember too all those who have taken part in the remarkable series of regional consultations preparing for this meeting; those who made a contribution to our work in the Rønde consultation bidding us to hold together the experience of the search for justice, peace and the mending of creation with the insights of Faith and Order. There are those, too, who wanted to be with us but who, for the sake of financial restraints, a lack of space and a decision not to favour those who could pay their own way, we had to turn away. We know that they, and many in our churches, hold us in their prayers and await what we shall say on the subject "Towards Communion in Faith, Life and Witness", for they sense the relevance of our theme amidst the injustices, violence and instability of our world.

It is in gratitude for our safe arrival in this resting place on our ecumenical journeying, and in the hope that we shall discover new vision and renewed commitment in our work for the unity of the church, that I open this world conference.

GREETING FROM THE CITY COUNCIL
OF SANTIAGO DE COMPOSTELA

PRESENTED BY THE DEPUTY MAYOR OF SANTIAGO DE COMPOSTELA

William X, Count of Aquitaine and Poitiers, wrote in the twelfth century a famous romance known as the ballad of Don Gaiferos de Mormaltán. This begins with the following verse:

> Where is that pilgrim going, where is my pilgrim going? He has taken the Way of Compostela, but I do not know when he will arrive.

Through this story of that Way of Compostela, and of all the journeys to Compostela, there emerges a new spirituality in which we seem to glimpse a path with differences in doctrine, a path both physical and symbolic, universal and personal, a journey for those who have faith and those who have no faith, those who do not have faith and do not seek it, but who may meet with faith on their journey, perhaps while quenching their thirst at a mountain spring, or stopping on the way at a humble chapel in which the lonely pilgrim, for centuries, has felt that the difficulties and hardships of the journey have been the means whereby he or she has triumphed personally.

We may well understand that at such times the great questions arise: Who am I? Who are we? Who is he, who is she? From whom do we come? What does it mean to be pilgrims, to be a human being, to have religious faith?

We want to sound the depths of this catharsis, this inner convulsion — be it intellectual, moral or religious — which makes us the person we are, able to tolerate and understand the other. We seem to perceive an experience which takes us beyond our own strength, our weaknesses, interests and power, and we recognize that the Way of Santiago, the path itself, helps us discover the truth of the symbol, the ecumenical road which leads to this "field of stars" [compostelas].

Alejo Carpentier has also written a beautiful story, the story of a pilgrim who never arrived at Santiago because there was always some business, some discussion which distracted him from the path. That pilgrim never came across the spring, or the old hermitage. He never realized that he was wasting his life away; for as he gained much wealth and power he was not aware that the things he "possessed" actually possessed *him* — and that they were of no lasting value.

Now that you have arrived in Santiago de Compostela you have the opportunity to "talk" with St James, who in the very stone of his statues symbolizes, as does no one else, unity in faith and harmony. The first can be understood only if you comprehend his serene glance towards the Gate of Glory at the plaza, that place of encounter among pilgrims, among the men and women passing through it; the second is to be found in the dialogue between the very stones from which the city of Santiago is built, the "language" and architecture of the buildings themselves showing how they are able to exist in harmony. And if the stones are capable of showing their identity to the world, what about you? What are *you* doing? What are *our* responsibilities today?

The ancient ballad of Don Gaiferos ends with the verse:

Where are you going, my pilgrim? Where do you want to go?

Don Gaiferos reached Compostela, practising a universal ecumenism and having as his dialogue partners his own faith and a love for the whole human community.

I am aware that we can free ourselves from prejudices and sterile dogmatisms only through a profound inner conversion; but each of us must choose — and find — his or her own way.

Thus I hope that in your meeting in our city, which is both the beginning and the end of your journey, you will discover the same inspiration which those persons of Mormaltán found more than a thousand years ago, and that you will seek the Way of Truth in this Land's End of Europe.

Santiago de Compostela, 3 August 1993

WELCOMING ADDRESS

DON MANUEL FRAGA IRIBORNE

Ladies and gentlemen, honoured members of this august assembly:

Permit me, as a layman with no specialized knowledge of the difficult theological questions raised by ecumenism today but, as a Christian believer, very interested in the success of this movement towards church unity, to recall the remarks made by the Catholic theologian Jean Daniélou and by Pastor Charles Westphal at the "rencontres"

His Excellency Don Manuel Fraga Iriborne is president of the Xunta of Galicia, Spain.

held in 1951 on humanity and culture in the twentieth century which, in my view, still hold good today on the threshold of the third millennium.

At that time Daniélou described the divisions among Christians as "not simply a tragedy for Christianity that is more serious than ever in the modern world, but also a tragedy for the whole of humanity". The famous French Jesuit was optimistic, however, emphasizing that

> unity is the will of God who made his church one, because the Spirit who lives in the church — and who is its soul — is seeking to reunite its separated members; because Christ is seeking with open arms to reunite his people.

Pastor Westphal fully supported the view of his "brother", Father Daniélou, on the divisions of Christianity, saying: "I am moved that we have been able to find such deep agreement in Jesus Christ." He then went on to examine the Christian image of humanity in the contemporary world and to warn that the road to unity could be a long one, calling for an "active faith moving forward in obedience"; a faith which, in the words of the great Calvinist theologian, Karl Barth, is sustained by a *theologia viatorum*, the theology of people on the move, of real pilgrims, walking in solidarity, in the hope of reaching the oikoumene, the inhabited earth, the universe in which we shall all be united and reconciled in Jesus Christ, according to the wish of the One who, in his "high-priestly prayer" before the Father, prayed "that they may all be one".

You could not have chosen a better place to hold this fifth world conference on Faith and Order; it was a wise idea to select the city of Santiago de Compostela which symbolizes the *theologia viatorum* propounded by Barth and many other Christian theologians. For historically, and still today, this city has been one of great places of Christian pilgrimage and precisely this year, in 1993, a jubilee year is being celebrated, a great year of forgiveness which includes a call to reconciliation among Christians.

The fact that some 350 qualified representatives of different Christian churches around the world are meeting here today to discuss the theme "Towards Koinonia in Faith, Life and Witness" is an event that represents hope and strength for all human beings who feel themselves pilgrims on this earth.

All of you who play an active role in the ecumenical movement show us an admirable example of humanity because, as we know, you attach central importance to dialogue as a method and attitude of mind that is essential to achieving your final goal; because you know that it is always possible "to share the truth, even when each one has not fully understood the other", as was pointed out by Prof. Juan Boch Navarro in his book *Para comprender el ecumenismo* ("Understanding Ecumenism").

At your ecumenical conferences — and of course at this world conference starting here in Compostela today — you have shown us clearly how right Reuel Howe is in his comments on the attitude of dialogue:

> ...dialogue is to love what blood is to the body. When the blood stops circulating the body dies. When dialogue stops, love dies and hatred and resentment are born. But dialogue can always revive a dead relationship.

And, no doubt, in the community life that naturally develops on a common pilgrimage, a march in solidarity towards the same goal, the attitude of dialogue that you advocate — the capacity to put oneself in the other's position — takes shape. Prof.

Juan Bosch reminds us in his book of the Iroquois saying that "no-one can judge another until he has walked at least a mile in his moccasins".

For all these reasons I believe that the history of the pilgrim way of Santiago — represented by thousands of people who continue to follow this route today from many different places — will help to foster a still greater atmosphere of dialogue at this conference so that we Christians may approach the third millennium with better prospects of unity, in accordance with the will of Christ expressed on the eve of his passion and death.

It is our hope that in this city of Compostela, this ancient place of pilgrimage, the "invisible monastery" for unity of which Paul Couturier spoke may constantly be active, in a spiritual climate of solidarity "as though the final time of the kingdom were already approaching, although in reality its fullness is yet to come."

I thank you.

WELCOME

ANTONIO MARIA ROUCO VARELA

Dear brothers and sisters, dear friends,

With great gratitude to our Lord and with joy I greet you and extend a warm welcome, in the name of the diocesan church of Santiago de Compostela, to all the participants in the fifth world conference on Faith and Order of the World Council of Churches.

We are *grateful to the Lord* because he has enlightened and accompanied your steps on the way to this church and this city, which has literally been born from the memory of one of the apostles of Jesus Christ, St James [Santiago] the Great. The book of Acts says of the apostles that "with great power [they] gave their testimony to the resurrection of the Lord Jesus" (4:33), to the point that they replied to the authorities of the town, who sought to keep them quiet, "we must obey God rather than any human authority" (5:29b; cf. 5:27-32) — a reply for which St James [Santiago] immediately became a martyr, for King Herod had him decapitated (12:2). This memory has attracted millions of pilgrims throughout the centuries, pilgrims who with their penitent footsteps have opened up the "Way of Santiago" throughout all of Europe as a way of reconciliation, unity and peace. Your presence in Santiago reminds us of this in a new and urgent way. The signs of our times require that we do not delay in this process — towards communion in the common apostolic faith, in a shared life in Christ, and in witness to the charity and love of Christ towards our brothers and sisters (especially the most humble and needy among those of this world) — which is demanded of us by the impulses coming today from the ecumenical movement and, above all, by the Spirit of the Lord.

The jubilee year which we celebrate thus becomes for us a call, to our archdiocese and to our sister dioceses in Spain, to a conversion to a more and more humble and authentic Christian identity, one which responds to the demand for ecclesial commun-

---

Archbishop Antonio María Rouco Varela is Roman Catholic archbishop of Santiago de Compostela.

ion and fraternal love amongst all of us who have been baptized in the name of the Father, the Son and the Holy Spirit.

And joy — *it is a profound joy* to be able to receive you in our house as brothers and sisters, "as the Lord". If there is any characteristic historical quality of this specific church of Santiago de Compostela, it is the fact that it understands and offers itself as a "house and home for pilgrims". John Paul II, when he came here in the summer of 1989 as a pilgrim, accompanied by a flood of young people anxious and thirsty for the gospel, exhorted us truly to *live* our vocation within the church. We want to *be* that for you, to share with you that true vocation, during these coming days: first through our prayers, and then by being available for you and by our humble service.

We would like to conclude in the best Christian spirit with the old Benedictine maxim, so deeply rooted here in this diocesan community of Santiago: *Hospes sicut Christus*. Welcome to Santiago de Compostela! In the name of the Lord, this is your house and your home.

STATEMENT OF WELCOME

ARTURO SANCHEZ

In the name of the Spanish Reformed Episcopal Church:

We extend to all the churches represented here the warmest welcome to our beloved country, and to the fifth world conference on Faith and Order meeting in this beautiful city of Santiago de Compostela.

We offer our heartfelt thanks and cordial welcome to the Commission on Faith and Order of the World Council of Churches. We are grateful to you for thinking of our country as the place to hold this important meeting. This is an admirable land, rich in symbolism, for the site in which you will study, pray and reflect on such a kerygmatic theme as our "communion in faith, life and witness".

We ask our God to illuminate and guide all the participants and pray that the blessing and inspiration of the Holy Spirit may make your work fruitful.

We long for the moment when our unity will become visible to the eyes of all humankind, in order that our deeds may manifest the greatness and glory of God in everyday life.

We wish with all our hearts that your stay in this beautiful city may be gratifying and that you will be able to enjoy its hospitality.

The Rt Rev. Arturo Sanchez is bishop of the Spanish Reformed Episcopal Church.

II

Faith and Order: Achievements, Vision and Promise

☐ Introduction

With the director's report which concluded plenary I the conference began to focus upon the work accomplished by Faith and Order since the previous Faith and Order world conference in Montreal in 1963, and the challenges and prospects for the future. This was developed in series of papers in plenary II, 4 August, 11h., vice-moderator Ms Veronica Swai presiding. The papers then enjoyed plenary discussion during the latter part of Plenary III.

Opening plenary II, Ms Swai called upon vice-moderator the Rev. Dr Paul A. Crow, Jr, to review the rules and procedures for plenary debate. He emphasized the three-minute time limit on speakers, noted that the sequence of speakers would be arranged so as to ensure a balanced discussion, and explained the right to speak as enjoyed by the delegates, plenary commission members, and younger theologians.

Moderator Dr Mary Tanner then presented her **paper**, which dealt with the work of the conference in the perspective of the future and offered a vision of the steps next needed in our ecumenical pilgrimage. This was followed by **complementary papers** delivered by the Rev. Mercedes Garcia Bachmann and the Rev. Dr Neville Callam. The plenary discussion of these texts is summarized on p. 35 below.

MONTREAL 1963-SANTIAGO DE COMPOSTELA 1993: REPORT OF THE DIRECTOR

GÜNTHER GASSMANN

Prelude

I prayed to God, sighing: "Lord, I've got 25 minutes to report on the thirty years of work done by Faith and Order from Montreal in 1963 to Santiago de Compostela in 1993. That's impossible!" And God answered: "In my history with you human beings, thirty years are but *one* second on the time-clock of the universe. You have 1,500 seconds. And in any case you've already written about these thirty years[1] — even if it's only in English — so concentrate on the essentials." "But what are the essentials?" I asked. And God said: "Just say it and the others will adjust what you have said and add to it."

So I was reminded once again that God's word gives us courage, but does not dispense us from making our own efforts. And it is in this perspective of God's will and gracious encouragement and our own theological efforts in response to them that I should also like to see the work of Faith and Order. In the past thirty years we have been able to serve God's history with his church and his world. We give thanks and praise to God that in the strength of the Holy Spirit we have been able to contribute something to the growing communion among the churches. We pray through Jesus Christ, our crucified and risen Lord, for forgiveness and for new strength wherever we have been too limited in our work and wherever we have failed to serve God's will boldly and effectively enough.

I should like briefly to outline a few essential aspects of the work of Faith and Order under the three headings of "differences", "continuity" and "new departures". It goes without saying that the work in question has always been done in the framework of the World Council of Churches and the wider ecumenical movement.

Montreal-Santiago de Compostela: differences

Just how far we have come in the past thirty years is most obvious if we look at the differences between today and the time of Montreal 1963. The conference in Montreal took place in the days when ecumenical thinking and action were still in the stage of development in the churches. The world confessional families and the Roman Catholic Church were just beginning to enter the ecumenical scene. National and regional councils of churches were only starting to be formed in many places. At the conference itself the representatives from the Orthodox churches and the participants from "third-world" countries were still a relatively small presence among 310 delegates, observers and youth delegates. Since Montreal the representation of the churches of Africa,

The Rev. Dr Günther Gassmann has been director of the secretariat of the Commission on Faith and Order since 1984. This paper was translated from the German by the WCC Language Service.

Asia, Latin America, the Caribbean and the Pacific region on the Commission and in our work has greatly increased. Besides Paul Minear, Oliver Tomkins and John Deschner, two prominent Orthodox theologians — John Meyendorff and Nikos Nissiotis — were moderators of the Faith and Order Commission during this time. Had not both been called away all too soon from this life they would certainly be with us today. In gratitude to God we remember them and Oliver Tomkins, who died last year.

From five observers at Montreal the Roman Catholic Church's participation and joint responsibility in Faith and Order became official in 1968, so we now have an official presence at this world conference, for the first time at an international ecumenical gathering. I see this as one of the most important differences between Montreal and Santiago de Compostela. The cooperation of Roman Catholic theologians has immensely expanded and enriched our work. We are hoping for a similar expansion with the increased involvement of theologians from Evangelical and Pentecostal churches and movements. In Montreal — I hardly dare say it and I hope I may have miscounted (not that it would change very much) — in Montreal there were three women among the participants: just one percent. Here the difference between now and then is likewise striking, even though we would have liked to see still more women among our participants. The growing number of women theologians in all the churches will make it possible to realize the goal of a true community of women and men in the work of Faith and Order also. And this enriching, God-given community will also make itself felt at this conference.

The theological discussion in Montreal was ahead of ecumenical thinking in the churches and their relations with one another. Discussion then turned on the question of intercommunion, which has become a reality today among many of the member churches; nonetheless its wider fulfilment must still remain one of the essential goals of our work. The important clarifications on the understanding of scripture, Tradition and traditions in Montreal were not really taken up by the churches and reappeared on the Faith and Order agenda in the eighties, with the responses to the Lima document on *Baptism, Eucharist and Ministry*.

There was one sphere, however, where the churches were ahead of the 1963 discussions in Montreal, and that was in the church union negotiations between churches of different confessions in different parts of the world, of which there were more than forty. Encouraged by the formation of the Church of South India in 1947, and no doubt also by the emphasis on the goal of organic unity or union in Faith and Order texts (e.g. Edinburgh 1937) these union negotiations were at that time an important form of ecumenical effort. In the years before Montreal the question of ministry, and more especially the office of bishop in apostolic succession, was already one of their most difficult problems, but it was not until Montreal that the question again appeared on our agenda.

A great deal more could be said about the differences between Montreal and Santiago de Compostela, especially in regard to the fundamentally altered ecumenical situation and, above all, the radical historical changes that have taken place in the world, to which we refer in the introduction to the discussion paper for this conference. But also the continuity in our work has in itself contributed to the fact that we are meeting here for this conference in a quite different ecumenical context.

Montreal-Santiago de Compostela: continuity

One thing has been clear from the outset in the Faith and Order movement in 1910: this movement — and since 1948 this Commission — is about church unity. But what kind of unity are we talking about? A first answer was that it was certainly not just an inward, spiritual, invisible unity but also an outward, visible manifestation of the unity that is already given us in Jesus Christ. The process of reflection on the conditions and the forms in which such visible unity could be expressed began already at the world conferences in Lausanne (1927) and Edinburgh (1937) and led to the statement on church unity prepared by Faith and Order and adopted by the WCC assembly in New Delhi in 1961, which was to be of such significance for the whole ecumenical movement. Faith and Order likewise prepared the way for the emphasis on a universal and conciliar form of Christian unity at the WCC assembly in Uppsala in 1968. A consultation in 1973 on "Concepts of Unity and Models of Union" developed the concept of a conciliar fellowship of churches, which was then incorporated into the report of section II at the WCC assembly in Nairobi in 1975. In 1978 the Commission meeting in Bangalore emphasized three requirements for visible unity: (1) a common understanding of the apostolic faith; (2) full mutual recognition of baptism, eucharist and ministry; (3) agreement on common forms of teaching and decision-making.

In 1990 the Commission prepared a new statement on the goal of visible unity which was revised and adopted by the WCC assembly in Canberra in 1991. Here the ambiguous term "unity" — which has acquired a certain negative resonance in the wake of recent developments in the socio-political field — is being interpreted by the concept of "koinonia". More clearly than unity, koinonia can be seen as an integral element in the wider context of God's saving action for the whole of humanity and of creation, which the church has to serve as sign and instrument. This view of church unity as koinonia is the central focus which is at the start and the finish of our discussions here at this world conference.

The three themes of baptism, eucharist and ministry have likewise been on Faith and Order's agenda since 1910. But discussion of them was more intensive in the period between Montreal and Santiago and was broadened by the involvement of Roman Catholic theologians. The various studies led in 1974 to the "Accra document" which was revised in the light of many comments. This work reached a decisive stage with the adoption of the texts on *Baptism, Eucharist and Ministry* (BEM) in Lima in 1982. Never before has an ecumenical document received such wide distribution and elicited such discussion and reaction in the churches. The responses say unanimously that the ecumenical theological dialogue has achieved an important ecumenical step forward. Discussion on BEM is continuing — the WCC recently published the 26th printing of the English edition. The text has helped to enrich and renew theological thinking, worship and practice in many churches. BEM has become an ecumenical reference text which is evoked in bilateral conversations and negotiations between churches. The text is continuing to have its impact. But some of the more deep-seated differences in the three areas, notably in the question of ministry in the apostolic succession, have yet to be overcome. The question of the ordination of women to the ministry of the church was rather inadequately dealt with in BEM, from both the theological and the ecumenical point of view, and the discussion on fellowship in the Lord's supper/intercommunion has not been continued in the work of Faith and Order since 1971. So the discussion of the Lima themes must continue, not least here at this conference.

Another line of continuity since Montreal can be seen in Faith and Order's commitment (ever since 1954) to reporting regularly on developments in united and uniting churches. These churches and union negotiations are important laboratories and expressions of ecumenical effort. But they do not have any worldwide ecumenical organization at their disposal. That is why, since 1967, we have undertaken to organize regular international consultations for the united and uniting churches. This enables them to benefit from one another's experience and reflect together on their specific contribution to ecumenical discussion. The sixth consultation is planned for 1995.

Shortly after Montreal, in 1965, the Joint Working Group between the Roman Catholic Church and the World Council of Churches was formed. Faith and Order has special ties with this Group, not just because the Commission is the only body in the WCC on which the Roman Catholic Church is officially represented, but also because we have been involved in a number of studies commissioned by the Joint Working Group: "Catholicity and Apostolicity" (1970), "Towards a Confession of the Common Faith" (1980), "The Notion of 'Hierarchy of Truths'", and "The Church: Local and Universal" (both 1990), and lastly, a booklet of ecumenical interpretations of the Canberra unity statement (1991), which we have brought with us for you.

Continuity is also reflected in the awareness that common prayer for Christian unity and reflection on the ecumenical significance of worship and spirituality are fundamental in all ecumenical efforts. This insight is not only reflected in many Faith and Order texts. Since 1966 it has been given tangible form in a yearly joint consultation with the Pontifical Council for Promoting Christian Unity at which the material for the Week of Prayer for Christian Unity is prepared and then made available to the churches. The reflection on worship between Lund (1952) and Uppsala (1968), at a consultation on "Worship in a Secular Age" (1968) should be taken up again and linked with the Lima document. We were involved in the preparation of the ecumenical hymnbook *Cantate Domino* (1974) and, together with the Sub-unit on Renewal and Congregational Life, in the compilation of the two ecumenical prayer cycles, *For All God's People* (1978) and *With All God's People* (1989). Although it was in fact prepared as the order of service for the closing worship at Lima in 1982, the so-called "Lima liturgy" has been surprisingly widely used at ecumenical gatherings, including Vancouver in 1983 and Canberra in 1991. This is probably due to the awareness that common prayer and common worship are not just a precondition for ecumenical effort but are also an expression and celebration of the communion/koinonia already achieved on the way towards full communion.

Continuity also implies development, change, new interpretations. Without that, there can be no true continuity in the church and in our work.

Montreal-Santiago de Compostela: new departures

Between Montreal and Santiago de Compostela new steps have been undertaken, taking up old questions in new ways and reacting to new insights and situations.

In the theological and historical context of Montreal, and above all Uppsala in 1968, renewed emphasis was placed on the perspective of God's purpose and action in universal history. The Uppsala statements accordingly set the efforts for church unity in the wider context of the renewal and unity of [hu]mankind. This was the starting point for a much-debated study by Faith and Order on "The Unity of the Church and the Unity of Mankind", begun in 1969. It related the question of church unity in a new way to the unity of the human race, to creation and history, also bringing in ecclesiological considerations such as the concept of the church as "sign". The inter-relation between the unity of the church and the struggle for justice, the encounter with other faiths, the struggle against racism, the place of the handicapped in the church and in society, and differences in culture were also discussed and some of these themes were dealt with in greater depth at consultations on each specific issue. Differences of opinion within the Commission prevented the elaboration of a comprehensive conclud-ing report. In 1974 a brief statement summarized some of the important insights of the study.

The subject of church and humanity did, however, reappear on Faith and Order's agenda in 1982, this time in the form of a study on "The Unity of the Church and the Renewal of Human Community". The main aim of the study was to investigate the inter-relation between the concern for the unity of the church and service for the renewal of human community in an overall ecclesiological perspective, examining its implications in concrete terms in the two areas of the struggle for justice and the community of women and men in the church. The text which concludes this stage of the study, *Church and World*,[2] is now available in English, German and French and will soon be ready in Portuguese and Spanish. It seeks to help the churches to reflect together on the fundamental theological inter-relatedness of their different ecumenical efforts. It is therefore one of the important preparatory texts for this conference.

The reason why the community of women and men was included in the study on unity and renewal (with three international consultations) was the continuation of another new departure in our work since Montreal. From 1974 to 1981 — despite, or perhaps precisely because of, the fact that there were only three women in Montreal — Faith and Order cooperated with the WCC's Sub-unit on Women in Church and Society in conducting a study on the "Community of Women and Men in the Church". Important consultations, for instance on the "Ordination of Women in Ecumenical Pespective" or "Towards a Theology of Human Wholeness" were part of this work which likewise involved local study groups, 150 of which sent a report to Geneva. The major consultation in Sheffield in 1981 marked the end of this study but the issue at stake in it remains on the ecumenical agenda and that of Faith and Order. Here, too, it is a matter of koinonia in faith, life and witness.

Another new departure after Montreal was the fact that Faith and Order did not deal only with the traditionally divisive issues and how to overcome them, but also tackled the task of jointly restating and confessing the fundamental convictions of the Christian faith. Without fellowship in the confession and life of the one faith all our ecumenical efforts would be built on sand. In 1971, after two initial projects on "Creation, New Creation and the Unity of the Church" and "God in Nature and History" a study was started on "Giving Account of the Hope That Is in Us". For the first time a deliberately contextual approach was used in conjunction with the more traditional Faith and Order method. This work led in 1978 to the widely-acclaimed statement "A Common Account of Hope".

In 1975 the WCC assembly in Nairobi requested the churches to "receive, reappropriate and confess together... the Christian truth and faith, delivered through the apostles" (section II, para. 19). Preliminary work on a common statement of our faith (1978), "Confessing the Common Faith" (1980), the *filioque* clause in the Nicene Creed (1978 and 1979) and on its ecumenical significance (1981) led the Lima meeting in 1982 to launch a new study entitled "Towards the Common Expression of the Apostolic Faith Today". The result of this is an ecumenical explication of the Nicene-Constantinopolitan Creed (381), *Confessing the One Faith*.[3] At present the book is available in English, German, French, Italian, Portuguese and Swedish, and it will shortly be published in Norwegian and Spanish. It is hoped that the document will help the churches to reappropriate the common apostolic faith, to recognize it in one another's faith and life, and on this more profound basis to confess it together in our present-day world. This task will continue to occupy our attention at this conference. Incidentally, I have not abandoned my long-cherished hope of publishing a short version of the insights and challenges emerging from these studies for use in local congregations.

Other new steps among those taken between Montreal and Santiago de Compostela include (and here I simply offer a list):
— the studies on the authority and interpretation of the Bible and on the relationship between the Old and New Testaments, which developed Montreal's fundamental clarifications on scripture and Tradition (1964-80);
— the widely-acclaimed work on the importance of the councils of the ancient church for the ecumenical movement and for the understanding of conciliarity (1964-74);
— work linked to both these areas on authority in the church (1974-77), which is now back again on our agenda;
— studies on "Spirit, Order and Organization" (1964-71) and "Church and State" (1976), which were unfortunately not taken further.

Lastly, after Montreal the ecumenical dialogue was considerably expanded by an ever-growing number of international bilateral dialogues started between the Roman Catholic Church and Christian World Communions, and then also between the latter. Forty-eight dialogue commissions have been at work to date. From 1964 to 1971 Faith and Order organized four consultations between the Orthodox and Oriental Orthodox churches in preparation for their official dialogue (started in 1985). The themes and goals of the bilateral dialogues largely correspond to those of the multilateral dialogue in Faith and Order. In order to promote relations between the two forms of ecumenical dialogue and encourage a sense of fellowship and complementarity, we have — amongst other things — organized five meetings of the forum on bilateral dialogues since 1978, at the request of the world communions. The sixth forum will take place in 1994. The reports of the bilateral dialogues and of the multilateral dialogue over the past twenty years show that a stimulating process of cross-fertilization has developed between the two.

Postlude

We can look back on an intensive and fruitful period of work. Our small staff and limited financial means have set many limits. It has proved impossible to continue certain lines of work. Our work has been considerably influenced by the themes and methods belonging to the history and theology of the churches in Europe and North America; this is understandable, that being the historical context from which the divisions in Christianity were exported all over the world. But it must not prevent us from including the theological questions and approaches of churches in other parts of the world in our thinking to a much greater extent than we have done up till now. We thank the governing bodies and our colleagues in the WCC for their support and cooperation. We thank the churches which have participated in so many different ways in our studies and made the necessary financial resources available.

Faith and Order has contributed considerably to the changed relationships and ways of thinking and action in the ecumenical community. But much remains to be done. We owe it to God and to our strife-torn world to be a credible communion in faith, life and witness, to the glory of God, and so that reconciliation, hope and true life may blossom wherever people are persecuted, humiliated and their lives bereft of meaning. In the cries of human beings God also judges our failure to be messengers of reconciliation and life for one another. If we are to make a reconciled and reconciling koinonia a reality, we will need the continued contribution of this unique, worldwide theological instrument which as the movement and the Commission on Faith and Order has become part of the church history of this century.

I read my report aloud to God and God said: "Your report is a bit dry, like so many reports. But that doesn't matter, because your sister Mary Tanner will add a lively counterpoint later on." "By the way," God added, "you forgot to mention the study on 'The Church and the Jewish People' (1967), and I'm glad Faith and Order is involved in work on that important subject again. You could also have said that Faith and Order has produced 120 publications since Montreal and held 148 meetings and consultations." I answered: "But I had so little time!" And God spoke: "I have time — but you people have to use it!"

NOTES

[1] Paul A. Crow & Günther Gassmann, *Lausanne 1927 to Santiago de Compostela 1993*, Faith and Order paper no. 160, Geneva, WCC, 1993, pp.15-31; Günther Gassmann ed., *Documentary History of Faith and Order 1963-1993*, Faith and Order paper no. 159, Geneva, WCC, 1993.
[2] Faith and Order Paper no. 151, Geneva, WCC, 1990.
[3] Faith and Order Paper no. 153, Geneva, WCC, 1991.

THE TASKS OF THE WORLD CONFERENCE
IN THE PERSPECTIVE OF THE FUTURE

MARY TANNER

Context and task

1. As we greet one another on this first day of the fifth world conference on Faith and Order, exchanging stories of the places and churches from which we come, we are aware that we gather together in the context of a dramatically changing world scene. This is not simply the backcloth against which this world conference takes place. It is woven into the daily lives of each of us. We are all caught up in the growing economic and social divide between North and South, the transfer of wealth from poor to rich countries, the turmoil caused by the breakdown of socialist systems in Eastern Europe. We are all affected, some more tragically than others, by bitter nationalistic and ethnic conflicts, terrorist violence, exploitation of the created order and the hardening of attitudes of those of one faith community towards another. Of course, there are individual acts of generosity and self-sacrifice, community acts of kindness and aid, as well as the near miraculous inventions of science and technology which help to alleviate suffering. Nevertheless, in these struggles do not the forces of selfishness and destruction appear to have the upper hand in the world — and often within ourselves? It is of paramount importance that consideration of ecumenical advance and of ecumenical strategy should never lose sight of the fact that this is the context in which, as Christians, we are absolutely required to show forth the possibility God has for all humanity and for all creation. Only in obedience to the requirements of this context can we hope to discover appropriate forms and images of the unity God gives.

2. The world conference takes place in the context of a restless ecumenical scene. Progress has been made in the thirty years since Montreal and we must celebrate that. The Roman Catholic Church's full participation for the first time in a world conference on Faith and Order gives a greater wholeness to our gathering, lacking in some other ecumenical meetings. The embracing of those so-called black-led churches and those of Pentecostal and Evangelical traditions also enriches the ecumenical community. Representation from Latin America, Africa, Asia and the Pacific as well as women, present in more just proportions, have helped Faith and Order since Montreal to integrate the contextual and liberation elements with the historical and systematic approaches to our work. Everyone has been talking to everyone else since Montreal in a complex network of bilateral conversations. Agreements have been reached in areas where differences once were thought intractable. Every regional consultation in the remarkable series of nine consultations leading to this conference had good stories to tell of cooperation between Christians in the region.[1] But these regional consultations

Dr Mary Tanner is general secretary of the Council for Christian Unity of the General Synod of the Church of England, and moderator of the Faith and Order Commission.

also spoke of growing disillusionment, not least of all with official ecumenism in the ecumenical movement. Every region spoke of competitive evangelism and proselytism of one Christian group by another. Some spoke of their anguish at the decision of Anglicans to ordain women to the priesthood and the episcopate — this action, so full of promise for some, for others appears to deny the achievements of the past. Experienced ecumenical theologians questioned the method of our work of seeking convergence in faith through dialogue; we seem to be arguing from different premises, asking different questions of the same texts or looking for more agreement than ever will be possible. Most unnerving of all are those who said that the search for visible unity itself is misplaced and unattainable: we should settle for good relations across denominational divides, cooperation in service and intercommunion.

3. It is within the context of a world in turmoil and a fragile ecumenical movement that we must consider the tasks of this conference. Whatever we say must speak to the realities of our world and the realities of this ecumenical scene. This is surely expected of us, for the aim of Faith and Order, set out in our by-laws, links the visible unity of the church with the destiny of the world. The aim is:

> to proclaim the oneness of the church of Jesus Christ and to call the churches to the goal of visible unity in one faith, and one eucharistic fellowship expressed in worship and in common life in Christ in order that the world may believe.[2]

The task of harvesting

4. Now is the time (as in Lausanne in 1927, Edinburgh in 1937, Lund in 1952 and Montreal in 1963) for Faith and Order to lay before this body of official delegates of the churches the work accomplished in the thirty years since Montreal. One task must be to review and harvest the work, summed up in the three studies: *Confessing the One Faith; Baptism, Eucharist and Ministry;* and *Church and World*.[3] These are not three unrelated studies: faith is expressed in liturgy, as well as in creed; in life, as well as in word; and we are sent out from the liturgy to witness in faithful discipleship in the common round of daily life. The agenda of these three studies is inextricably bound together: each relates to one of the "characteristics" or "requirements" of visible unity.

a) Towards communion in faith

5. The apostolic faith study aims to draw us together into a "communion in faith". We whose lives are lived in isolation must necessarily find ways of building confidence that, at the level of faith, we do believe the same God, Father, Son and Holy Spirit, the same Christ, mediator of salvation, the same Holy Spirit, pulsator of life, the same one, holy, catholic and apostolic church, and we share a common hope in the age to come.

6. Here in Santiago, we must ask: is the ambitious task of explicating the biblical faith through the "prism" of the Nicene-Constantinopolitan Creed in fact helping our churches to recognize the apostolic faith in their own lives? Is it helping our churches to recognize that same faith in the lives of others — whether they formally recite the creed or not? Is the text of explication, *Confessing the One Faith*, proving to be an instrument capable of provoking recognition of the faith? Is it an instrument of passage which will lead us, beyond recognition of the faith in our own lives and in each other, to common confession?

7. There are those who doubt whether it will ever be possible to achieve *common* confession of the apostolic faith. Even when it is clearly stated that there will always be different expressions of the one faith, "where", they ask, "does content end and expression begin?" We need to be careful not to sound as if the hurdle of faith commitment is being raised higher and higher: we seek only that which is "sufficient and required". Here we have an opportunity to show that the ecumenical symbol is a potentially exciting, basic faith symbol. Far from imprisoning us in a bygone age, it has the power to release us to live together in the present and into the future in continuity with the past. The symbol maps out for us the central matters of faith which we are to confess together — not as a bare formula of words, but as a faith inseparable from its expression in liturgy and its expression in life.

8. Many of our churches have hardly begun to respond to this study. What more should Faith and Order do to make this work accessible? This world conference provides a timely opportunity to repeat the challenge of the Canberra statement:[4]

> to move towards the recognition of the apostolic faith as expressed through the Nicene-Constantinopolitan Creed in the life and witness of one another.

When we have responded to this challenge we can move beyond recognition to *common* confession.

b) Towards communion in life

9. Here we must review and harvest the work done to draw us into a communion in life, focused in sacramental life — a sacramental life inseparable from the total life of discipleship in the ordinary stuff of everyday living. Central to this task is assessing *Baptism, Eucharist and Ministry*. Since Lima in 1982 churches have identified issues that need further work (underlying issues of scripture and Tradition, sacrament and sacramentality, ecclesiology; as well as issues in each of the three areas that need revisiting: the relation of faith to baptism, the ordination of women to the priesthood, apostolicity and succession, etc.). Again, we need to take care that we seek only that agreement which is "sufficient and required". A Roman Catholic participant in one of the regional consultations gave a timely warning: "This is my dream of Santiago de Compostela — that churches should withdraw from any maximalistic demand to provide a full theological and canonical agreement on all the points where they have inherited different positions and views from the past and move to closer living."

10. This world conference must consider the challenge given by my two predecessors, Nikos Nissiotis and John Deschner.[5] How are we to get beyond speculation, beyond theorizing about BEM and find direct and tangible effects on the life of the churches? We must reconsider BEM's potential as "an instrument of convergence" in life, finding time to encourage one another with stories of where that text has already been used to supply building blocks in forming closer relationships: used in the bilateral dialogues to note agreements in faith; used as a basis for shared living in cooperating parishes and local ecumenical projects; used in the various regions of the world in new bilateral agreements such as the Meissen agreement in Europe and the agreement in the USA between Anglicans and Lutherans; used in the formation of more inclusive councils of churches. All of these moves are supported by the convergences expressed in the BEM text. This relativizes the accusation that conver-

gence methodology has had its day. And these new partnerships in ecumenical living, at least for some of us, make clear that there is no way back.

11. But Faith and Order itself cannot effect change in our churches' relations with one another. We can however, here in Santiago, *re-present* BEM, pleading that our churches, which sponsored its production and engaged in its maturation, give much more serious consideration to developing relationships on the basis of its firm foundations. We should reiterate the challenges of the Canberra statement:
— to recognize each other's baptisms;
— to consider, wherever appropriate, forms of eucharistic hospitality, gladly acknowledging that some who do not observe these rites share in the spiritual experience of a life in Christ;
— to move towards a mutual recognition of ministries.
Rightly linked to this are challenges to a life of discipleship:
— to work for justice, peace and the integrity of creation, linking more closely the search for sacramental communion of the church with the struggles for justice and peace.

12. We shall, however, not get far with this conversation without stubbing our toes on the familiar divide between those churches which feel able to take steps towards eucharistic hospitality and a shared ministry on the basis of a degree of agreement in faith, and those churches which look for agreement in faith on *all* the interconnected elements of unity before moving to sacramental hospitality, given or received. The mark of maturity in ecumenism is surely that we respect each other's positions. Pilgrims together on the road need sustenance and yet at the same time the gathering around the one table will express the fullness of the unity God gives. Acknowledging this must not stop us from asking, are there appropriate occasions where eucharistic hospitality could be extended? And, if we are unable to grow in sacramental hospitality in certain ecclesial relationships, how can those same relationships mark, in other appropriate ways, the degree of shared faith that we know already binds us together? Unless *all* our churches find ways of turning the ever-growing pile of ecumenical texts into shared life, will not new divisions appear between those who do find ways to progress and those who do not? There will be a greater divide between the world of "private ecumenism" in interchurch families, women's groups, local Bible study groups, house churches and the formal, structural ecumenism most of us represent. More and more, especially the young, will "vote with their feet". It will be little wonder if disillusionment grows with the distinctive doctrinal task of Faith and Order and the ecumenical movement becomes limited to one of social involvement and activity: "a movement of movements".

c) Towards communion in witness

13. We must review and harvest the work focused in *Church and World*. This is the study which most helps us to understand the essential link between the vocation of the church and the destiny of the world in the perspective of the kingdom. Without this work we should be in danger of spending too much energy on what it means to become churches together, apart from the world, rather than churches together *in* and *for* the world. Without this work, we should be in danger of concentrating only on becoming Christians together and losing sight of being Christians together *among* and *with* those of other faiths. *Church and World* lays much emphasis on the church as "mystery" and

"prophetic sign" in the midst of a world in which we are not separate, but, *in* and *with* the whole creation, a part.

14. Since Montreal studies on the handicapped, race and, most strikingly, the "Community of Women and Men" have demonstrated the need for renewal in the community of the church if the church is to be a credible "prophetic sign".[6] They show how human divisions influence the very language and images with which we express our faith, the way we celebrate the sacraments, exercise the ministry, order our lives, serve the world and engage in mission. Becoming a communion in witness entails not only breaking down the walls of partition between our churches, but also the constant renewal of our lives by the overcoming of human divisions which penetrate the life of the church. Becoming a communion in witness is about being "renewed into unity" — learning to live together a life of constant repentance of sin and constant renewal into unity. The struggle to keep the work of unity and renewal within the orbit of Faith and Order is one of the success stories of the period since Montreal. This world conference will do well to ask whether the insights, particularly of the community study, have radically influenced our understanding of visible unity.

15. As we struggle to understand the relationship of church to world, we need to establish a more intentional relationship with the work of other parts of the ecumenical movement. The experience of those engaged in the conciliar process on JPIC and the experiences of those engaged in common mission and dialogue with those of other faiths, have important insights about the sort of visible unity that would best be "prophetic sign". For example, the joint consultation between JPIC and Faith and Order (the Rønde consultation) challenges us to consider unity in terms of "moral community".[7] In the perspective of the future the regional consultations suggested that the work of *Church and World* needs now to study the place of racial, ethnic and national differences. The allying of ethnic and racial differences with denominational differences plays an insidious and deadly part in contemporary conflicts, contradicting the vocation of the church as "prophetic sign". Here is an important agenda opening up if we are to enrich our understanding of the sort of visible unity that will best be "sign" for the world of its own possibilities.

16. So, one task of this world conference is to "harvest" the work of the years since Montreal asking: what has been achieved, what are the outstanding stumbling blocks, what more remains to be done? However, in planning this conference, Faith and Order has not sought simply to "harvest" three separate studies. We have been much more ambitious. The three studies have been brought within a single framework in such a way that each is seen to contribute an overall "portraiture" of visible unity: each contributes to a cohesive ecumenical vision. To the question where are we going in the ecumenical movement, the answer given is "towards a communion in faith, life and witness".

The task of envisioning

17. The theme of koinonia is no new one to Faith and Order. From Lausanne to Santiago our documents contain classic statements from Orthodox, but not only Orthodox members. It is increasingly a central theme in the work of bilateral dialogues and in the self-understanding of many world communions. It is the most promising theme of contemporary ecumenical theology, resonating with contemplative experi-

ence and the experience of close human relationships. It seems the theme most likely to breathe new life into the search for visible unity.

18. Koinonia draws our attention away from our divisions directing us to that giving and receiving life and love which flow between the persons of the Holy Trinity. This mysterious life of divine communion is one in which the personal and relational are prior; in which multiplicity is perfectly held together so that there is no separation, while at the same time the very unity is enriched by the multiplicity, so that it never degenerates into arid uniformity. It is a communion at the heart of which is a cross and it is a communion which is dynamic, always sending and being sent, stretching out to embrace and enfold within its own life.

19. As we come, through contemplation in prayer and through experience of life in community, to a shared understanding of that divine Trinitarian life we shall get hold together of a deeper understanding of the unity of the church. For the unity we are to live out is none other than the "grace of our Lord Jesus Christ, the love of God and the fellowship of the Holy Spirit". That is the life into which we are enfolded through baptism as we die with Christ and rise to new life in him and that is the life we are to make visible in the unity of the church. We must not be diverted from the quest for visible unity but rather ask, what sort of communion in faith would testify to this sort of God? What sort of communion in life would be "prophetic sign" of this sort of God? What sort of communion in witness would portray this sort of God? It is as we interpret what we have already understood about visible unity in the light of koinonia that we are most likely to revitalize the portrait of visible unity and provide a "cohesive ecumenical vision".[8]

20. If visible unity is about living in the world the communion of God's own Trinitarian life, then our portrait of visible unity must demonstrate that the personal and relational are prior to the institutional and organizational. Without the institutional, the personal and relational are hampered. But we cannot grow in unity unless that springs from a growth in personal relations at every level of the church's life. Personal and relational attitudes are the "living tissue" of our unity and a sign that our unity is grounded in God's own life flowing in us. We must be at peace with each other, we must learn to forgive, trust and expect the best of one another, above all we must love one another.

21. If visible unity is about living in the world the communion of God's own life, then our portrait of visible unity must astonish us with its diversity. We seek a diversity in the expression of the faith, a diversity in life and a diversity in witness, by which the gospel is lived in each place authentically in the bodies, skins, dances, languages and thought-forms of that place. The battle sparked off at the Canberra assembly by the theatrical, dramatic presentation of Prof. Chung Hyun Kyung led to a fierce debate on whether there are limits to diversity in inculturating the faith in different regions of the world.[9] That suggestion for some speaks of exclusion in a faith which by its very nature marvellously seeks to include.[10] And yet, is not the decisive reason for "limits" a proper insistence on the imperative to maintain a unity in the faith community through the ages, as well as a proper distinction between truth and error? Without this insistence will not new divisions appear between the churches and between groups within the churches?[11]

22. If visible unity is about living in the world the communion of God's own life, then our portrait of visible unity will show a church always in dialogue, always

searching to discern the truth of God and the right conduct of life with one another. We must risk living with the provisional, for the truth of God and the mystery of the divine Trinity are wonderfully complex, delicately balanced, infinitely subtle. They can never be trapped in hard-edged, inflexible moulds. We must not expect fundamentalistic certainties. There has to be ceaseless cultural reinterpretation, both linguistic and conceptual. The same gospel story must be told, the same credal symbol recited but these are reinterpreted as proof that the same apostolic tradition is alive and still relevant today.

23. If visible unity is about living in the world the communion of God's own life then our portrait of visible unity must show that tension, even conflict, will always be part of life this side of the kingdom. "Sharp things that divide us can paradoxically turn out to be gift... The world with all its divisions is not used to such a possibility as this: that those on opposing sides should stay together, should remain in dialogue, bearing each other's burdens, even entering one another's pain."[12] If we are able, by grace, to live together bearing the cost of difference, we shall get hold, at a deeper level, of a communion with a God who suffered and we shall be rewarded with an experience of communion which is grounded in the communion of the Holy Trinity at whose heart is forever a cross.

24. If visible unity is about living out the communion of God's own life then our portrait of visible unity must be of a church never turned in on itself, obsessively concerned with preserving itself apart from the messiness of the world. It will be a church always prepared to risk moving outwards expecting to find God in the world. It will be a church always sending out in order to welcome and embrace within the inclusive community of the church.

25. I have spent much time on this second task of "re-visioning" the goal of visible unity for so much is at stake here. Faith and Order's vocation is at stake, the vocation to call the churches to visible unity and to keep this vision alive at the centre of the work of the World Council of Churches and the wider ecumenical movement. Visible unity, reinterpreted by koinonia, breathes new life into the portrait of the unity we seek. Moreover, koinonia reorders our priorities — God, the world, the church, reminding us that communion is grounded in the order of creation itself and is realized in part in the natural relationships of family and kinship, of tribe and people and in the good things of creation. The life of communion in the church builds upon and transforms but never wholly replaces communion in the order of creation. The visible communion of the church is to demonstrate what God intends for the whole of humanity and creation — a foretaste of the kingdom. Here is the rationale for our distinctive Faith and Order work and the rationale which interprets all the other dimensions of Christian unity, not least of all the search for justice, peace and the mending of creation.

The task of fomulating an agenda

26. A third task of this world conference is to indicate an agenda for the next period of Faith and Order's work. Already we have seen things that need to be continued and developed in relation to *Confessing the One Faith*, *Baptism, Eucharist and Ministry* and *Church and World*. This ought not to depress us. Faith and Order's work has always been characterized by the patient and persistent nurturing of an agenda related to those basic requirements for unity, however unpopular and unfashionable this may appear.

27. But as we look to the future one element is lacking in the portrait of unity. Some find threatening the language of "structures of decision-making and teaching with authority" as a requirement for visible unity. Yet structures of conciliar communion are needed to serve a church always in dialogue, always searching to discern truth afresh under the Spirit's guidance. What bonds of communion, "personal, collegial and communal" at the different levels of church life, working according to subsidiarity, would enable the church to live in fidelity to the apostolic faith, keeping us mutually accountable and enabling us to serve and witness in the world?[13] If Faith and Order fails to take up this agenda it will fail in its task of providing the bilateral dialogues with an over-arching context in which each may view its own work on authority. Most important of all it will fail to fill out the one part of the portrait of visible unity without which the rest remains incomplete. It will be an uncomfortable agenda. Each church will have to face questions of structure and leadership and the exercise of power that belong to conciliar communion (not least of all issues of primacy) which test their own self-understanding and practice. No church has a perfect model of conciliar life. Are not all our structures in need of reformation? Nevertheless, it is strangely this characteristic requirement of visible unity that may prove most receptive to the notion of koinonia. To call for a study on this unfinished agenda, within a study of ecumenical perspectives on ecclesiology, would surely give wise direction for the next decade.

28. Any developing of Faith and Order's work will need attention to both method and structure. The Latin American consultation called for a deconstruction of the classical Faith and Order method, stressing the need to begin with the experience of Christians gathered together in base communities to read the scriptures and to act in service together. This experience indeed renders profound truths about a life of unity. But what is the relation of this to that truth discovered through going back together to scripture and Tradition? Our work must surely take account of continuity from the apostolic community until now by looking at history, events, experience, liturgy, for that inner meaning, that "nerve centre" that makes us apostolic. But, if it is not possible to form doctrine from perpetual newness, it is equally impossible to form doctrine today by simply restating old categories without explication in relation to that perpetual newness. We should be challenged in Faith and Order to find an ecumenical method which lives more in the "in between", constantly living the tradition handed on through the ages and constantly open to new ways of understanding and living the faith of the church in today's world. In this way we shall remain apostolic and catholic in the sense of what all in every place and at every time believe. For that, we need a more inclusive community for reflection and interpretation, open to every culture and ecclesial tradition. We need to ask who is missing from our circle — and whom do we silence *within* our circle?

29. The future work of Faith and Order needs right method. It also needs structures that will enable its work. Like every institution the World Council of Churches is subject to restructuring. In 1947 Bishop Headlam (of my own church) feared that the integration of Faith and Order into the WCC would mean diminution of its distinctive task and witness. We must seek more effective partnership with other parts of the WCC while continuing to be focused on the distinctive task we have been given: we must seek to be interdependent and yet retain a degree of autonomy. Faith and Order has a special mandate in seeking to overcome those things that divide churches and to

act as "a continuing, identifiable and persistent reminder and advocate of the central task to call the churches to visible unity".[14] Faith and Order also has a duty to represent those who have no voice within the structures of the World Council of Churches. Our time together provides, as earlier world conferences have all done, for a discussion of just these issues.

The task of challenging

30. A fourth and last task of this world conference is to challenge the churches we represent. We can reiterate those sharp challenges of the Canberra statement. These relate most specifically to the work on faith and life and witness urging convergence in faith to go hand in hand with convergence in life.

31. Our theme of koinonia helps us to recognize that, in spite of our continuing ecclesial divisions, we do already share a real, though not full communion. It is a communion given in baptism and built on all that we already share in faith and in life. We must urge the churches to honour and protect that very real communion which exists and not to slip back from that which has been achieved. We must live now sensitive to each other's needs and perceptions, even when we disagree over developments in their lives. The mark of our communion is surely that we never again say "I have no need of you", but consult each other, continue in honest and critical dialogue, remaining open to new possibilities offered by the other.

32. Perhaps the most important challenge of all will be to look for recommitment to the goal of visible unity — reinterpreted, revisioned by an understanding of koinonia. Do our churches really want unity and if so are they prepared to take costly steps towards koinonia in faith, life and witness? If we as individuals and if our churches are serious about visible unity then we must accept that this requires *metanoia*, a deep and constant conversion of heart and mind on the part of ourselves and the Christian communities from which we come.

What lies before us?

33. So what lies before us? What lies before us are ten gifted days together in which in worship and Bible study, surrounded by a much larger company of pilgrims in this city, we shall experience something of the communion of God's own life and love about which we talk. The days provide time for harvesting; time for charting new directions; time for challenging and, most important of all, time to reaffirm commitment to a communion in faith, life and witness.

34. What lies before us? What lies before us is a world in which millions are homeless and go hungry, where people betray one another, where they rape, murder and torture, where women and children are used as human shields in battle. What we say and do will be judged by the message of hope and reconciliation, the possibility of a better way, which we hold out to that world, God's world.

35. What lies before us? What lies before us is the communion of God's own life and love in the consummation of the kingdom. This fifth world conference on Faith and Order in Santiago de Compostela is only one more pilgrim resting place on our ecumenical pilgrimage. Our pilgrimage is towards communion in faith, life and witness — a foretaste of that full communion that we believe and trust will be ours in the kingdom of God.

NOTES

[1] *Regional Consultations in Preparation for the Fifth World Conference on Faith and Order: Summary of Reports,* eds Thomas F. Best & Günther Gassmann, Geneva, WCC, 1993.

[2] See this volume, p.308.

[3] *Confessing the One Faith,* Faith and Order paper no. 153, Geneva, WCC, 1991; *Baptism, Eucharist and Ministry,* Faith and Order paper no. 111, Geneva, WCC, 1982; *Church and World: The Unity of the Church and the Renewal of Human Community,* Faith and Order paper no. 152, Geneva, WCC, 1990.

[4] *Signs of the Spirit,* official report of the seventh assembly of the WCC, Geneva, WCC, 1991, pp.172ff.

[5] Nikos Nissiotis, "A Credible Reception of the Lima Document in the Churches", in *The Reception of BEM in the European Context,* Geneva, CEC, 1986, and John Deschner, "What Could Santiago Accomplish?" in *The Ecumenical Review,* vol. 45, no. 1, January 1993, pp.105ff.

[6] Geiko Müller-Fahrenholz ed., *Unity in Today's World: Faith and Order Studies on: Unity of the Church — Unity of Humankind,* Faith and Order paper no. 88, Geneva, WCC, 1978; and Constance Parvey ed., *The Community of Women and Men in the Church,* the Sheffield report, Geneva, WCC, 1983.

[7] *Costly Unity: Kononia and Justice, Peace and the Integrity of Creation,* Geneva, WCC, Units I and II, 1993.

[8] S. Mark Heim, "Montreal to Compostela: Pilgrimage in Ecumenical Winter", in *The Christian Century,* April 1992, pp.333ff.

[9] *Signs of the Spirit, op. cit.,* pp.37ff.

[10] Melanie May, "Fire or Ice? Or, How Will We Stay Together?", in *The Ecumenical Review,* vol. 45, no. 1, January 1993, pp.114ff.

[11] J.-M. Tillard, "Was the Holy Spirit at Canberra?", in *One in Christ,* vol. 29, no. 1, 1993.

[12] Elizabeth Templeton, "The Unity We Seek", in *The Truth Shall Make You Free,* London, ACC, 1989.

[13] *Baptism, Eucharist and Ministry,* Faith and Order paper no. 111, Geneva, WCC, 1982, Ministry 26.

[14] Gunther Gassmann, "From Montreal 1963 to Santiago de Compostela 1993", in *The Ecumenical Review,* vol. 45, no. 1, January 1993, pp.27ff.

THE TASKS OF THE WORLD CONFERENCE IN THE PERSPECTIVE OF THE FUTURE: REFLECTIONS

NEVILLE CALLAM

There is community in God's being. The pre-existent and eternal persons of the Trinity mirror community and model for us true koinonia. The awareness of the ecclesiological implications of Trinitarian understandings fuels the engine of the church's passionate commitment to the search for visible unity. In the power of the Holy Spirit, the church strives to become what it is — the body which participates in and expresses the communion of God's own life — and today the marks of the church's vitality are being characterized as koinonia in faith, life and witness.

We are met as a pilgrim people at a pilgrimage site to challenge the church to gather up the gains which have been made, over the last thirty years, on the road to visible unity. We traverse the journey from Montreal to Santiago de Compostela. We read again the signposts on the journey, and celebrate the accomplishments which have been recounted and canvassed again and again. We ask whether these accomplishments represent the consensus which finds expression in theoretical constructions of mind and intellect rather than in the readiness to appropriate instruments of change based on the convergence we claim to have achieved. The need is urgent for the consensus statements minted out of bilateral and multilateral conversations to find concrete expression in the life of our churches "that the world may believe".

In the process of evaluation, hopefully, we will better understand the nature of the progress registered and the reasons for it, as well as the demands which the stewardship of church unity imposes on us all.

Those of us who will undertake the work of this world conference represent a wide cross-section of the church. Here, East and West, South and North, converge, not to seek the sameness which yields the boredom of uniformity but to pursue the unity which lives and breathes in the rich texture of our diversities — that is, the diversities which enrich unity, not those which rob it of its appeal and disengage it from its anchor in the reality and being of the Triune God. In the quest for visible ecclesial unity we must ask, concerning the common confession of the faith, not only whether the reality represented in one formulation of the faith is a shared reality, but also whether we recognize the same faith in churches that do not use that particular credal formula. This way, our ecumenical symbol will become not an instrument in the oppression of cultures, but a glad affirmation of our continuity in the faith of the saints throughout the ages.

The resolve to appropriate the progress made to date should provide the backdrop for the commitment to adopt the steps that need so urgently to be taken as we come face to face with our stewardship in respect of the future.

The Rev. Neville Callam is a pastor in the Jamaica Baptist Union.

The self-congratulatory ecumenical mood which cramps the spirit of daring, the equanimity which is ignorant of the anguished feelings of disappointment experienced by many Christians who yearn for the visible unity of the church, the gleeful celebration of the gains registered by initiatives aimed at ecumenical cooperation which is unmindful of the challenge and the demand of engagement in the present for the sake of visible ecclesial unity — all these reduce the prophetic people to the childhood of preoccupation with the minimum that is acceptable if church unity is to be demonstrated, and result in the abdication of vocational commitment.

Many of the people of our world are in captivity to despair as the spring of ethnic, racial, nationalist and gender prejudice joins forces with the summer of our numbed resolve to take concrete action for justice and peace, and the autumn of our worldly worship at the altar of the kind of development which is underpinned by the idolatry of progress. We are fast approaching a richly-deserved winter of ecological destruction. In this situation, we dare not ask the wrong questions. For example, we must ask, concerning the problems marking North-South relations, not how kindness may be expressed, but how justice may be established.

Involvement in the struggle for respect of human rights and concern for responsible discipleship must mark the church's life, if the witness of the church is not to be compromised. In this regard, the divisions which the church helps to entrench by the conflicting positions adopted on moral issues need urgently to be acknowledged and fearlessly to be addressed. Some may desire to shirk this responsibility out of fear that the salutary gains already achieved in the quest for visible church unity will thereby be nullified. They seem to forget that the unity of the church does not depend ultimately on human formulations of ecclesiastical compromise. What we are claiming is that the contradictory positions the church adopts on moral issues are a hindrance to the visible unity of the church. If this is so, whatever the risks involved, the time is ripe for the church to launch into the sea of moral pluralism and examine whether and how the reality of ethical pluralism strengthens or hinders the expression of ecclesial oneness with and under the Lord God revealed to us as Creator, Redeemer and Sanctifier.

As we envision a meaningful future of ecumenical engagement we need to address unity in terms of "moral community", as was so well expressed at the Rønde consultation. Participation in the communion of God's own life requires the affirmation of partnership in the search for obedient unity — the affirmation which breaks down dividing walls and reflects the commitment vigorously to engage in the search for the visible ecclesial unity which knows its roots, accepts its purpose and fulfils its mission. The diaconic and "marturetic" dimensions of the unity of the church cry out for expression.

Let this conference in Santiago de Compostela urge the churches to examine their understanding of the church's teaching authority and let us propose an agenda to tackle the divisions engendered by the disparate teaching which the church imparts on matters of morals. This way, the process of harvesting the fruit of the work of the last thirty years, of envisioning the goal of visible unity, of formulating an agenda for future Faith and Order work, and of presenting a challenge to the churches from which we come — a task expertly defined in Dr Mary Tanner's presentation — will bear much fruit. "Costly unity" will reflect the true unity patterned for us by the koinonia in the divine community of the one God who brooks no rivals and calls us to manifest the ecclesial unity which God bestows as both gift and demand.

THE TASKS OF THE WORLD CONFERENCE IN THE PERSPECTIVE OF THE FUTURE: REFLECTIONS

MERCEDES GARCIA BACHMANN

Coming from a country colonized by Spain, and my father's surname being Garcia, from the port of Vigo very near here, some of the Spanish poets (Federico García Lorca, Juan Ramón Jiménez, and especially Antonio Machado) have been a great attraction to me. Machado's poem quoted below, "Eulogy to José Ortega y Gasset" (from the first decades of this century), came to my attention because of its ending. It belongs to a period where ecumenical relationships — ·such as are possible now even between persons who hold very different concepts and viewpoints — were not yet really in vogue:

To you Laurel and Ivy
Be crowned, beloved one
of Sofía, architect.
Chisel, hammer and stone
and masons to serve you, the mountains
of the Guadarrama, cold
may offer you the blue of their inmost recess,
musing over another sombre Escorial.
And that austere Felipe
on the border of his regal sepulchre
appears to see the new architecture
and bless the fruit of Luther.[1]

Poets and dreamers outside their "time", and heterodox theologians like Machado, are those who help us "dream dreams and see visions", as Joel prophesied and as those who partook at Pentecost could observe; these remind us that it is not always necessary to be so formal in our vision of God and God's plan; because, after all, religious language about our experience of God and God's saving love are not the exclusive property of theologians. And thank God for that!

One thing I rarely see in Europe, but do see in Buenos Aires, is the diesel locomotive. When it begins to function and is warming up, the rest of the train remains static, producing a series of squeaks, bumps and jolts, until at last the whole train gets going; meanwhile in this process the locomotive has lost its initial extra "push". It now moves together with the rest of the cars — as it must if the whole train is to proceed. It is exactly this process that the churches seem to be living through. In technical language we call it "reception" — or, at least, that is the way I would like to see the problem that others have called the "ecumenical winter", or the "cooling off" of enthusiasm or the situation which has resulted from this.

The Rev. Mercedes Garcia Bachmann is a Lutheran pastor in Argentina.

I would like to share with you two experiences that I have lived through as a pastor, some years ago, in a university city in Argentina: two experiences related to the same church, where differing ecumenical attitudes, and a different degree of openness to concepts different from one's own, led to opposite results in practice.

The first experience was when I took part in a mixed wedding ceremony. Everything was going quite well, until the minister found out that the other minister would be... a woman! Then he did not even allow me to read the Bible during the ceremony. His argument was that if the women of his church should see me, there would be no way of stopping them when they too expressed the wish to be ordained...

The other experience was working for many years in a university ecumenical youth group, with people of at least seven denominations — Bible studies, liturgical celebrations and diaconal work.

It is due to this kind of experience that I — a Lutheran pastor, bearing a responsible position in a church with a strong, solid faith and practising the type of ecumenism known as "reconciled diversity" — learned that koinonia is a gift of God, much greater than theology. In other words, if it is necessary for the locomotive to lose part of its own "push" in order for the carriages to start moving, it is still worthwhile. So if, in order to establish a real unity, imperfect as it may be, it is necessary to put aside some sacred customs, the effort is well worthwhile — for in the end it is not the great, ultimate questions or fundamentals which usually are the stones in our path.

It was also Machado who wrote:

Look for your complementary
who always marches with you —
and he is usually your opponent.[2]

This leads me to the second challenge I would like to propose to you.

Ecumenism in action

Ecumenism must become alive at the roots of our churches. It must show itself not only in agreements signed by church hierarchs, but also, in all our churches, we must find the way to make ecumenism concrete, real and committed.

Many men and women not only live in a divided and angry world, but also often experience those very divisions within their own families — and that due to their religious beliefs. If the catholicity of our church, if our prayers for peace and unity, if our liturgical celebrations, if concepts like koinonia, reconciliation, plurality, do not reach such men and women, then our testimony will continue to lose its authenticity.

As for politicians, experts in economy and those who sanction the status quo, none of these are believed now by anybody. Latin America, at least, has lately seen a proliferation of churches — not to speak of sects — many of which have emerged because of dissent amongst church leaders and the tactics they use to separate themselves rather than settle their differences. As a consequence, one can observe the confusion caused among those who are "outsiders" from the church.

How can we arrive at a united witness without giving up the particularities which belong to each one of our churches? How do we show ecumenical goodwill without becoming one more denomination or *ekklesia* within the church? In my humble opinion, as someone who sees the WCC from outside, we should not look so much at what we lack but rather at what we have accomplished, and look for true ways to bring these accomplishments into our own families. When this has been done, new roads towards dialogue and work together will appear. A home divided against itself cannot bear witness to anything.

Otherwise, how do we witness in the face of those who feel far away from any denomination? In other words, the time has come to stop acting like ostriches and to start looking around us. And better than looking, we must start listening — listening to those voices which, because they bothered us, we had stopped listening to. We have acted as we do when we are travelling on a bus and a child is screaming and crying all the time: we cannot get off (or throw the child out of the window!) so we end up trying to ignore the child in order not to hear him any more.

Who is that neighbour who bothers us, and whom we would like to ignore? Due to lack of time, I shall only mention two types. One is the sects, from the pseudo-Christians to those who are openly non-Christian. They bother us because they are dangerous to our own constituency, and because we can find no way to dialogue with them.

> An old saying asserts that "the sects are the unpaid bills of the church" — which is not far from the truth. Often the emergence of sects is due to the fact that some elements of the truth have been neglected by certain Christian denominations. These sects have then mistakenly put the emphasis on these overlooked sayings, or marginalized aspects of the faith...[3]

The others who bother us are the scientists and professionals, not only because they *are* professionals but because they are absorbed by a culture and a vision of the world that is determined by science. Sometimes I feel that we who are immersed in the life of the church are the only human beings who do not recognize this change in our companions in dialogue.

> ...the church must rethink its message in today's language for any scientifically educated society. That does not mean only the so-called "first world". Increasingly scientific education, an understanding of the natural history of the world, has become spread throughout all cultures. The old images, although they are meaningful to those brought up in the bosom of the church, no longer sound at all credible to those outside.[4]

Dialogue with science and technology would be most profitable for us men and women of the churches, because it would help us to refashion some of the areas in our theologies where we might be a bit weak (for example, the theology of creation, epistemology, the most appropriate symbols for the twenty-first century, biblical texts in relation to the present cosmic vision). To that effect, I would like to recommend to you the suggested proposals on this topic which were discussed in a consultation towards the end of 1987.[5]

Dialogue on science and technology would also be beneficial for people who, while understanding themselves as Christians, put themselves "in advance" of the church in some areas. Theology and church could provide them with the ethical and prophetic elements necessary for science to be of service to the whole of humanity and the entire creation, not only to serve some people, some countries or some enterprises.[6]

I resort once again to Antonio Machado:

Reason says: Let us look for Truth.
And the Heart: Vanity.
Truth we already have.

Reason: O, who reaches the Truth!
The Heart: Vanity.
Truth is hope.
Says Reason: You lie.
And the Heart answers:
The one who lies is you, Reason,
Who says what you do not feel.
Reason: we will never be able
to understand each other, Heart.
The Heart: We shall see.[7]

Once again the question arises: How do we obtain it within our ecumenical limits, where we very often cannot reach substantial assent? And others, more sceptical, will ask themselves: Why bother with so much dialogue when we have so many other pressing problems such as hunger, war, xenophobia, the arms race, the unification of Europe over against the rest of the world? Will there be someone who will pay attention to our humble results?

A few Sundays ago, the text indicated in the ecumenical lectionary was the parable of the sower. Basically this invites all those who hear to discover that the growth of the seed in good soil was abundant, although it may seem meagre compared to what was lost in the barren ground. Humble and meagre as this yield may make us feel, we dare not lose it. Certainly we are beggars for love and for God's salvation. We are pilgrims, as are so many others in this "field of stars" [campo de la estrella], in Santiago de Compostela.

In my loneliness
I have seen things clearly
That are not true.

Your truth? No, real truth,
And come with me to search for it.
Yours, keep it.[8]

NOTES

[1] Antonio Machado, "Elogios: Al joven meditador José Ortega y Gasset", in Antología Poética, Estella, Spain, Biblioteca Básica Salvat, Salvat Editores, 1970.
[2] Antonio Machado, "Proverbios y Cantares", XV, in Antología Poética, op. cit.
[3] J.K. Van Baalen, "El Caos de las Sectas", T.E.L.L., Jenison, USA, 7th printing, 1988, p.363.
[4] Arthur Peacocke, "The Challenge of Science to Theology and the Church", in The New Faith-Science Debate, ed. John M. Mangum, Minneapolis, Fortress Press, and Geneva, WCC, 1989, pp.21-22.
[5] Ibid.
[6] Various authors, The New Faith-Science Debate, op. cit., cf. esp ch. 10.
[7] Machado, "Profesión de fe".
[8] Machado, "Proverbios y Cantares", XXII and LXXXV, Antología Poética, op. cit.

☐ Plenary discussion

In a brief period of discussion five persons addressed issues raised by the opening presentations. One speaker called attention to the continuing vitality of the united and uniting churches, challenging any suggestion that work with them "represented a phase in the life of the commission which is now past". He expressed his doubt that koinonia is a clearer concept than unity, as suggested in the director's paper. In addition he commended the moderator's recognition of the need for "structures of communion". In response, the director affirmed the continuing work of Faith and Order with the united and uniting churches.

Another speaker drew attention to the challenge inherent in the question raised in the moderator's presentation: "Do our churches really want unity and if so are they prepared to take costly steps towards koinonia in faith, life and witness?" Speaking more generally, others expressed appreciation for the work done on the apostolic faith, and the importance of the Nicene-Constantinopolitan Creed was stressed. One speaker suggested that "continuity in apostolic faith" need not necessarily imply apostolic succession through the laying-on of hands; it was the continuing "koinonia in faith" which was crucial. Another expressed concern that the phrase "unity-in-diversity" might become simply an alibi for our continuing divisions: while there is a proper diversity of cultural, social and psychological expressions of the faith, "unity requires that the same meaning be represented in [those] diverse expressions".

III

The Biblical Witness to Koinonia

☐ Introduction

The biblical background of koinonia was the subject of plenary III, 4 August, 4h., and plenary IV, 5 August, 9h15. Prof. Nicolas Lossky, acting in place of vice-moderator V. Rev. Emmanuel Clapsis, who was unable to be present, presided at plenary III, and vice-moderator the Rev. Araceli Rocchietti presided at plenary IV.

In plenary III Prof. Lossky introduced the Rev. Prof. John Reumann, whose **paper** offered an exhaustive and detailed survey of the biblical material on *koinnia* and cognate terms. The latter part of plenary III was devoted to discussion of the papers delivered in plenaries I and II, as explained above. The Rev. A. Rocchietti in plenary IV introduced three **papers** giving personal visions of koinonia based upon particular biblical texts. These were presented by Most Rev. John Onayeikan, the Rev. Dr Dorothy Lee and the Dr Simon Chan. The brief plenary comments on this material are recorded on pp.91 below.

KOINONIA IN SCRIPTURE:
SURVEY OF BIBLICAL TEXTS

JOHN REUMANN

To Professors Paul Minear, Ernst Käsemann
and Raymond E. Brown, S.S., New Testament scholars
who contributed to the Faith and Order movement

The Rev. Prof. John Reumann (Lutheran) teaches at Lutheran Theological Seminary, Philadelphia, USA.

I. INTRODUCTION

1. When the apostle Paul came to the Greek city of Corinth, probably about A.D. 50, the stage was set for the theme of *koinōnia* to make its way into Christian faith, life and witness, a development stretching till today. Paul's missionary message centred in Christ, who
> died for our sins in accord with the scriptures, was buried,
> and was raised on the third day in accord with the scriptures

and who then appeared to Cephas, the twelve, and other witnesses, including Paul, so that they might make proclamation and thus people might come to faith (1 Cor. 15: 3-8). This gospel called on Jews to confess the stumbling block of "Christ crucified" (1 Cor. 1:23) and Gentiles to turn "from idols to serve a living and true God, and to wait for his Son from heaven, whom he raised from the dead — Jesus who rescues us from the wrath [or judgment] that is to come" (1 Thess. 1:9-10).

2. In the ensuing encounter with Greek culture in Corinth, *koinōnia* came first to the fore. It was not a word used by Jesus. At best the Greek root could be used in our gospels to describe James and John as "partners" (*koinōnoi*, Luke 5:10; cf. 5:7 *metochois*, NRSV also "partners") in the fishing business with Simon. It was a term with no precise Hebrew counterpart in the Old Testament, rare even in the Greek translations of Israel's scriptures. Its earliest usage in Christian documents occurs in 1 Corinthians.

3. So typically Greco-Roman is *koinōnia* that no one way to translate it suffices in modern languages. The Dublin text for Faith and Order ("Towards Koinonia in Faith, Life and Witness: Draft of a Working Document", April 1992) was well advised to transliterate the Greek so as "to avoid slanting its meaning" (p.4). The revised dicussion paper for this conference has opted for the translation "communion" as a synonym (p.10, note on terminology). But it is widely held that the Greek *koinōnia* is only partly like the Latin *communio*, for it is also partly like the Latin *participatio* ("participation", rather than "communion"); and it is to yet another Latin word, *societas* ("association"), that the oft-used German rendering *Gemeinschaft* corresponds (Hahn 1979:13-14 = repr. 1986:120-21). We know that we are in translation troubles when two major English Bibles translate "the *koinōnia* of the Holy Spirit" in 2 Corinthians 13:14 (13) four different ways: "fellowship" (RSV text 1946), "participation in" (RSV note); "communion" (NRSV text 1989), and "sharing in" (NRSV note). I shall regularly cite the Greek but often seek to translate it appropriate to the context.

A. Faith and Order 1963: *koinōnia*, methodology and aim

4. Thirty years ago the report of the fourth world conference on Faith and Order (pp.57-58, no. 66) said, with an eye to Eastern and Afro-Asian churches:

> When the Word became flesh, the Gospel came to man ["humanity" we would say nowadays in inclusive language] through a particular cultural medium, that of the Palestinian world of the time. So when the Church takes the Tradition ["the act of God in Christ..., the Christian faith itself...; the revelation in Christ and the preaching of the Word", no. 57] to new peoples, it is necessary that again the essential content should find expression in terms of new cultures.

With regard to *koinōnia*, we must say that already in the New Testament period the gospel was moving from the Palestinian to the Greco-Roman world and so new inculturation and indigenization were occurring, paradigmatic for us.

5. The 1963 section reports at Montreal sometimes employed *koinonia* (e.g., no. 25 "the *koinonia* of true eucharistic worship"; no. 71 "faithfulness to the whole *koinonia* of Christ's church"; no. 133 "our *koinonia* within councils of churches in general and the WCC in particular"). I recall its use in my youth for "fellowship", especially in World Student Christian Federation circles. It has continued as a jargon term for "fellowship groups" in local congregations. But in the last decade or so *koinōnia* has become a cinderella term in ecclesiology and beyond, both beloved and under assault.

6. Statistically, in scripture, even the New Testament, *koinōnia* and related terms occur in but moderately frequent numbers (see box; Old Testament totals are for the Septuagint or "translation by the seventy" [LXX]). *Koinōnia* itself occurs 19 times in the New Testament, primarily in Paul (13 ×, all in unquestioned letters). If related terms are included, there are 36 New Testament occurrences. If stretched to the absolute limits by including passages where *koinos*, meaning "(in) common", involves the idea of "profane" or "unclean" (and the verb *koinoun*, as in Matt. 15:11,18,20, "defile" a person), a total of 64 occurrences is possible. But not all of even the 36 involving *koinōn*-terms are theologically significant. These data place *koinōnia* words between, for example, "righteousness/justification" terminology (over 300 New Testament examples of *dikaioun/dikaiosynē*, *adikein* terms) and "reconciliation" (only 13 New Testament instances of [*apo*]*katallagein* derivatives). It is a "middle-level" word in terms of frequency, slightly more frequent than *oikonomia* (some 20 New Testament examples, plus many more, of course, of *oikos/ oikia* = "house", part of the root of this term for "household management"; 20 OT examples).

---

koinōnia (noun) — 19 ×, 13 in the Pauline corpus, all in acknowledged letters; OT = 3 ×;

koinōnein (verb) — 8 ×, 5 in the Pauline corpus, 4 in acknowledged letters; OT = 14 ×;

koinōnos (adjective) — 10 ×, 5 in the Pauline corpus, all in acknowledged letters; OT = 8 ×;

koinōnikos (adjective) — 1 × (1 Tim. 6:18, "generous"); OT none;

for a total of 38 occurrences, 22 in letters by Paul himself;

plus compound forms:

sygkoinōnein (verb) — 3 ×, 2 in the Pauline corpus; OT none;

sygkoinōnos (adjective) — 4 ×, 3 in the Pauline corpus, all in acknowledged letters; OT none;

for a grand total of 45 examples. Even if the adjective *koinos* ("common") is added, there are only 14 more examples (4 in Paul, all in acknowledged letters; OT = 20 instances), and if the verb *koinoun* ("make common, declare profane") is added, 14 more examples (none in Paul; OT 1 possible example); the overall grand total would be 73 for the NT, 46 for the OT.

7. The aim of this presentation must, then, be to set forth biblical teaching on *koinōnia* and related terms, in New Testament context. This involves material that is for all Christians basic and formative; indeed, for some, the biblical witness that is supremely authoritative, God-given (*jure divino*, by divine right), which we can but obey (Acts 4:19-20). It is material to be weighed, to varying degrees, in the spirit of the Montreal conference, along with the Tradition or Gospel, the traditioning process in the church, and our separate traditions. One of its strengths is precisely that *koinōnia* cuts across many traditional lines. A particular concern must be to examine *koinōnia* as defined biblically first of all, not by church fathers of the fourth century or positions of the sixteenth or even late twentieth century. There must not be, as Father Raymond E. Brown, S.S., warned at Montreal in 1963, "an oversimplified picture of the continuity and uniformity of New Testament ecclesiology" (*New Testament Essays*, p.72, cf. p.64), or as Prof. Ernst Käsemann put it on the same occasion, "no romanatic postulate, dressed up as *Heilsgeschichte*", for "all New Testament statements concerning the Church have their particular historical locus" (*Novum Testamentum* 6 [1963] 295, 290 = *EVB* 2:265, 262).

8. At Faith and Order, Montreal, 1963, both Brown and Käsemann reflected the fruitful contributions then of historical-critical study of the Bible for ecumenism (e.g., Brown, pp.60-61; Käsemann 290, no *ecclesiologia perennis* or perennial, single, permanent doctrine of the church in the New Testament). In spite of suspicions in some quarters about historical criticism, its contributions have been enormous in bilateral dialogues and multilateral discussion like Faith and Order's Lima statement (*Baptism, Eucharist and Ministry*), often moving us beyond old impasses. Yet in the last thirty years new emphases in biblical studies themselves have emerged, at times overshadowing historical criticism and making it seem tame (Reumann 1992). Prominent among these new methods are literary/narrative approaches. But these are of little help on *koinōnia* since the word rarely occurs in biblical narrative; even in Acts the few examples are in summary statements (2:42; 4:32). Social-world setting has, however, long been emphasized (as early as 1913 by Carr). Some structural/linguistic analysis has been applied (cf. Di Marco 1988; Franco 20-21). Rhetorical approaches prove beneficial in Pauline letters. Liberation and feminist theology have had less to say on the subject, but New Testament ecclesiology assumes a *koinōnia* of women and men in Christ. Yet by older or newer methods, *koinōnia* theology remains both praised (e.g., Tillard) and criticized (e.g., S. Brown).

9. In order to understand why there are no precise Old Testament parallels to New Testament *koinōnia* and no use by Jesus, we must look to origins in the Greek world for a term that burst into prominence in 1 Corinthians. Then, because more than three out of four New Testament examples of *koinōn*-terms are in the Pauline corpus, we shall spend more space on Paul's letters than on the rest of the New Testament combined. Briefer treatment will be in order on 1 John, Hebrews, Peter's letters, and Acts, in moving towards a possible "*koinonia* theology" and ecclesiology.

II. BACKGROUNDS, ESPECIALLY IN THE GREEK WORLD

10. From a root meaning of "common", often in contrast to what is "private" (Greek *idios*), *koinōn*-words went through an amazingly broad series of applications from the seventh-century on, in "public" life, community, the state, business partner-

ships, marriage as a life-association, and society. *Koinōnia* could refer to all sorts of relationships, even sexual intercourse. It frequently meant "having a share" in something and thus "*participation*"; more rarely in the classical world, "giving a share" of something and thus "imparting". A whole cultural outlook was embodied where "common life" and "common good" were related to a complex of factors such as "justice" *(dikaiosynē)*, "order" *(kosmos)*, what is fitting or beneficial *(sympheron*, 1 Cor. 6:12, 7:35, 10:23), and the significant relationship of friendship *(philia)*. A communal economy was often involved, equality *(isotēs)* at least for citizens of a city-state, a contrast with private greed. By the philosophers, notions were held aloft of a community where goods and possessions were shared in an ideal society or brother-hood, a community where "all things (are) in common for all" *(koina gar pasi panta*, Pythagoras; Iamblichus, *Vit. Pyth.* 30. 168). That "friends have all things in common" *(koina ta philōn)* echoes over the centuries. Sometimes a *koinōnia* of gods and human beings was asserted, even, in the mystery cults, to the point of union with the deity through certain rites. Plato spoke of how "heaven and earth and gods and people comprise the *koinōnia* and friendship and orderly behaviour and self-control and justice" *(Gorgias* 508a); Epictetus (1.19.27), of "*koinōnia* with Zeus"; and papyrus invitations exist "to dine at the table of Lord Sarapis" (POxy. 1.110), a background for the "table of demons" to which Paul refers in a *koinōnia* passage (1 Cor. 10:18-22,27).

11. Time does not permit spelling out here the variations of what Plato said of his ideal society, or Aristotle on political *koinōnia*, derived from nature itself, prior even to family and the individual. Or of how the fall of the city-state *(polis)* (fourth century B.C.) led to a certain crisis in Hellenistic society, opening up both more individualistic tendencies and more cosmopolitanism, as well as producing a quest for new small groups within society. Reports circulated of ideal communities in a lost "golden age" or in far-off lands like India. There were Pythagorean communes, with their order derived from cosmic order; a widespread Stoic emphasis on humans as "communal beings" *(koinōnikon zōon)*; and Cynics who gave up all private possessions for a life as wandering teachers. The Hellenistic cities where Paul and other itinerant missionaries worked were thus full of social and cult groups, brotherhoods, or *synodoi*, talking of, and promoting, *koinōnia*. This rarely meant participation in divine gifts in daily life, but might imply communion or actual union with the god(s), through sacrifice and common meals. More often it implied fellowship with others in the group (Nock, on "hero cults") and a certain ethical programme or life-style. In government one heard of "the league *(to koinon)* of Asia", with which the Asiarchs of Acts 19:31 were connected, or "the assembly *(to koinon)* of the Jerusalemites" (Josephus, *Vita* 65,72,190,254). A recent investigation would place *koinōnia* in one of Paul's letters, Philippians, in close connection with political and military rhetoric (Geoffrion, comparing Phil. 1:27-30, 4:1, 3:20 *politeuma*, with ancient speeches by a general to his troops, e.g.). It was a world familar with the searchings for, and offers of, *koinōnia* with one another and sometimes with a deity. People encountered the term not only through popular philosophies but in daily life. To Paul's description of "many gods and many lords" in Corinth (1 Cor. 8:5), one could add, "many *koinōniai*" too.

A. Contrasts in Israel and Judaism

12. It now becomes apparent how different Israel's outlook was. This people had their identity on the basis of God's call, election, deliverance through the exodus, and

fulfilment of promises in a covenant, land, and kingship. One did not talk of fellowship with Yahweh but of God's lordship and the people's servanthood. Righteousness was an attribute of God; it worked for Israel's salvation (Isa. 46:13, 51:5,6,8). There was no Greek concept of, or networks for, "friendship" in Israel. The root *koinon-* therefore has no exact equivalent in Hebrew; the closest is the root, *chābar*, to "join together, bind, unite". But *chbr* seems oriented to "event", *koinōn-* to "being" (Popkes 1125). Of the some 65 occurrences of *chbr* and derivatives in the Hebrew scriptures, only a dozen or so are rendered by *koinōn* terms in the Greek Septuagint (e.g., Ezek. 37:16,19, the tribes "associated with" the stick of Joseph). Even here the examples may be pejorative (Isa. 1:23 "companions of thieves"; Mal. 2:14 "your companion and your wife by covenant", but in the context of unfaithful behaviour). *Koinōnia* is not used for Israel's communion with Yahweh but rather for fellowship with pagan deities (Hos. 4:17 "Ephraim is joined to idols"; Isa. 44:11, Theodotion's translation, "all who have fellowship with [an idol]"). Examples of *koinōnia* words in the Greek Bible increase in later wisdom books like Ecclesiastes and Proverbs and in deutero-canonical works under Hellenistic influence. E.g., 3 Maccabees 4:6 "share married life"; Wisdom of Solomon 6:23 "envy does not associate with wisdom"; 8:18 there is "renown in sharing wisdom's words".

13. The Hebrew root produced a noun, *chăbûrah*, used by Pharisees in particular. It referred to an elite fellowship or group in a town or village dedicated to more strict obedience to the Law, often in terms of ritual purity and tithing. A teacher and a group of disciples might be called a *chăbûrah*, a conventicle, separate from others, rigorists in obedience. Their fellowship was with one another. The Qumran community employed *chbr* terms only occasionally (5 × in extant texts) and never in relation with God. But because an ordered life and shared possessions marked their existence, Hellenistic Jewish writers like Philo used the term *koinōnia* to describe the Essenes in a way that Greek readers would readily understand, as if they were a Pythagorean society. Qumranites understood themselves, however, not in "friendship" terms but as a priestly, covenantal community called by God. It is in the Hellenistically-oriented Josephus and above all Philo that *koinonia* terms are found among Jewish authors. They employ them for groups like the Essenes and Therapeutae; in describing marriage; for Moses as "friend of God" (in light of Exod. 33:11); and in Israel (God the benefactor makes those in need sharers [*koinonon*] in the convivial company with the priests who offer sacrifices, *Spec. Leg.* 1.221; cf. 131). But to Palestinian Judaism the *koinōnia* concept was not indigenous or widely adopted. Hence it played no part in Jesus' teachings and the life of the Palestinian church (for Acts 2:42 see below). But since the Greek concept of *koinōnia* had at points infiltrated Hellenistic Judaism, Saul of Tarsus could have known the term.

III. *KOINŌNIA* IN PAUL'S LETTERS

A. The oldest pre-Pauline formula, as used by Paul (1 Cor. 10:16)

14. When Paul evangelized in Corinth, he taught, as elsewhere, about the crucified and risen Jesus, who, as Lord, reigns and continues to be present, for example as

deliverer and judge at the Lord's supper. Paul handed on the tradition (now recorded at 1 Cor. 11:23-25) that

> the Lord Jesus on the night when he was betrayed took a loaf of bread, and when he had given thanks, he broke it and said: "This is my body that is for you. Do this in remembrance of me." In the same way he took the cup also, after supper, saying: "This cup is the new covenant in my blood. Do this, as often as you drink it, in remembrance of me."

His converts took the meal of Jesus to heart and sought to understand it in terms more familiar to their world. In 1 Corinthians 10:16 we have, as restated by Paul, what seems a Hellenistic Christian assertion about the bread and cup which puts the meaning in *koinōnia* terms. This formulation was probably drawn up for catechetical purposes (Häuser), possibly by the Corinthians themselves (Klauck). Paul approves this formulation by citing it in his argument. It ran, in parallel sentences:

> The bread which we break is a participation (or sharing, *koinōnia*) in the body of Christ.
> The cup of blessing over which we say a blessing (to God) is a participation (or sharing, *koinōnia*) in the blood of Christ.

The "body of Christ" was that which Jesus offered on the cross; "the blood", that poured out at his death. Eating bread and drinking wine is to proclaim the Lord's death until he comes at the parousia (or future coming of Christ, 11:26) and to partake of its benefits and blessings.

15. Paul employs the formula at 10:16 as part of his presentation for "sensible people" (10:15) on the problem of "food sacrificed to idols" (8:1,4,7-8, 10:14,19,25-30) and the conscience of Christians of strong or weak faith (8:9-13). Paul has put the two catechetical statements as questions and reversed their order. Why? To make rhetorically a point about "the body of Christ" as involving not only Jesus' body sacrificed on the cross (16b) but also the community in Corinth as "body of Christ" (17b; 12:12-27). Paul thus moves from Christology, soteriology, and "sacrament" to *ecclesiology*. But the "church emphasis" in v.17 is there for a purpose: to encourage *unity* among Corinthian Christians with one another, in the face of divisiveness between or within their house churches (11:17-22). *Koinōnia* was the operative word or proprium in the formula, participation in the one loaf of bread. Paul moves the emphasis to the commonality as all partake of (*metechomen* in 17c) the one bread as one body. Unity in the church is a major theme, but there are others.

16. The first letter to the Corinthians 10 also carries with it a note of *exclusivity*, as in OT use of *koinōnia*: you cannot participate in the table of idols or demons and that of Christ. It is a matter of Christ alone! To participate has meaning (10:18,20, *koinōnoi*; v.21 "partake" = *metechein*). (Since this alternate term, *metechein*, is used in v.17 of Christians and in 21 of both the table of the Lord and the table of demons, it is difficult to establish a clear distinction from *koinōnia*, except that *metechein* emphasizes "have a share in".) This key passage in 10:16 has been made the basis of a "sacramental ecclesiology" based on the eucharist. It is scarcely implied, however, that the community of Jesus is "church" *only* when it celebrates the Lord's supper or even solely *because* it celebrates the Lord's supper. For the note of *baptism* also undergirds the discussion, in 10:1-4; cf. 12:12-13. Other verses point to the "*judgment* theme": with most of those delivered in the exodus "God was not pleased" and "they were struck down" (10:5). Christians even with baptism and the Lord's supper

should take heed lest they fall (10:6-13; cf. Heb. 6:4-12; 1 Cor. 11:27-32). Yet the passage is pre-eminently about *receiving* a share in Christ and his gifts of grace and the Spirit (12:4-11); about *having* a share or being partners with each other "in Christ" (belonging to the Lord and to the ecclesial body of Christ); and realizing the fellowship and freedom of the new creation when one is "in Christ" (10:25-26; 2 Cor. 5:17; Hahn 1981:166).

17. Ecclesiologically, the unity that Paul calls for in this *koinōnia* at Corinth involved, we must remind ourselves, diverse house churches there. It is not here in chapters 8-11 a matter of Corinth and other churches elsewhere or a "universal church". Much of Paul's concern in this and other letters was with getting Christians to worship and function together in a single city — be it Corinth (in the face of factions there), Philippi (where Euodia and Syntyche quarrelled and believers need to be "of one mind", 4:2, 1:27, 2:2), or Thessalonica (where there were "idlers", 5:14). "The church of God in Corinth" (1:2) involved active, lively house congregations of some variety. (There were probably two to four in Corinth, two or three in Philippi, and as many as eight in Rome; cf. Rom. 16; Klauck 1981:34-40.) Keeping them in communion with each other, the weak with the strong, Jewish and Gentile Christians, and, for all we know, achieving (on occasion?) all-city eucharistic celebrations (cf. Klauck, Branick) were no small tasks. Everything that Paul does is kept in a gospel- and mission-setting by his remark at 1 Corinthians 9:23: "I do it all for the sake of the gospel, so that I may share (*sugkoinōnos*) in its blessings" — and others too in the gospel.

B. In Paul's prayer reports

18. The first letter to the Corinthians 10:16 moves the *koinōnia* theme in the direction of a eucharistic emphasis, but in the service of unity in the face of divisions. It does so on the basis of common participation in the same Lord who died for all and who now adversely judges contempt against the poor (11:22) and failure to live with sensitivity in Christian love and freedom (10:25-32). But Paul places this *koinōnia* reference in the middle of 1 Corinthians *after* a prior passage at the very outset of the letter where he gives thanks to God for the *koinōnia* with Christ that marks the faith, life and witness of all Corinthian believers (1:9). Similar references occur at the beginning of three other letters from Paul, making the "thanksgiving" section of his epistles the most common locus for speaking of *koinōnia*. These opening passages help interpret later statements in a letter. We must note, however, the variety with which such references are tailored to the situation of those addressed. The fact that in 2 Corinthians *koinōnia* also occurs at 13:13 (see sect. 23 below) suggests a "framing device" or frame of reference within which other passages like 1 Corinthians 10:16 should be understood.

19. The first letter to the Corinthians 1:9 is the climax of a letter-opening where Paul thanks God for the saints at Corinth:

> God is faithful; by him you were called into the fellowship (*koinōnia*) of his Son, Jesus Christ our Lord.

While the *koinōnia* is with Christ, the verse is really a statement about **God**, beginning with assertion of the divine fidelity, as at 10:13, "God is faithful, who will not let you be tempted beyond your strength..."; cf. 2 Corinthians 1:18; 1 John 1:9;

and similar verses (2 Thess. 3:3; 2 Tim. 2:13; Heb. 10:23, 11:11). Here in 1 Corinthians the emphasis is on God's **call**, an Old Testament theme, as at 1 Thessalonians 5:24: "The God who calls you is faithful, and he will do it", that is, "keep you blameless" at the parousia. But the *koinōnia* at 1:9 is not just a matter of the future. For "you were called", in a past action by God, individually and collectively, called to be a holy people (1:2), a status Paul understands as "sanctified [now] in Christ" (1:2), through **baptism** (6:11, "washed", sanctified, justified). As in chapter 10, baptism thus brings a relationship with Christ called *koinōnia*, an encounter with, and a continuing tie to, Christ, the Son of God, the common Lord of all who "in every place call on" his name (1:2). Since the "you" in v.9 is plural, those addressed are a community "in Christ" (1:2,4,5), though the term "church" is used only in v.2. The *koinōnia* verse emphasizes God's fidelity and call, Christology and the continuing effects of soteriology as holiness. Standard English translations prefer "fellowship" at 1:9 (KJV, RSV, NRSV) or "to share in the life of" the Son (NEB, REB). Since more than an associative sense is involved, some prefer "communion" here (Häuser). God's call in the past provides the point of departure; the grace and grace-gifts granted (1:4-5,7), a continuing historical development (which, however, can go awry, ch. 10); and God's promise to see believers through to the end, a future conclusion (v.8) (Franco 27-28). Meanwhile there exists *koinōnia* with the Son.

20. A second example of *koinōnia* in a prayer report occurs at Philippians 1:5. Paul thanks God for the saints there

> because of your sharing *(koinōnia)* in the gospel from the first day until now.

The verse spans the period from the day when some at Philippi were first converted till the time when Paul writes. "Sharing" covers the two possible senses implied in the response of the Philippians to, literally "for (into, Greek *eis*), the gospel". On the one hand, they shared in the message about Christ that Paul preached, by believing, so that a local "fellowship in the gospel" (KJV) or community of house churches resulted. On the other hand, the Philippians also shared the gospel with others (RSV "your partnership in the gospel"; NEB, REB "the part you have taken in the work of the gospel"; cf. 4:15-16, 2:25-30, money and persons, including a congregational *apostolos*, 2:25, NRSV "messenger"). *Koinōnia* thus involves **sharing in the gospel** for salvation and sharing it with others in **mission**. *Koinōnia* was a reality for the Philippians, originating in God's grace (1:7), in which "all of you share *(sugkoinōnous)*", making the community fruitful (1:11) in present witness and missionary labour (1:6), and to be brought to completion in God's future (1:6-7,11) (Panikulam 84-85).

21. The third example of *koinōnia* in a prayer report comes at Philemon v.6. In this personal note Paul records his thanks to God for Philemon's love and faith towards God and all the saints (v.5) and then goes on in what has been termed the most obscure verse in the letter. This is because of debate over what "the *koinōnia* of your [singular] faith" means and the terseness of what follows, literally "every good that [is] in us for Christ". The RSV had:

> I pray that the sharing of your faith may promote the knowledge of all the good that is ours in Christ.

NRSV begins the same way but ends very differently:

> I pray that the sharing of your faith may become effective when you perceive all the good
> we [*or* you] may do for Christ.

Clearly Paul prays not for fellowship but participation in *faith*. The phrase has
been taken as (a) "contributions that spring from faith", such as the Philippians
shared with Paul; (b) "communication of the faith" to others (cf. KJV); (c)
"fellowship with other Christians, created by faith"; (d) "communion with Christ by
faith"; (e) Philemon's share in the faith; or (f) "participation of other Christians in
your faith" (O'Brien 1982: 279-80). Since v.5 affirms Philemon's faith in God, the
koinōnia of his faith in v.6 includes his sharing in the common faith and the spread
of it, together with Paul his partner (*koinōnos*, v.17) and others, effectively. But
"spread of" precisely what? "All the good that is ours in Christ" (RSV) contemplates
the blessings of faith and fellowship with Christ, not individually in the heart of each
person, but "among us", plural, in the community. The NRSV rendering "all the
good that we may do for Christ" includes both mission (sharing the faith) and
hospitality and *benevolence* (vv.4,7b, refreshing the saints). In this way *koinōnia*
here begins to approach the sense of financial sharing, to be noted more specifically
below.

22. A fourth instance involves *koinōnia* at 2 Corinthians 1:7 in that letter's
somewhat differently shaped thanksgiving prayer (1:3-11).

> Our hope for you is unshaken, for we know that as you share (*hōs koinōnoi este*) in our
> sufferings, so also you share in our consolation.

The theme of tribulation and consolation is here extended into future hope.
Communion with Christ reflects his sufferings and comfort available for believers
(1:5). The apostle has recently himself personally experienced peril and rescue (1:8-
10). If one belongs to Christ and labours for the gospel, afflictions may well come. In
a related passage in another letter, Paul speaks autobiographically of his own
experience of "righteousness from God based on faith" and of his witness to the cross
of Christ (Phil. 3:9,18), in order finally

> to know Christ and the power of his resurrection and the sharing (*koinōnia*) of his sufferings
> by becoming like him in his death, if somehow I may attain the resurrection from the dead.
> (Phil. 3:10-11)

Koinōnia for the person who is a baptized believer (cf. Rom. 6:4) and a witness
involve *suffering* and *future hope*; cf. also Phil. 4:14 "share my distress".

C. The benediction of 2 Corinthians 13:13 (14); cf. Philippians 2:1

23. Paul's letters regularly close with a benediction, usually "the grace of our
Lord Jesus Christ (be) with you (all)"; so, e.g., 1 Corinthians 16:23. Only in
2 Corinthians is this expanded into a triadic form, by adding "... the love of God
and the *koinōnia* of the Holy Spirit". The Christo-primary order of Christ, God and
Spirit suggests the usual form has been further developed here (cf. 1 Cor.
12:5,6,7). Behind grace as "love in action" stands God. Grace from Christ and
agapé from God are obvious enough. But is it *koinōnia* from the Spirit (a
community created by the Spirit) or *koinōnia* of which the Spirit is the object

(participation in the Spirit)? The multiplicity of meanings in standard translations has been noted above (sect. 3). Each rendering has its champions, with able reasonings for each choice. Those favouring "community" stress the church as created by the Spirit; it comes from God, as grace does from Christ and love from God. Those stressing "participation" in God's Spirit and gifts (an emphatic feature of Corinthian Christianity) see individuals and community sharing in these as a basic form of blessing for life. Some commentators suspect that both senses are present. But context is against a solely ecclesial meaning, for what sense would there be in saying "... the church created by the Spirit be with you all"? At best one could claim "communion created by the Spirit". But more likely is: "May participation in the Spirit continue to characterize the life of each of you and the life of all of you together" (cf. 1 Cor. 1:9 "participation in the Son" as a parallel to such participation in the Spirit; the salvation-experience involves receiving the Spirit and spiritual gifts; Schnackenburg 68).

24. For understanding 2 Corinthians 13:13, appeal can be made to Philippians 2:1, where "Christ", "love", and "Spirit" also appear:

> If then there is any encouragement in Christ, any consolation from love, any sharing in the Spirit (*koinōnia pneumatos*), make my joy complete: be of the same mind....

Paul's several grounds for appeal include the fact that every Christian shares in God's Spirit (by baptism). This reference brings us to *koinōnia* in *paraenesis* (admonitions and exhortations for congregational life).

D. In exhortations and admonitions *(paraenesis)* for congregational life

25. Greek concepts of *koinōnia* often included ethical components for "life together", for to agree to share something in common was a positive value-judgment. Good things might include justice, order and the "mean" between extremes, or the obligations of guest-friendship; later, peace, harmony, equality, and care for others as part of humanity and even care for animals. Clubs and associations had philanthropic goals, including honours and proper burials for members (references in Popkes 1106-08, 1111-12, 1117-18, 1122). In Paul and the New Testament generally, *koinōn*-terms are little used for direct commands ("imperatives") about how to live. *Koinōnia* serves rather to motivate (cf. Phil. 2:1). The implications are indirect, *implied* actions stemming from fellowship with Christ, his saving death and contemporary community; from participation in the Spirit; from sharing in the gospel or in faith. We have already been able, from the context of *koinōnia* passages, to list above involvements for Christians such as the spread of the gospel or mission, hospitality and benevolence, attitude towards suffering and hope. Paul's most pointed references will involve financial sharing (E, below). There is also some use of our terms for "partners" in various aspects of Christian mission — Paul with Philemon (Philemon 17), Titus with Paul (2 Cor. 8:23, *koinōnos emos*; cf. Titus 1:4 "my loyal child in the faith we share [*koinēn pistin*]"). Involvement in the tasks of *koinōnia* was thus based on faith as the reply to God's call; one may compare Jesus' disciples who followed him and formed with him an "eschatological family of God", which supersedes natural, family ties (Mark 3:21-35). Many commentators describe *koinōnia* in first "vertical" terms (for the relationship with God), followed by "horizontal" associations (with other human beings, almost always in our literature

Christians), including tasks together. This can be sketched in chart form (cf.
Panikulam 39,57,79; Franco 240):

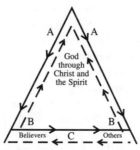

A = Communication from God in Christ and the gospel
B = Response in faith, participation in Christ and the Spirit by believers
C = Reciprocal participation, with each other, giving and taking a part in this undertaking or that

In Paul and the New Testament generally, the *koinōnia* relationship is limited to
those in Christ or to evangelization by them to others. Galatians 6:10 is as far as the
Pauline outlook goes with regard to the world in general or creation, given the
imminent eschatological expectations of the day: "Let us work for the good of all, and
especially for those of the family of faith."

26. Galatians 6:6 is the one clearly imperatival use of the verb *koinōnein* in the
New Testament (on Rom. 12:13, see sect. 29 below):

> Let the one who is taught in the word share *(koinōneitō)* all good things with the one who
> teaches. [NRSV has, for inclusive language reasons, changed it to a plural and inserted
> "must".]

The verse has been variously assessed. Panikulam omits treatment because he takes up
only passages with nouns. Betz (1979:304-06) sees a maxim akin to Pythagoras's
"friends share everything in common", applied possibly to an "educational institution"
among the Galatian churches. Hainz (1982:62-89) sees the verse as setting forth "the
Pauline principle" of *koinōnia*. 6:6 is part of the *paraenesis* section of Galatians,
specifically in the unit that begins: "Let us be guided by the Spirit" (5:25-6:10). All
Christians have their own tasks (6:2). Some "teach the word". This involves probably
not just baptismal instruction in a household but broader teaching and preaching of the
gospel, over a long enough period of time to call for financial support by those taught.
While local teachers are involved, Paul and members of his missionary team could
also be in view (cf. 1 Cor. 9:14, "those who proclaim the gospel should get their living
by the gospel"). In Galatians the menace of false teachers with a different gospel is
also prominent (1:6; 5:12); hence teaching the word is under the eye of a God who will
not be mocked (6:7-8). Nonetheless the teaching task in the Galatian churches must go
on, individually and corporately. The sharing is a reciprocal matter, Hainz argues, a
partnership of giving and receiving material and spiritual goods. The teacher who
brings spiritual blessings of the gospel is to receive material support in exchange; cf.
1 Corinthians 9:11, sowing "spiritual good", reaping "material benefits". Paul himself
may not have made use of such a right (1 Cor. 9:12b), but Hainz views it as a principle
of all-encompassing *koinōnia* in Paul's churches, here seen in the particular relationship and obligation of teaching. The principle is reciprocity, spiritual and material.

While Paul elsewhere cited somewhat forced Old Testament texts in support of Christian apostles and teachers having "hope of a share in the crop" (*metechein*; 1 Cor. 9:9-10, cf. Deut. 25:4 and Sir. 6:19?), teaching for pay was common among Greek sophists, and reciprocity characterized friendship practices. But at 6:6 it is not, as in idealized Greek societies or Acts 2-5, that people must put all their possessions in common; Hainz (81-84,87) sees here a modified form of sharing, as in 1 Corinthians 9:4-14: one gives a portion of one's goods, as well as thanks, faithfulness and obedience, but it is not required to tithe or to turn all over to a central administration.

27. Hainz's claim of a "*koinōnia* principle" involves a rather sweeping reading of Galatians 6:6, but he goes on to apply it thoroughly to (1) *koinōnia* as *Gemeinschaft* (association or community) with someone through common participation in something (Phil. 1:5, 3:10; 2 Cor. 1:7); (2) *koinōnoi* as people who stand in a relationship of *Gemeinschaft* to one another because they have common participation in something (1 Cor. 10:18,20; 2 Cor. 8:23; Philemon 6, 17); (3) *koinōnein* as a verb meaning to have or obtain *Gemeinschaft* through reciprocal giving and receiving a portion (Rom. 15:27; Phil. 4:15; Rom. 12:13); and (4) the compounds *sygkoinōnos* and *sygkoinōnein* as *Gemeinschaft* relationships or conduct on the basis of common participation in something such as the apostle's distress (Phil. 4:14), grace (Phil. 1:7), or the promises of the gospel (1 Cor. 9:23; Rom. 11:17). This yields the understanding that fellowship or communion *(Gemeinschaft)* comes through participation (173), all of which Hainz views in light of the two-sided fact that there is no fellowship in the body of Christ (the community) without common participation in the body of Christ at the Lord's supper (1 Cor. 1:9, 10:16-21). His is, however, but one possible arrangement of the Pauline evidence. Panikulam settles for a vertical/horizontal sequence: the "call to *koinōnia* with the Son awaits response through *koinōnia* on our part"; i.e., Christology, followed by the communitarian dimension (108). Franco (289-90) found the proprium or heart of the Pauline concept of *koinōnia* in the gospel (Phil. 1:5; 1 Cor. 9:19-23); new existence as a Christian and the experience of the interpersonal relationships of communion led to articulation by Paul along vertical/horizontal, historical/eschatological, passive/active lines for "communion and participation". Or should one say "participation and communion"? Or that "participation *is* communion"? Or that it is from a human point of view "participation", leading to communion with God and others, and then further common participation, in a diastolic rhythm?

E. Financial support, the collection (2 Cor. 8-9)

28. Since *koinōnia* in the classical world could refer to a business relationship or even financial partnership, it is not surprising to find *koinōn* words used for support of the Pauline mission through money and personnel and (sect. 29) for Paul's collection for Jerusalem. The clearest example of such support for Paul comes in the section of Philippians (4:10-20) where the apostle responds, somewhat as in a Greek "letter of friendship", with regard to the help sent to Paul "more than once" in Thessalonia (4:16) and now during his imprisonment.

> ...it was kind of you to share my distress *(sygkoinōnēsantes mou tē thlipsei)*. You Philippians indeed know that in the early days of the gospel, when I left Macedonia, no church shared with me *(ekoinōnēsen)* in the matter of giving and receiving, except you alone. (Phil. 4:14-15)

The Philippians stand in *koinōnia* with him (v.14), they have expressed their solidarity once and again in pecuniary support. Paul uses technical business terms here to describe their involvement, something quite appropriate with *koinōnia* language. M. Jack Suggs indeed began his discussion of "Koinonia in the New Testament" for an ecumenical audience with such references to "material goods" (351-52) but also brought out the sense of empathy and kindness in the Philippians' identifying with Paul's needs and suffering.

29. The history, details and debate over the collection project we need not assess here, in paying attention to actual uses of *koinōnia* to denote sharing in this financial appeal. Examples occur in 2 Corinthians 8 and 9 and in Romans. The second letter to the Corinthians 8:4 speaks of "the privilege *(charin)* of sharing *(koinōnia)* in this ministry *(diakonia)* to the saints". The verse piles up a series of words, notably "grace" and *koinōnia*, that take on particular meanings in the account of how the Macedonians (8:1), impoverished and afflicted themselves, responded graciously in participating quite specifically and objectively in this service. The second letter to the Corinthians 9:13 attests to the "generosity" of the people in the province of Achaia (around Corinth, 9:2) in "sharing with *(koinōnia)*" the saints (in Jerusalem). The addition in 9:13 of the words "and with all others" could imply additional gifts to Christians elsewhere, out of "obedience to the confession of the gospel of Christ". In Romans 12:13 the participle *koinōnountes* can be taken as an imperative: "Contribute to the needs of the saints." Romans 15:26-27 pulls these references together and adds another idea:

> Macedonia and Achaia [the two provinces mentioned in 2 Cor. 8-9] have been pleased to share their resources *(koinōnian tina poiēsasthai)* with the poor among the saints in Jerusalem. They were pleased to do this, and indeed they owe it to them; for if the Gentiles have come to share *(ekoinōnēsan)* in their spiritual blessings, they ought also to be of service *(leitourgēsai)* to them in material things.

(NRSV suggests another instance when it renders 9:8:

> God is able to provide you with every blessing in abundance, so that by always having enough of everything, you may share abundantly in every good work.

But the verb is not *koinōnein* but another one, to "abound", *perisseuein*.) The idea in 15:27, of reciprocally sharing spiritual and material things, we have encountered before, in Galatians 6:6. The suggestion that Jerusalem was imposing a "church tax" receives lesser support in recent discussions than it once did. Indeed, that the giver is inferior to the recipient does not fit patron-client relations in the ancient world, where it was the weaker party who initiated the tie to the patron (Furnish 413). The collection, however, was more than a charitable appeal for the poor or even an expression of solidarity. Paul saw the project as a means for his Gentile churches to show how they had come of age and, as recipients of the same gospel and same Lord with Jerusalem, to demonstrate the unity of churches made up of Jewish and Gentile believers. That Paul was acting with an understanding of the collection as a key step in salvation history (Munck) remains debated, as does what eventually happened in Jerusalem with the endeavour. (Acts is silent about the collection.) Paul's project was not "worldwide", involving a "universal church", but concerned Paul's half-dozen or so congregations and Jerusalem ("the poor" meaning all the saints there, not just a lower economic level of church members). But ecumenical rapprochement, in the face of doctrinal variations over gospel or law, and involving economics, ethnicity, cultures and language, was difficult already in Paul's day.

F. Ecclesiology, especially Galatians 2:9

30. *Koinōnia*, to review, has not by itself in Paul proven to be a synonym for "church" *(ekklēsia)*, except via 1 Corinthians 10:16 (we as one body partake of one bread), unless 2 Corinthians 13:13 is taken as "the community created by the Holy Spirit". The word usually refers instead to that to which believers are called, namely fellowship with Christ and the Spirit, participating in the blessings of Jesus' death and being a part of Christ's body, through faith, with responsibilities for mission, care of the saints locally and in Jerusalem, and hospitality and benevolence. These are all aspects of the church but not a definition. It has also been pointed out above that Paul's concerns for *koinōnia* as sharing in evangelization and unity involved first of all the multiple house churches in a given urban area; then, their combined support of Paul's mission (Phil. 4:15); and in the collection, a group of Aegean churches contributing to the saints in Jerusalem (Rom. 12:13, 15:26-27; 2 Cor. 8-9). One cannot as yet speak of a "universal" church (Hainz 1981:41; 1982:148-61) or of a worldwide communion either as existing or even as a goal to be sought, but only of *koinōnia* in existing churches expressed in various ways (cf. Brown 1985; *Unité*). Occasionally there have been attempts to explain Paul's *koinōn*-language, particularly in Philippians, along the lines of a business venture (Fleury) or, more important, as a "consensual *societas*" under Roman law (Sampley 1977, 1980); on this reading, Paul and the Philippians would have entered into a legal agreement for the support of his mission. But that would yield an unparallelled ecclesiology, uniquely Philippian, hardly applicable elsewhere, tied to mission and dissolved upon the death of any member. Further consideration (White) has tended to see this case as incomplete and Philippians as fitting better into a "friendship" paradigm (Fitzgerald, Mitchell 1991); in my opinion (1993:455-56) the *philia*-connections were quite naturally developed by the Philippians but somewhat modified by Paul. A network or "society" of friends does not do justice to the full *koinōnia* contents in Paul's letters.

31. Are there implications for leadership structures in the church from Paul's use of *koinōnia*? In broad terms, yes, in that the concept implied that all believers participate in the realities of gospel, Christ, Spirit, and faith, and so, with the sense of equality present in the Greek concept of *koinōnia*, share reciprocally in goods both spiritual and material. The Greek background carried with it also a sense of order, and so we find Paul emphasizing that all should be "of one mind", indeed "the same mind", the same spirit, and all things done "decently and in order" (Phil. 1:27, 2:2; 1 Cor. 12:4-14, 14:40). Hence there are hints of leaders in the congregations' life. Galatians 6:6 points to teachers (preachers). For shepherding the collection to Jersualem, in impeccable fashion, there were congregational delegates, and Paul may have acceded to a congregation itself electing its representative for the task in Greek democratic style (1 Cor. 16:3; 2 Cor. 8:19 "appointed by the churches" = *cheironētheis*, literally by raising the hand; Betz 1985:74-75). But in Paul's congregations there was great variety in other leadership structures — for Thessalonica, *proïstamenoi* (5:12, "those who labour among you and 'manage' [better: care for] you"); in Corinth, probably house church heads (cf. 1 Cor. 16:15-19); in Philippi, *episkopoi* and *diakonoi* (1:1, probably locally evolved overseers and agents); never in

Paul *presbyteroi* or elders — suggesting that the apostle came with no fixed plan of organization but let each congregation develop its own leadership out of local practices (Reumann, 1993:446-50).

32. The use of *koinōnia* by Paul at Galatians 2:9 is a final piece of evidence on an early Christian understanding of the churches in Judea (1:22) and Jerusalem (2:1) and those of Paul in Galatia (1:2) as sharing gospel-unity and mission strategy. It comes in a letter where Paul is battling against interlopers with roots in Jerusalem (2:4,12,13, 1:6-9, 4:21, 5:2-4,7-12), against whom he defends his law-free gospel of justification (2:15-21, 3:5-29) and his own apostleship and authority (1:1,15-2:14). Paul recounts how he went up to Jerusalem, in accord with a revelation (2:2), to set before leaders there (2:2 RSV "those who were of repute") the gospel he proclaimed, one *not* demanding circumcision for Gentiles (2:3, 3:3, 5:2-6). The result of the consultation was that the Jerusalem leaders added nothing to change Paul's message or approach to Gentiles. The actual words of the agreement may be preserved in vv.7-8 and 10, about how Paul was entrusted with the gospel and should go to the uncircumcised or Gentiles, and Peter was entrusted with the gospel and should go to the circumcised or Jews, God working in both of them. Paul records his own description (v.9a) of the outcome (9b-10):

> [9b] when James and Cephas [Peter] and John, who were acknowledged pillars, recognized the grace that had been given me, they gave to me the right hand of fellowship *(dexias* [supply *cheiras]… koinōnias)*, agreeing that we should go to the Gentiles and they to the circumcized.   [10] They asked only one thing, that we remember the poor, which was actually what I was [*or* had been] eager to do.

The verses certainly set missionary strategy for the two great segments of humanity (in Jewish opinion) and build in Paul's collection project. Left out are other missionaries to the Gentiles, like Stephen and the "Hellenists" (Acts 6-8, 11:19-21), so even in Galatians 2 one cannot speak of a "universal" church and officers (*Gesamtkirche*, Hainz 1981a:41). "The right hand of fellowship" has been variously interpreted, as a merely personal handshake of agreement or, at the other extreme, the sealing of a legal contract. It can be debated whether the gesture is confirming and extending previously-existing agreement or that fellowship is now for the first time established (Betz 1979:100). It may best be read as carrying further an existing agreement on the gospel (1:18-19) and confirming a future intention of cooperative mission for the gospel (cf. Hainz 1981a:39). The second of the two purpose-clauses, in v.10, care for the poor, is not surprising when one considers the financial side of *koinōnia*. The *koinōnia* of Galatians 2:9 rests, then, on common participation in the one gospel (cast at 2:16 in terms of justification by grace through faith; cf. 3:6; as promise at 3:14-18,21-22,29, 4:23,28; as freedom and life in the Spirit, 5:1,13,16,22-25). Participation in the gospel marks the church of Jews and Gentiles in Christ. Unity has to do with "the truth of the gospel" (2:6,14), not juridical categories of the law or merely those of friendship. Kertelge (1981) would therefore set kerygma and *koinōnia* side by side in the theological description of the church of the New Testament, a "diastasis" of teaching and common faith-experience under the word of God.

33. Our survey of *koinōnia* in Paul has thus far omitted 2 Corinthians 6:14:

> Do not be mismatched with unbelievers. For what partnership *(metochē)* is there between righteousness and lawlessness? Or what fellowship *(koinōnia)* is there between light and darkness?

This omission is in part for historical-critical reasons: many (e.g., Hainz 1982:204-5) think 2 Corinthians 6:14-7:1 a non-Pauline fragment, with Qumran affinities (like the name "Beliar" in 6:15; R.P. Martin 1986:190-95, sees a borrowed piece of Essene writing). If included, 2 Corinthians 6:14 warns strenuously against *koinōnia* with unbelievers and calls for holy separateness from the world of the unclean. It reflects the biblical idea of not sharing in evil deeds (Matt. 23:30, taking part in shedding the blood of prophets; 1 Tim. 5:22, "Do not participate in the sins of others"; Eph. 5:11; 2 John 11; Rev. 18:4). Romans 11:17 strikes a more positive but mixed note, with regard to Gentiles and Israel, viewed as a branch and olive tree, respectively:

> If some of the branches were broken off, and you, a wild olive shoot, were grafted in their place to share *(sygkoinōnos)* the rich root of the olive tree, do not boast....

Much of Israel is here regarded as broken off but some branches and the roots of the patriarchs like Abraham remain, into which Gentiles are now grafted, by grace, in a *koinōnia* relationship of participation in the root and life of God's planting.

G. Doxological summary

34. Ettore Franco (p.295) has sought to weave together Paul's *koinōnia* references in a prayer form, stressing the sequence of communion and participation:

> We return thanks to you, our Father
> because you have called us to communion with your Son (cf. 1 Cor. 1:9)
> and because you have granted us the downpayment [first instalment] of the Holy Spirit (cf. 2 Cor. 1:22, 13:13)
> to make of us,
>> through communion with the body and blood of Christ,
> a single body, your church (cf. 1 Cor. 10:16-17).
> For this we pray you:
>> that our participation in the gospel (cf. Phil. 1:5) may become effective
>> in acknowledging all the good that is among us in relation to Christ (cf. Philemon 6)
> and that our love grow ever more (cf. Phil. 1:9),
>> contributing to the needs of the poor (Rom. 12:13),
> and being able with one mind to think the same thing (Phil. 2:2),
> in manner becoming so through communion with the passion of Christ,
>> co-participants in his resurrection (cf. Phil. 3:10-11; 1 Cor. 1:7).
> To you be glory through Jesus Christ our Lord
>> in the unity of the Holy Spirit,
>> now and for ever. Amen.

H. Other (Deutero-) Pauline writings

35. Somewhat surprisingly, the later Pauline letters, often attributed to his pupils, not the apostle himself, employ *koinōn*-terms very little. In the pastoral epistles, 1 Timothy 5:22 has already been cited (sect. 33) as *paraenesis* to Timothy not to participate in others' sins. In the same letter 6:18 advises the rich to be "generous and ready to share *(koinōnikous)*." Ephesians 5:11 is a warning like 1 Timothy 5:22: "Take no part *(mē sygkoinōneite)* in the unfruitful works of darkness." It is striking that Ephesians, as the great epistle of the almost cosmic church, never uses *koinōnia* (even if Paul Lehmann has based his *"koinonia* ethics" and "politics of God" upon it; cf. Fischer).

IV. *KOINŌNIA* IN OTHER NEW TESTAMENT WRITINGS

A. The Johannine school

36. Although the fourth gospel could be presented as stressing the believer's having a part in God's love and life through Christ (e.g., 1:16; the true vine of chap. 15) and the need for unity (17:11,21-23), perhaps in the face of existing divisions, as Schnackenburg has suggested (1978; 1979:80-93), the book presents its narrative theology without any use of *koinōn*-terms, though there is some "friendship" language (e.g., 15:13-15). In the Book of Revelation, John the seer describes himself (1:9) as "your brother who share[s] *(sygkoinōnos)* with you in Jesus the persecution and the kingdom and the patient endurance". The persecution note was heard in Paul; the connection with *the kingdom* is a new theme here. The second letter of John 11 has already been listed (sect. 33) about *not* offering *hospitality* to false teachers, "for to welcome [a deceiver who preaches a gospel that goes beyond the teaching of Christ] is to participate *(koinōnei)* in the evil deeds of such a person". The love-command extended to receive itinerants (John 13:34; 3 John 5) thus has its limits where doctrine is concerned. Hospitality becomes an "evil deed" when it abets heretical teaching and thus breaks the unity of a congregation and threatens proper love with one another in the community (1 John 2:15, 4:7-11, 20-21).

37. It is in 1 John 1:2-3,6-7 that a concentration of four examples of *koinonia* occurs. As in Paul, they revolve around the vertical and horizontal connection with *the Father* (a designation for God not used in Pauline *koinōnia* passages) and with the Son, something which grounds a reciprocal linking with fellow-believers. The opening paragraph (1:1-5), about the word of life, the word that brings life, tells the nature and purpose of the revelation in Christ:

> This life was revealed, and we have seen it and testify to it, and declare to you the eternal life which was with the Father and was revealed to us — we declare to you what we have seen and heard so that you also may have fellowship *(koinōnia)* with us, and truly our fellowship *(koinōnia)* is with the Father and with his Son Jesus Christ. (1:2-3)

The pattern is that of a two-dimensional relationship. Life was manifested vertically from above, when the Father sent Christ. This calls for a response of witness, declaration, or proclamation by the recipients to others. But they and we are to have fellowship with one another, horizontally, as well as with the Father and the Son. The claim of the Johannine community to have fellowship with God was, however, taken by some in the group to mean participation in God but then doing whatever you want in life, forgetting the sister and the brother; in their view, no matter what you do morally, it is no sin for those who enjoy such vertical fellowship with the Father. Some slogans of these perfectionists are quoted in vv.6 and 8 and then refuted by a *koinōnia* theology that stresses the horizontal, ethical aspects, as well as the truth about our relationship here and now with God:

> [6] If we say, "We have fellowship *(koinōnia)* with God", while we are walking in the darkness, we lie and do not do what is true. [7] But if we walk in the light as Christ is in the light, we have fellowship *(koinōnia)* with one another, and the blood of Jesus his Son cleanses us from all sin.

This is to say that the Johannine community is a *corpus permixtum*, a mixed body of people pressing on but never in this age attaining perfection. They remain relatively perfect — in but not of the world; sin no longer holds them but they may still commit acts of sin. Verses 8-9 refute the claims of the opponents about life-style and attainment, while pointing to the continually saving work of Christ in a "God-is-faithful" statement (cf. 1 Cor. 1:9, above, sect. 19):

> [8] If we say, "We have no sin", we deceive ourselves and the truth is not in us.   [9] If we confess our sins, (God) who is faithful and just will forgive us our sins and cleanse us from all unrighteousness.   [10] If we say, "We have not sinned", we make God a liar, and his word is not in us.

Koinōnia is, then, relational with God *and* with each other. Yet even in the community of the word of life there are broken relations and the need of cleansing, which God has provided (2:1-2). *Koinōnia* brings life, from and of God. Witness is there in terms of proclamation and love for one another, including sharing this world's goods with sisters and brothers (3:17). The command is to believe and love (3:23). About ministerial structures there is little until 2 and 3 John, when an elder is mentioned. Estimates of a Johannine view on "sacraments" range from non-existent (in the "gospel of the Spirit") to an extremely sacramental, mystical interpretation (which, at Montreal, Raymond Brown sought to solve by saying John "presupposes sacraments in the Church", p.62). The Johannine literature has thus provided grounds for subsequent Pentecostal emphasis on the Spirit, Reformation emphasis on the word, and Catholic sacramentology. But, unlike Paul's writings, *koinōnia* is not here brought into relation with the eucharist. The attempt has been made to show that all of 1 John is constructed around the theme of *koinōnia* (Malatesta), but even in 1:1-4, where half of the *koinōnia* references in the entire epistle occur, the subject is "life" as well as "fellowship", and the spiralling structure of the rest of the document and the subsequent lack of *koinōn*-terms after 1:7 makes such a claim exaggerated.

38. Doxologically the Johannine references to *koinōnia* could be put together thus as a prayer:

> We to whom eternal life has been revealed (1 John 1:1-2)
> and who have seen the glory of the word (John 1:14)
> declare with joy the fellowship that is ours
> with the Father and with his Son, Jesus Christ (1 John 1:3b).
> At the same time that we declare our fellowship with God (1 John 1:6)
> we know that we must walk in the light (1 John 1:7)
> and live in fellowship with one another (1 John 1:3,7).
> Yet we must confess that we do sin (1 John 1:8,10)
> against God and the sisters and the brothers,
> and so we look to God's forgiveness (1 John 1:9)
> and the blood of Jesus to cleanse us from all sin (1 John 1:7).
> Let us therefore love one another, in word and deed,
> sharing this world's goods, and practice hospitality
> but not with those who teach falsely (2 John 11).
> We thank you that in Jesus we can share in the kingdom, persecution,
>   and patient endurance (Rev. 1:9),
> abiding in Christ, through the Spirit-Paraclete.

B. Hebrews

39. As in Paul and 1 John, *koinōnia* references here can be analyzed in terms of (1) fellowship with regard to God or Christ, and (2) fellowship with reference to our

fellow human beings (Popkes 1131-32) or, otherwise put, vertically and horizontally. Those addressed by this "word of exhortation" (13:22) are themselves "partners of Christ" (3:14 *metochoi... tou Christou*), who have grown somewhat complacent (2:1-3a, 3:12-14, 6:1-12). They still partake of *(metochon)* milk when they should be on solid food (5:12-14). Yet earlier in their Christian existence they had endured sufferings well, sometimes "publicly exposed to abuse and persecution, and sometimes being partners *(koinōnoi)* with those so treated" (10:32-33). In presenting Jesus as the Son of God subjected to suffering and death to bring about salvation, the author of Hebrews insists on a real **incarnation**. At the same time it is insisted that the saviour and those saved "have all one origin" (2:11 RSV, or as NRSV puts it, "the one who sanctifies and those who are sanctified all have one Father"). There follow three Old Testament quotations to show how Jesus identified with the brothers and sisters whom he saves. The last one, in Hebrews 2:13, from Isaiah 8:18: "Here am I and the children whom God has given me", is picked up in 2:14, one of the few places in the New Testament where a *koinōnia* reference builds on an Old Testament verse:

> Since therefore the children share *(kekoinōnēken)* flesh and blood, Jesus himself likewise shared *(meteschen)* the same things [flesh and blood], so that through death he might destroy the one who has the power of death, that is, the devil, and free those... held in slavery....

Jesus shared our human existence in order fully and effectively to work salvation. Here *koinōnein* and *metechein* are synonymous. (Cf. also 7:13, Jesus "belonged to [*metescheken*, partook of] another tribe", Judah, not a tribe of Israelite priests.) Hebrews 2:14 is, along with 1 John 1, as close as *koinōnia* passages come to the topic of **anthropology**, what human beings are, here "flesh and blood". The final reference in Hebrews is paraenetic:

> Do not neglect to do good and to share *(koinōnias)* what you have, for such sacrifices are pleasing to God. (13:16)

The admonition follows references to Christ's high-priestly death (13:12) and then to our proper response, praise to God and "lips that confess his name" (v.15) and then the virtue of sharing. "To do good" means "mutual love" (*philadelphia*, 13:1), and "sharing" here may especially suggest compassion and solidarity with those suffering persecution (10:33, 13:3).

40. The limited Hebrews material on *koinōnia* might be construed thus in a prayer:

> We remember, O God, how Jesus shared our flesh and blood
> in order to destroy the devil and to deliver us from death
> and bring many flesh-and-blood children to glory (2:10-15).
> Praise be to you as we confess your name
> and share what we have with our persecuted, imprisoned brothers and sisters (13:16),
> our partners in faith, pilgrimage, and struggle (10:33, chap. 11).

C. 1 and 2 Peter

41. The two letters of Peter may be treated together, although many critics think that 2 Peter is pseudonymous (written not by Peter but in the name of "Simeon Peter") and very late in the New Testament period (perhaps as late as A.D. 140). Some even claim 1 Peter is not by Peter and is Pauline in content. In any case, 2 Peter builds on the first letter (see 2 Pet. 3:1); it defends Paul against misinterpretations (3:15b-17) and

defends the faith (1:1) against false teachers of the day (2:1). The first letter of Peter, addressing Christians throughout Asia Minor (1:1), rejoices in hope through the resurrection of Jesus Christ (1:3-5), in the face of imminent or present persecutions (1:6, 2:20, 3:14-17, 4:12-19). There is frequent appeal to confessional statements about Christ's passion, death, and resurrection (2:21-24, 3:18-19,21c-22). The *koinōn*-reference in 4:13 urges joy now, during *sufferings*, and future joy at Christ's parousia:

> Rejoice insofar as you are sharing *(koinōneite)* Christ's sufferings, so that you may also be glad and shout for joy when his glory is revealed.

The thought is akin to that of Philippians 3:10 and 2 Corinthians 1:5-7 on suffering. The first letter of Peter has previously alluded to unjust suffering as a Christian (2:19-21, 3:17-18). But whereas Paul speaks of the sufferings of Christ for us and our sufferings for Christ's sake (2 Cor. 1:5,7; Phil. 3:10), 1 Peter 4:13 relates more closely Christians' having a part, by suffering, in "the sufferings of Christ" *(ta pathēmata tou Christou)* and in his subsequent glory (cf. 1:11, 5:1; but in Paul see also 2 Cor. 4:10-11; Rom. 8:17; cf. Col. 1:24). The thought rests, not on a "passion mysticism" or imitation of Christ, but upon baptismal identification with Christ (1:3, 23 new birth; 3:21) (Goppelt 1978:297-98,323). Joy *in* suffering, here for Christ, reflects not only Old Testament, especially apocalyptic, thought (4:14b = Isa. 11:2; cf. Isa. 25:6-10, 26:16-19 on joy *after* suffering) but also the teaching of Jesus in the Synoptic tradition (with the beatitude of 4:14a, cf. Matt. 5:10-12). The adverb *katho*, translated "insofar as", prevents full or automatic identification of the Christian's situation with that of Christ; obedience to Christ and faith or trust in God, while doing good, mark Christian existence, while awaiting vindication at the end (4:15-19). In 5:1 Peter's self-description personalizes the twin emphasis on sufferings and glory (cf. also Luke 24:26):

> ...a witness of the sufferings of Christ, as well as one who shares *(koinōnos)* in the glory to be revealed....

Looking back to Jesus' passion, amid present participation in persecution, one expects to share in the future glory. Eschatological *koinōnia*, now and in the future (10), is the basis for exhortation (4:15-19, 5:1b-9).

42. The address in 2 Peter is quite general: "to those who have received a faith as precious as ours through the righteousness of our God and Saviour Jesus Christ" (1:1b). Here the old biblical phrase "the righteousness of God" (Deut. 33:21; Matt. 6:33; Rom. 1:17, 14:17) has been expanded to include Christ as its source; or if Christ is viewed as "God", its sole author. The *prooimium* or opening that follows in 1:3-11, in place of the thanksgiving in an epistle, is structured around (a) the historical-theological grounding of salvation (vv.3-4) in the divine power and acts "of God and of Jesus our Lord" (1:2); (b) the ethical implications (vv.5-10) in a chain of eight virtues, beginning with faith and reaching a climax in brotherly love *(philadelphia)* and agape (1:7); and (c) a future eschatological expectation (v.11, "entry into the eternal kingdom... will be richly provided"). In this context a *koinōn*-reference occurs in v.4:

> [3] His [God's and Jesus'] divine power has given us everything needed for life and godliness, through the knowledge of him who called us by his own glory and good-

ness.   [4] Thus he has given us, through these things [God's glory and goodness or all things] his precious and very great promises, so that through them you may escape from the corruption that is in the world because of lust, and may become participants of the divine nature *(theias koinōnoi physeōs)*.

(NRSV has not done well here on inclusive language; it also reverses the two final ideas in v.4; in the Greek word order "fleeing the corruption" in the world comes after "become participants of the divine nature".) Exegetes agree that the verses are full of language and ideas from the Greco-Roman world and its philosophies, not only *koinōnia* but also "divine nature" and the dualistic view of the world as corrupted by lust so that the saved must flee from it. Some (e.g., Käsemann 1952) therefore condemn 2 Peter for going too far in accommodating the gospel to "the strongly syncretistic and pluralistic environment of the decline of antiquity" (Fornberg 88), by succumbing to a programme oriented to human hopes for deification in a metaphysics that discards this world of God's creation. Yet while stressing "knowledge" *(epig-nōsis)*, the passage does retain God's call, gifts and promises, and the righteousness of God-in-Christ, through faith. Some argue that v.4 does not refer to "participation in *God* but in the nature of heavenly, immortal beings", in a world *like* God (Bauckham 181). Some (Wolters) would interpret 1:4 as "partners of the Deity" in "covenant fellowship", but it is truer to the text to go the route of Greco-Roman "friendship" philosophy, since the word for covenant *(diathēkē)*, surprisingly rare in the New Testament, never occurs in 2 Peter. More to the point is the futurist eschatology, not a process in this life but an outcome at the end. We "become" such (aorist infinitive in Greek, single decisive action) at the End (1:11, by God's providing). The goal of the sequence of virtues (vv.5-7) is not yet *theōsis* or deification but love, here and now, in the community. The second letter of Peter as a whole is very much oriented to futurist eschatology; see especially chapter 3, vv.4ff., "the promise of Christ's coming", as the future hope. What we have in 2 Peter 1:4 is Peter's own hope, as expressed in 1 Peter 5:1, writ large and applied to all true Christians who obtain faith (2 Pet. 1:1). To participate "in the glory that is going to be revealed" has been here put in Hellenistic philosophical terms, as an outcome of the hope in 1 John for *koinōnia* with God the Father — a claim there subject to overstatement by the opponents (1 John 1:6, people who say "I know God", 1 John 2:4), which the author of 1 John nuanced in ethical terms and 2 Peter has in eschatological ones. Is the bridge that 2 Peter has built to ideas and philosophies of the day too risky when not hedged by the qualifications in 2 Peter itself and the rest of the Bible? Resurrection and new creation differ from apotheosis and a world left to corruption and lust. For 2 Peter's own answer on cosmic renewal and "new heavens and a new earth, where righteousness is at home", see 3:5-17.

   43. A prayer for the Petrine letters might run:

Blessed be the God and Father of our Lord Jesus Christ (1 Pet. 1:3)
who by Jesus' resurrection and our baptism has given us a living hope!
Even as we share in Christ's sufferings,
may we rejoice and shout for joy at the glory to be revealed (1 Pet. 4:13, 5:1).
May God's power, glory, goodness, call, and promises,
   which offer us faith, love, and everything needed for life and goodness,
richly provide entry into the eternal kingdom and,
escaping this world, participation in the divine world (2 Pet. 1:3-11).

D. The Acts of the Apostles

44. The single reference to *koinōnia* in Acts at 2:42 has often been taken as a starting point for New Testament usage, though with a variety of interpretations. The passage reflects Luke's fondness for summary statements, such as those about the spread of the word of God (Acts 6:7, 12:24, 19:20) or the growth of the churches (9:31, 16:5). There are also summaries about the nature of church life in Jerusalem. That at 2:42 comes after the baptism at Pentecost of 3,000 persons (2:41). Their house-church life is thus described:

> They devoted themselves to the apostles' teaching and fellowship *(koinōnia)*, to the breaking of bread, and to prayers. (2:42)

Cf. 2:44-47:

> All who believed were together and had all things in common *(koina)*; they would sell their possessions and goods and distribute the proceeds to all, as any had need. Day after day, as they spent much time together in the temple, they broke bread at home [*or* from house to house] and ate their food with glad and generous hearts, praising God and having the good will of all the people. And day by day the Lord added to their number those who were being saved.

Cf. also 4:33:

> Now the whole group of those who believed were of one heart and soul, and no one claimed private ownership *(idion)* of any possessions, but everything they owned was held in common *(autois panta koina)*.

A traditional interpretation of 2:42 found here four aspects of church life: the apostles' teaching, *koinōnia*, the breaking of bread (identified as the agape meal or the eucharist or both or every meal by households as a time of praise to God, v.46), and prayers. Some made the second item more specifically liturgical: (1) apostolic teaching; (2) apostolic liturgy, i.e. (a) breaking the bread and (b) prayers.

How *koinōnia* has been interpreted here constitutes almost a history of scholarship for the term. Panikulam (123) documents four lines of understanding: (a) fraternal communion with each other, fellowship; (b) communion (of the faithful) with the apostles ("hierarchic communion"); (c) table fellowship, a communitarian agape; (d) communication of material goods (which Panikulam himself accepts as "concrete external realisation" of fellowship based on faith and cult). In addition, *koinōnia* has been taken as "a self-designation" of the earliest Christian community, "the Fellowship" (Anderson Scott), and more recently for the church as (sacramental) communion ("the eucharist makes the church", J.-M. R. Tillard). At times the Pharisaic *chăbûrah* has been invoked to suggest ancient Palestinian origins of the church as fellowship-communion. But what we have in Acts 2-5 is rather different from a Jewish *chăbûrah* (above, sect. 13). Tillard allows that to define the church as *koinōnia* comes from the church fathers, not the New Testament (1987:34-35 n.54; Eng. tr. 18-19, n.54). The Lukan summaries have come to be regarded more and more in scholarship as the evangelist's own compositions, not based on sources (Panikulam 112-13). Finally J.D.G. Dunn speaks for many in distinguishing the "instruments of catholicity" like sacraments and creeds from the source of unity in the "common experience of the Spirit" — surely the setting at Pentecost (Acts 2:1-4,17,33,38), along with Peter's preaching of the word (2:14-36, 38-40).

45. The various understandings of *koinōnia* in 2:42 have given way, to a considerable degree, to the one that Luke makes apparent by his vocabulary.

Koinōnia, which appears along with apostolic teaching in v.42, is explained in v.44 by reference to how "all who *believed*" were together *(epi to auto)* "and had all things *in common*" *(koina)*. The praxis is made specific in v.45, they "sold possessions" and "distributed the proceeds" to those in need. Onlookers were impressed (v.47). Luke's second summary on the Jerusalem community in 4:32 says nothing of prayers (having illustrated this in 4:24-31) or of the breaking of bread but does emphasize how, among those who believed, all gave up private ownership of possessions and held everything in common. Luke then illustrates this facet of early Jerusalem church life by narratives: Barnabas's sale of a field provides a positive example when he shares the proceeds (4:36-37); the way Ananias and Sapphira withhold proceeds offers a dire negative warning (5:1-10), so that the church and all who heard stood in awe. This economic interpretation, as a Lukan description of the Jerusalem community in a way that makes it appealing, even awesome, to Gentile readers, has been borne out in recent work on the "friendship" theme from Greek antiquity. Unity among believers is a feature of the story, expressed in such phrases as "together" *(epi to auto* 2:44, 47 [NRSV "to their number"]; *homothymadon* 2:46, 5:12) or "of one heart and soul" (4:32) (Panikulam 125-26); we now recognize these as emphases common in the topic of friendship. Luke uses such language, including *koinōnia*, it has recently been well argued (Mitchell 1992), to urge friendship among believers with one another across "status divisions". Luke employs "friendship traditions" as a vehicle "to encourage upper status people in the community to benefit those beneath them" and to do this without expecting reciprocity (cf. Luke 6:34-35a "lend, expecting nothing in return"; 14:12-14). In that way Luke seeks to build communal unity across lines of social rank and wealth. In the subsequent chapters of Acts the crossing of boundaries will continue, over barriers of race, class, wealth and poverty, but the Jerusalem "community of goods" will not be mentioned again. Was the poverty among the saints in Jerusalem that later necessitated Paul's collection for them caused at least in part by selling all and thus exhausting capital? Luke's account, like Paul's letters (sect. 26), seems to end up with a modification of what was claimed in Greek idealized societies. Such a reading of Acts 2 may diminish the view that in the New Testament the word *koinōnia* means "church". But such a view never did work well in Acts 2:42, for it would make the church one item, along with teaching and prayers and the breaking of bread, on a list. In the history of scholarship, it must be remembered, those who argued for "the Fellowship" as translation here and a name for the community (notably Anderson Scott), took the term not as "the church" but as *a step towards* the later "organized Ecclesia", which came about only when Christians separated from "the Jewish church" (1922:129-30). Does one wish to say the *koinōnia* of 2:42 was but a step towards the church, much as the agape might be regarded as a step towards the Lord's supper.

46. The Jerusalem church, according to Luke in Acts, might have prayed:

Sovereign Lord, creator, who spoke by the Spirit
   about your anointed servant, Jesus,
     crucified and risen, according to your plan:
grant to your servants to speak your word boldly (4:24-29)
   according to the apostles' teaching,
     exercising a community of goods, using our possessions for those in need,
     devoted to meals together and to prayer (2:42),
so that your word may spread (6:7)
and the churches everywhere be strengthened in faith and grow (16:5).

V. CONCLUDING OBSERVATIONS

47. While each of us may bring questions or conclusions to the data from the biblical tradition out of our varied traditions, the following observations can likely command considerable assent.

1. Faith and Order is well grounded in the New Testament in speaking of *koinōnia* **in faith, life and witness.** There are ample ties to *witness*, both in the sense of evangelization for the Christian gospel (e.g., Phil. 1:5; Philemon 17; Gal. 2:7-9) and of service to those in need (2 Cor. 8:4; Rom. 12:13; Gal. 2:10; Acts 2:42). The theme is directly tied to *faith* not only in that believers are addressed but also because all rests on God's fidelity (1 Cor. 1:9); this means both personal faith and attachment to the content of faith (traditionally *fides qua*, the faith with which one believes, 2 Pet. 1:5; and *fides quae*, the faith which is to be believed, Acts 2:42, apostolic teaching; both senses at Philemon 6). There is *koinōnia* in *life* in that Jesus Christ is involved (1 Cor. 1:9, 10:16; Heb. 2:14), the Spirit (2 Cor. 13:13), and the Father (1 John 1:3b), with divine gifts now (2 Pet. 1:3) and the hope of glory to come and the eternal life of the ultimate kingdom to come (1 Pet. 4:13, 5:1; 2 Pet. 1:4); it is also life here and now, with each other, in community (1 John 1:3a,7; 1 Cor. 10:17), including solidarity in suffering (Phil. 4:14, 3:10, 1 Pet. 4:13, 5:1), and that without minimalizing this present world and its goods, indeed bluntly emphasizing it by urging the sharing of money and self for the needy (Gal. 6:6; Rom. 15:27; Phil. 4:15; 2 Cor. 8-9, esp. 8:5; Acts 2:42-47).

48. **2. It goes beyond what the New Testament says to equate** *koinōnia* **with the church, particularly later structural definitions of the** *ekklēsia,* **or with the inner life of the Trinity.** These and other definitions, we all know, were forged in later theology, but we must be careful not to confuse New Testament teaching with later assertions, or, e.g., confuse *koinōnia* with *oikonomia* (as at Eph. 3:9, where some manuscripts have *koinonia* [KJV "fellowship of the mystery"], but *oikonomia* or "plan of the mystery" [RSV] is to be read) and so read God's total economy into every occurrence of a *koinōn*-word. The one term, *oikonomia*, looks at things from the vantage point of God's plan for salvation and the divine administration or arrangement of matters, whereas *koinōnia* looks from the human standpoint towards having a share in the gospel, fellowship with Christ, sharing in the Spirit, and partnership with one another in the church ("in Christ") for mission and service. *Koinōnia* and *oikonomia* overlap at times, as when they refer to the incarnation (for *koinōnia* see Heb. 2:14), but they are not the same in outlook. On *koinōnia* and ecclesiology, see sections 50-51 below; as to the Trinity, 1 Corinthians 1:9 speaks of our *koinōnia* with Christ, 2 Corinthians 13:13 with the Spirit, 1 John 1:3 with the Father, but no New Testament passage speaks about *koinōnia* of Father, Son and Spirit with one another. At the same time we must not leave *koinōnia* a cipher into which everyone pours in the meaning that each wants. It cannot mean everything or just anything. The history of research is full of attempts to make it mean "grace" (Currie); covenant; fellowship in the sense of warm friendly ties within a group or association; sacramental ecclesiology (often eucharistic, without due attention to baptism); participation or communion without the ethical response of giving shares with others; or primarily ethical response involving material goods (cf. Suggs). Is there a way in which equation with the Latin *communio* has set the course for some lines of interpretation, and equation with *societas* or

communicatio for other lines of meaning in the West? The Greek word is itself multivalent, but its several aspects can be listed, even if no one of them was exclusively dominant in the New Testament. That is why the exegetical finds above, especially as displayed in point 1, are important.

49. **3.** Are there sufficient biblical references to provide a *"koinōnia* **theology"?** **In Paul**, yes, provided other even more common Pauline emphases are not omitted and provided one is cautious about the "word-field" that is posited around the term (so Schenk 62-65,95 n.29, in contrast with Hainz). Franco (241-48) speaks of a "theological vision" in Paul. Part III, above, represents an attempt to show the considerable scope of Paul's *koinōnia* references. They deal with God, Christology, the Spirit, salvation, the life in Christ, in community, around the word of God especially as encountered in baptism and the Lord's supper; and human response, particularly with material possessions for those who teach and those in need. The data in 1 John, Hebrews, 1 and 2 Peter, and Acts, as outlined above, can be used to **supplement** this basic outline on *koinōnia*. One does not find in the various biblical theologies that have been written in the last century or so any further extension of *koinōnia*. Old Testament theologies (rightly) do not mention the term or pack other themes under it as a heading. Theologies of the New Testament mention the word only occasionally, then descriptively, chiefly in connection with the sharing of goods and property in the early Jerusalem church. Hence biblical theologies of both testaments rarely even refer to *koinōnia*. Hans-Ruedi Weber, e.g., in his ecumenically-oriented volume, *Power* (136), speaks only of a "community of sharing" as part of a "preferential option for the poor". In Brevard S. Childs's recent *Biblical Theology* of the canon, see pages 81-82 for hints for a development of which he himself may not be aware (God's reality, which is primary, "has no true being apart from communion, first within God's self, and secondly with his creation"). An interesting attempt has been made (by Bojorge) in terms of the first-person plural pronoun, "we". He views the ecclesial society as growth from an initial or "proto-we", consisting of Father and Son, as seen in the passion, to a "deutero-we", involving disciples, and then a "trito-we", of the divine, apostles, and the ecclesia, via faith in the preaching of the apostles and by baptism. A "macro-we" is reflected in the sharing of goods. But such first-person plural language seems often read into the *koinōnia* passages.

50. **4.** Is there, in the New Testament, a *"koinōnia* **ecclesiology"**? It has been concluded above that *koinōnia* is not a name for an interim step called "the Fellowship" on the way to the Christian church, or a name for the ecclesia itself. (The latter point holds even for the church fathers; cf. Lampe's *Patristic Greek Lexicon* 762-64.) *Koinōnia* is instead an early and important aspect of the church and its unity, in faith, witness and life, including baptism and Lord's supper. Believers share in the results of Christ's death (1 Cor. 10:16) as they all share in one bread and are one body, because they are "in Christ" by baptism. Common participation in the gospel, Christ and Spirit mark their life together. Even if 2 Corinthians 13:13 is taken as "the communion", in the sense of community, created by the Holy Spirit, that implies an association that is based on a common experience of the Spirit and charismatic gifts. But theories of a legal *societas* in Philippi (Sampley 1977, 1980) have been denied above; friendship theory provides a fuller analogy for Philippi and elsewhere in the New Testament.

51. Parts of what later definitions for the church have seen as crucial — especially specific structures of ministry — are simply not present in New Testament *koinōnia* passages. That things be done "in order" in the Pauline and other communities follows from the classical background (*kosmos*, order) and Paul's specific words at 1 Corinthians 14:40; cf. 14:33, a God "not of disorder but of peace". The many Greek examples of *koinōniai* in society and government provide no single or even dominant model for structure. Nor, even if we invoke associations of Pharisees, did the *chăbûrah*, except for teacher and disciples. As a practice in Galatia, at least, if not as a general principle, Paul called for financial support for Christian teachers by those taught the word. His congregations each developed leadership structures, but different, as far as we know, in every case. Ecclesial sharing in Paul's churches began within and among the house churches in a given city (like Philippi) or area (Galatia), and expanded through an "Aegean network", to include Jerusalem. That is as "universal" as his *koinōnia* references get. But Paul's churches did have local leaders, likely house-church patrons and benefactors, and in Philippi "*episkopoi* and *diakonoi*", but no presbyters. Acts and 1 Peter speak of "apostles and elders". The Spirit-filled Johannine community reflects virtually nothing about leaders; only in 2 and 3 John do "elders" appear. *Koinōnia* ecclesiology in the New Testament herefore involves variety in church structures. Cothenet (1972b) finds that the New Testament's ecclesiology of communion has two points of reference: adherence to "the word of truth" and faith, imposing on believers tasks to be performed and hope to be sustained.

52. **5.** Since ecumenically today *koinōnia* has been used in an effort to deal with **"intercommunion"**, we must ask whether the New Testament communities profiled above would have **shared fellowship**. If groups praying the characteristic prayer summaries on *koinōnia* (above, sects. 34,38,40,43,46) met in, say, Ephesus, would they have received each other with hospitality and eucharistic sharing? This is to ask, not, as we usually do, about a New Testament composite on *koinōnia*, but for how the view of "having and going shares" works out in the clash of one "particular historical locus" with another. We may hazard the guess that Pauline, Johannine, Petrine, and other Christians would have found broad agreement on *koinōnia* in Christology (Jesus' incarnation, death, and resurrection), the Spirit (and gifts of the Spirit through baptism for each Christian), access to the Father and at the end the life God intends for those who have believed the gospel; as well as agreement on the necessity of faith, mission, sharing with each other, and doing good for those in need. Experience may have led one community to stress some aspects more than, or rather than, others, but there was wide agreement on eschatology ("already and not yet"), the human situation in Christ (rescued, on the way, but not yet perfected), and a common life, including prayer, solidarity, and doing good. Structural uniformity, however, simply did not exist. The tendency in *koinōnia* thought is to work from the local, actual communal situations of those in communion with Christ, involving what is "in common". The lack of structures "from above" does not prevent rigorous resistance to false teaching, misplaced hospitality and rejection of "another gospel". What stands over all and is shared in common is the Christ-event as the way to God.

53. **6. Can *koinōnia* bear the weight we wish to put on it** when the term and concept are virtually non-existent in the Hebrew scriptures and not used by Jesus himself? Yes, I suggest, for ecclesial purposes and understanding God. For it is precisely the God now known in Christ after Easter and through the Spirit, and the

community that results from *koinōnia* with the Father, Christ and the Spirit, which must be involved in a Christian understanding. Admittedly, *koinōnia* references do not stress, but certainly do not deny, continuity with Israel. But we should not be startled that faith, life and witness *in Christ* involves a "new creation" (*kainē ktisis*, 2 Cor. 5:17), yet from the God who is the faithful Creator and Redeemer of Old Testament faith, life and witness. Where better to begin a fresh understanding of the church for today than from the days when the church was fresh and new, in the theologies of Paul and John, aided by Peter, Luke and Hebrews?

54. **7.** A good deal has been made in the presentation above of *koinōnia* as a term and concept that reflects **crossing the boundaries**, from Palestine to the Greco-Roman world, from Semitic to Hellenistic thought, from agrarian Galilee to urban centres. *Koinōnia* involved for New Testament Christians the expression of a world of shared gospel experiences and associations in Christ and the Spirit, but presented in the vocabulary and ideas of Greek thought. Thus the Greek term was brought into the service of the gospel. The gospel, in turn, reshaped the social categories of that word and its world, with new emphases on solidarity with suffering, the poor, and human needs. The appeal in Luke-Acts was a new one, to benefit others without expectation of return, across divisions of status. Our world and our ecclesiology can benefit from such crossing of boundaries today, and perhaps not the least step can be **ecclesial friendship** and hospitable sharing that is as inclusive as that of Pauline, Johannine, Petrine, and other churches of the decisive and normative New Testament era.

BIBLIOGRAPHY

Aherns, Barnabas, 1960, "The Fellowship of His Sufferings (Phil. 3:10)", *Catholic Biblical Quarterly*, 22, 1-32.

Anderson Scott, C.A. See Scott.

Banks, Robert, 1980, *Paul's Idea of Community: The Early House Churches in their Historical Setting*, Grand Rapids, MI, Eerdmans.

Barclay, William, 1964, *New Testament Words*, Philadelphia, Westminster, pp.173-176.

Bauckham, Richard J., 1983, *Jude, 2 Peter*, Word Biblical Commentary 50, Waco, TX, Word Books.

Benkö, István, 1951, *Sanctorum communio: Eine dogmengeschichtliche Untersuchung über das Symbolsglied*, Basel (printed Innsbruck, Felizian Rauch). Trans. by Stephen Benko, *The Meaning of Sanctorum Communio*, Studies in Historical Theology 3, London, SCM, and Naperville, IL, Allenson, 1964.

Betz, Hans Dieter, 1979, *Galatians*, Hermeneia, Philadelphia, Fortress.

Betz, Hans Dieter, 1985, *2 Corinthians 8 and 9*, Hermeneia, Philadelphia, Fortress.

Bojorge, H., 1975, "Koinónia-Communicación en el Nuevo Testamento. Como Contexto Estructural de la Communidad y el Liderazgo", *Revista Bíblica*, 37, 33-47.

Bori, P.C., 1972, *Koinōnia. L'idea della comunione nell' ecclesiologia recente e nel Nuovo Testamento*, Testi e ricerche di Scienze religiose 7, Brescia, Paideia.

Branick, Vincent, 1989, *The House Church in the Writings of Paul*, Zacchaeus Studies, New Testament, Wilmington, DE, Glazier.

Bria, J., 1976, "Koinonia als kanonische Gemeinschaft — Aktuelle Perspektiven", in *Auf dem Weg zur Einheit des Glaubens: Koinonia, Referate und Protokolle*, Stiftungsfond Pro Oriente, Wien, in Zusammenarbeit mit dem Orthodoxen Zentrum des Ökumenischen Patriarchats, Chambésy, und dem Sekretariat für die Einheit der Christen, Innsbruck, Tyrolia-Verlag, pp.137-47.

Brown, Raymond E., 1963, "The Unity and Diversity in New Testament Ecclesiology", originally in *Novum Testamentum*, 6, 1963, 298-308; reprinted in Brown's *New Testament Essays*, Garden City, NY, Doubleday, Image Books, 1965, 60-73.

Brown, Raymond E., 1985, "New Testament Background for the Concept of Local Church", in *Proceedings of the Catholic Theology Society of America*, 36, 1981, 1-14, contributed to "The New Testament Background for the Emerging Doctrine of 'Local Church'", in Brown's *Biblical Exegesis and Church Doctrine*, New York/Mahwah, NJ, Paulist, 1985, 114-34.

Brown, Schuyler, 1976, "Koinonia as the Basis of New Testament Ecclesiology?", in *One in Christ*, 12, 157-67.

Campbell, J.Y., 1932, "KOINŌNIA and its Cognates in the New Testament", in *Journal of Biblical Literature*, 51, 352-82.

Carr, A., 1913, "The Fellowship *(Koinōnia)* of Acts II,42 and Cognate Words", *Expositor*, 8th series, 5, 458-64.

Childs, Brevard S., 1992, *Biblical Theology of the Old and New Testaments: Theological Reflection on the Christian Bible*, Minneapolis, Fortress.

Cipriani, S., 1971, "La chiesa come comunione (koinōnia) nel Nuevo Testamento", in *Presenza Pastorale*, 41, 163-79.

Coppens, J., 1970, "La koinōnia dans l'Eglise primitive", in *Ephemerides theologicae lovanienses*, 46, 116-21.

Cothenet, E., 1972a, "La 'communio' nel Nuovo Testamento", in *Communio*, 1, 13-21.

Cothenet, E., 1972b, "La Communio Sanctorum. Partage de la foi et de la mission de l'Église", in *Maison-Dieu*, 112, 28-53.

Currie, Stuart D., 1962, *Koinonia in Christian Literature to A.D. 200*, dissertation, Emory University, Atlanta, USA.

Davies, J.G., 1958, *Members One of Another: Aspects of Koinonia*, London, Mowbray.

Dewailley, L.M., 1970, "Communio — Communicatio: Brèves notes sur l'histoire d'un sémantème", in *Revue des sciences philosophiques et théologiques*, 44, 46-63.

Dewailley, L.M., 1973, "La part prise à l'Évangile (Phil 1, 5)", in *Revue biblique*, 80, 247-60. See also *Svensk exegetisk årsbok*, 37-38, 1972-72, 274-83.

Di Marco, A., 1980, "Koinonia — Communio: Flp 2,1", in *Laurentianum*, 21, 376-403.

Di Marco, A., 1988, "*KOINŌNIA PNEUMATOS* (2 Cor 13,13; Flp 2,1)-*PNEUMA KOINŌNIAS*: Circolarità e ambivalenza linguistica e filologica", *Filologia neotestamentaria*, 1, 63-75.

Dobbeler, Axel von, 1987, *Glaube als Teilhabe: Historische und semantische Grundlagen der paulinischen Theologie und Ekklesiologie des Glaubens*, Wissenschaftliche Untersuchungen zum Neuen Testament 2/22, Tubingen, Mohr-Siebeck.

Dunn, J.D.G., 1989, "'Instruments of Koinonia' in the Early Church", in *One in Christ*, 25, 204-16.

Dupont, Jacques, 1972, "La koinônia des premiers chrétiens dans les Actes des Apôtres", in *Comunione Interecclesiale. Collegialita. Primato, Ecumenismo. Acta Conventus Intern. de Historia Sollicitudinis omnium ecclesiarum Romae 1967*, eds G. D'Ercole & A. M. Stickler, *Communio*, 12, Rome, 41-61.

Endenberg, Pieter J.T., 1937, *Koinoonia, En Gemeenschap van Zaken bij de Grieken in den Klassieken Tijd*, Amsterdam, H.J. Paris.

Fischer, G.-D., 1971, "Zum Koinonia-Charakter christlicher Gemeinde", in *Theologie und Glaube*, 61, 39-44.

Fitzgerald, John T., 1992, "Philippians, Epistle to the", in *Anchor Bible Dictionary*, New York, Doubleday, 5:318-26.

Fleury, Jean, 1963, "Une société de fait dans l'Eglise apostolique (Phil. 4:10 à 22)", in *Mélanges Philippe Meylan*, vol. 2, *Histoire du Droit*, Lausanne, Université de Lausanne, pp.41-59.

Ford, H.W., 1945, "The New Testament Conception of Fellowship", in *Shane Quarterly*, 6, 188-215.

Fornberg, Tord, 1977, *An Early Church in a Pluralistic Society: A Study of 2 Peter*, Coniectanea neotestamentica 9, Lund, Gleerup.

Franco, Ettore, 1986, *Comunione e Partecipazione: La koinônia nell'epistolario paolino*, Aloisiana 20, Brescia, Morcelliana.

Furnish, Victor Paul, 1984, *II Corinthians*, Anchor Bible 32A, Garden City, NY, Doubleday.

Geoffrion, Timothy C., 1993, *Philippians: A Call to Stand Firm! An Investigation of the Rhetorical Purpose and the Political and Military Character of Paul's Letter to the Philippian Christians*, Lewiston/Queenston/Lampeter, Mellen Biblical Press.

George, A. Raymond, 1953, *Communion with God in the New Testament*, London, Epworth.

Goppelt, Leonhard, 1957, "Kirchengemeinschaft und Abendmahlsgemeinschaft nach dem Neuen Testament", in KOINONIA: *Arbeiten des Ökumenischen Ausschusses der Vereinigten Evangelisch-Lutherischen Kirche Deutschlands zur Frage der Kirchen- und Abendmahlsgemeinschaft*, Berlin, Lutherisches Verlagshaus, pp.24-33.

Goppelt, Leonhard, 1978, *Der erste Petrusbrief*, MeyerKEK 12/1, Göttingen, Vandenhoeck & Ruprecht. Trans. by John E. Alsup, *A Commentary on I Peter*, Grand Rapids, MI, Eerdmans, 1993.

Groenewald, Evert P., 1932, *Koinōnia (Gemeenskap) bij Paulus*, Delft, W.D. Meinema.

Hahn, Ferdinand, 1979, "Einheit der Kirche und Kirchengemeinschaft in neutestamentlicher Sicht", in F. Hahn, K. Kertelge & R. Schnackenburg, *Einheit der Kirche: Grundlegung im Neuen Testament*, Quaestiones Disputatae 84, Freiburg, Herder, pp.9-51.

Hahn, Ferdinand, 1981, "Teilhabe am Heil und Gefahr des Abfalls: Eine Auslegung von 1 Ko 10,1-22", in *Freedom and Love: The Guide for Christian Life (1 Co 8-10; Rm 14-15)*, ed. L. de Lorenzi, Monographic Series of "Benedictina", Biblical-Ecumenical Section 6, Rome, St Paul's Abbey, pp.149-71, with discussion following.

Hahn, Ferdinand, 1986, "Thesen zur Frage einheitsstiftender Elemente in Lehre und Praxis des urchristlichen Herrenmahls", in Hahn's collected essays, *Exegetische Beiträge zum ökumenischen Gespräch: Gesammelte Aufsätze 1*, Göttingen, Vandenhoeck & Ruprecht, pp.232-41.

Hainz, Josef, 1981a, "Gemeinschaft (koinōnia) zwischen Paulus und Jerusalem (Gal 2,9f.): Zum paulinischen Verständnis von der Einheit der Kirche", in *Kontinuität und Einheit* (Festschrift for Franz Mussner), eds P.-G. Müller & W. Stenger, Freiburg, Herder, pp.30-42.

Hainz, Josef, 1981b, "*koinōnia, koinōneō, koinōnos*", in *Exegetisches Wörterbuch zum Neuen Testament*, Stuttgart, Kohlhammer, 2:749-55. Trans. *Exegetical Dictionary of the New Testament*, Grand Rapids, MI, Eerdmans, 1991, 2:303-305.

Hainz, Josef, 1982, *Koinonia: "Kirche" als Gemeinschaft bei Paulus*, Biblische Untersuchungen 16, Regensburg, Pustat.

Hamer, Jerome, 1962, *L'Eglise est une communion*, Unam Sanctam 40, Paris, Editions du Cerf. Trans. *The Church Is a Communion*, London, Chapman, 1964.

Hauck, Friedrich, 1938, "*Koinos,... koinōnia, sugkoinōnos,... koinoō*", in *Theologisches Wörterbuch zum Neuen Testament*, 3, 789-810 = *Theological Dictionary of the New Testament*, 3:789-809, supplement in *Theologisches Wörterbuch*, 10/2:1145-46.

Häuser, Götz Ludwig, 1992, *Communion with Christ and Christian Community in 1 Corinthians: A Study of Paul's Concept of KOINONIA*, dissertation, University of Durham, England.

Hertling, Ludwig, 1972, *Communio: Church and Papacy in Early Christianity*. Trans. with introduction by Jared Wicks, Chicago, Loyola University Press. German originally in *Xenia Piana: Miscellanea historiae pontificiae 7*, 1943, 1-48, later "Communio und Primat", *Una Sancta*, 17, 1962.

Hinnebusch, P., 1964, "Christian Fellowship in the Epistle to the Philippians", in *The Bible Today*, 3, 793-98.

Holl, Karl, 1921, "Der Kirchenbegriff des Paulus in seinem Verhältnis zu dem der Urgemeinde", SAB Berlin, reprinted in Holl's *Gesammelte Aufsätze*, 2, Tübingen, Mohr, 1928, 44-67, and in *Das Paulusbild in der neueren deutschen Forschung*, ed. K.H. Rengstorf, Darmstadt, Wissenschaftliche Buchgesellschaft, 1964, 144-78.

Jourdan, G.V., 1948, "Koinōnia in 1 Corinthians 10:16", in *Journal of Biblical Literature*, 67, 111-24.

Käsemann, Ernst, 1952, "Eine Apologie der urchristlichen Eschatologie", originally in *Zeitschrift für Theologie und Kirche*, 49, 272-96, reprinted in his collected essays, *Exegetische Versuche und*

Besinnungen, Göttingen, Vandenhoeck & Ruprecht, vol. 1, 1960, 135-57. Trans. by W. J. Montague, "An Apology for Primitive Christian Eschatology", in Käsemann's *Essays on New Testament Themes*, Studies in Biblical Theology 41, London, SCM, 1964; reprinted Philadelphia, Fortress, 1982, pp.169-95.

Käsemann, Ernst, 1963, "Einheit und Vielfalt in der neutestamentlichen Lehre von der Kirche", in *Ökumenische Rundschau*, 1964, 58-63, reprinted in Käsemann's *Exegetische Versuche*, 2, 1964, 262-67. Trans. "Unity and Multiplicity in the New Testament Doctrine of the Church", in *Novum Testamentum*, 6, 1963, 290-97, reprinted in Käsemann's *New Testament Questions of Today*, Philadelphia, Fortress, 1969, 252-59.

Kertelge, Karl, 1974, "Abendmahlsgemeinschaft und Kirchengemeinschaft im Neuen Testament und in der Alten Kirche", in *Einheit der Kirche*, pp.94-132. Originally in *Interkommunion — Konziliarität. Zwei Studien im Auftrag des Deutschen ökumenischen Studienausschusses*, Beiheft zur Ökumenischen Rundschau, 25, 20-51.

Kertelge, Karl, 1981. "Kerygma und Koinonia: Zur theologischen Bestimmung der Kirche des Urchristentums", in *Kontinuität und Einheit* (cited above under Hainz 1981) 327-39.

Klauck, H.-J., 1981a, "Die Hausgemeinde als Lebensform im Urchristentum", in *Münchener theologische Zeitschrift*, 32, 1-15, reprinted in his collected essays, *Gemeinde • Amt • Sakrament: Neutestamentliche Perspektiven*, Würzburg, Echter Verlag, 1989, 11-28; summary trans. in *Theology Digest*, 30, 1982, 153-57.

Klauck, H.-J., 1981b, "Eucharistie und Kirchengemeinschaft bei Paulus", in *Gemeinde • Amt • Sakrament* (cited above, under 1981 listing), 331-47.

Klauck, H.-J., 1982a, *Herrenmahl und hellenistischen Kult. Eine religionsgeschichtliche Untersuchung zum ersten Korintherbrief*, Neutestamentliche Abhandlungen New Series 15, Münster, Aschendorff.

Klauck, H.-J., 1982b, "Gütergemeinschaft in der klassischen Antike, in Qumran und im Neuen Testament", in *Revue de Qumran*, 11, 47-79.

Klauck, H.-J., 1991, "Kirche als Freundesgemeinschaft? Auf Spurensuche in Neuen Testament", in *Münchener theologische Zeitschrift*, 42, 1-14.

Klinger, J., 1976, "Die Koinonia als sakramentale Gemeinschaft — Aktuelle Perspektiven", in *Auf dem Weg zur Einheit des Glaubens* (see above, under Bria).

Krause, W. von, 1957, "Was sagt uns das Neue Testament zur Frage der Kirchen- und Abendmahlsgemeinschaft?", *KOINONIA* (as cited above under Goppelt, 1957), 34-41.

Lampe, G.W.H. ed., 1961-68, *A Patristic Greek Lexicon*, Oxford, Clarendon.

Lehmann, Paul L., 1963, *Ethics in a Christian Context*, New York, Harper & Row. Cf. also Nancy J. Duff, *Humanization and the Politics of God: The* Koinonia *Ethics of Paul Lehmann*, Grand Rapids, MI, Eerdmans, 1992.

McDermott, J.M., 1975, "The Biblical Doctrine of KOINŌNIA", in *Biblische Zeitschrift*, N.F. 19, 64-77 and (II. Part) 219-33.

Malatesta, E., 1973, *The Epistles of St. John: Greek Text and English Translation Schematically Arranged*, Rome, Gregorian University Press.

Marco, A. di, see under Di Marco.

Martin, Ralph P., 1986, *2 Corinthians*, Word Biblical Commentary 40, Waco, TX, Word Books.

Meyer, Rudolf & Konrad Weiss, 1974, *"Pharisaios"*, in *Theological Dictionary of the New Testament*, ed. G. Friedrich, Grand Rapids, MI, Eerdmans, 9, 11-48, esp. 16-17.

Mitchell, Alan, 1991, "'Greet the Friends by Name': New Testament Evidence for the Greco-Roman Topos on Friendship", Society of Biblical Literature Hellenistic Moral Philosophy and Early Christianity Group, publication forthcoming.

Mitchell, Alan, 1992, "The Social Function of Friendship in Acts 2:44-47 and 4:32-37", in *Journal of Biblical Literature*, 111, 255-72.

Munck, Johannes, 1954, *Paulus und die Heilsgeschichte*, Copenhagen, Munksgaard. Trans. by Frank Clark, *Paul and the Salvation of Mankind*, London, SCM, and Richmond, VA, John Knox, 1959.

Muñoz-Iglesias, S., 1953, "Concepto bíblico de *Koinōnia*", *XIII Semana Bíblica Española. El Movimento Ecumenistico*, Madrid, 195-224.

Murphy-O'Connor, Jerome, 1977, "Eucharist and Community in First Corinthians", in *Worship*, 51, 56-69.

Neusner, Jacob, 1963, *Fellowship in Judaism: The First Century and Today*, London, Vallentine, Mitchell.

O'Brien, Peter T., 1978, "The Fellowship Theme in Philippians", in *Reformed Theological Review*, 37, 244-45.

O'Brien, Peter T., 1982, *Colossians, Philemon*, Word Biblical Commentary, 44, Waco, TX, Word Books.

Panikulam, George, 1979, *Koinōnia in the New Testament: A Dynamic Expression of Christian Life*, Analecta Biblica 85, Rome, Biblical Institute Press.

Popkes, Wiard, 1976, "Gemeinschaft", in *Reallexikon für Antike und Christentum*, Stuttgart, Hiersemann, 9, 1100-1145.

Reumann, John, 1992, "After Historical Criticism, What? Trends in Biblical Interpretation and Ecumenical, Interfaith Dialogues", in *Journal of Ecumenical Studies*, 29, 55-86.

Reumann, John, 1993, "Contributions of the Philippian Community to Paul and to Earliest Christianity", in *New Testament Studies*, 39, 438-57.

Rodger, P.C. & Lukas Vischer, 1964, *The Fourth World Conference on Faith and Order, Montreal 1963*, New York, Association Press.

Roloff, Jurgen, 1990, "Heil als Gemeindschaft. Kommunikative Faktoren im urchristlichen Herrenmahl", in his collected essays, *Exegetische Verantwortung in der Kirche: Aufsätze*, ed. M. Karrer, Göttingen, Vandenhoeck & Ruprecht, 171-200.

Sampley, J. Paul, 1977, "Societas Christi: Roman Law and Paul's Conception of the Christian Community", in *God's Christ and His People*, festschrift for Nils Dahl, eds J. Jervell & W. A. Meeks, Oslo/Bergen/Tromsö, Universitetsforlaget, pp.158-74.

Sampley, J. Paul, 1980, *Pauline Partnership in Christ: Christian Community and Commitment in Light of Roman Law*, Philadelphia, Fortress.

Schattenmann, Johannes, 1967-71, "Gemeinschaft/*koinōnia*", in *Theologisches Begriffslexikon zum Neuen Testament*, eds L. Coenen et al, Wuppertal, Brockhaus, Studienausgabe (7th ed. 1986) 495-99; trans. ed. Colin Brown, *The New International Dictionary of New Testament Theology*, Grand Rapids, MI, Zondervan, 1975, 1:639-44.

Schenk, Wolfgang, 1984, *Die Philipperbriefe des Paulus: Kommentar*, Stuttgart, Kohlhammer.

Schnackenburg, Rudolf, 1979, "Die Einheit der Kirche unter dem Koinonia-Gedanken", in *Einheit der Kirche*, pp.52-93. Cf. his earlier paper in *Massstab des Glaubens. Fragen heutiger Christen im Licht des Neuen Testaments*, Freiburg, Herder, 1978, 88-118.

Scott, C.A. Anderson, 1922, "What Happened at Pentecost?", in *The Spirit*, ed. B.H. Streeter, New York, Macmillan, 115-53.

Scott, C.A. Anderson, 1923-24, "The 'Fellowship', or Koinōnia", in *Expository Times*, 35, 567.

Scott, C.A. Anderson, 1927, *Christianity According to St Paul*, Cambridge, Cambridge University Press.

Seesemann, H., 1933, *Der Begriff KOINŌNIA im Neuen Testament*, Beihefte zur Zeitschrift fur die Neutestamentliche Wissenschaft 14, Giessen, Töpelmann.

Sieben, H.J., J.M. McDermott, M. Manzanera, H. Bacht & J.-M. Tillard, 1974, "Koinônia: Communauté-Communion", in *Dictionnaire de spiritualité ascétique et mystique*, Paris, Beauchesne, 8:1743-69.

Stählin, Gustav, 1970, "*philos*, etc.", in *Theologisches Wörterbuch zum Neuen Testament*, 9, 144-169; *Theological Dictionary of the New Testament*, 9, 1974, 146-71.

Stanley, David, "Koinônia as Symbol and Reality in the Primitive Church", in *Comunione Interecclesiale* (as cited above, under Dupont), 83-99.

Suggs, M. Jack, 1984, "Koinonia in the New Testament", in *Midstream*, 23, 351-62.

Thornton, Lionel S., 1942, *The Common Life in the Body of Christ*, London, Dacre Press, 4th ed. 1963.

Tillard, J.-M.R., 1987, *Eglise d'églises: L'ecclésiologie de communion*, Paris, Editions du Cerf. Trans. by R.C. De Peaux, *Church of Churches: The Ecclesiology of Communion*, Collegeville, MN, Glazier, Liturgical Press, 1992.

Unité et Diversité dans l'Église. Texte officiel de la Commission biblique pontificale et travaux personnels des membres, 1989, Teologia e Filosofia 15, Rome, Libreria Editrice Vaticana.

Vischer, Lukas. See Rodger.

Vischer, Lukas, 1981, "Die lokale Kirche — Ort der Gegenwart Christi in der Kraft des Heiligen Geistes, Der Beitrag der orthodoxen Kirche und Theologie zur ökumenischen Diskussion über ein zentrales Thema der Ekklesiologie", in *Eglise locale et Eglise universelle. TOPIKĒ KAI KATA TĒN OIKOUMENĒN EKKLĒSIA*, Chambésy-Genève, Edition du Centre Orthodoxe du Patriarcat Œcuménique, pp.297-307.

Wall, Robert W., 1992, "Community: New Testament *Koinōnia*", in *Anchor Bible Dictionary*, New York, Doubleday, 1:1103-1110.

Weber, Hans-Ruedi, 1989, *Power: Focus for a Biblical Theology*, Geneva, WCC.

Weiser, Anton, 1990, "Basis und Führung in kirchliche Communio", in *Bibel und Kirche*, 45, 66-71.

Weiss, Konrad. See Meyer.

White, L. Michael, 1990, "Morality between Two Worlds: A Paradigm of Friendship in Philippians", in *Greeks, Romans, and Christians* (Festschrift for Abraham Malherbe), eds D.L. Balch & Wayne Meeks, Minneapolis, Fortress, pp.201-15.

Wolters, A., 1990, "'Partners of the Deity': A Covenantal Reading of 2 Peter 1:4", in *Calvin Theological Journal*, 25, 28-44.

Wolters, A., 1991, "Postscript to 'Partners of the Deity'", in *Calvin Theological Journal*, 26, 418-20.

Wood, W.S., 1921, " Fellowship", in *Expositor*, 8th series, 21, 31-40.

THE BLESSING PROMISED TO THE NATIONS: THE CALL OF ABRAHAM
Genesis 12:1-9

A Personal Vision of Koinonia

JOHN ONAIYEKAN

Introduction

Koinonia as used in the theme of this fifth world conference of Faith and Order is, strictly speaking, a New Testament concept. It has to do, in my view, with the fellowship of the followers of Christ with God the Father, through the Lord Jesus in the Spirit, and their fellowship with each other on the basis of their relationship of faith and love with the Triune God. The detailed and sustained reflection on the epistle of St Paul to the Galatians which forms the biblical framework of the programme of the conference will lead us, we hope, straight into the heart of the matter. We should find ample material in that epistle to inspire and challenge us on the journey towards greater koinonia in faith, life and witness.

My assignment is to share with this conference a "personal vision" of koinonia based on an Old Testament passage.[1] Every major New Testament theme has ample illustration and is foreshadowed in the Old Testament. There is a basic unity between the Old and New Testaments. Drawing on the teaching of St Augustine on this point, the Second Vatican Council, in its Dogmatic Constitution on Divine Revelation, *Dei Verbum*, paragraph 16, declares: "God, the inspirer and author of both Testaments, in his wisdom has so brought it about that the New should be hidden in the Old and that the Old should be made manifest in the New."[2]

Of the many Old Testament passages which highlight and open up perspectives on the New Testament theme of koinonia, I have chosen the text of Genesis 12:1-9: the story of the call of Abraham. The story deals not only with the call and choice of a person, but also shows how this call and choice open out to embrace and involve others; the descendants and ultimately all of humanity. My hope is to draw attention, from the story of the call of Abraham, to the open-ended and ultimately universal scope of koinonia with and in God.

We shall first of all examine the biblical text and its context, highlighting elements that are relevant to our theme. Then we shall briefly survey the varied understanding of this biblical episode in the development of the history of Israel in the Old Testament. We shall next examine the New Testament, re-reading and reinterpreting the story. Finally, we shall try to identify the significance of this passage for us today, as we move towards a koinonia in faith, life and witness, both within and beyond the strict boundaries of the Christian community.

1. The call of Abraham

The story told in Genesis 12:1-9 is simple, straightforward and very familiar. It is nevertheless a powerful story with far-reaching implications in the history of the

---

The Most Rev. Dr John Onaiyekan is Roman Catholic bishop of Abuja, Nigeria.

Israelite nation and of humanity as a whole. We shall take the story as it is in the inspired text, prescinding from the complex and hardly conclusive speculations of so-called "high criticism" on issues like authorship, hypothetical sources and trends of tradition. On the question of historicity, suffice it to say here that the most recent scholarship and research have tended to confirm rather than disprove the traditional position that Abraham and the patriarchs were true and real historical figures. This does not necessarily exclude elements of fiction in the literary presentation of the story. But according to the canons of ancient historiography, the story of Abraham is no less historical than any other contemporary historical record available to us today. As for the story itself, we want to draw attention to three major elements: the call, the mission, and the promise — all in the context of and in relation to koinonia.

1.1. The call

The previous chapter (Gen. 11) gave a sketch of the early life of Abraham: his Semite genealogy, his immediate family background, his migration with his father Terah from Ur of the Chaldeans towards the land of Canaan, but halting in Haran (see Gen. 11:10-32). There is nothing in this early history to single out Abraham for the dramatic statement of Genesis 12:1: "Yahweh said to Abram..." As far as this Genesis passage is concerned, the call of Abraham was a totally gratuitous choice by God. Some later Old Testament traditions would try to "improve" on this simple story by making the call of Abraham a reward for his uprightness in the midst of a confused and wicked world (Wis. 10:5; Sir. 44:19-23; 1 Macc. 2:52). The koranic version of the call of Abraham develops this trend with even greater details.[3] But there is no basis in the original story for this effort. Paul was later to stress the gratuitousness of God's promise to Abraham (Rom. 4:16).

The Genesis account is as simple as it is dramatic: "Yahweh said to Abram." Yahweh picked Abraham and made him a "friend" (Isa. 41:8). There is no evidence that he had a higher spiritual understanding or more sublime morality than the other people in his clan and family. Indeed, Abraham's comportment at the court of Pharaoh in the next story (Gen. 12:10-20) seemed to have scandalized even the Pharaoh himself to the extent of earning Abraham immediate deportation.

We often imagine Abraham as a select individual worshipping the true God in the midst of a world of polytheistic paganism. The story, no doubt, presents the call as a deep personal experience of God on the part of Abraham. But when we examine the text on how he actually practised his religious life, he appears very much a man of his times. The idea of a God who is a personal and family patron and protector seems well known among the nomads of ancient Mesopotamia.[4] The shrines connected with Abraham's journeys through the land of Canaan are now known to have existed as sanctuaries long before Abraham. The traditions of theophanies associated with the Palestinian sanctuaries like Sichem (Gen. 12:6) and Mamre (Gen. 13:18), Beersheba (26:23-25) and Bethel (Gen. 28:19) cannot therefore be read in isolation from the religious context of those holy places. The incident of Melchizedek (Gen. 14:17-20), "a priest of God Most High" who blessed Abraham and received tithes from him, shows that Abraham acknowledged the validity of at least some elements of the religious system he met in Palestine.

Thus the religion of Abraham and of the patriarchs has been described, I think correctly too, as a synthesis of the religion of their original home in Mesopotamia and that of their new land of sojourn in Canaan, a synthesis inspired and guided by the unique religious experience of the call of Abraham.[5] From their Eastern origins they brought "the God of our fathers", a personal divinity, typical of a nomadic existence. This divinity is always present to the devotee everywhere, a God of history who controls human destinies and events. In Canaan, they met the nature-God, associated with some identifiable holy place with a specific title in each shrine, e.g., apart from El Elyon of Jerusalem (Gen. 14:18), we hear of El Olam in Beersheba (Gen. 21:33). This is a religious system that fits in well with the sedentary existence of Canaanite city-dwellers. Abraham effected the synthesis of the two images of God by identifying, in the El of the Canaanite sanctuaries, the God who called him in Mesopotamia.

All the foregoing considerations point to the strong suggestion that the God who called Abraham was not a new unknown God either to Abraham or to some of those with whom he had religious interactions. Often, God's call reaches us within the normal context of our lives. But that does not make it any less demanding.

1.2. The mission

"Leave your country, your kindred and your father's house for a country which I shall show you." Abraham was called for a purpose: to be sent on a *mission* that demands faith in God's loving plans.

Attention has often been drawn to the personal risk which the command of God entailed for Abraham. He had to leave behind and break through those concentric circles of human relationships that ensure personal security: the nation, the clan and the family. For the nomad, it was a double risk. But for Abraham, it was a calculated risk, since he leaves to follow the guidance of the God who calls. As for the exact nature of this divine guidance, the text gives no details. We are simply told that Abraham left Haran and "set off for the land of Canaan" (Gen. 12:5).

We note that God's guidance took Abraham along the usual contemporary route of migration. Ur-Haran-Canaan is a well-known trade route around the eighteenth century B.C. Even if its historicity is at times disputed,[6] the information about Terah's migration from Ur with Canaan as destination (Gen. 11:31) is instructive in this regard. The movement of Abraham appears as a continuation of a previous migration. "He set off for the land of Canaan and arrived there" (Gen. 12:5), while Terah had the same intention and only arrived in Haran, where he settled. Again we see here the hand of God in what may well have been the most natural thing to do.

"Abram went as Yahweh told him" (Gen. 12:4) but he did not go alone. He had with him Lot, his nephew, his wife Sarai and "the people they had acquired in Haran" (Gen. 12:5). There was, therefore, already a form of community at the very beginning of Abraham's mission. There is always a community dimension to our most personal relations with God. Of all the persons drawn into Abraham's faith history, we know a bit of the story of Sarai and Lot. I wonder what all this meant to "the people they had acquired in Haran". That they too were later affected by the law of circumcision (Gen. 17:27) would suggest some amount of personal commitment to the faith of Abraham.

But Abraham still felt alone without a son of his own at the age of seventy-five. The arrival of Ishmael through the slave woman, Hagar, turned out to be a poor and unsatisfactory substitute (21:12).

1.3. The promise

Abram's faith was founded on the promises of God. At the moment of the call, all these promises referred to the future; promises of land, nation and blessing. Abraham saw only a glimpse of the fulfilment of these promises during his lifetime. He saw the promised land but owned no more of it than the plot he acquired as a tomb for his family (23:3-20). The promise of a nation hung precariously on his only free-born son, Isaac. In his promise of blessing, God commits himself to Abraham's cause:

> I shall bless you, I shall bless those who bless you and shall curse those who curse you. (v.3)

But there is also the universal dimension to this blessing: "all clans on earth will bless themselves by you" (v.3). God's blessing embraces all creation; but he often channels his universal love through some chosen persons. Ultimately, the blessing of Abraham makes sense only in such a universal perspective.

The biblical story of the call of Abraham contains powerful lessons about how God deals with his chosen ones. His choice is free and gratuitous; but he expects on our part a response of faith and trust. Special call is for a mission that is as limitless as God's love is all-embracing. Unfortunately, there is always the human tendency to restrict the scope of God's saving love and to exclude those we believe do not belong. The story of the descendants of Abraham is an eloquent illustration of this.

2. The descendants of Abraham

2.1. The patriarchs

In the biblical narrative about the patriarchs, we are presented with the story of the family of Abraham. The promises of the blessings on the family are reconfirmed to Abraham (Gen. 17:4-8) and repeated to Isaac (26:2-5), and to Jacob (28:13-15) and thus create a strong sense of family destiny.

But the inheritance of the promise was not determined by blood descent alone: the element of divine choice continued in the three generations of Abraham-Isaac-Jacob. Isaac was singled out among the children of Abraham, and Jacob was preferred to Esau, his elder twin brother. Thus, it turned out that many "children of Abraham" were excluded from the promise. Even these too, however, were not excluded from the loving care of God, e.g. Hagar and Ishmael in Genesis 21:17-21 and Esau in Genesis 36:6-8.

Tradition later presents most of the pagan neighbours of Israel as descendants of these other sons of Abraham. Despite frequent instances of wars and antagonisms, the memories of some ethnic affinity remained. It is now difficult to say how much historical basis there is beneath these traditions of ethnic affinity.

2.2. The Israelite nation

Jacob, whose name was changed to Israel (Gen. 35:10), went with his twelve sons into Egypt at the invitation of Joseph. There, amidst the ups and downs of their political fortunes, they became a nation strong and numerous enough to constitute a threat to their host country. Their oppression under a Pharaoh "who had never heard of Joseph" (Ex. 1:8) enhanced their sense of common identity even more than their earlier experience of prosperity and privilege. With the emergence of Moses as leader of the people, a new phase began in the history of the Israelites.

Moses, too, like Abraham, was called by God. This is the same God of his ancestors: "the God of Abraham, the God of Isaac and the God of Jacob", who according to Exodus 3:13-15 revealed his name, now generally written as "Yahweh". The promise of God to protect Abraham and his descendants was, as it were, resumed in the divine wonders of liberation from Egypt under the leadership of Moses, culminating in the covenant at Mt Sinai. There, with the memories of the divine exploits of liberation still fresh in their mind, the "House of Jacob" welcomed God's promises of further blessings and committed itself to God. "Whatever Yahweh has said, we will do" (Ex. 19:8). The law thus became an integral part of the covenant, indeed a condition (Ex. 19:15).

We note here that the descendants of Abraham have been narrowed down to the house of Jacob, while the unconditional promises of God to Abraham have become a general background for the Sinaitic covenant and Mosaic Law. There is, however, a basic continuity with the story of Abraham. The Yahweh of the Exodus is the God of Abraham and of the fathers. The divine exploits in the Exodus are seen as God ensuring that his promise to Abraham shall not be in vain.

If the promise to Abraham of a great nation can be said to have been substantially fulfilled at the foot of Mt Sinai, the promise of a land still remained a future hope. The story of the "conquest" of the land of the Canaanites under Joshua and the Judges is meant to show how that promise too was fulfilled. But there is as much theology as there is history in the Books of Joshua and Judges.

There is enough evidence to uphold the theory that the Israelite settlement in Palestine was more a matter of gradual infiltration than of a massive conquest.[7] It has been suggested, for example, that apart from the group who left Egypt under Moses, we might think of:
a) clans related to Israel who never left Canaan at all;
b) components of some possible earlier minor "exoduses" that may have entered the land from the south;
c) non-Israelites who joined the Israelite victory caravan during the exodus, e.g. Caleb (Josh. 14:6-14);
d) Canaanite inhabitants who made peaceful treaties of association with the Israelite conquering invaders, e.g. the Gibeonites of Joshua 9 and very likely Sichem, about which there is no tradition of Israelite conquest.

The great assembly at Sichem (Josh. 24) was crucial in welding together these heterogeneous groups under the common religious banner of Yahweh. Joshua puts before them various options — the religions of Mesopotamia, Egypt, Canaan, or Yahweh. They all replied: "We too shall serve Yahweh, for he is our God" (Josh. 24:18). All this points to the fact that the concept of "the sons of Israel" is more fluid than it may appear at first sight. Furthermore, it means that it was always possible to *become* part of God's holy people, provided certain conditions were met.

Later on, as Israel tried to "become like other nations" (1 Sam. 8:20) with king and palace, temple and priestly caste, standard civil service and a standing army, and other paraphernalia of world power statehood, the boundaries of Israel widened to include even more peoples and nations. This development invariably brought with it a decrease in the level of religious fervour and orthodoxy. It became very difficult to keep together for long an over-extended Israelite nation. The challenge of not losing fervour with growing numbers is a constant experience of living in koinonia.

The traditions around the Davidic kingdom claim there is a special relationship between God and David. This is a reflection of the call of Abraham. God called David and promised: "Your dynasty and your sovereignty will ever stand firm before me, and your throne will be for ever secure" (2 Sam. 7:16). But David's election is placed securely within the context of God's concern for his chosen people. In the long run, it is the people and God's promises to them that matter.

We see this even in the words of the Prophet Nathan: "I am going to provide a place for my people Israel" (2 Sam. 7:10). The legitimacy of the king is based on the fact that the people acknowledged him as God's chosen shepherd for his flock, Israel. Thus, the monarchy entailed a tripartite pact between the king, the people and Yahweh: "King David made a pact with them (the elders of Israel) in Yahweh's presence at Hebron" (2 Sam. 5:3). In Israel, the king can rule only in the name of God.[8] Among the people, there was always the strong consciousness of being heirs to a divine promise to Abraham, their ancestor. This was also a powerful basis for the feeling of belonging together as God's chosen people.

2.3. Breakdown of koinonia

The latent fragility of Solomon's empire manifested itself in the schism that resulted from the struggle for his succession (1 Kings 12). The House of Israel broke up into two rival and warring kingdoms around 930 BCE, never again to be totally reintegrated. In their dividedness they fell, one after the other, easy prey to invading forces. The Northern Kingdom of Israel, riddled with dynastic instability, was the first to be swept off the stage of world history. The Southern Kingdom of Judah, thanks to its royal ideology of God's promise of an eternal throne of David and his house, enjoyed relative stability. But it only outlived the Northern Kingdom by about a century and a half and thereafter crumbled in its turn under the weight of Bablyonian might.

The seventy years of exile in Babylon turned out to be also an occasion for God's miracle of restoration of the sense of national identity. By the rivers of Babylon, the exiled people continued to think of Jerusalem (Ps. 137) and trusted in the Lord to rebuild its walls (Ps. 51:18). A faithful remnant, through God's powerful intervention, returned to the land of promise, to rebuild the holy city and the nation. "Indeed, it was like a dream" (Ps. 125).

The history of Israel is an abiding lesson on what it means to be in a special relationship with God: its privileges and responsibilities; its joys and demands. It shows human infidelity in the face of God's irrevocable commitment of love and mercy. It also shows the fragility of our human relationships so long as our position with God is not clear or consistent. Here we touch the most crucial issues of koinonia in the community of faith.

2.4. Reminders of universalism

On the whole, the people of Israel tended to restrict the scope of God's blessing. The prophets, on the other hand, often reminded them that the God of Israel is the God of all nations and of the whole universe. The great prophets warned against too much complacency over being a chosen people (e.g. Isa. 22). They also looked forward to a future when not only the Israelites but all the nations of the world would be reconciled to God (Isa. 19:23-25). The book of Jonah is a powerful story illustrating at the same time God's concern for non-Israelites and the responsibility of Israel to proclaim God's merciful love to all nations.

Parallel to this prophetic line is the wisdom tradition which cuts across national and religious boundaries. It opened Israel up to the universal truth about God, about humanity and about creation; though in Israel every true wisdom comes from God.

Thus, through these two trends, the universal dimensions of Abraham's blessing were kept alive at every stage of Israel's national history. The messianic expectations heightened with the passage of time after the return from the exile. Their expectations always included a future hope of a universal scope of God's promise, a future in which the descendants of Abraham were to have a special destiny.

3. The descendant of Abraham

3.1. Jesus Son of Abraham

Saint Matthew opens his gospel with a "genealogy of Jesus Christ, son of David, son of Abraham" (Matt. 1:1). By bringing out these two ancestors, he stresses from the beginning that Jesus is the Davidic messiah, and the great descendant of Abraham in whom the promises of God are to be fulfilled. Abraham is at the head of the line of ancestors. Luke (Luke 3:23-28) works his own list the other way round, and goes back beyond Abraham to "Adam, son of God". But in both lists, the fact of Jesus being of the stock of Abraham and of David's royal line is affirmed.

3.2. Greater than Abraham

Jesus is not only a descendant of Abraham; he claims to be greater than Abraham. "Before Abraham ever was, I am" (John 8:58). He is the fulfilment of the promises to Abraham. St Luke, in the Magnificat hymn of Mary, sees the great things which the Almighty has done as being "according to the promise God made to our ancestors, of his mercy to Abraham and to his descendants for ever" (Luke 1:55). In the same gospel of Luke, Simeon, carrying the baby Jesus in his hands, praised the Lord, the God of Israel; and sees in Jesus, "the oath he swore to our Father Abraham" (Luke 1:73). The joy of Mary that "from now onwards all generations will call me blessed" re-echoes the promise to Abraham in Genesis 12:3, "and all clans on earth will bless themselves by you".

St Peter, in his sermon to the people outside the Jerusalem temple, recalled the promise to Abraham and declared its fulfilment in Jesus who was raised up by God and "sent... to bless you" (Acts 3:25). God has started a new thing in Jesus as he did in Abraham.

The gospels, especially that of St John, celebrate the intimate relationship between Jesus and his heavenly Father. "The Father and I are one" (John 10:30). By faith, the believer becomes one with Jesus, and through Jesus with God. Here is the sublime basis of the New Testament koinonia. We now have a new way of being heirs to the promises of God to Abraham: in Jesus.

3.3. The new children of Abraham

Despite its political and economic inferiority and oppression, the Israelite community into which Jesus was born was proud of its spiritual pedigree. "We have Abraham as our Father" (Luke 3:8; cf. John 8:39) was a common formula of ethnic and religious pride. Jesus himself affirms the dignity that belongs as of right to a descendant of Abraham, whether a "daughter of Abraham" (Luke 13:16) or a "son of Abraham" (Luke 19:9). Peter told the "men of Israel" at the temple portico: "You are the heirs of the covenant of God made with your ancestors", through Abraham (Acts 3:25). Even St Paul devotes a long passage of Romans to demonstrating that the Jews are still the chosen people (Rom. 9-11).

But that is no longer the end of the story. Blood connection is not the decisive factor: "God can raise children for Abraham from these stones" (Luke 3:8). The long and heated debate between the Jews and Jesus in John 8:31-59 was to make the point that without faith Abraham's blood connection is useless (see also Rom. 9:6-8). On the other hand, those who follow Abraham's example of faith and accept Jesus, become heirs of Abraham's blessings. These blessings are meant for all the clans of the earth (Gen. 11:3). That is why the message of Christ must be preached to all nations: "Go, make disciples of all nations" (Matt. 28:19). Thus, the bond of Christian fellowship of grace embraces all of humanity; it is deeper and wider than that of the Old Testament Israelite identity.

4. Abraham and the "wider ecumenism"

4.1. Abraham and Christian unity

At our present stage in the ecumenical pilgrimage, it is right that we face with both realism and serenity those factors which keep the Christian family in a state of scandalous dividedness. At the same time, we should celebrate those things which we share. We all share the spiritual inheritance of Abraham: renewed, deepened, widened and radically transformed by the Lord Jesus, as we see in the traditions and teachings of the New Testament. Having reflected on Abraham, his faith and the impact of this on his physical descendants, there are some basic lessons we can and should learn in our desire for the blessing of fellowship with one another in Christ. We have highlighted some of these in earlier parts of this paper. Others will emerge with further discussion and reflection. We are all children of Abraham.

4.2. The wider ecumenism

Koinonia cannot be treated as an exclusive concern of Christians in their internal relations. God's grace of fellowship is intended for all. Perhaps if we were more aware of the huge challenges of these wider dimensions, we would have greater courage and Christian incentive to promote more vigorously the koinonia within the church and among the churches. Humanity has suffered a lot as a result of divisions on a religious basis. We must explore and exploit any opportunities which religion offers to bring people closer together.

The greatest of such factors is precisely faith in God, the Father of all. The tragic irony is that many wars have been fought "in the name of God". That should not, however, stop us from pursuing justice, peace and love "in the name of God".[9]

The religious personality and patrimony of Abraham can be a bridge across the gaps separating the three great monotheistic religions — Judaism, Christianity and Islam. They all have a special place for Abraham as a man of faith.

4.3. The stock of Abraham

The physical stock of Abraham survives and thrives today in the Jewish race. "Of their race according to the flesh, is the Christ" (Rom. 9:5). For this reason alone, the Christian community cannot be indifferent to its relations with the Jewish community today. The past history of Jewish-Christian relations shows that the tremendous implication of the place of Abraham for both communities has not always been sufficiently appreciated. Today, there is more effort being made to improve relations on a religious basis. The imperatives of the New Testament faith demand that the Christian ought not to hesitate in taking initiatives and offering the hand of fellowship. Many churches, including my own, have well-articulated channels of dialogue with the Jewish community.[10] That is as it should be. Greater dialogue among the churches, in view of this other dialogue with the Jewish faith, may be to the mutual advantage of all concerned.

4.4. The Islamic community

In many parts of the world, Christian-Muslim relations pose serious challenges for peace and national unity. The spiritual personality of Abraham is an area of partial but important convergence between the two faiths.

Of course, we cannot overlook the basic difference between Islam and Christianity: namely the person of Jesus Christ. By rejecting the divinity of Christ, Islam rejects the very basis of the Christian faith. There is little scope for dialogue on this point.

Furthermore, even in the issues where similarities exist, such similarities often go with major differences. Abraham is a case in point. In the Koran, Abraham is mentioned in about 245 verses. He is called the "friend of God" (Khalil Allah), and is reputed to be the first "submissive one", that is, the first "Muslim" (Koran 3:67).

But there are many important differences between the biblical and koranic pictures of Abraham. In the Koran, there is no mention of the land and posterity. Ishmael rather than Isaac is the son of sacrifice. The greatest difference is theological. This can be stated as follows: whereas in the Bible, God seeks out and finds Abraham, in the Koran it is Abraham who seeks and finds God. In each case, however, a personal decision of faith is taken, to cast his lot on God, abandoning his own. Thus, the same Abraham unites and divides Christians and Muslims.[11] But one can say that he unites more than he divides. The French Catholic church some years ago published a booklet to present Islam to Christians in a positive light with a view to fruitful dialogue. The title of the booklet was appropriately *Tous fils d'Abraham* — all children of Abraham.[12]

4.5. The land promised to Abraham

The land promised to Abraham and his descendants is today a land of conflict and violence. The conflict seems basically political and racial. But there is an obvious religious dimension. The three monotheistic religions are involved. The Israeli-Arab conflict is not simply a Jewish-Muslim affair. There is a sizeable Arab Christian community who are sharing the political lot of their Muslim fellow-Arabs. This Christian Arab community is often forgotten in Christian circles. We hear there are also a few Israeli Christians. Even if these are few, their very existence is of great symbolic significance.

The three religions see Abraham in more or less different ways. But Abraham still remains a recognizable common religious symbol — with great potential for reconciliation and peace. Here again, the responsibilities of the Christian communities in this region are great; perhaps greater than their numbers and influence. They, at least, have a clear perspective of the promise to Abraham as being addressed to all people. If to all peoples, surely to all who live in the land of God's promise.

Conclusion

We live in a world torn apart by all sorts of divisions and discriminations, rivalries and rifts, clashes and conflicts. The boundaries of all these cleavages criss-cross in all sorts of tangled webs. The beautiful world of order and harmony created by God and disrupted by sin is still groaning for its restoration and reconciliation in Christ (Rom. 8:22).

In this world conference, we are concerned about the divisions and disunity within the Christian fold. What is the ultimate objective of our search for unity? Surely not simply and only to feel warm and cosy with one another. The Lord prayed for the unity of his followers "so that the world may believe" (John 17:21) that in Jesus is the route to reconciliation and peace. Koinonia in the church is for the sake of the world — this world which God loved — and loves — so much! (John 3:16). The divine project called the church is not an end in itself. It is nothing if it is not a sign and an instrument of the kingdom of God on earth.[13] Our task must go beyond reaching out to each other.

At another level, we might also ask: what is the quality of the koinonia we already claim to enjoy in our different Christian communities? Christians, even of the same denomination, are divided and kept apart also by social, economic and political differences. In concrete terms, what does "koinonia in life" mean for a Christian community that is as divided as the rest of the world into rich and poor, powerful and weak, free and shackled? After our beautiful and moving "fellowship" here in Santiago de Compostela, we shall all disperse to our respective little corners. Shall we remain there and continue business as usual? How shall we be able to join hands in a "koinonia of witness" to God's kingdom of love and peace?

Jesus links Abraham with the eschatological table fellowship in his future kingdom to which all men and women of good will shall be admitted. Reclining on the "bosom of Abraham" at that eschatological banquet will be not only the poor and patient Lazarus (Luke 16:20-22) but also "many from the east and the west" (Matt. 8:11). Then shall the promise to Abraham have its complete fulfilment. Our koinonia in faith, life and witness shall then have its full realization. In the meantime, we are on pilgrimage, with our eyes set on our heavenly destination.

NOTES

[1] We emphasize that this is only a personal view, stressing only an aspect of koinonia, and not necessarily the most important one even for the author.

[2] St Augustine of Hippo expresses it in his characteristic poetic Latin prose as follows: *(Deus)... ita sapienter disposuit ut Novum in Vetere lateret et in Novo vetus pateret. Quest. in Hept.* 2:73, P.L. 34:623.

[3] For a modern progressive presentation of the koranic image of Abraham in the context of dialogue with Christianity, see M. Talbi, "Foi d'Abraham et foi islamique", *Islamochristiana*, 5, 1979, 1-5.

[4] R. De Vaux, *Histoire Ancienne d'Israël*, Paris, J. Gabalda, 1971, 256-73. See also M. Haran, "The Religion of the Patriarchs: An Attempt at a Synthesis", *ASTI*, 4, 1965, 30-55.

[5] *Ibid.*, 261-69.

[6] On the historical value of these migration narratives see *ibid.*, 180-87.

[7] For a competent discussion of the conquest/infiltration debate see *ibid.*, 613-19.

[8] On covenant theology in the context of kingship ideology in Israel see D.J. McCarthy, *Old Testament Covenant*, Oxford, Blackwell, 1973, esp. 45-52.

[9] Pope John-Paul II, with his personal experience of the human tragedy of atheism as state ideology, is particularly sensitive to the crucial importance of shared faith in God in the promotion of world peace, e.g., the social encyclical *Centesimus Annus* of 1 May 1991, para. 13, as well as many of his messages for the World Day of Peace issued every New Year's day.

[10] For the Roman Catholic Church, there is a Commission for Religious Relations with the Jews. It is significant that this commission operates *not* within the Pontifical Council for Inter-Religious Dialogue, which deals with non-Christian religions, but rather within the Pontifical Council for Promoting Christian Unity.

[11] B. Huber, "Abraham eint — Abraham scheidet", in *Cibedo*, 6, 1992, 176-77; see also G. Demeerseman, "La rencontre 'abrahamique' de Cordoue", in *Islamochristiana*, 13, 1987, 192-93. He comments on the inter-religious consultation on Abraham held in Córdoba, Spain, as follows: "Une fois épuisés les désirs pieux et les provisions de bonne volonté, il a bien fallu constater les limites théologiques des convergences possibles autour d'Abraham, pourtant vénéré typologiquement par toutes les confessions représentées", 192.

[12] CNER-SRI, *Tous fils d'Abraham: Pour un regard chrétien sur l'Islam*, Paris, Chalet, 1980. Reviewed by M. Borrmans in *Islamochristiana*, 6, 1980, 218-20.

[13] One of the key insights of Vatican II with far-reaching implications for contemporary Catholic ecclesiology is the concept of the church as a sacrament, "a sign and instrument, that is, of the communication with God and of unity among all men..." See the Vatican II Dogmatic Constitution on the Church, *Lumen Gentium*, 1.

A VISION OF KOINONIA:
THE ANOINTING AT BETHANY
John 12:1-8

DOROTHY A. LEE

[1] Six days before the Passover Jesus came to Bethany, the home of Lazarus, whom he had raised from the dead. [2] There they gave a dinner for him. Martha served, and Lazarus was one of those at the table with him. [3] Mary took a pound of costly perfume made of pure nard, anointed Jesus' feet, and wiped them with her hair. The house was filled with the fragrance of the perfume. [4] But Judas Iscariot, one of his disciples (the one who was about to betray him), said: [5] "Why was this perfume not sold for three hundred denarii and the money given the poor?" [6] (He said this not because he cared about the poor, but because he was a thief; he kept the common purse and used to steal what was put into it.) [7] Jesus said: "Leave her alone. She bought it so that she might keep it for the day of my burial. [8] You always have the poor with you, but you do not always have me." (NRSV)

Introduction

The vision of koinonia I would like to share with you comes from an unusual source, the story of the anointing at Bethany (John 12:1-8). The word koinonia is not found in this story, nor is it found anywhere in John's gospel. But, like Paul, John also has a vision of a community of love, and this story captures something of that vision. Mary of Bethany anoints Jesus' feet with perfumed oil and wipes them with her hair. When Judas Iscariot objects, Jesus defends Mary in the most affirming way. As I hope to show, the story of the anointing focuses on the communion or fellowship which takes place between Jesus and the family at Bethany. Significantly, that fellowship occurs in the context of a meal.

Koinonia as gratitude for life

There are three ways in which koinonia operates in this story. First, koinonia begins in gratitude for Jesus' gift of life. In the previous chapter, John has told us the story of Lazarus' death and the grief of his sisters, Martha and Mary. We learn of Jesus' love for the two women and their brother, and their love for him as disciples. After Lazarus dies, Jesus visits the grieving sisters. In conversation with Martha, he reveals himself to her as the resurrection and the life (11:25-26). Martha responds with the highest confession of faith we have yet heard in the fourth gospel, a confession which parallels that of Peter in the Synoptic gospels: "Yes, Lord," she says, "I believe that you are the Messiah, the Son of God, the one coming into the world" (11:27).

Jesus then meets Mary with a crowd of mourners (11:28-37). She falls at his feet in grief and disappointment. While she too loves Jesus, she shares with her sister Martha the sense of being abandoned by him in her hour of need. The harmony of her love for

---

The Rev. Dr Dorothy A. Lee (United) lectures in New Testament at the United Faculty of Theology, Melbourne, Australia.

Jesus has broken down: because he delayed his coming, because Lazarus died as a consequence. Mary, though one of his disciples, is alienated. She weeps and the mourners weep, and Jesus too begins to weep, sharing their grief (11:35). He accompanies them to the tomb and summons Lazarus from the dead (11:38-44). Many people come to faith as a result of this, many take offence against Jesus, and the religious leaders plot to kill him (11:45-57).

The banquet described in chapter 12, therefore, belongs to the story of the raising of Lazarus. Once again, we find Mary sitting at Jesus' feet, just as she was in the previous chapter; only now everything is different. Now she expresses a love without grief or alienation. Now she pours out her gratitude for the gift of her brother's life. For John the koinonia of this meal begins in the loving and grateful recognition that Jesus is the giver of life. The family circle, broken by sickness and death, is here restored by the life and healing which Jesus brings.

The picture of Jesus giving life is relevant for us today. The Christian community is also broken and surrounded by symbols of death: by sin and alienation, by injustice and intolerance, by grief and pain. We are disciples of Jesus, we have been given life in baptism, yet our struggle remains. Unlike the Bethany family, we do not share full table-fellowship with one another. Although Martha presides at the table and at the meal, we in the church still find it hard to embrace the ministry of women. Is the seamless robe of Jesus divided after all? As John reminds us throughout the gospel, and particularly in the farewell discourse (chapters 13-17), communion is a gift of God: the gift of Jesus who is sent to us from the Father, the gift of the Spirit who gives birth to the church. Only God can re-form the circle of koinonia, broken by sin; only God can bring wholeness to our fragmentation. Koinonia begins for us, as it does for Mary of Bethany, in the grateful recognition of God's gift of life: the gift of resurrection life reaching out to us in our experience of death.

Koinonia as cross-shaped

Secondly, this gift of life, this koinonia, is linked profoundly to Jesus' death. Mary of Bethany's action in anointing Jesus is more than just the expression of gratitude, important though that is. It is also the perceptive recognition of Jesus' death. That is why, at the end of the story, Jesus says to those who attack her: "She bought it [the perfume] so that she might keep it for the day of my burial" (v.7). The wording of this statement is awkward but the meaning is clear: Mary has anointed Jesus for death. Her action is not an unconscious one, as many have suggested. Jesus defends her precisely because she does know what she is doing. She realizes that Jesus has given life at the cost of his own life. She knows that his journey to Lazarus' tomb is the journey to his own death (11:7-16). The cross lies at the heart of Jesus' life-giving mission to the world.

All this is central to our understanding of koinonia. The gift of unity comes at great cost: the giving of God's beloved Son to death. The cross is not something we put behind us, once we have achieved a degree of unity in the church. On the contrary, it is the basis for our ongoing life together. It makes that life and that unity possible at every stage of the journey. Because of it, we name the conflicts between us and do not run away from them — as we would prefer to do — or try and paper over the cracks. The cross prevents our koinonia being superficial: a smiling sense of being together which pretends there is no suffering, no injustice, no wounds in the body of Christ.

Through the cross, we face the sin of our division and are reminded of how vulnerable we are. Through it, we are embraced by the forgiving love of God; we are given as gifts to each other, like the mother of Jesus and the beloved disciple at the foot of the cross (19:25-27); we are nourished by the blood and water from Jesus' side (19:31-37). The cross is the place where we encounter both our own suffering and the life-giving glory of God.

This nexus beneath life and death — the life given to Lazarus, the death faced by Jesus — is emphasized in the perfume: "The house was filled with the fragrance of the perfume" (11:3). The fragrance is so strong that it pervades the whole house. As we have seen, Mary's anointing of Jesus is associated with death, with his death. In the ancient world — as in parts of the modern world — women anointed the bodies of their loved ones with spices and fragrant oils, as a way of mourning their death and expressing their grief. But women also anointed their dead for reasons of life: because they hoped for a world where death would no longer hold sway.

In the same way, Mary's anointing is as much about life as death. The perfume is a symbol of life and hope. The fine fragrance wafting through the house contrasts with the smell of death at the tomb of Lazarus in chapter 11 (v.39). In that story Martha, for all her faith, wants to protect everyone from the smell of death, the unbearable smell of our mortality. But Jesus reveals to her that, unless we confront it, the odour of death can never become the fragrance of life. In this experience Martha's faith is deepened: now in chapter 12, she breathes in the perfume of life. The stench of death now becomes the fragrant odour of life, and it does so only through Jesus' death and resurrection. True koinonia faces the reality of death and finds life at its centre, a life whose fragrance is infinitely stronger than the cloying scent of death.

The same point is made with Judas Iscariot (12:4-6). There is a powerful contrast between the two main characters in the story: Mary and Judas. Both are disciples of Jesus, and both are present in the restored intimacy of the family's life. Both, in an ironical way, are connected with Jesus' death: Mary because she proclaims Jesus' death in faith and love, and Judas because he betrays Jesus and brings about his death. Just as Mary is the model disciple, so Judas is the type of the false disciple. But of course Judas' objection is not allowed to stand; it is neither sincere nor valid. Judas is a thief and has no concern for the poor. Even if he had, his words would not lessen the greatness of Mary's action. In John's gospel, koinonia is not found primarily in sharing possessions with the poor but, as Mary of Bethany shows, in sharing intimacy with Jesus.

Judas' response to Mary plays an important role in the story. It represents the way in which evil tries to damage the life of the community. Here koinonia is threatened, not by the external powers of death, but rather by the internal forces of petty-mindedness and jealousy. They come from one who claims to be a follower of Jesus. John warns us that, even in the community of faith, there are ungenerous and destructive forces at work that would turn the fragrance of life into the smell of death. But Jesus defeats the attempt to destroy koinonia. The One who gives the gift also protects and nourishes it. In defending Mary, Jesus defends the unity of the community.

Koinonia as costly love

Thirdly, koinonia calls for a response from us as individuals and as the church. In anointing Jesus, Mary symbolizes the communion of faith, the church. What she does is to make a symbolic confession of faith. In the story of the raising of Lazarus, we remember, Martha makes the gospel's central confession — that Jesus is the Christ — in *word* (11:27). That confession of faith is now parallelled by Mary, who makes her confession of faith in *deed*. Each faith-confession is equally important for John, since word and action belong together.

But there is more in this story than the unity of word and action. We have seen that Mary recognizes the cost of Jesus' action in raising Lazarus: the result is that the authorities plot to kill Jesus (11:46-53). Mary not only recognizes that cost, however; she also mirrors it in the costliness of her action (12:3). It is not some cheap scent that she pours over Jesus' feet, but the best perfume money can buy — perhaps the whole of her life's savings. As a true disciple, Mary responds to the costliness of Jesus' gift of life with the costliness of her own gift. John's theology of mutual love is summed up in this symbolic action. Disciples are not servants, but friends and beloved of Jesus: "I do not call you servants *(douloi)* any longer... but I have called you friends *(philoi)*", Jesus tells his disciples later in the gospel (15:15).

Mary's anointing of Jesus is a model for us in the church, a model of discipleship and ministry. It symbolizes the mutual love which exists between Jesus and the church, a love that is immensely costly. Koinonia is based on reciprocal love — between us and God, in the first place, and between us as churches. A genuine and mutual love is costly on both sides. The cost is not just on God's part, but also on ours. It is costly because it demands our whole selves, given to God and given to one another across denominational barriers. Not that we lose our identity in this process: self-surrender means that we know who we are and can thus give our deepest selves. True mutuality, like the give-and-take between lovers, empowers us to give and receive in a way that restores and enriches our identity, rather than undermining it. This reciprocal dynamic is the basis of our spirituality and is also to be the way we relate to each other. As Christians, we are to abandon the barricades we hide behind, and open ourselves to the Spirit and to one another. Like Mary of Bethany, we are to give to each other in a radical way, and not withhold out of fear or pride or even low self-esteem. Without such costly self-giving, koinonia is just a game we play.

Conclusion

There are three aspects of koinonia that we can articulate from John's story of the anointing. First, koinonia begins in God's gift of life, binding us together in a community of love as we receive it in gratitude from the Lord. Secondly, the cross lies at the centre of koinonia, bringing the fragrance of life where there was once the smell of death. Only Jesus' death makes sense of our suffering and struggle, and only his resurrection gives us joyful hope and life-giving unity. Thirdly, koinonia involves us in a mutual and reciprocal love that shares itself in a costly way and opens us to the other, through the divine Spirit. All three dimensions of koinonia are essential for our self-understanding as the church and they are all, as we would expect from John's gospel, profoundly sacramental. Through the symbolic action of Mary of Bethany at this celebratory meal, we gain a vision of that koinonia which lies at the heart of the Trinity: the self-giving love of God given to us in Jesus, and made real for us in the loving embrace of the Spirit.

SHARING THE TRINITARIAN LIFE
John 17:20-26, 1 John 1:1-4

SIMON CHAN

I have been asked to present a personal perspective of the biblical vision of koinonia. But before I begin, it would only be fair to the audience to be informed briefly about the background that shaped this personal perspective. I am an Asian living in a context that can be best described as modern and cosmopolitan. It is a world very much shaped by modern development, by science and technology and the world economic system; in economic parlance, the NIEs (newly industrializing economies), one of the four "little dragons". It is in view of this that the reflection tries to take seriously the problem of depersonalization. I am also a Christian by conversion and a Pentecostal (in that order). This means that Christianity, for me, as a lived experience, has much in common with what is traditionally called enthusiasm. I therefore bring to the reflection a heritage that values a more intense (though, hopefully, not individualistic) kind of personal engagement.

The two passages from the Johannine corpus are chosen for the obvious reason that they provide a vision that is quite perennial to the ecumenical movement, namely, the visible unity of the church. They also address a concern more particular to this conference, namely, the relationship of koinonia to the life, faith and witness of the church. The choice of those texts is based on the conviction that the reality of the Trinitarian life is utterly basic to these concerns. John 17 and 1 John 1 epitomize our theme. They singularly focus on our common life as a life derived from the inner life of God and linked to it in a certain way. But in point of fact, the nature of the Trinitarian life is imprinted throughout the Johannine corpus, so that our discussion must first take this larger context into consideration. So we begin with a consideration of:

The nature of the Trinitarian life

The Western tradition has often tended to emphasize the undifferentiated equality between the Father, Son and Holy Spirit, their equality in honour, power, glory, etc. But what we see in John is an equality that is obviously differentiated. The relationship between the Father and the Son is supremely an intense, intimate and dynamic relationship — a relationship characterized by humble service, generosity, mutual respect, deference, and disposability; in short, love.

The Father sends the Son (8:28); the Son freely consents to and carries out the will of the Father, speaking just what the Father wants him to speak and always doing what pleases him (8:29). The Father testifies to the Son (5:37; 8:18) while the Son reveals the Father (8:18; 14:7-9). The Son honours the Father (8:49), and the Father honours

Dr Simon Chan (Pentecostal) is lecturer in systematic theology at Trinity Theological College, Singapore.

the Son by committing all judgment to the Son (5:22,23); and the reason for the Father's honouring the Son is because of the Son's complete disposability to his Father's will.

> Now is the Son of man glorified, and in him God is glorified. If God is glorified in him, God will also glorify him in himself, and glorify him at once. (13:31,32)

Jesus speaks here of mutual glorification in reference to his death. Here is an act of ultimate disposability: his death for others in keeping with the will of the Father (cf. 10:11; 15:13). Such is the relationship between the Father and the Son that those who serve the Son in the same way as the Son serves the Father will be honoured by the Father (12:26). The relationship could also be described in terms of accessibility and openness. Jesus is conscious of the Father's complete accessibility to him. Before the tomb of Lazarus he declares: "Father, I thank you that you have heard me. I knew that you always hear me" (11:41). He on his part is fully accessible to the Father so that he can claim his Father as his witness (8:18).

In this relationship where does the Holy Spirit come in? One of the most interesting features of Johannine pneumatology is that while the Spirit is referred to in the most explicitly personal terms, yet his role is largely a hidden one. The "farewell discourse" of Jesus portrays the Spirit mainly in a supportive role. The Spirit testifies, guides, comforts and convicts; yet these activities serve more as pointers to the central role played by the Father and the Son. He is "another Comforter" (14:16), implying a substitutionary role. He will "remind you of everything I have said to you" (14:26), again suggesting that it is what *Jesus* said that is the primary focus. He will "testify about me" (15:26) and "bring glory to me by taking from what is mine and making it known to you" (16:14). In the prayer of John 17, more than one commentator has pointed to the conspicuous lack of reference to the Spirit. His work is referred to, but only implicitly; e.g. "sanctify them through thy truth; thy word is truth" (17:17) may be taken as an oblique reference to the Spirit who is the Spirit of truth (14:26). If the disciples are to be made holy in truth, it must be the Holy Spirit who does it (cf. 2 Thess. 2:13: "God chose you from the beginning to be saved through *sanctification* by the *Spirit* and belief in the *truth*"). The implicit work of the Spirit is again seen in v.26. Here Jesus makes known the Father to the believers so that "the love you have for me may be in them and that I myself may be in them" (cf. Rom. 5:5: "God has poured out his love into our hearts by the Holy Spirit whom he has given us").

The Spirit may be pictured as the hidden "glue" that binds together the Trinitarian fellowship. The reality of the Spirit is not directly focused upon but is implicitly recognized. He makes possible the fellowship, giving to it a certain concrete structure. He may well be called the "spirit" of the fellowship. We recognize the "ethos" of the Father-Son relationship, but only when we (to use an expression from Michael Polanyi) attend "from" the Spirit "to" the life of God revealed in the Father-Son relationship. We must not conclude, however, that seeing the Spirit thus will reduce the Spirit to an impersonal force. Precisely because the Spirit is seen in relation to the intra-personal life of God, his presence is always personal. Only together with the Father and the Son is the Spirit worshipped and glorified, that is, revealed as person — so says our creed. In fact excessive focus on the Spirit, which isolates the Spirit from the Father and the Son, has tended to result in the depersonalization of the Spirit to "a power for service" or a "cosmic Spirit" diffused across the universe. In either case, it is a denial of Trinitarian theology.

Christian koinonia in the Trinity

Christian koinonia is an extension of *this* Trinitarian life. The new community that comes into existence through the Trinitarian drama of redemption is called upon not only to exemplify the Trinitarian mode of existence but also to partake of the Trinitarian life. The Trinity is not only the *pattern* ("that all of them may be one, Father, *just as* you are in me and I am in you", v.20a) but also the *potential* for the new community ("may they also be *in us*...", v.21b). The latter is perhaps the more compelling picture in John. The original koinonia is now expanded to embrace the community. The glory which unites the Father and Son (v.22) is now shared with the believers: "I in them and you in me" (v.23). Take, for example, the matter of divine accessibility. It is not only that there is mutual openness between the Father and the Son; there is also to be openness and accessibility towards the community. Thus, Jesus extends friendship to the disciples, calling them "friends" and letting them into the divine "secrets": "I call you friends, for everything that I learned from my Father I have made known to you" (15:15). The first letter of John 1 puts the matter more prosaically: We proclaim the word of life so that you may have fellowship with us, and our fellowship is with the Father and with his Son, Jesus Christ.

As the pattern, the relationship between the Father and the Son as shown in the behaviour of the Son provides the model for Christian koinonia: "I have set you an example that you should do as I have done for you" (13:15). We would be missing the real import of Jesus' oft-repeated commandment to love if the divine *exemplum* is not presupposed. There is something to be said here for the much-neglected idea of *imitatio Christi*. As the potential, the hidden Spirit in the Trinitarian life is also the Spirit of the community, infusing it with supernatural life and drawing it into the koinonia of Father and Son (cf. the Pauline "fellowship of the Spirit" in the Trinitarian benediction, 2 Cor. 13:14). The community becomes a part of the extended divine family through the indwelling Spirit. Thus it is in connection with the sending of the Spirit that Jesus could assure his disciples: "I will not leave you as orphans; I will come to you" (14:18, cf. v.17).

But how is the community taken into the intra-Trinitarian life? The answer is the "word". The believers "know" and live by the firm conviction of the true identity of Jesus because he gives them the words from the Father: "For I gave them the words you gave me and they accepted them. They knew with certainty that I came from you" (17:8). We referred just now to Jesus' words of command in terms of *exemplum*. But these words are more than merely instructions to be carried out or chores to be borne. Jesus, as *exemplum*, certainly did not understand the Father's words in such a manner when he said: "My food is to do the will of him who sent me and to finish his work" (4:34). Rather, the words reveal the will of the Father and give the community access to the Father. The commandment-obedience dynamic must now be seen also as defining the structure of Trinitarian koinonia. The words of command are in reality words of welcome! For the word which communicates, expresses, goes out to the other; the word of free and open exchange that characterizes the Trinitarian fellowship; the word of the original Speaker of Genesis 1 — that word enables the enlargement of the koinonia by becoming flesh and dwelling among us. It is he, the incarnate Word, who now gives us the words of the Father so that we may become veritable partners in the Trinitarian conversation. The divine accessibility culminates in God's word of welcome through Jesus to join in the conversation. God has included us in his "inner circle"! The very prayer in chapter 17 illustrates this fact. It is so structured that the reader becomes aware of being "party to a heavenly family conversation" (Raymond Brown). (Perhaps we may note parenthetically, by way of contrast, that the Fall could be seen as the privatization of life, the loss of conversation and the abuse of language for selfish and destructive purposes (cf. modern advertising), while Pentecost is the restoration of creative conversation: "We *hear* them speaking in our own native language" (Acts 2:8)).

The outworking of the shared Trinitarian life

As we reflect on the koinonia of believers based on the extension of the Trinitarian life, we become more fully aware of the significance of the characteristically Johannine paradoxes and their implications for the life and witness of the church.

First, there is an inclusion as well as an exclusion in the Trinitarian koinonia. Our being included as full partners in the divine conversation also involves the exclusion of the cosmos. In John the exclusion motif is just as pervasive as the inclusion motif (cf. the light-darkness theme). John is deeply conscious of the dark side of reality which disrupts, alienates and destroys. He speaks of it not only from a cosmic perspective (ch. 1) but shows up the "world" in a number of smaller, down-to-earth ways. For example, in the discourse on the good shepherd, the fellowship of the sheepfold is threatened by the presence of thieves, robbers and hirelings (10:10,13). In the midst of the community of humble servants (13:1ff.), there stands Judas Iscariot (vv.2,18). In the midst of his discourse concerning the Spirit that binds the community in fellowship, he also identifies the Spirit as a Spirit "the world cannot receive because it neither sees him nor knows him". Only those who share the divine life know him "for he dwells with you, and will be in you" (14:17). The healing of the blind man is understood as a sign of the coming of the true light which divides faith and unbelief.

> For judgment I came into the world, that those who do not see may see, and that those who see may become blind. (9:39)

Our problem, perhaps, is not so much the inability to know *what* the cosmos is and what it stands for, as the inability to know *where* it is, to discern it when we are face to face with it, and to say a firm "no" to it. At a time when it is popular to talk about a "world-affirming" religion, we stand in danger of succumbing to an all-embracing cosmism that knows little of an "exclusive" koinonia. It is only in Trinitarian inclusion that we become sensitized to the excluded cosmos. And the cosmos will be excluded as long as it remains the *kosmos*. The "only hope for the *kosmos* is that it should cease to be the *kosmos*" (Barrett).

On the other hand, inclusion in the Trinitarian life makes involvement in the expanding circle of koinonia inevitable. Even though Christian theology tells us that the Trinity is self-sufficient, it is not a smug self-sufficiency but seeks to draw others in to share its inner life. In this sense it is not exclusive. This is the mission of the Father which the Son came to fulfil; and the mission of Christ is now extended to the church: "As the Father has sent me, I am sending you" (20:21). The two have become inseparable, so that reception of the church's mission is also reception of the mission of the Father through the Son (13:20).

The second paradox is found in John's double meaning of glory. The glory Christ receives from the Father and which he shares with the community is a glory acquired through and expressed in suffering. It is in the suffering of the Son that the character of God, namely the Trinitarian disposability towards a sinful world, is most poignantly revealed. Jesus often speaks of "the hour" of his death as precisely the point when the Father is glorified (12:23-24,27-28, 17;1). His exaltation consists in his being "lifted up from the earth" upon the cross (12:32). The glory of suffering, it must be stressed, comes through the activation of the redemptive drama. It is a revealed glory. In other words, we may say that God's suffering comes from his attempt to accommodate us in the divine conversation. God has to bear with our infirmities. This is portrayed in Jesus' bearing us in his intercessory prayer that "they be one". The prayer, in effect, is for the Trinitarian life to be fully embodied in the community so that believers can become full partners in the conversation with God and one another.

Perhaps we could press the logic of conversation still further to show the central place that suffering occupies in koinonia. Speaking and listening are what real conversations are about, but the difficulty is that we are often better at speaking than listening. We have all too quickly acquired a tongue like "the pen of a ready writer", sought to be a "prophetic voice" without a pair of "prophetic ears" — long-suffering ears. We refuse to listen because we cannot share the pain of the other. Listening is one of the most basic forms of suffering in a koinonia distinguished and bound together by the "word". Listening is painful, but by refusing, the conversation breaks down. There is more sombre truth in what C.S. Lewis said half in jest: "It is easier to pray for a bore than to go and visit him." With God, however, he first *heard* the cry of his people, then he spoke (Ex. 3:7). This is the pattern in the unfolding drama of redemption. We can indeed speak of being changed "from glory to glory" (in the positive sense) as we share in the divine conversation since conversation opens up our persons and makes us accessible to other persons. But even such a transformation does not come without participation with "unveiled faces" (2 Cor. 3:18), that is, with no holds barred, with complete accessibility. This is a risky — and painful — undertaking, yet progress in koinonia demands that we take such a risk. Sharing the Trinitarian life is unavoidably a koinonia of Christ's sufferings (Phil. 3:10). Such a fellowship is a much more powerful witness to the world which knows only the "success syndrome" as the measure of positive life.

The third paradox is the unity and diversity in the Trinitarian life. The fact that the church's life is an extension of the life of the three-in-one God means that we need to give full play to both diversity and unity in the church and more especially in our ecumenical effort. In this respect, I share the concern of my European brothers and sisters that diversity must be taken "more seriously", that it should be "received as a gift, not just tolerated or seen as a threat".[1] To see diversity only in terms of unity or vice-versa does not reflect faithfully our Trinitarian theology. The divine unity-in-diversity or diversity-in-unity is in fact the pattern and potential of the church's koinonia.

Three things, about which we can speak with some degree of confidence, may be said about this unity. First, it is achieved by the power and action of God. The fact that Jesus prayed for the church's unity suggests that ultimately it is not brought about by mere human effort but rather by the perfect concurrence of the will of the Father and the Son. The church's life is primarily a supernatural life, so that the best of human efforts must be acknowledged as means of grace and not as a primary cause of the unity. Secondly, the form of unity anticipated in the prayer of Jesus must at least attain a measure of visibility in order for the world which "does not know" the Father (v.25) to "know" that the Father sent the Son (v.23). The unity must take concrete shape in a vibrant, loving community. A purely inner, spiritual unity is no more conceivable than a purely invisible love relationship. Thirdly, the unity that Jesus prayed for does not necessarily guarantee the world's conversion (Jesus consciously excludes the cosmos in his prayer, 17:9), but it poses the most compelling challenge to the world which, while hating the believers (17:14), is yet forced to acknowledge the reality of the koinonia based on love originating from the Father through the Son and to the community (v.23b).

Diversity, on the other hand, is a little more difficult to predicate, and part of the reason for this is that it can so easily become an excuse for disunity, a justification for self-interest or even simply an acquiescence to chaos. Yet diversity has to be taken seriously because it is a reality in God. Traditionally, we speak of different roles, of generation and procession and of coinherence. But they all point to the singular fact of diversity. The Trinitarian life is rich, deep and challenging precisely because Father, Son and Spirit are *also*, in a way, not the same, and they sustain a relationship to each other which points the way to and realizes the richness and depth of our own koinonia.

Yet, if I may hazard to point out one way in which diversity may be accepted and even celebrated, it is this: there is a wide diversity (note well!) of views among commentators on how the unity in verses 22 and 23 is to be conceived, and whether it refers to ecumenical unity at all, although its implication for ecumenism is generally acknowledged. I would like to think that this very fact reflects the richness of Trinitarian koinonia and should be viewed positively as long as it is set in a healthy tension with the fact of unity. In other words, to take seriously the Trinitarian koinonia means that the church must live at two levels of consciousness, the consciousness of unity as well as the consciousness of diversity. And if these two levels are faithfully pursued, then whatever final form of "complete unity" that Jesus desires for his church emerges, we can be confident that it will be just the form he desires. For it will be a real extension of Trinitarian life into the church's life:

> You whom he ordained to be
> Transcripts of the Trinity
> Charles Wesley

NOTE

[1] *Regional Consultations in Preparation for the Fifth World Conference on Faith and Order: Summary of Reports*, eds Thomas F. Best & Günther Gassmann, Faith and Order paper no. 162, Geneva, WCC, 1993, p.9.

☐   Plenary discussion

In a discussion devoted mainly to the conference theme and sub-themes, two speakers addressed the biblical presentations. One expressed satisfaction with these, including the Bible studies on Galatians during the morning worship. It was noted that in reflecting on the theme and sub-themes all of the conference material and input should be considered, not only the discussion paper. Another speaker registered particular appreciation for Dr Chan's description of "the love shared between the Father and the Son", noting that a reference to the *kenosis* theme in Philippians 2:5ff. would have been apposite.

IV
Towards Koinonia
in Faith, Life and Witness

□ Introduction

Presentations on the conference theme and sub-themes occupied plenary V, 5 August, 11h., vice-moderator the Rev. Prof. Jean-Marie Tillard, O.P., presiding; plenary VI, 5 August, 16h., vice-moderator the Rev. Dr Paul A. Crow, Jr, presiding; and plenary VII, 5 August, 18h., Prof. Nicolas Lossky presiding.

In plenary V the Rev. Prof. Tillard, O.P. introduced **papers** on the conference theme of koinonia by the Most Rev. Desmond Tutu and Metropolitan John of Pergamon. These were complemented in plenary VI as the Rev. Dr Crow introduced three **papers** treating the conference sub-themes of faith, life and witness delivered by Prof. Dr Wolfhart Pannenberg, Ms Elizabeth Templeton and Metropolitan Georges Khodr, respectively.

Plenary VII was devoted for the most part to a discussion of these presentations; this is recorded on pp.127-128 below.

TOWARDS KOINONIA IN FAITH, LIFE AND WITNESS

DESMOND TUTU

Preamble

It has become trite to observe that we have experienced momentous changes in the world in recent years. Perhaps we tend to become blasé too easily. You might recall a cartoon in *Newsweek* which depicted two Russian astronauts conversing in space. The one says: "I am looking forward to returning home when President Gorbachev will welcome me," and he is told that President Gorbachev is no longer in power. And then he says: "Ah well, I look forward to going home to the Soviet Union," and he is told that there is no longer any Soviet Union, and he sighs and says he looks forward to drinking his vodka, and he is told it will cost him a zillion roubles. Poor chap.

But the fact of the matter is that the church's context, its *Sitz im Leben*, has changed quite dramatically in just a matter of a few years. There is now no longer any Berlin wall, no longer two Germanies, but one united state and one people, although from some accounts it has not been as simple a matter as one would have imagined to reintegrate a people who are one racially and were one before the Berlin wall was built. The fact to celebrate is that the wall has been breached, a wall that symbolized Churchill's "iron curtain", separating the globe into two spheres of influence, ideologically and militarily hostile to each other with serious repercussions for the people of the world.

We have entered a different and new epoch with the end of the cold war and the collapse of the communist bloc. The split of the world into Eastern and Western power blocs had a significant impact on a whole range of situations. It determined who were friendly nations, what was to be spent in the defence budget and the obscene arms race and who would receive what aid. It had an important bearing on Western imperialism and Soviet expansionism. When the elephants, the two superpowers, were fighting the grass invariably suffered. Many regional conflicts were really an extension of the cold war when surrogates of the super adversaries fought to advance the course of their overlords. Morality hardly featured at all. You did not ask questions about justice, equity and freedom. The most important consideration was that of global superpower politics — did it benefit this or that power bloc? Repressive governments were supported and maintained in office despite a horrendous record of human-rights violations, as long as they claimed to be anti-communist. And so the West armed UNITA to oppose a duly elected but Marxist MPLA government in Angola, or certain client elites in Somalia, and so on, etc. Now we are reaping the consequences of these policies in the carnage in Angola, in Somalia, in Afghanistan, etc., etc.

We can say that there is both good news and bad news to proclaim. We must celebrate the end of the cold war, looking to see what the so-called peace dividend is

The Most Rev. Desmond Tutu is Anglican archbishop of Cape Town, Republic of South Africa.

likely to be, and welcome what significant changes have followed in the wake of the collapse of communism. Freedom has broken out in so many and in such unlikely places. Western patronage has come to be linked with respect for human rights and so we have witnessed the transformation of many military one-party dictatorships into multiparty democracies, especially in Africa (although we should add that multiparty-ism is not necessarily the same thing as genuine participation by the broad mass of the people in political decision-making). Namibia has become independent. Reasonably free and fair elections have taken place in, for example, the Seychelles, Madagascar, Zambia, Benin, Kenya, Angola, Lesotho, Burundi, Kampuchea, Haiti and so on. And of course the world rejoices with what has been happening in South Africa to vindicate the anti-apartheid movement. Captured in the moment when the world united as it rarely has, we watched Nelson Mandela step out of prison. It was a giddy moment when humanity experienced an exhilaration — we were all proud to be human. There was a nobility we all shared then, as when again we thrilled to see an unarmed student force a tank to keep changing direction in Tiananmen Square in Beijing. We are all waiting with bated breath for the end of apartheid and the establishment of a new dispensation in South Africa, democratic, non-racial and non-sexist.

Yes, there is much to be thankful for in the new milieu in which the church finds itself. Unfortunately we are not permitted the luxury of euphoria for there is much, far too much, that is sombre. The economy of the world is in lingering recession. When the economy is in poor shape, people look for scapegoats. That is how Hitler could pick on the Jews in Nazi Germany. It is not surprising then that there should be a resurgence of racism and xenophobia all over Europe, spectacularly exemplified by the skinheads assaulting and killing Turkish persons and other foreigners in Germany. Wonderfully, thousands of decent Germans have come out in massive demonstrations against this evil. It is a time of flux, when the old order is changing, giving place to the new. Familiar landmarks are no more and people are uncertain and apprehensive as they venture into the unknown. There is the turmoil and instability in transition periods when people want to assert their distinctiveness and their peculiar identity and cling to something that is reasonably familiar and reassuring.

And so there is a resurgence of nationalism seen in its most virulent form in the "ethnic cleansing" in the mess that is the disintegrating former Yugoslavia and in the breaking-up and fighting in the former Soviet Union. We are seeing it in the restrictive and plainly racist immigration and naturalization policies of some European countries, in the marginalization of the so-called third world as the West seems to concentrate on bailing out Eastern Europe. Is it a case of blood being indeed "thicker than water", as reflected in saturation media coverage of the awfulness of Bosnia with scant attention to like events elsewhere in the world? It is in some ways like what is happening in South Africa — that the papers no longer make too much of a fuss about the killings of several blacks but will make a meal of those occasions when whites are the victims. Every violent death should be one too many. Hardly any positive reporting of the third world happens. When Africa gets in the news, as if to comply with a stereotype, it will be only the bad news that hits the media. People ask why the UN has seemed able easily to take military action to try to apprehend a warlord in Somalia, and yet seemed so impotent in Bosnia? Is it because in the one case it is blacks who are involved, and it is whites in the other? Why is it so easy for the US to attack Iraq for an alleged attempted crime, and yet Palestinians can be treated so harshly elsewhere?

In a time of uncertainty and perplexity when the familiar reference points have disappeared, it is not surprising that there will be resurgence of religious fundamentalism which gives people what they want — certitude in simplistic answers to what are often complex situations. Intolerance accompanies fundamentalism because other possible options and answers merely call in question the "orthodox" position, and would exacerbate the uncertainty which the fundamentalism was designed to deal with effectively. And why should we be surprised that there is an increase in violence?

The unity of the church in its koinonia may have something to offer to a world that is rapidly disintegrating in some places. Our identity as Christians which transcends all sorts of barriers and distinctions could give hope to those who are floundering in this time of flux, wondering who they are.

The collapse of communism has in some quarters been equated with the triumph of Western capitalism. Good theology is almost always a subversive thing, questioning the shibboleths of this or that status quo. Perhaps Christian theology will be obliged to have a prophetic stance against the ready assumption of Western capitalist triumphalism. There have been spectacular scientific and technological advances. Any euphoria accompanying these has had to be tempered by the sobering fact that modern sophisticated medicine stands, so far, baffled by the pandemic of AIDS. Genetic engineering, surrogate motherhood, artificial insemination by donor or father and test-tube babies are presenting novel moral and ethical problems. And yet in some respects the more things change the more they remain the same.

We still have repressive, unrepresentative governments in Africa, in Latin America and elsewhere. Human-rights violations still give rise to a ragged file of refugees walking wearily in search of asylum. There are many who are victims of natural and man-made disasters — the Kurds, the Croatians, the Sudanese, the Liberians, the Angolans, the Somalis, the Kampucheans, the Burmese, the people of the Dalai Lama of Tibet. There is factional strife still in Northern Ireland and ethnic turmoil in Sri Lanka and the Middle East. There are still too many of God's children without decent homes, adequate health care and nutrition, clean water and the security to lead normal fulfilled lives. And somehow it happens that the affluent North manages to get richer and the poor South poorer, carrying an enormous burden because of neo-colonialism and a hopelessly unjust international economic system, with the World Bank and the IMF often imposing conditions that are totally oblivious of the massive suffering they cause to the ordinary people — as if persons did not really count. The social cost has been far too exorbitant in numerous cases when the cure has been worse than the disease, or has led to the death of the patient.

The nuclear accidents at Three Mile Island and Chernobyl, our reckless pollution of the atmosphere and of our waters, and wanton destruction of irreplaceable rain forests and wanton use of fossil fuels show we have not begun to take seriously our ecological obligations as God's stewards. Our irresponsible conduct is resulting in the hothouse effect and damage to the ozone layer through the reckless use of CFCs. It is this fascinating, changing, perplexed world and these times which form the context, the *Sitz im Leben* of the church.

Towards koinonia

Our Lord prayed solemnly for the unity of his followers because the credibility of his own mission depended on it. Hence it cannot be a matter of indifference for

Christians, this issue of the reunion of Christians. We have no option but to work and pray that we might all be one. And yet there seems to be a universal inertia in the ecumenical movement. There are conversations, discussions and plans galore, but hardly anywhere has anything of much significance actually happened. There have been near-betrothals and engagements but hardly any nuptials, least of all consummations. We have had failed attempts or near attempts. There have been COCU, ARCIC, CUC (in South Africa), conversations between, say, Anglicans and Methodists, Anglicans and Orthodox, Anglicans and Lutherans, Anglicans and Baptists, etc., and such bilateral talks could be replicated for other denominations, confessions or communions. Often and again a remarkable degree of agreement or consensus has been reached, and yet, and yet... they have somehow lacked something to propel them to take the logical next step — organic union, becoming one, in any sense that is of significance to their members or to a world looking on with desultory and waning interest. It has seemed that toes have been dipped in the water and then the courage or the will to take the plunge into the stream has failed.

Often we have heard people say that the world has been impatient of ecclesiastical tinkering with church structures; that the world was shouting an agenda for the churches, that God's children were hurting out there and it was almost obscene to appear to be obsessed with domestic trivia when God's children were hungry for justice and food and peace. The church deserved to be marginalized if it was consuming its energies on academic pursuits of interest to a peculiar elite, as if the scriptures had declared that God so "loved the church"... rather than "God so loved the world..." This particular concern for justice, for getting priorities right, was an important corrective but it was posing a false set of alternatives. It should never have been a question of *either* unity *or* justice. It should have been a case of "both... and". It was God who indeed loved the world who set the agenda for the church which Christ loved so much that he had bought it with his own precious blood to present it as a pure bride for himself, God who determined that the church was intended to be God's agent for justice and peace.

People did grow impatient with what seemed an unconscionable concentration on apparently academic theological issues. They felt we ought to get on with the business of redeeming the world, making it more hospitable for human beings, making it a more humane environment where there was room for love, compassion, joy and laughter, peace and prosperity, sharing and caring — in short, the kind of world which clearly was becoming more and more what God intended it to be, a part of his kingdom.

Unity and justice

Our experience, which would probably be repeated elsewhere, has been that you really should not separate church unity from the pursuit of justice or, even more starkly, that that pursuit is made infinitely more hazardous and difficult, perhaps even impossible, when the church is divided. When our church held a consultation on mission our overseas partners declared categorically "apartheid is too strong for a divided church".

Some of our more exhilarating moments in the struggle for justice, peace and freedom in South Africa have occurred when the churches have been involved in united witness against the iniquity of the vicious system of apartheid. I recall how an ecumenical group of about fifty clergy were arrested in Johannesburg for demonstrating against the detention of a colleague. As we waited in the cells below the magistrate's court for our case to be heard, we held a prayer service. The late Rev. Joseph Wing, the general secretary of the United Congregational Church and secretary of the church unity commission (and known affectionately as Mr Church Unity) broke down and with tears streaming down his face said: "I have been working many years for church unity. I have never experienced it to such an extent as now." We even took a collection because Leah, who had disobeyed her husband and joined our protest march, had met a young woman who would go to jail unless she paid her fine. It was a rare moment when a church collection had such immediate and dramatic results.

When the South African government banned most popular political organizations it did not think that the churches would do anything particularly significant. It must have been shocked when an impressive phalanx of church leaders, representing a very wide spectrum of church affiliation, descended on Cape Town and was arrested as it left the Anglican cathedral of St George to march on parliament next door. At the height of apartheid's repression when its perpetrators should have expected that the stuffing had been knocked out of our people, they must have been totally flabbergasted by the defiance campaign to disobey all apartheid laws under the aegis of the mass democratic movement. The churches participated in all this through the South African Council of Churches' inspired "Standing for the Truth" campaign. Church leaders, especially in Cape Town, were trying to get arrested with varying degrees of failure. Those were heady days. The South African government realized that it would have to increase the level of repression to an intensity that would be quite unacceptable to the international community.

A reasonably united church witness together with the resilience of the people must have helped to persuade Mr de Klerk to undertake his remarkable and very courageous initiatives, including the release of Nelson Mandela and others, and then announce to parliament on 2 February 1990 the unbanning of political groups such as the ANC, PAC, SACP, etc. The subsequent exciting developments in South Africa therefore are in part due to the witness of the churches, a witness more potent because relatively united. Indeed there might have *been* no apartheid in South Africa had some churches not sought to provide theological justification for this immoral and evil system.

From our experience, then, there can be no question at all that a united church is a far more effective agent for justice and peace against oppression and injustice. It may be that we will find our most meaningful unity as we strive together for justice and peace. Just imagine what could happen in Northern Ireland and elsewhere if the churches could indeed speak and act as one, for religious differences have exacerbated political, social and economic differences.

Unity: a practical imperative

It may be that we should sit far more loosely to huge international schemes and conversations and invest our resources more and more on regional, national and, even more effectively, on local initiatives and schemes. It would be what could be called "ecumenism at work", a kind of bottom-up approach. There is no reason why Anglicans in Namibia should not go ahead into a far closer relationship with Lutherans than might necessarily be the case in, say, the Republic of South Africa, because their experience during the liberation war threw them willy-nilly into a close network of cooperation to survive as they ministered to people facing a common enemy. It may be that we should not expect to see spectacular developments at the international — what you might call the macro — level. It will happen mostly on the micro level as Christians face together the daunting problems in their locality. Sometimes the momentum will slacken because the enemy or the problem has been dealt with. Perhaps we must expect fluctuations in ecumenical zeal and enthusiasm. Facing a common enemy or problem tends to concentrate the mind. We must not be over-agitated when the zeal flags.

Our unity is ultimately like that of the divine Trinity. Some theologians made a distinction between the essential Trinity and the economic trinity — the trinity of revelation, of salvation and sanctification, or what we might call the trinity "at work". Maybe we should consider making a like distinction — between the essential ontological unity of the church and that unity as revealed in praxis.

The Faith and Order Commission has done a superb job with *Baptism, Eucharist and Ministry*. A very substantial consensus has emerged about what the churches believe regarding baptism, the eucharist and ministry. I once asked when I was still a member of the Standing Commission: "Just what is sufficient consensus, such that the churches would be willing to take the leap of faith to embrace one another?" That is still a pertinent question. How much agreement is considered sufficient to justify going forward? It just might be that we cannot be argued into oneness, just as you cannot argue someone into faith in Jesus. Perhaps having done all we could cerebrally, we have to be like Philip and Andrew in their evangelistic method and say: "Come and see!" Come and experience what it can be to be one.

I once suggested that those churches which found that they had developed strong links through cooperating in witness should go ahead and take the risk of behaving "as if" they were united, and then let the theologians sort out the mess, such as it might be. In fact in a way the so-called united churches (that is to say, congregations or parishes) are doing precisely this kind of thing. They may be anomalies in relation to the polity of their constituent churches, but they could blaze the trail in all their awkward ecclesiastical untidiness.

Do we accept the validity of one another's baptism as the sacramental act by which each person is grafted into the body of Christ? Do we think we mean much the same things about our faith when we recite the Apostles' and the Nicene Creeds? If the answers to these questions have been in the affirmative, then we share crucial elements that constitute conciliar fellowship. In addition we share a belief that the holy scriptures of the Old and New Testaments are a unique record of God's saving revelation. So far as I can tell, almost every denomination declares that even if it does not accept the sacramental validity of the ministerial orders of others, it acknowledges their efficacy in so far as God somehow vouchsafes his grace through those ministers.

I wonder how long we are going to keep making this distinction between an almost juridical *validity* and efficacy — how long *can* we do this without seeming to be ridiculous to a world watching us appear to be fiddling whilst our various Romes are burning? I have sometimes tried to imagine what would happen to, say, Anglicans if all their threefold-ordained ministers were swept away in a special flood and only those churches remained whose orders Anglicans did not recognize as valid. Would the surviving Anglicans refuse to receive "invalid" sacraments, I wonder. What about Roman Catholics, if the only surviving ministers were, say, Methodists or any others whom they did not believe stood in the apostolic succession ministerially? Don't we say God is not bound by his covenanted means of grace? Why don't we come together to pray that God will supply to all our churches whatever it may be that we believe the others might be lacking?

Unity and variety

We should each hold on to the things that we believe made us distinctive. I am fond of the Adam and Eve story — when God remarks that it is not good for man to be alone. Then Adam is asked to choose a mate from among the animals. He rejects all of them and it is only when God produces that delectable creature, Eve, from his rib that Adam exults and finds fulfilment. The story speaks fundamentally about how we need other human beings in order to be human, for none of us comes into the world fully formed. In our African idiom we say "a person is a person through other persons". We are made for interdependence. We are different so that we may know our need of one another. We are made for complementarity. Consequently we should realize that we seek unity, not uniformity, which thing we have asserted *ad nauseam*, and yet somehow we seem to give the impression that we cannot stand diversity in theology, liturgy, styles of worship, polity, etc., etc. We forget again that our unity is meant to reflect the unity of the Triune God, a unity in the diversity of persons. Most of us tend to be appalled by what is untraditional, unfamiliar and what is peculiar in theological thinking, in liturgical practice, in the ordering of church life, and so on.

The unity of the church is supposed to be celebrated as a foretaste of the kingdom of God that is surely characterized by that glorious diversity in which God calls people from all nations and races to worship him. We might have something to say to those who are worried about political schemes that would obliterate their distinctiveness if we hold up a paradigm of unity in diversity, and so stem the tide of fragmentation and fissiparousness. We could too, as the body of Jesus Christ where there is neither Jew nor Greek, etc., whose members although many form one body, put forward an example of profound unity where peculiar identity is not done away with but is subsumed under a unity that transcends all that tends to separate.

When in September 1989 we had a massive march in Cape Town against the police shootings of those who had been protesting against the racist elections, I marched with a Jewish rabbi on one side and a Muslim imam on the other. In our common quest for justice and peace we realized that our ecumenism was intended to embrace the oikoumene, the inhabited world and all its denizens, that God's concern was for all his people whatever their faith or ideology, for the Bible depicts God making the Noahic covenant with all humankind. We worship a God who could regard an Assyria as the rod of his anger and who could exalt a Cyrus to the position of being his "anointed", a God whose mercy and compassion were not the preserves of Christians alone. The rabbis tell how, after the episode of the Red Sea when the Egyptians were overwhelmed and the Israelites were celebrating their deliverance, Yahweh said: "How can you rejoice when my children have drowned?"

Yes indeed, God so loved the *world*, not the church... We cannot be serious about winning the world for God if we are not concerned about Christian unity. And we cannot be serious about ecumenism if we are not in earnest about interfaith dialogue. We must be unanimous in calling for secular states in which all religions are treated equally and even-handedly, with none enjoying unfair advantages over others. This will almost always be so in those countries where Christians are a majority. We hope that adherents of other faiths will want to do likewise in those countries where they are dominant, but whether they do or not we are obliged by the imperatives of our faith to do what is right in our own situations. Religious freedom and religious tolerance are precious things. We must be vigilant to resist the backlash of conservative Christian fundamentalism in the face of the proselytizing zeal of other faiths. Christianity must be commended to non-believers ultimately by the attractiveness of the lives of its adherents and not because it enjoys the patronage of the state.

Solidarity — spiritual and material

One of the most wonderful things about being harassed and in trouble with your government because of trying to be obedient to your Lord and Master, is discovering the exhilarating reality of being a member of the church of God. Ecclesiology comes alive. You realize that our Lord's promise to Peter, to those who have left all to follow him, that they will have sisters and brothers, etc., more than they can number, is not frivolous. That it is true — that you have all this family round the globe most of whom you will not meet this side of death, and that they are praying for you, and that they love you, and uphold you. It is almost a physical sensation and you recall the vision in Zachariah when Yahweh promises that the restored Jerusalem will be so populous that it would not have conventional walls, but that Yahweh would be like a wall of fire round Jerusalem. We have experienced a like "wall of fire" in the love, prayers and concern of our sisters and brothers around the world. That is the deepest level of our koinonia, sharing in the life of the Spirit at this intimate level and that is why one of the most important things that has come out of WCC has been the ecumenical prayer cycle.

When I was general secretary of the SACC in some of our darkest moments of apartheid's harassment, I received the newsletter of a Lutheran parish in Alaska, no less. And there I heard that we were being prayed for and the newsletter contained our names. We were being prayed for by name in Alaska — well, how could we not eventually win?

I once asked a solitary contemplative to tell me a little about her life. At the time she was living in the woods in California. Her day started at 2.00 a.m., and she said she prayed for me. Well, well — here was I being prayed for at 2.00 a.m. in the morning, in the woods in California and I thought: "What chance does the South African government stand?" Part of the South African government's harassment led to its appointing a judicial commission, the Eloff commission, to investigate the SACC. The purpose was so to discredit us that none of our overseas friends and partners, nor our South African member churches, would want to touch us with the proverbial barge pole. As it happened the government was hoisted with its own petard, for through making a few international telephone calls we had the most impressive array of overseas church leaders and delegations to descend on South Africa in a long time, to testify on behalf of the SACC. That was a tremendous act of solidarity and the government ended up with considerable egg on its face.

Thank you, dear friends, for your love and support of economic sanctions and other forms of pressure, together with your fervent prayers, which have brought us to this point when a new South Africa is about to be born. You have a substantial share in that victory.

We need to help the churches develop their best and greatest asset — their spiritual resources. We should do all we can to develop and support the growing retreat movement for deepening our spiritual life. We must become more and more in our churches power houses of prayer where vigils and fasts are normal, matter-of-course occurrences. We should grow in holiness and in stillness and contemplation for we are exhorted: "Be still and know that I am God." Our warfare is not against flesh and blood. To take on the powers and principalities we have to put on the whole armour of God. As we grow closer to God, so we will draw closer or, rather, we will be *drawn* closer to one another. An authentic Christian existence is quite impossible without an authentic spirituality when we put God where God belongs — first and in the centre of our personal and corporate lives. Such a spirituality, such an authentic encounter with God, will invariably send us away to look with the eyes of God, to hear with the ears of God, and to feel with the heart of God, what is happening in God's world so that we can become God's fellow workers, his agents of transfiguration to transform the ugliness of this world, its hatred, its alienation, its poverty, its hostility, its hunger, its fears and anxieties, its competitiveness, its evil, injustice, wars — all into their glorious counterparts so that there is more caring, more joy, more laughter, more compassion, more sharing, more justice, more peace, more love.

Friends, sisters and brothers, we are members of one family, God's family, the human family. An important characteristic of the family is that it shares. We have benefitted from the generosity of our friends in the more affluent parts of our globe. Thank you. And yet we must admit that there is something not right when the poorer countries are having to pay out to the richer a great deal more than they are receiving because of the enormous debt burden they are carrying.

It is a theological issue about stewardship, about justice. It is a moral issue of right and wrong. You, our friends from the North, have been marvellous in your enthusiasm for the anti-apartheid movement. I want to suggest that the next critical issue of like global proportions is the question of the international economic system and especially the debt burden on third-world countries. I want to suggest that perhaps a year's moratorium on repayments be called. Those countries which in that period engage seriously in the process of democratizing, in upholding basic human rights and in appropriate development benefitting the majority of their populations, should then have their debt cancelled. I call on the ecumenical movement to take this up as a major concern.

We have received so much from the North and have given hardly anything in return. I want to suggest that the West might consider a small gift we in Africa just could offer. It is the gift of *ubuntu* — a term difficult to translate into occidental languages. But it is the essence of being human, it declares that my humanity is caught up and inextricably bound up in yours — the Old Testament spoke of the "bundle" of life. I am because I belong. My humanity does not depend on extraneous things. It is intrinsic to who I am. I have value because I am a person and I am judged not so much on the basis of material possessions but on spiritual attributes such as compassion, hospitality, warmth, caring about others.

The West has made wonderful strides in its impressive technological achievements and material prosperity. But its dominant achievement/success ethic is taking its toll. People feel worthless, are often considered worthless, if they do not achieve. The worst thing that can happen to anyone is to fail. You must succeed at whatever cost.

Profits, things, are often prized above people. *Ubuntu* might remind us of a biblical truth — all that we are, all that we have is gift. We are because God loved us, loves us and will love us for ever. We don't have to do anything to earn God's love, we don't have to impress God. We can do nothing to make God love us less. We can do nothing to make God love us more.

Friends, sisters and brothers, Christianity is not a religion of virtue. Christianity is a religion of grace. Can we help as the church to transform our societies so that they are more people-friendly, more gentle, more caring, more compassionate, more sharing? Then we will see the fulfilment of that wonderful vision of Revelation 7:9-11:

> After this I looked, and behold, a great multitude which no one could number, from every nation, from all tribes and peoples and tongues, standing before the throne and before the Lamb, clothed in white robes, with palm branches in their hands, and crying out with a loud voice: "Salvation belongs to our God who sits upon the throne, and to the Lamb!" And all the angels stood round the throne and round the elders and the four living creatures, and they fell on their faces before the throne and worshipped God, saying: "Amen! Blessing and glory and wisdom and thanksgiving and honour and power and might be to our God for ever and ever! Amen."

THE CHURCH AS COMMUNION:
A PRESENTATION ON
THE WORLD CONFERENCE THEME

METROPOLITAN JOHN OF PERGAMON

Introduction

1. It is a privilege for me to address this world conference of Faith and Order, the fifth in a series of such conferences beginning with that of Lausanne in 1927. This conference, coming as it does at a time when the Faith and Order movement no longer follows the initial comparative confessionalistic approach to the problem of church unity which was evident in Lausanne and Lund, is called to see how the common roots of our biblical and patristic tradition can help the sacred course of the restoration of church unity.

It is against the background of this approach to the problem of church unity that we should appreciate the emergence of the concept of koinonia as a key notion in the theological language of Faith and Order. No Christian can doubt the biblical and patristic origins of this concept. Although not all Christian traditions can claim the same degree of appreciation and use of this concept in theology, its application to ecumenical discourse can hardly be attributed to the influence of any specific Christian tradition. As an Orthodox I cannot but rejoice at the employment of such a concept in ecumenical discourse, given the depth and the richness that it has in the theology of the Greek fathers. But at the same time, I am bound to admit that the idea of communion is equally present in the Latin fathers of the church, such as Ambrose, Augustine and others, as well as in the Reformers. Even those of us who would attach more, or even exclusive, importance to the holy scriptures can hardly overlook the important place of the theme of koinonia in the Bible. We are, therefore, dealing with a theme which is deeply rooted in all Christian traditions, i.e. with a truly ecumenical, in the old sense of the word, theme. All of us can profit from the careful and profound study of this concept as we try to find ways of overcoming division in the church of Christ.

2. The emergence of the concept of koinonia as a key notion in the theological language of the eumenical movement, and of the Faith and Order movement in particular, is not an accidental fact. It is, I think, closely connected with a major shift, or development, that took place between Edinburgh and Montreal with regard to ecclesiology. Both Lausanne and Edinburgh focused ecclesiology on Christology. Lund 1952 built on that focus, and emphasized the Christological approach to ecclesiology: "Because we believe in Jesus Christ, we believe also in the church as the body of Christ." The influence of eminent theologians at that time, such as the late Father Georges Florovsky, is evident here: "Ecclesiology is nothing but a chapter of Christology," he wrote. We should not forget that even the basis of the World Council of Churches was still at that time strictly Christological.

Metropolitan John (Zizioulas) of Pergamon is a prelate of the Ecumenical Patriarchate and professor at King's College, London, and the University of Thessaloniki, Greece.

Things begin to change at New Delhi in 1961. The basis of the WCC was broadened to include reference to the Holy Trinity, while Orthodox theologians, such as the late Nikos Nissiotis and others, strove to shift the focus from Christology to pneumatology in ecclesiology. The Faith and Order world conference in Montreal (1963), in its report of section I, stressed that our understanding of the church should not derive only from Christology but from the Trinitarian understanding of God.

We were still at that time away from any clear reference to the notion of koinonia in connection with the church. And yet, not much later, the event of the Second Vatican Council took place, paving the way towards a theology of communion for Roman Catholic theology. Through a convergence of Roman Catholic, Protestant and Orthodox theology, this concept of koinonia is now becoming central in ecumenical discussions. The present world conference on Faith and Order is being faithful to this fact in choosing koinonia as its main theme.

But why is the concept of koinonia so important for Faith and Order at the present phase of its history? What can this concept contribute to the promotion of the cause of Christian unity at this moment? This is the question I should like to raise in this address. In my attempt to suggest an answer to such a question, I shall inevitably draw from my own theological tradition, as well as from the tradition of the fathers of the church. My purpose will be to share with you some reflections on how the problem of the church's unity would appear and be approached if placed in the light of koinonia.

Koinonia as a theological concept

What do we mean when we use the concept of "koinonia" in theology? How does this term differ from the secular use of the idea of "communion" or "fellowship"? This question must be answered before any attempt is made to apply this concept to ecclesiology and the problem of the church's unity. The very fact that the Greek original of the term has been chosen for official use in this world conference indicates some uneasiness with the common use of "communion" or "fellowship". Indeed koinonia, taken directly from its original use in the Greek scriptures and patristic tradition, bears a specific meaning which should be taken into account in its application to ecclesiology. The basic ingredients of the concept of koinonia can only be drawn from theology, and it is on this point that convergence should begin in the ecumenical movement. What are these basic ingredients of a theology of koinonia?

A. Koinonia derives not from sociological experience, nor from ethics, but from *faith*. We are not called to koinonia because it is "good" for us and for the church, but because we believe in a God who is in his very being koinonia. If we believe in a God who is primarily an individual, who first *is* and then *relates*, we are not far from a sociological understanding of koinonia; the church in this case is not in its *being* communion, but only secondarily, i.e. for the sake of its *bene esse*. The doctrine of the Trinity acquires in this case a decisive significance: God *is* Trinitarian; he is a relational being by definition; a non-Trinitarian God is not koinonia in his very being. Ecclesiology must be based on Trinitarian theology if it is to be an ecclesiology of communion.

B. Koinonia is decisive also in our understanding of the person of Christ. Here the right synthesis between Christology and pneumatology becomes extremely important. What does it mean that Christ is a "pneumatic" being, a person "born by the Spirit", anointed with the Spirit, etc., if not that he is in his very being a relational being? The

Spirit is a Spirit of koinonia. If we cannot have Christology without pneumatology, this means that we must stop thinking of Christ in individualistic terms and understand him as a "corporate person", an inclusive being. The "many" are a constitutive element of the "one". The "head" without the "body" is inconceivable. The church is the body of Christ, because Christ is a pneumatological being, born and existing in the koinonia of the Spirit.

The church as "koinonia"

We can now raise the ecclesiological question on that basis. If the very being of God in whom we believe is koinonia, and if the person of Christ in whose name we human beings and the whole creation are saved is also in his very being koinonia, what consequences does this faith entail for our understanding of the church? How does the notion of koinonia affect the church's identity, her structure and her ministry in the world? How can this understanding of the church as koinonia affect our efforts towards visible unity and the overcoming of the scandal of division? Finally, how can the understanding of the church as koinonia affect her mission in the world, including her relation with the entire creation? These are the questions we propose to reflect upon in this address, hoping that in this way we might serve the purpose of this conference, which is

> to encourage the churches to affirm and live the already existing, though partial, communion with each other... to identify and struggle with those issues... which still remain barriers to full communion.[1]

1. The identity of the church is relational

If we study carefully the use of the term *ekklesia* in the New Testament, we are struck by the fact that it is normally accompanied with the genitive "of", and this in a double direction. St Paul, who seems to be the first one to use this term extensively, speaks on the one hand of the "church of God (or Christ)", and on the other hand of the church or churches "of a certain place" (Salonika, Macedonia, Judea, etc.) There is no church which can be conceived in herself, but only in relation to something else — in this case to God or Christ and to a certain locality, i.e. to the world around her.

The genitive "of God" shows clearly that the identity of the church derives from her relation with the Triune God. This relation has many aspects to it. In the first place it means that the church must reflect in her very being the way God exists, i.e. the way of personal communion. The demand that we should "become as God is" (Luke 6:36 and parallels) or that we should be "partakers of divine nature" (2 Pet. 1:4) implies that the church cannot exist and function without reference to the Holy Trinity, which is the way God is (cf. the definition of the persons of the Trinity as "mode of being" by the Cappadocian fathers). The fact that God reveals to us his existence as one of personal communion is decisive in our understanding of the nature of the church. It implies that when we say that the church is koinonia, we mean no other kind of communion but the very personal communion between the Father, the Son and the Spirit. It implies also that the church is by definition incompatible with individualism; her fabric is communion and personal relatedness.

On the other hand, the fact that the genitive "of" applied to the church is equally used in the Bible with reference to Christ, shows that the church cannot be a reflection of God's way of being apart from the "economy of the Son", i.e. the sonship given to us in Christ. The church is not a sort of Platonic "image" of the Trinity; she is communion in the sense of being the people of God, Israel, and the "body of Christ", i.e. in the sense of serving and realizing in herself God's purpose in history for the sake of the entire creation. This purpose makes the church a sign of the kingdom which is the final goal in the divine "economy". The church as a communion reflects God's being as communion in the way this communion will be revealed fully in the kingdom. Koinonia is an eschatological gift. During her historical existence, the church strives to model herself on the pattern of the kingdom, and should never cease to do so. But the achievement of full and perfect communion in history is a matter of constant struggle with the powers that threaten it. Any complacency concerning this fight for communion can be destructive for the identity of the church.

2. The structure of the church is relational

How does the structure of the church look if it is placed in the light of communion? Here we ought to distinguish two levels of structure: the local and the universal. On both of these levels communion is crucial. On the local level an ecclesiology of communion would mean that no Christian can exist as an individual exercising a direct communion with God. *Unus christianus nullus christianus*, to remember an old Latin saying. The way to God passes through the "neighbour", who in this case is the fellow-member of the community. The church is conceivable only as a structured local community. All Christians must agree on this if there is to be unity in the church.

The structure of the local church must be such that two things would be simultaneously guaranteed. On the one hand, *unity* and *oneness* must be safeguarded. No member of the church, whatever his or her position in it, can say to another member "I need you not" (1 Cor. 12). There is absolute interdependence among all members of the community which means that, simultaneously with unity and oneness, there is in the church *diversity*. Each member of the community is indispensable, carrying his or her gifts to the one body. All members are needed but not all are the same; they are needed precisely because they are different.

This variety and diversity can involve natural and social as well as spiritual differences. At the level of nature, race, sex and age are all differences which must be included in the diversity of communion. No one should be excluded on account of racial, sexual or age differences. Communion on the local level involves variety in respect of all such matters. This is true about social differences too: rich and poor, powerful and weak, all should be accommodated in the community. The same must be said about the variety of spiritual gifts. Not all in the church are apostles, not all are teachers, not all have the charism of healing, etc. And yet *all* of them are needful of one another. Spiritual elitism — which was condemned by St Paul in Corinth — has never ceased to tempt the churches. It is to be excluded from an ecclesiology of communion.

But are there no limits to diversity? Does communion sanction diversity in an unconditional way? This is a delicate question, and one that concerns directly the ecumenical problematic. It must, therefore, be given careful consideration.

The most important condition attached to diversity is that it should not destroy unity. The local church must be structured in such a way that unity does not destroy diversity and diversity does not destroy unity. This appears at first sight to be a totally unrealistic principle. And yet, the careful balance between the "one" and the "many" in the structure of the community is to be discovered behind all canonical provisions in the early church. Here the importance of the ministry of episkope becomes evident, and its proper understanding in the light of communion crucial. All diversity in the community must somehow pass through a ministry of unity, otherwise it risks running against unity. Ordination, as an act of confirming the place of a certain minister within the community, must be restricted to one minister if it is to serve the oneness of the community. Equally, this one minister should be *part* of the community, and not stand above it as an authority in itself. All pyramidal notions of church structure vanish in the ecclesiology of communion. There is *perichoresis* of ministries, and this applies also to the ministry of unity.

The same principle of relationality applies also to the structure of the church on the regional and universal levels. One community isolated from the rest of the communities cannot claim any ecclesial status; there is *one* church in the world, although there are *many* churches at the same time. This paradox lies at the heart of an ecclesiology of communion. The proper relationship between the "one" and the "many" is at stake once again. How is it to be worked out both in theory and in practice?

From the viewpoint of theology, we have here to do with a proper synthesis between Christology and pneumatology (or even a proper understanding of the "one" and the "many" — the Three — in the Holy Trinity). The Holy Spirit particularizes the one body of Christ by making each local church a full and "catholic" church. Whenever pneumatology is weak or dependent in relation to Christology (a sort of "filioquism" in ecclesiology), there is bound to be a submission of the local church to a universal church structure. The "koinonia of the Holy Spirit" suffers in this case. Equally, if the local church is not related to the one church of God in the world, this is a sign of submission of Christology to pneumatology (a sort of "Spirituquism" in triadology as well as in ecclesiology). If we attach to Christology and pneumatology an equal importance, we are bound to recognize full catholicity to each local church (the *totus Christus*) and at the same time seek ways of safeguarding the oneness of the church on the universal level. How can this be done?

The answer to this question is to be found in the right understanding of two things: the synodal system and the ministry of primacy. It seems to me, at least, that in the ecumenical movement these two issues cannot be avoided if the approach of an ecclesiology of communion is adopted.

The first thing that must be emphasized is that, in an ecclesiology of communion, neither synodality nor primacy can be understood as implying structures or ministries standing above the ecclesial community or communities. Only by a structure or a ministry that would involve the community of each local church can synodality and primacy be realities of communion.

The model offered to us by the early church with regard to the synodal structure can be extremely helpful. If we do not wish to copy it, we might at least seek inspiration from it. The substance of the model is to be found in canon 34 of the so-called "Apostolic Canons" (belonging probably to the fourth century C.E.), which provides that in each region the heads of the local churches — the bishops — must recognize one of them — the bishop of the capital city — as *primus (protos)* and do nothing without him. The latter, however, must do nothing without these bishops, so that, the canon concludes, the Triune God may be glorified.

The importance of this model lies in the fact that, through it, synodality and primacy are affirmed in such a way that the fullness and catholicity of each local church, expressed through its bishop, is fully safeguarded. Could this not serve as a guide for the divided Christians in their way to visible unity? Without synodality, unity risks being sacrificed in favour of the local church. But a synodality which suppresses the catholicity and integrity of the local church can lead to ecclesiastical universalism. The same must be said about primacy. Can there be unity of the church without primacy on the local, the regional and the universal level in an ecclesiology of communion? We believe not. For it is through a "head", some kind of "primus" that the "many", be it individual Christians or local churches, can speak with one voice. But a "primus" must be part of a community; not a self-defined, but a truly relational ministry. Such a ministry can only act together with the heads of the rest of the local churches whose consensus it would express. A primacy of this kind is both desirable and harmless in an ecclesiology of communion.

3. Authority in the church is relational

It follows from what has just been said that authority in the church resides not in any office *per se*, but in the event of communion created by the Spirit as the Spirit forms the believers into the body of Christ, both locally and universally. It is traditionally admitted, at least by Roman Catholics and Orthodox, that the highest authority in the church lies in the ecumenical council. But no ecumenical council is authoritative simply as an institution. Reception of its decisions by the local churches is required for it in order to be authoritative. The example of Ephesus 449 and Ferrara-Florence, which possessed all the institutional requirements of an ecumenical council (universal representation, etc.), and yet were not received by the church as a whole, is well known. It is true that without some kind of institution, which would teach and decide authoritatively, there could be no unity in the church. But the final decisions of such an institution must be tested through their reception by the communities before they can claim full and true authority. Like everything else in an ecclesiology of communion, authority must be relational.

This observation applies equally to matters of *doctrine*. Doctrine, too, passes through the body of the church, because the dogmas of the church are not logical propositions to be tested and approved by the minds of the individual believers, but doxological statements to be part of the worship and the life of the communities. The creed is not there for theologians to study, but for communities to sing.

4. Mission in the church is relational

For quite a long time, Christian mission was regarded as a kind of sermon addressed to the world. It is, of course, true that the church is not *of* this world and that the world hates Christ and his church. But the relation of the church to the world is not just negative: it is also positive. This is implied in the incarnation and ideas such as the recapitulation of all in Christ to be found in the Bible (Eph., Col., etc.), and in the fathers (Irenaeus, Maximus, et al.). In the Orthodox tradition, in which the eucharist is so central, the world is brought into the church in the form of the natural elements as well as the everyday preoccupations of the members of the church. If communion is made a key idea in ecclesiology, mission is better understood and served not by placing the gospel over against the world, but by inculturating it in it. Theology must seek ways of *relating* the gospel to the existential needs of the world, to whatever is human — and not only. Instead of throwing the Bible or the dogmas of the church into the face of the world, it would be best to seek first to feel and understand what every human being longs for deep in their being, and then see how the gospel and doctrine can make sense to that longing.

This relationality of mission should not be limited to human beings. It must be extended to include *creation* also in its non-human form. Sensitivity to the integrity of creation has not been traditionally part of the Christian mission. We now realize that it ought to be. The church as koinonia relates also to the animal and the material world as a whole. Perhaps the most urgent mission of the church today is to become conscious of, and proclaim in the strongest of terms, the fact that there is an intrinsic koinonia between the human being and its natural environment, a koinonia that must be brought into the church's very being in order to receive its fullness.

5. Communion in time

The church is not an entity living outside time. Communion is not only a matter of the relatedness of each local church with the rest of the churches in space or with the rest of the world at a given time, but of koinonia with the communities of the past as well as of the future. As far as the past is concerned, the church needs *Tradition* in order to exist as koinonia. When Tradition is itself affected and conditioned by communion, it ceases to be a formal transmission of teaching and life and becomes a reinterpreted and re-received reality in the light of the particular context into which it is transmitted. This makes Tradition acquire the form of traditions (small "t", cf. the fourth Faith and Order world conference at Montreal), and in this way diversity becomes part of the picture. The church in this case must raise the question of what is decisive in discovering Tradition behind or underneath traditions.

The criteria applied by the churches differ and cause great difficulties in achieving full communion. Some think that only whatever is explicit in scripture is the criterion for Tradition. Others see scripture as part of Tradition, which they regard as a broader reality. In an ecclesiology of communion, time is not broken down into past, present and future. The end of time is time redeemed from this kind of brokenness through the intervention of the kingdom between the past and the present. The true criterion of Tradition is, therefore, to be found in the revelation of what the world will be like in the kingdom. As St Maximus the Confessor put it in the seventh century: "The things of the past are shadow; those of the present *eikon*; the truth is to be found in the things of the future." Are we prepared to seek the criteria of Tradition in the vision of the kingdom, and not simply in what has been transmitted to us from the past? Communion in time would require in this case a vision of the kingdom, and the church would be called to be a sign of it in the world.

Similar observations apply to *apostolic succession*. Communion with the apostolic *kerygma* and mission is not just a matter of a chain of ordinations or of keeping the apostolic faith in its original form. Apostolic succession itself passes through the community of the church (hence the requirement that all ordinations should take place in the presence of the community, especially in its eucharistic form); it is a succession of communities and not of individuals, and it is a succession that comes to us via the kingdom as it is portrayed and foretasted in the eucharistic gathering. It is in *this* way that the communities of the past meet those of the present as well as those of the future. Without this meeting there is no true communion.

6. *Communio in sacris*

There can be no full communion without communion in the sacramental life of the church, and above all in the eucharist. "Intercommunion" should be replaced by "communion" in order to do justice to an ecclesiology of communion. Full communion means in the first place eucharistic communion, since the eucharist is the recapitulation of the entire economy of salvation in which past, present and future are united, and in which communion with the Holy Trinity and with the rest of the churches as well as with creation takes place. Baptism, chrismation or confirmation and the rest of the sacramental life are all given *in view of* the eucharist. Communion in these sacraments may be described as "partial" or *anticipatory* communion, calling for its fulfilment in the eucharist. It is not without significance that in many languages, including modern Greek, *koinonia* or communion is a synonym for partaking of the eucharist (*theia koinonia* — holy communion).

These remarks seem to me to echo the significant word "towards" which is found in the theme of this world conference. We are still in a process *towards* full communion which means, finally, eucharistic communion. Communion, however, is the fabric not only of the goal but also of the way towards the goal. If we share nothing already, we cannot hope ever to share everything. And if we wish to move in the right direction, we must never lose sight of the final goal.

Conclusion

Let us now try to draw some concluding points from this modest theological reflection.

1. If we are to seek unity on a stable and healthy basis, we need a sound doctrine of God as Trinity and of the divine economy in Christ in relation to the work of the Holy Spirit. These doctrines are not simply dogmatic formulations for theologians, but indispensable presuppositions for an ecclesiology of communion as well as for all efforts to overcome division with the help of such an ecclesiology. It is crucial, therefore, that there should be essential agreement on faith, particularly with regard to these matters. The progress made in Faith and Order in connection with the project on apostolic faith and the Nicene-Constantinopolitan Creed is very welcome and ought to be deepened further. Trinitarian theology must enter more fully the agenda of Faith and Order. Experience with the Roman Catholic-Orthodox dialogue has shown how important this can be.

2. One of the areas in which the concept of koinonia appears to have considerable potential for ecumenical progress is that of tackling questions of church structure, ministry, authority, etc. As I have tried to suggest here, the concept of communion can help us overcome traditional dichotomies between the institutional and the charismatic, the local and the universal, conciliarity and primacy, etc. This concept, if it is used creatively in ecclesiology, would destroy all legalistic and pyramidal views of ministry, authority and structure in the church, which hinder progress towards unity.

3. The theme of koinonia can add a quality of life and existential relevance to church unity. The church is a relational entity: she is the church "of God" but exists

as the church *of a certain place*. The Christian view of koinonia is inseparably linked with the *koinōnia tōn pathematōn* (communion in the sufferings) of Christ (1 Pet. 4:12-19) for God's world. The love of God the Father and the grace of our Lord Jesus Christ cannot be separated from the koinonia of the Holy Spirit; they form one reality.

These are a few modest reflections on a vast theme. Communion is an inexhaustible subject in theory as well as in life. It reminds us of our ultimate goal as well as of our way to this goal.

NOTE

[1] *Towards Koinonia in Faith, Life and Witness: A Discussion Paper*, Faith and Order paper no. 161, Geneva, WCC, 1993, p.5.

COMMUNION IN FAITH

WOLFHART PANNENBERG

All Christians are united with each other by the one Lord Jesus Christ in a worldwide community. Our faith in the one Lord unites us across all the differences and oppositions that otherwise often divide people — differences between nations and cultures, between classes and races. The one Lord in whom we believe unites us even beyond the divisions that exist between the Christian churches. This is the basis of the ecumenical movement. That Christians wage war against each other — as is happening today in Ireland or in Yugoslavia — is bound to give all of us the feeling of a shameful defeat of our faith. The fact that the differences between our churches still continue to divide us — even though today we recognize each other as Christian sisters and brothers — humiliates us, because it reveals the weakness of our faith. If all of us were more committed to the faith and therefore were united through that faith to the one Lord, then as a united Christian community we could give testimony to the world of the truth of our faith in a new way.

Throughout the world of Christianity there is a need today for a renewal of faith in the new life from God that became apparent in Jesus Christ. There is a need for the renewal of that joyful confidence of faith — which, according to the witness of John, has overcome the world. The period of half-hearted compromise with the spirit of a modernity that departs more and more from Christianity must come to an end. There is no reason why Christians should be afraid that their faith may be intellectually inferior to the spirit of modern culture. Precisely the opposite is true. Contemporary Christians can be confident again that their faith is in alliance with true reason as in the period of the patristic church. Therefore we have no need of any brand of fundamentalism to protect us against experiential evidence of the knowledge of our world and against an unprejudiced investigation of the biblical traditions. What we need is new confidence, the rigour of unabashed trust in the truth of God that nourishes our faith. It is only the vigour of a renewed faith that can overcome the divisions that have occurred in the body of Christianity in the course of past centuries.

Confessing our common faith

The communion with the one Lord that we enjoy through our faith in him unites us within the one body of his church across all our divisions. Communion through the one Lord, however, can only be ascertained through communion in one and the same faith. Christians have to hold in common what they believe, at least the core of it, not only in the worldwide family of Christian churches today, in the entire community of Christians on earth, but also through the process of time, starting from the origins of

---

Prof. Dr Wolfhart Pannenberg (Lutheran) is professor of systematic theology at the University of Munich, Germany.

the church until the parousia of our Lord. The faith of contemporary Christianity cannot be a different faith from that of the apostles and of the fathers of the ancient church. Therefore, even today we express our faith in the words of the fathers of the patristic church, who in the symbol of Nicea and Constantinople summarized the apostolic faith on behalf of the entire Christian community, with a claim to authority for all Christians in every place, but also for all future times until the return of our Lord. This claim has been recognized by the Christian churches over the centuries, in spite of the unjustified and deplorable addition to the affirmation of the third article concerning the procession of the Holy Spirit. This addition, which was unilaterally introduced into the text of the creed by the Western church as from the ninth and tenth century, constituted a break in the union of the faith expressed in its ecumenical symbol and should therefore be abandoned by Western Christianity today. It is the original text of the symbol of Nicea and Constantinople that we have to recognize as the authoritative expression of the unity of faith of the entire community of Christians through the centuries.

The unity of faith does not exclude differences in the form of expressing its affirmations and in the theological interpretation of its content. As early as the apostolic period there were deep differences between various ways of explicating the one faith, differences that became documented in the New Testament writings, for instance in the contrast between the theology of the Johannine writings and the Pauline letters, but also in the different theological perspectives of the individual gospels. In places there are considerable tensions, but these differences are held together by the unity of faith within which each New Testament witness contributed in its own way to the polyphonic abundance of the apostolic witness. Even in the apostolic age, however, the apostles and the churches had to struggle for the unity of faith in order to prevent the differences and tensions in expressing the faith from jeopardizing its unity. This struggle for the unity of faith was continued in later centuries. In the course of events it came to painful separations — where the unity of faith was no longer recognizable. Even today we consider some of these separations as unavoidable, e.g. in the case of the church's struggle with gnosticism and with Arianism. In other cases, however, we have to recognize today that they constituted tragic events in Christian history, separations that could and should have been avoided. These include the separation between the Christian East and West in the eleventh century, but also the separations that occurred in the fifth century after the council of Chalcedon and, later, the break-up of the Western church in the sixteenth century. With regard to the latter cases, better knowledge of the course of events has rendered it increasingly doubtful that these separations were really necessary in order to protect the fundamental truths of the faith. Insufficient awareness of the positions on both sides of the controversy combined with human passions had tragic effects. The entire community of Christians has had to pay for it in the catastrophes of Christian history.

The overcoming of the consequences of these separations has become the principal aim in the ecumenical movement of our century. The restoration of Christian unity is both necessary and possible on the basis of our common faith in the one Lord. The need to restore Christian unity is based on the explicit commandment of our Lord himself and expresses the fundamental importance of unity of all Christians within the one church in faithfulness to her Lord. The possibility of restoring Christian unity exists, however, provided that we contemporary Christians allow the appropriate space for legitimate diversities in theology and liturgical life and administration of the individual churches according to their historical development, rather than mistaking unity in faith for the uniformity in its expression and in the overall institutional structure of the church.

Confessing our common faith *today*

The common Christian faith was expressed in the symbol of Nicea and Constantinople in a way that was to become authoritative for all later periods of the church. As distinct from other symbols of the faith from the patristic periods this text was formulated with the intention and claim to provide a representative summary of the faith for the whole church. This is why the Commission on Faith and Order turned to this ancient document in order to attempt an explication of this text by the combined efforts of delegates from so many member churches. The alternative of producing a common statement on the content of our faith was considered from a contemporary perspective. But such a new symbol of the faith we have in common could never fulfill the function which the symbol of Nicea and Constantinople has had in the life of the church. At best a new symbol of the faith could express a consensus among the contemporary churches but not unambiguously the unity of the faith of the church through the centuries. Each new expression of faith has to be questioned to see whether it expresses the same faith that the church professed through the centuries in the words of the symbol of Nicea and Constantinople. With regard to the efforts to express the faith of the church today by different, supposedly more contemporary words, one may also ask whether such a new confession of faith does not perhaps give expression to a different faith. This need not be, but questions of this kind inevitably arise as soon as a different text is offered in place of the ecumenical symbol of Nicea and Constantinopole as a summary of the faith of the church from the perspective of its contemporary understanding. It is preferable therefore to concentrate on a common explication of the creed of Nicea and Constantinople, in keeping with contemporary insights into its content and with an awareness of the contemporary challenges that all Christians have to meet.

Such an exposition of the symbol of Constantinople should not confine itself to historical intepretation, although a responsible explication must not neglect the historical profile of its wording. The symbol claims to summarize the apostolic faith of the church. Therefore it requires an explication on the basis of the biblical witness to the revelation of God in Jesus Christ that the church proclaims and professes. The focus on the expression of the faith of the church in the ecumenical symbol of Constantinople cannot stand in opposition to the witness of scripture. Rather, the wording of the ecumenical symbol has to be interpreted in the light of that witness. If such an attempt is made, it becomes apparent that many particulars that belong to the witness of scripture do not appear explicitly in the symbol of Constantinople. Thus the symbol does not mention the Pauline doctrine on justification by faith nor the eucharistic liturgy of the church in memory of Jesus' last supper, and the story of Jesus is summarized in the second article with just a few data, focusing on the incarnation, crucifixion and resurrection of the Lord, but without a single word on his baptism by John the Baptist and on his earthly ministry. These are central issues, however, in the Christian faith. Does that mean that the symbol of Constantinople is an incomplete summary of the apostolic faith?

In a sense, a certain incompleteness has to be admitted. If we set out today to summarize the basis and content of the Christian faith, those issues would receive a stronger emphasis. They are not simply absent from the symbol of Constantinople, however, but are present by implication. Thus the entire doctrine on justification is implied in the one sentence on baptism for the forgiveness of sins. The one, holy, catholic and apostolic church is unimaginable without the eucharistic liturgy at the centre of her life. The message of Jesus proclaiming the nearness of the kingdom, and even its being at hand in his own ministry, forms the basis for the profession of the true divinity of Jesus Christ in essential unity with the Father. It is only on the basis of scripture and in the light of its witness that the affirmations of the creed can be properly read and understood.

This is especially true in the case of the new emphases in the Nicene Creed that go beyond what is explicitly said in the scriptures. The famous example is the affirmation of the essential unity of Jesus Christ with the Father. The Trinitarian faith of the church, forming the core of the symbol of Nicea and Constantinople, makes explicit what the biblical affirmations on the presence of the kingdom of God in Jesus of Nazareth and on his relationship as Son to his heavenly Father contain by implication. This is the substantial basis for the emphasis on the incarnation of the eternal Son in the human person of Jesus who was born of Mary and crucified under Pontius Pilate. Do not these affirmations give expression to what Jesus' historical proclamation implied concerning himself, concerning his peculiar authority and the mystery of his own person?

Similar considerations apply to the confession of the true divinity of the Spirit. Here again, the symbol of Constantinople goes beyond the explicit words of the New Testament witnesses. And yet what is said on the Spirit in the New Testament implies that the eternal Father is never without his Spirit. It is well known that the intention of affirming the same thing in relation to the Son was the reason for including a reference to the activity of the Spirit in the very begining of Jesus' life in the second article of the text of Nicea.

The Christian faith: a Trinitarian faith

By its Trinitarian affirmations the church of the fourth century successfully expressed the implications of the apostolic witnesses of the New Testament with regard to the identity of God himself, and there is every reason for contemporary Christianity to reaffirm this Trinitarian faith of the church as expressing the concrete monotheism characteristic of the Christian faith, a concrete monotheism that has proved its spiritual power again in the discussions on the true nature of God in our own times. It is the Trinitarian understanding of God in the symbol of Nicea and Constantinople that secured the ecumenical authority of this symbol in the church. This is because Christians profess the Trinitarian God when they really profess Jesus Christ as their Lord. Professing Jesus cannot be separated from professing his heavenly Father, the God who created heaven and earth, nor can it be separated from professing the Spirit through whom the risen Lord himself is present for his church, and who was in the beginning the origin of life and will reveal to us in the eschatological future the new and imperishable life to which we have been reborn in our baptism.

Professing Jesus Christ has always been a confession of his person, taking sides for Jesus in the public controversy surrounding his person. To those who confess him in this way Jesus himself promised the reward of eternal life. After his death on the cross nobody could then confess Jesus Christ without professing him to be risen from the dead, and nobody could join the church in calling upon her living Lord without professing him as the pre-existent Son of his eternal Father, who became incarnate among us in the form of this one human being. Professing the resurrection of the crucified one and professing the incarnation of the eternal Son in Jesus Christ have become the two main biblical roots that gave rise to the Trinitarian profession of the church as expressed in the ecumenical symbol of Nicea and Constantinople. This symbol is not only the summary of New Testament affirmations of the Christian faith. It professes at the same time the Trinitarian God who was revealed for humanity in Jesus Christ, and who is present through the Spirit in the church of Jesus Christ in order to communicate salvation to all believers. The profession of the Trinitarian God recapitulates the entire content of the symbol, and it is for its sake alone that the individual affirmations of the symbol are important. We cannot profess Jesus without professing the Trinitarian God revealed in him, and vice versa. Only those who confess Jesus Christ, the incarnate and risen Son of the eternal Father, present through the Spirit in the church to bring about eternal life in his believers — only those truly confess the Trinitarian God.

Faith and Order's endeavours to provide a common explication of the ecumenical symbol of Nicea and Constantinople aim at encouraging the contemporary churches to pledge themselves anew in communion with each other to the one Trinitarian God revealed in Jesus Christ, by professing together the words of this symbol. Certainly, many of our member churches use this creed in their liturgies, be it regularly or on particular occasions. But many Christians consider this symbol an ancient formula, the affirmations of which have become strange to them. It needs explication so that we may recognize in the phrases of this symbol the living faith of the church, which is our own faith, too, if we are serious in pledging ourselves to Jesus Christ. A common explication of this symbol by the hitherto-separated churches is required to enable them to recognize in the words of the symbol the unity of the faith that unites us all. On the basis of such a common explication the common profession of this symbol will become an act of common confession in pledging ourselves to the Trinitarian God who was revealed in Jesus Christ. It is a profession that confronts a world that is not yet, or is no longer, prepared to accept the Christian witness to the truth of God, but it is made in the confidence of the unity of faith that unites us Christians in spite of all differences that may otherwise exist among us.

TOWARDS THE REALIZATION OF COMMON LIFE

ELIZABETH TEMPLETON

Common life is about birth and death and all that goes on between. It is about living under the sky, with sun and rain sustaining or destroying. It is about desire fulfilled and frustrated; about the pain and joy of child-rearing; the responsibility of finding bread; the mellowness or bitterness of old age; about war, land, exile, the use and abuse of power.

Common life is about tiredness and singing songs, about making money and playing with children and washing socks. It involves all the concrete diversity of existence summed up by Sartre as "the glory, the horror and the boredom of being human".

We belong to a common world, not just in the accelerated twentieth-century sense of the global village, touched by the winds of Chernobyl, spanned by telecommunications, faced by one ecological menace and orphaned by escalating AIDS — but in the deeper sense that in the humanness of any of us we have to recognize the humanness of each. As Shylock voiced it, against his anti-Semitic environment:

> Hath not a Jew eyes? hath not a Jew hands, organs, dimensions, senses, affections, passions? fed with the same food, hurt with the same weapons, subject to the same diseases, healed by the same means, warmed and cooled by the same winter and summer as a Christian is?

Shakespeare, *The Merchant of Venice*
Act III, scene 1

If Faith and Order has a contribution to make to the life of the world, it is by articulating how this common life is not accident or mere human construct, but gift and invitation, grounded in the communion of God's own life as it reaches out to touch and welcome all that is created, nourished by its access to that life, and finally, we hope, transfigured and purged into inalienable belonging in that context of freedom and love which, clumsily, we name as the kingdom of God.

Deep in the vision and documentation of Faith and Order is the sense that the existence of the church, the vitality of the sacraments and the specificity of apostolic order is about making this affirmation palpable, about tasting, and giving to be tasted, the consummation of all things in the strangeness of God's future, earthed by Christ in the very stuff of the cosmos, and made present to us in the dynamic gift of his Spirit, who opens into their eschatological possibilities all the patternings of being which space and time and culture and history throw up for us.

Nothing much less than such a vision could sustain people through the hours of blood and sweat and toil and tears which go into the construction of ecumenical

---

Ms Elizabeth Templeton is a theologian in the Church of Scotland, Edinburgh.

paragraphs! Nothing else could vindicate the centuries and decades of wrestling, across massive gulfs of tradition and language, to achieve the recapitulation of past divisions in shared ecumenical documents like *Baptism, Eucharist and Ministry*, or *Church and World*. The jet-polluted air and the despoiled forests on which we produce our pre-millennial utterances demand contrition, unless our work contributes to the real credibility of that hope.

But does it?

The present situation: a challenge to Faith and Order

My experience of the dedication and passion of ecumenical encounter at all the levels I have been privileged to share makes clear to me that cynicism is an unworthy response. The easy criticism that ecumaniacs fiddle while multiple Romes burn recognizes nothing of the depth of desire for a manifest earthing of the koinonia of God, and of commitment to that.

Yet not necessarily in cynicism, but in sadness and sometimes in desperation, the world in which our common life is lived asks us how on earth what we are doing can be seen as constructive of a shared future. Where is the touchdown, what French airline notices call the *atterrissage*?

For we live in a world where dogma, faith, religious identity are bound up with some of the most dehumanizing situations of our planet; where Christians kill and rape Muslims in the former Yugoslavia, apparently only because they are Muslims; where the Middle East and Ireland and the Sudan and countless other places seem to fragment because of self-identifications which are in part religiously partisan. To many who watch this from the outside, and even to some who live inside the hope that the church exists to heal creation, this is an almost unbearable irony. For, de facto, our actual ecclesiastical institutions and traditions manifest themselves as obstacles to the unity of peoples rather than as signal of it. De facto, the sacramental practice we observe, instead of anchoring the whole earth in the communion of God, seems to reserve his generosity for a *part* of it, conditional upon right belief, right practice or right discipline. Even the Trinitarian horizon of Christian faith, instead of meeting and challenging the world's yearning with its own immeasurable enlargement, becomes, as heard, a cramping dogma, a shibboleth, an elitist Christian password to which most of the earth has no access.

To suggest therefore that *Baptism, Eucharist and Ministry*, if it could only find a way to resolve the remaining internal questions documented in the volumes of responses, would thereby have elucidated the form of our common life, seems to me to under-estimate the credibility- and communication-gap we have to bridge, those of us who invest energy and hope in the Faith and Order process.

I am not speaking merely about the obvious and perennial gaps between theory and practice which blot church history. Most adults who live in the world with their eyes open know that we live, institutionally as well as individually, *simul iustus et peccator*, that vision and aspiration often exceed capacity to sustain; and that we walk a knife-edge between proper self-forgiveness and the exploitation of cheap grace.

So the challenge to Faith and Order is not just the challenge of a naive utopianism, nor the impatience of a mortally foreshortened perspective on the things of eternity. (Though some, indeed, might be tempted to retort that professional ecumenicals are temperamentally disposed to over-estimate the patience of God, and loathe to hear the urgency of one who was hungry for figs on the tree even out of season!)

I overhear a deeper malaise sometimes, among churchmen and -women who have devoted lives to ecumenical communication, that they doubt whether, in principle, Faith and Order can deliver the goods for the church, let alone for the world's common life. It seems to me that we must not brush this critique aside as malicious or superficial, even if, in the long run, we resist it. For if our documents are to move off the page and out of the conference to vibrate in that shared life, then we have to grapple with several issues in what I would call the *apologetics of ecumenism*.

By that I do not mean the process which our presentation-conscious world calls *packaging*. I mean engagement with the deep scepticism there is about the methods and processes of formal ecumenical theology, most specifically when that means doctrinal exchange and ecclesiastical negotiation about mutual recognition.

The search for new methods

The very structuring of this conference title expresses the traditional priorities: first faith, then life, and then witness. And faith is elaborated doctrinally, certainly with constant reference to the cries of the world for peace and justice, and in commitment to spelling out the shared faith in diakonia and lives of costly reconciliation. But still, whether we share the same faith is tested by whether we can use the same sentences to affirm what we believe.

I think there is a great risk in this — that we commit, albeit at a more sophisticated level, the error of all fundamentalism, and perhaps all confessionalism, of confusing our statements about God with God himself. Supposing the whole world were struck dumb tomorrow. Would our common life cease? Of course not! Would we be incapable of worship? Of course not! Would we be less vulnerable to the splits in human community which arise because of difference of endowment or greed or competition or fear or diverse aesthetic sensibilities or the absence of a sense of humour? I doubt it! Would we be further from a common faith? I suspect not!

Even in a speaking world, we register often enough that it is sometimes easier to share deep life with those who do not share our credal or confessional positions than with some who do. It was a poet, a lover of words, who registered the pathos of our speaking:

> Words strain,
> Crack and sometimes break, under the burden,
> Under the tension, slip, slide, perish,
> Decay with imprecision, will not stay in place,
> Will not stay still.
>   T.S. Eliot, *Four Quartets, Burnt Norton*, V

This is not to argue that words are to be reckoned a handicap; an irony that would be indeed for a faith which has *word* as a central category! But it is a real question whether, when words get in the way of life, they become demonic. And I think we have not yet articulated in a way which is convincing to the outside world why it *matters* twopence whether or not you believe in the *filioque*, or whether you think that churches need bishops, or can admit women into the apostolic succession of clerical priesthood.

When people overhear such debates, they think, more or less sympathetically: "There goes a group of human beings defending its identity against violation." If they are one kind of person, they think that it's important to have such boundaries defined in black and white, so that people know where they are with one another and with God. If they're another kind of person, they wish the boundaries weren't there, or believe them to be a regressive tendency in human beings, inimical to the openness of God and unfaithful to his inclusiveness.

Certainly, within all our churches, both responses are found, complicated of course by the fact that some identify the separating creeds and confessions and practices of sacramental life with God's self-revelation, while others find that idolatrous. This division does not align denomination against denomination, but marks a more subtle and, I suspect, a more problematic fault-line which cuts through all our communities of faith.

This fault-line has on the one side people who believe that, whatever disputes remain about doctrine, order, praxis, they are trivial in the light of the confidence that we *are* one in Christ, and that we could and should be already exploring that confidence in sacramental life, exchangeable ministry and common service. On the other side are those who find it mere pious or sentimental fiction that we are all one, until we can wrestle into concrete agreed articulation what we believe, how we structure our discipline and liturgical life, and sanction our practice in the light of God's self-disclosure. None of the affirmations about rich and legitimate diversity clarifies what it is, but the hidden fault-line is not far below the theological crust.

It must be a major part of Faith and Order's agenda to expose, explain and, if possible, close this fault-line. For, unless it can be closed, common ecclesiological life in this pre-eschatological world seems impossible. Yet I have a niggling fear that the more successful Faith and Order is in producing celebrated texts like *BEM* or *Confessing the One Faith*, the more the fault-line is going to be masked — rather like the twigs and grass which cover the hole in the ground from the unsuspecting boar, but cannot bear the weight of his charge! (For who, longing for unity, and knowing anything of the delicate, painful, dedicated work, not to speak of the time and money that go into ecumenical dialogue, is going to abandon hope that the next document might just close the fault-line by a millimetre, until, millimetre by slow millimetre, we stand on common ground.)

And yet there are yawning distances in perception and reception of the faith we share which will not be closed by these carefully-negotiated texts until we can fill in more of the holes from the bottom up.

Some specific challenges

Let me, in closing, name some of the "holes" about which we have to be candid if we are to find that there is solid ground for us to walk on together. And I hope they are named not in a spirit of destructiveness, but so that we may face the challenge which the French call *reculer pour mieux sauter*.

1. There is the "hole" identified by liberation theologians, among others, namely that theological method is distorted if it works from exegesis and authoritative tradition

to praxis, and not the other way round. Our working document for this conference clearly takes on board the rich lesson of that voice, demanding that all true doctrine must have a palpable bearing on how we stand in solidarity with the poor, the marginalized, the unloved. But it does not quite hear the sharpness of it, the conviction of many who live each day with the slenderest hold on life, that it doesn't matter a fig whether you subscribe to the doctrine of the Trinity, or affirm the hypostatic union, provided that you give yourself to the struggle for justice, peace and a sustainable future for the whole earth.

2. Nor does it grasp the nettle of the conspicuous fact that most of the traditional Faith and Order issues have been tabled by the relatively powerful presence of those who are predominantly male, predominantly clerical, predominantly European in thought-form, predominantly with most control of, and most investment in, the disintegrating structures of Christendom. I have little time for conspiracy theories of theology; and it is part of my hope against hope that ecumenism involves us in so entering one another's being and life that *representation* is redefined, not in these disgusting terms of quota allocations per category — male, female, young, old, lay, clerical — but in terms of the learning of each, from whatever place, to make *his* or *her very own* the humanness of the other, so that to make any decision which excludes or constrains them is like losing one's own life. (It is, for example, in this context that we properly carry together the ecclesiological question about women's ordination into the threefold ministry, not in terms of a power-struggle between winners and losers on that issue.)

3. Yet while the intentionality of the Faith and Order movement is, at its best, i.e. at its most free and loving, not to do with power, but with truth and fidelity responsive to God's initiative, we *do* all have considerable skill at spotting other people's specks of ecumenical manipulation while ignoring our own domestic planks. We must face the kind of culture-shocks which so rocked the Canberra assembly, *the outrageous questions to our own cultural presuppositions* which arise from letting people speak in their own idiom, especially if that relativizes idioms about which we have become complacent.

4. Most specifically, I think that the Montreal recognition of the area of hermeneutics as one demanding more attention has not yet been boldly enough addressed, though everyone is aware of it, and hit-and-run references pepper the BEM text and the work on the Nicene Creed. But there is a long way to go here. I suspect it is still unintelligible to some Christians why others believe that what is called the *historical-critical method* should be taken seriously. It is unintelligible to others how it can be dismissed. And to yet others, that whole debate is as irrelevant as the angels-on-pinheads controversy. Until we not only understand, but can stand in one another's shoes on that deep procedural question, I wonder if our substantial doctrinal consensus can bear much pressure.

In all this, of course, I have to acknowledge and can only offer the perspective of my own theological training and ecclesiastical formation: European, academic and Reformed; though I have had enough ecumenical benediction to know that I owe my survival in Christian life to more exuberant explorations of the love and freedom of God.

It is because we do sometimes taste in theological encounter the quickening of love and enlargement of imagination which are the real raison d'etre of Faith and Order that we must resist both the abuse of doctrine as an ecclesiastical straitjacket for our common life and the dismissal of it as a footnote to ethics. We are wrestling together with the mystery of the church as a vehicle of life for the world, and of dogma and concrete form as vehicles of life for the church. But these are not self-evident truths, and they often look like falsehoods. To test their reality in the teeth of the world's pain, in the complex opening of interfaith engagement, and in the robust suspicion of those who think, inside and beyond the church, that theology is a menace, is a task to keep Faith and Order in business. But not, I hope, with a sense of leisure. For our own redundancy might be a signal of the kingdom's immanence, at least if it meant that we had discovered the unconditionality of the common life we are charged with as stewards of God's future.

KOINONIA IN WITNESS

METROPOLITAN GEORGES OF MOUNT LEBANON

Witnessing together arises out of our being together. Since apostolic times churches, such as Corinth, united by the tradition of the apostles and the breaking of bread, have, through their internal divisions, produced a counter-witness. Even more so, the churches which have experienced divisions, from the schism of the fifth century until the Reformation, are apparently unable to show forth the power of their love to the world, thus obscuring the face of the Lord. What then can be the meaning, apart from common action, of communion in witness?

Love is a reality which is beyond all knowledge and which determines it. In the first letter of John we find a perfect correlation between communion with God, doing the truth, communion with one another, knowledge, abiding in God, obedience to the new commandment, and victory over the world. In fact, the originator and locus of witness is the Holy Spirit itself. If we are together the bearers of the Spirit, we are manifesting in community the life of the Trinity. The Spirit seals our unity and makes us into a single manifestation of God. Now, that only becomes possible if believers, drawn close to one another in love, attain to the full flowering of their understanding, which enables them to enter into the mystery of God (Col. 2:2). It is through sharing in this mystery that we can work "so that the body of Christ may be built up until we all reach unity in the faith and in the knowlege of the Son of God and become mature, attaining to the whole measure of the fullness of Christ" (Eph. 4:12-13, NIV). This progression towards being the church in the sense of a community in communion takes place through a vision of the mystery of the church as a place where people look forward in expectation to the full light (not a half light) and to the feast where the two parousias come together — an impossibility in our present divided state.

We do not approach the world together in a joint planned cooperative effort. It is rather identity of being in the eucharist, which is a sign of our common faith, that forms in us the same face with identical features and enables us to present that same face to the world. The divine nature, in which we share by constantly ascending, in creating our identity creates our unity. It is not simply our minds which are enlightened by the gospel teachings, but our hearts which are purified by being liberated from human passions. "The divine light itself received into the very foundation of my being and yours exhibits henceforth the energy common to God and his elect," says St Maximus the Confessor, "or, rather, there is from now on only God alone in the measure in which, as befits love, he invades with God's whole being the whole being of his elect."

Metropolitan Georges (Khodr) is metropolitan of Mount Lebanon, Lebanon (Patriarchate of Antioch). This paper was translated from the French by the WCC Language Service.

Koinonia: God's creation

God thus creates koinonia between those believers whom he is already glorifying, to whatever church they belong. Koinonia in witness is the characteristic of an ecclesial community constituted in God himself. Unity in action is a consequence of unity of vision. The world is sensitive only to perfection of life, from wherever it comes. That by no means relativizes the importance of dogma as a sign of orthodoxy in the faith and as the normal soil in which holiness grows. But the Spirit blows where the Spirit wills and holiness in the sense of enlightenment and glorification can be received by all people everywhere. The body of Christ is comprised of the sum total of those men and women who have attained in the mystery to the communion of the Holy Spirit. If we wish for a patristic definition of the church, we could say that it is the whole community of deified human beings, who, because they have become impassible to human passions, have become the abode of the most holy Trinity. They have entered into the internal life of the Trinity, according to the words of our Lord: "No one knows the Son except the Father, and no one knows the Father except the Son and those to whom the Son chooses to reveal him" (Matt. 11:27). The process is thus: Jesus, rooted eternally in the vision of the Father, appoints us witnesses "through the Spirit of holiness... with power" (Rom. 1:4) in that we share already in resurrection from death. Witness given solely in identical spoken words carries no weight. If the flesh of witnesses does not become a word transforming the whole person eucharistically, then no message is transmitted. Even in the Old Testament, the word was never external to the prophet. The prophet's personality was transfigured by the word, which became breath within him. That is why all prophets have their own feast days and their own icons.

Our witness becomes God's witness to the extent that we renounce ourselves. That is why, if the church becomes the community of the meek, it will remove the veil from the face of Jesus, who, by his death, was constituted both Lamb of God and Shepherd. That is why the church becomes a prophetic sign ultimately only by martyrdom. The great Russian philosopher Vladimir Soloviev goes further and places the unity of the church in the future in an eschatological vision. In *Three Conversations* and *Narrative on the Antichrist* the three principal characters symbolize, as their names suggest, the three major Christian families: Catholic, Orthodox and Protestant. After being killed by the antichrist they are raised from death together and restore the unity which had been lost. I think that the basic difference between prophecy under the old covenant and under the new covenant in Christ is that our Lord only fully became a prophet by his death. Similarly, by renouncing violence, the church recovers its femininity, in which it surrenders to Jesus and receives the breath of his Spirit.

The church sent out into the world calls the world to what it has itself tasted, i.e., the joy of having lived with Jesus in the wedding chamber. Because of these mystic nuptials, it experiences opposition to the world, in the Johannine sense. The kingdom it inaugurates creates a break in the fabric of history. There is a veritable denial of the present age when the "cloud of witnesses" who live in it, in their denial of idolatry, proclaim to it the promise of the age to come. God's action in history is not simply the passage of time, but a succession of divine manifestations in the loyalty of the Spirit to itself in the midst of history's unpredictability. It is here that the inspiration of prophecy operates against the demonic forces at work in the world. It is tragic that sin is simply described and analyzed as a mere human weakness and no longer as seduction by the serpent, the source of human disintegration leading to death.

There is also, however, the world viewed as a harmonious and beautiful paradise, according to our Lord's words, "God so loved the world that he gave his one and only Son" (John 3:16). It is poetry, revelation, a divine book, a manifestation of the eternal wisdom of God and of diakonia, an inexhaustible source of that culture which leads to virtue (as Origen put it), and of that refinement which takes us to the threshold of the kingdom, despite the ambiguity of culture and our insatiable thirst for beauty. Viewed thus, church and world are not two separate spaces nor do they belong to two different ages. The church, aware of Jesus' love for it, travels as a pilgrim through time and space. Its only location is in the world. That is why Origen correctly wrote: "Christ is the cosmos of the church and the church is the cosmos of the cosmos." Thus understood, the church is not placed over against the world. Nor is it in the world. The world is in the church. The church is its logos, its meaning. The church leads the world to its destiny, because she can understand it and become the place where it is transfigured.

The world lives by the mystery of the church because of the saving remnant. A considerable number of Christians are faithless, but the remnant live in expectation of the kingdom and recreate the world. The kingdom is a treasure which is often hidden, but there is a witness of silence, of singing, of indescribable zeal by ardent individuals wounded by the love of Jesus with a wound which, according to Ibn Arabi of Andalusia, will never heal. In certain countries where Christians are a minority there has been no apparent strong Christian presence in their history. But the gospel has been lived out there in a daily communal confession of faith, and non-Christians testify in their literature to what they have received from this evangelical poverty which was truly present.

There are periods when God visits God's people and faith increases, when people's perception of the divine mysteries is sharpened, when there is a more intense thirst for God's word. The church takes on a new beauty and the world sees this beauty and slowly and imperceptibly changes. One could say that the world is at present caught up in a destructive self-sufficiency. It establishes its own moral values, which do have, however, a certain link with the gospel. But, clearly, the Spirit has its own ways in a society which is developing its own civilization without Christian language and symbols and is totally alien to the mystery of death and the hope of resurrection.

Christian witness: challenges for the future

Re-evangelization of the post-Christian world will not ignore the legitimate development of science and technology, of freedom and of human rights, but will exercise vigilance arising out of a critical understanding of the mythology of developed societies. Such societies have also an irrational element in them and are experiencing decadence in the form of racial discrimination, exploitation of the third world and applying double standards in their dealings with the South. If the churches do not break out of this Machiavellianism of secure power, Christian witness is doomed to be sterile. The presence in non-Christian countries of foreign Christians who have been arrogant and powerful has been a failing and an error for the local people associated with them. Moreover, peoples who have gained independence are hardly ever attracted by Christianity. It thus seems to me that mission and indeed the dialogue associated with it are no longer effective. Social change is seen as a secular task in the context of international solidarity and no longer as an expression of the gospel. At the present day, we do not know how to fulfil the Lord's command: "Go and make disciples of all nations" (Matt. 28:19). But that great commission of Jesus remains a definite command, and, whatever may be our understanding of other faiths and their possible place in God's purpose, Christ remains the one way to the Father. The eschatological encounter with the followers of the various religions will take place in him.

Obviously, organized mission is not conceivable in those vast regions of the world where religious freedom is not recognized and the weight of a majority-established religion rules out any conversion. Christian witness is, however, not unknown even in such places. It is seen as people live together, work as citizens together, in art, literature and the genuine piety of simple folk. Real gospel values are shared. Dialogue, whether at an elementary or academic level, opens up minds and hearts to an imperfect but real perception of the truth of the gospel.

In such openness Christians of all confessions are engaged together if they offer the same essential witness. In pluralist societies Christians are not interested in our dogmatic differences. Those who live on the frontier are free of all political allegiances which alienate non-Christians from them, particularly if Christianity is seen as a turning in on oneself, or if it is presented as an extreme assertion of identity. Sharing in the culture of the nation, being subject to the same trials as one's fellow citizens can make the message heard. Christians achieve credibility by their confident commitment to justice and peace out of a desire for national and social liberation, and not by simply struggling for their own exclusive rights as Christians. Love proves itself in dialogue in the form of shared lives.

Dialogue for truth can be established. Christian adherence to Christ as the truth should not obscure the truths scattered in the religious traditions surrounding them. All these truths spring from the same divine source. We should welcome all spiritual life-giving nourishment, not as a human word but as bread from heaven. All discourse resists different discourse, and all scriptures resist different scriptures. That is why the aim of dialogue is above all, by going beyond religious traditions, to seek the divine truth latent beneath different words and symbols. That is not to relativize the Christian messsage: it is not syncretism, it is the same Christ we worship as he journeys through the infinite spaces of other religions. This requires us to have a kenotic attitude. Kenosis is witness without words and can be fruitful.

In dialogue the church opens up, goes deeper and comes to know itself. Dialogue is not a didactic or tactical means to incorporate others into the church. It is in any case the only contact possible in a pluralist society. Even in countries historically Christian, atheism, mysticism and sects have become traditions which are religious in nature so that direct mission, in the form of attacking the objects of their worship, is no longer valid. Christians create the world inwardly by the power of the Spirit. Renewed by this same Spirit they share in the common task of humankind. They will go in pilgrimage through all created things, all history, with an inward freedom, charmed by the face of Christ. It is only by belonging passionately to the world and the kingdom that Christians will be able to expand the world so that it assumes the infinite dimensions of the kingdom. We do not gain the kingdom by turning aside from the world. The world will never be saved except by the entire power of the coming Christ. This creative tension is the secret of those who witness.

☐ Plenary discussion

In the discussion a total of fifteen persons spoke. Particular approval was expressed for Metropolitan John's articulation of "unity-in-diversity" (strikingly, Prof. Pannenberg in introducing his paper had said that Metropolitan John had presented an ecclesiology with which he would not take issue on a single point). Several speakers responded favourably to Bishop Tutu's call for a greater emphasis upon prayer and spirituality, even as we engaged in work for justice and peace. His proposal for a day of fasting to express our support of those who suffer from oppression and need was widely commended. One speaker asked for clarification of Metropolitan Khodr's statements on spirituality in relation to religions other than Christianity.

Other speakers addressed the treatment of koinonia in the presentations. One speaker felt that the approach which he had so far experienced in the world conference was too "rational", with too little emphasis upon the experiential and spiritual, and encouraged study of specific efforts to achieve koinonia, for example in the "post-denominational" situation of the churches in China. Another speaker expressed approval that the conference was not only analyzing the theme of koinonia, but also exploring how churches and Christians are struggling to *live* koinonia in their distinctive situations. A third warned against using koinonia too generally, thus avoiding "the more difficult issues of structural and visible unity". The importance of baptism in relation to koinonia was stressed.

Two speakers encouraged the conference to face squarely the question of eucharistic sharing. One spoke of the continuing pain of being excluded from the eucharist, a pain which is all the "more intense and widespread because of the deeper koinonia [now] existing in a wider circle of Christians". There was, he said, a proper impatience arising from the inclusive hospitality extended by Jesus himself, from the power of the gospel to breach fundamental barriers (such as that between Jews and Gentiles — as our study of Galatians was showing), and from the fact that (as we learn from the Orthodox) in the eucharist, "all human alienation is overcome". Another speaker, stating that our expression of the faith is already "compromised by divisions between rich and poor, higher and lower castes, black and white", emphasized the importance of defining "boundaries within which different expressions of the apostolic faith are acceptable".

One speaker challenged what was taken to be general assumptions lying behind the various papers with regard to creeds, ministries, sacraments, and the parousia. Christians in some traditions, such as Quakers, understand these realities differently (for example "they believe in Christ's realized eschatological presence with us [here and now], not in a 'second coming'"), and this perspective needs to be more widely acknowledged within the ecumenical movement.

In a challenging but also moving and gracious speech a delegate from a Spanish Protestant church drew attention to the difficulty felt by many at a hymn of St James sung in the opening worship; though (he was sure) the intention had not been to give offence, the song was heard by many as triumphalist and unecumenical. He went on to point to the need for the reconciliation of memories of past alienations and hostilities.

Calls were heard for further work in several areas: ecumenical hermeneutics, the church in relation to Israel, the European "conquest" of the Americas remembered particularly in 1992, and the recent Roman Catholic statement on communion. There was an appeal for closer cooperation between Faith and Order and work within the World Council of Churches on mission and evangelism; this was important in relation to "a time of renewal and evangelism — not proselytism — in secularized Europe". Through a heartfelt testimony, the conference was reminded of the long association of the Russian Orthodox Church with the Faith and Order movement, and the church's present witness within a complex and difficult situation.

V

The Future
of the Ecumenical Movement

☐ Introduction

The conference turned its attention to the future prospects for the ecumenical movement in plenary IX, 10 August, 11h.30, moderator Dr Mary Tanner presiding; and plenary XI, 12 August, 11h.15, vice-moderator Ms Veronica Swai presiding.

In plenary IX Dr Tanner introduced Dr Anna Marie Aagaard, who delivered one of three **papers** on the future of the ecumenical movement. The second was presented by His Eminence Edward Idris Cardinal Cassidy, while the third came in the form of a **Message** from Archbishop Iakovos of North and South America.

(The archbishop having been prevented by illness from attending the world conference, his text was read to the conference by the Rev. Dr Milton Efthimiou. The moderator emphasized that as Faith and Order sent Archbishop Iakovos best wishes for his health and strength it was also grateful for his recent initiative, "The Archbishop Iakovos Endowment Fund for Faith and Order". The purpose of this programme is to raise funds for the Faith and Order programmes of both the World Council of Churches and the National Council of the Churches of Christ in the USA. The moderator then invited Bishop James Matthews to address the conference. Bishop Matthews explained the origins, process and goals of this important project, emphasizing how it hoped, by securing a sound financial basis for Faith and Order work, to contribute to the cause of Christian unity.)

In plenary XI Ms Swai introduced three further **papers** on the theme of the future of the ecumenical movement. The first was by the Rt Rev. Dr S.B. Joshua, the second by the Rev. Dr Rena Weller Karefa-Smart. The third was brought by a team representing the younger theologians and other younger participants in the world conference. The presenters included Mag. Phil. Christian A. K. Ayivi, Ms Claudia Bruweleit, Mr Stylianos Tsobanidis, the Rev. Flora Winfield and Lic. Dalila C. Nayap-Pot.

REALITIES, POSSIBILITIES — AND THE WILL

ANNA MARIE AAGAARD

In the city of Hamburg there was recently an exhibition of contemporary art. The pieces were named "figurations". These astonishing constructions were built of familiar and well-known elements, but something was shaking, and shaking up, the visitors' reading of everyday material and objects. The visions and realities of a technological world had led painters and sculptors to create artforms intended to make the spectators react, and I take the title of the exhibition, "Post Human", to be a provocation. The art was meant to make us aware that we were standing here, now, with these human feelings of dizziness, curiosity and sometimes revulsion, that we were standing at crossroads between possibilities, realities and our will. The artforms raised questions about what *may* happen in a future world in the light of what *can* happen; but at the same time it helped cast out paralyzing fears by pointing to the present: you are standing *here*, with your reactions. Ideological, "happy-end" scenarios of the future have gone. The present is ambiguous, but not fixed. Things might get worse, but they can also get better. Nothing is too late, even if it may be high time.

The exhibition read our turbulent times as configurations of possibilities, realities and will. And that makes sense, not just in abstract theories but also in the real world, where stability and chaos, new vistas and old preferences, constantly intersect in politics as well as in science and in culture. We do experience a poly-centred, shifting world with no single, overarching world-view, belief system or political ideology.

Instead of bemoaning these facts the artists lifted up the human responsibility to construct and to build, and thus to make new configurations emerge. They pointed to our responsibility to find new ways of combining (on the one hand) the will to give the present — and hence the future — a chance with (on the other hand) the real and the possible.

I have chosen to introduce some musings on the ecumenical movement by referring to the Hamburg exhibition because it might help us to understand both facts and fictions about the ecumenical situation if we borrow that exhibition's reading of history, and interpret the ecumenical movement as configurations of possibilities, hard realities and will.

"And yet it moves"

One of the pieces at the exhibition made the visitors see a man standing in a corner. Another man, seated on an airport scooter — one of those little vehicles that whisks people down those long corridors — was passing him. The head of that hurrying driver

---

Dr Anna Marie Aagaard (Lutheran) teaches systematic theology at the University of Aarhus, Denmark. She is a president of the World Council of Churches.

was transparent, like glass. On the floor there was a road-sign: the sign for danger. An easy, one-dimensional interpretation would take this work of art to suggest a humanity moving, with faces turned away and with empty heads, towards unacknowledged abysses. But who placed that danger sign, and what if the driver stopped the scooter? What would happen if the man in the corner became aware of the scooter, and decided to turn around? The interpretation is open-ended.

It is possible for a congregation or a church to "stand in a corner", like the first man in that work of art, and claim that the ecumenical movement is in crisis. Nothing moves — because nothing moves here in our corner. We are not moving, and we do not want to move. But this is an inadequate attitude. The artist makes us understand that it is a fiction. The man on the scooter moves, and hence also the standing man is made a part of a new whole, a new configuration.

Standing in the "corners" of inherited traditions and ecclesiastical business as usual is, indeed, the intended — or unintended — reality of most Christians in the world. But because a minority of Christians and churches respond to the call to discipleship by moving towards koinonia in faith, life and witness then the Christians and churches who stand "in the corner" also become parts of new configurations of churches and traditions. New configurations do emerge, and no tradition and no church can count itself unaffected, although these configurations may sometimes be unwanted and sometimes be generated behind somebody's back. The idea of ecumenical "corner-standing" is an illusory fiction, because possibilities of witness, the realities of Christian cultures, and the will to heed the call to be faithful disciples of Christ constantly rub against each other. Something new emerges, and whatever the vocabulary (whether we speak of imperfect, wounded or impaired koinonia) — these new configurations are indeed real.

When the British and Irish Anglican churches and the Nordic and Baltic Lutheran churches articulate a common understanding of the nature and purpose of the church, and now move towards formalizing their relationship, a new configuration is emerging, a new relationship that will effect the traditions which are involved.

Because somebody moves, because new configurations are manifested in common worship of the Triune God and in common witness which is both truthful and relevant to the painful struggles of the human community, the inherited ecclesial traditions also undergo change, become renewed, tested and sorted out. Ecclesial traditions are never merely "corner-standing" givens. They are complicated processes of construction, reception, and human relationships. Through these processes inherited ways of obeying the gospel become influenced by the emergence of a deepened koinonia manifested in common prayer, in common service of the destitute and the despairing, and in common endeavours to clarify the Christian faith. And conversely: if the new configurations within the people of God are realities of grace and faith, then they are emerging from the koinonia-generating ways of renewing the tradition in order to live in Christ's way in a brutal world. If new configurations are spiritual realities of faith, and not merely theological make-believe or conglomerates of social programmes, then they emerge from the living faith handed on in eucharistic communities which dare to become involved in the present agonies of humankind, communities in which the ultimate questions raised by ecological disasters, spiritual voids and angry violence challenge the traditional ways of living and probing the gospel.

And so: the ecumenical movement is not at a stand-still, in spite of the magnitude of the unfinished ecumenical tasks. Because the issues of world and humanity are no fictions, because the living faith in eucharistic communities makes disciples respond and new configurations of koinonia emerge, both traditions and the ecumenical movement move.

Clear heads

Let me return to the work of art at the Hamburg exhibition. The head of the moving man, the driver of that scooter, was transparent. But was it an empty head? or was it the clear head of one who knows what he is doing?

Much criticism of the ecumenical movement claims that it has lost its focus in an empty-headed proliferation of programmes, organizations and one-issue concerns which are unrelated to any model of the unity we seek. So many are moving towards the achievement of particular goals, but where is the willingness to be challenged by a wider community? Where is the acknowledgment of being a part of a configuration of communities?

True it is that there are many different responses to the ecumenical calling; but instead of lamenting the fact, ecumenical instruments (and among them Faith and Order) need to foster a clear-headed conversation on catholicity. I am neither suggesting a repeat of Uppsala 1968 and its section report on "The Holy Spirit and the Catholicity of the Church",[1] nor making a plea for yet another round of abstract unity-diversity discussions. What I am after is a theological reflection on the catholicity expressed in the real and concrete configurations of communion which already exist in prayer and praxis, in worship and ministry, and in the commitment to explore further ways in which that already-existing communion may be expressed authentically.

Catholicity is predicated of existing, particular realities; it is a concrete term, and not an ideal or a hope for an eschatological future. The Uppsala assembly described it as "the quality by which the church *expresses* the fullness, the integrity, and the totality of life in Christ".[2] But neither the Uppsala assembly, nor any other contemporary ecumenical document I know of, have claimed that catholicity has been manifested in an unsurpassable way at any given point in time or in any given tradition. Catholicity involves an imperative: *to express*, in this complex and savage world, the wholeness of the unifying grace of the Holy Spirit which unites the disciples of Christ in faith and diakonia. Catholicity is an analogous rather than an univocal concept. It can only be predicated of particular, historical expressions of the full, divine gift which is received.

But this implies that the cultural traditions, the heterogeneous social universes of an unfair and unjust world, the various forms of piety, and the different clues used to interpret both world and gospel, all become the material in which the gift of catholicity takes shape.

If the eyes of faith cannot see any new configurations of which catholicity may be predicated because they — in their particular, sometimes awkward and stumbling, ways — express in some measure the gift of the fullness of grace, then the ecumenical movement is indeed a fiction. If new realities of communion do not, in fact, exist, then ecumenical instruments like the Faith and Order Commission are superfluous structures; but if they do exist, then we need to focus on ways of:

— recognizing the expressions of catholicity;

— discerning the impact of these expressions on the inherited understandings of catholicity as a mark of God's church;
— and helping the new configurations clarify, test and express authentically the communion which they already live.

To be specific: common worship and prayer is a matrix in which communion emerges. In praise of God and in prayer for the coming of the kingdom we receive the gift of reconciliation and the courage to live what we pray in intercessions for the killed and the crying. Unless all such gathering together is considered a frivolous hoax, it expresses the gift of catholicity in particular ways which are shaped by the concrete features of traditions, pieties, cultures, pains and aspirations. It has often enough been claimed that it is in worship and prayer that the emergent realities of a deeper and fuller communion are expressed most authentically. And there is much liturgical material which justifies this claim. But *what* is it that new configurations affirm together, in however-unusual liturgical language? Who are, and where are, the clear-headed ecumenical instruments which help to study, test and clarify the understanding of faith, the use of Bible and tradition, and the contours of ecclesiology and ethics herein embedded? And where is the funding for such undertakings?

Another point: ecumenical history is full of examples of failed attempts to keep Faith and Order and Life and Work, ecclesiology and ethics, together. There is a history of focusing *either* on doctrinal traditions *or* on a common praxis for the sake of humanizing a world torn by racism, discrimination, hunger, greed and outright atrocities. I consider it a "must" that ecumenical instruments go beyond general affirmations of the church as a "moral community" and begin to find out, test and clarify how the concrete involvement in particular struggles of the human community generates koinonia, enlightens doctrine, and shapes specific ways of expressing the undivided gift of God's grace. *Costly Unity*, the report from the 1993 JPIC/Faith and Order consultation on koinonia in Rønde, Denmark, suggests that:

> The WCC should continue to consider the ways different traditions express in their ecclesiologies binding and shaping approaches to ethical questions...[3]

But then it goes on to say:

> This process should, however, be directly linked to local experiences of the interconnectedness of faith and action and move between an investigation of the moral substance of traditions and the moral experience of the people of God today.[4]

Clarifying the linkage between ecclesiology and ethics cannot be done in an abstract way. Only empty heads — empty as opposed to clear — can overlook or ignore the new configurations of koinonia.

My third point is much more controversial. If the new koinonia-configurations are not fictions, but evident to the eyes of reasoned faith, the Faith and Order Commission must begin reconsidering the Toronto declaration.

> [The] Toronto [declaration] remains an important tool for reflection, but questions were raised about its *adequacy* (its "negative affirmations have stood the test of time better than its "positive" ones), its *scope* (though ecclesiology is the heart of the matter, Toronto sidesteps ecclesiology) and its *status* (it is not a dogmatic formulation and should not be treated as one, though Orthodox churches often link it inextricably with their WCC membership).[5]

New realities of communion are emerging, and the Toronto declaration is out of date as a tool which can articulate adequately the basis on which the churches stay together and grow together in the World Council of Churches. What have we learnt since 1950, through the new configurations, about the church and the churches, about the one, catholic church and the particular ways of expressing "the fullness, the integrity, and the totality of life in Christ"? Clear heads ought to help answer that question. Failure to revise the Toronto declaration would only reinforce an assumption that the churches remain together in the World Council of Churches on the basis of canonized formulations, statements which legitimate their "standing in the corner", looking on, not accepting new developments — rather than on the basis of the ecclesial reality they already have in common because of God's gifts and the experiences of living together, as disciples of Christ, in new configurations of response to those gifts.

And the will?

In a recent speech Václav Havel, the president of the Czechs, pointed once again to the necessity of exercising the will to take responsibility for meeting the challenges of the present "post-communist nightmare", with all its xenophobia, nationalisms, primitive consumerist cults, and self-affirmation at all costs.[6] Neither anonymous collectives nor the "invisible hand" of classic liberalism will, by inevitable "happy-end" processes, create a more civil world. But a more civil world may — just may — be the outcome of exercising the human will to engage in positive action, however partial it may be, to humanize the face of the earth.

The instruments of the ecumenical movement also will have to learn to learn to find satisfaction, even intense joy, in the uncertainties of positive partial action.[7] Things might get worse, because the hard realities of "standing in the corner", as many have been doing, may intimidate women and men from recognizing, clarifying and formalizing new configurations of koinonia. Things might get worse, with ecumenical instruments ending up in a self-destructive "implosion" where competing pressures and programmes will finally destroy each other in a cacaphony of conflicting purposes. But things may also get better. We are standing *here*, now, at the crossroads between realities, possibilities and our will to discipleship.

NOTES

[1] Norman Goodall ed., *The Uppsala 68 Report: Official Report of the Fourth Assembly of the World Council of Churches, Uppsala, July 4-20, 1968*, Geneva, WCC, 1968, pp.7-20.
[2] *Ibid.*, para. 7, p.13.
[3] *Costly Unity: a World Council of Churches Consultation on Koinonia and Justice, Peace and the Integrity of Creation*, Geneva, WCC, 1993, appendix II, "Suggestions to the World Council of Churches", para. 2, p.24.
[4] *Ibid.*
[5] Marlin VanElderen, "Towards a Common Understanding and Vision", *The Ecumenical Review*, vol. 43, no. 1, January 1991, p.140.
[6] *New York Review of Books*, 27 May 1993.
[7] Cf. R.C. Fernandez, "Back and Forth to 'Civil Society'", unpublished paper, January 1993.

THE FUTURE OF THE ECUMENICAL MOVEMENT

EDWARD IDRIS CARDINAL CASSIDY

Whatever assessment might be made about the future of the ecumenical movement, one thing is sure. The success of the ecumenical movement ultimately depends on God's grace. The quality of our participation in the shaping of the ecumenical future will depend on the degree to which we respond to God's grace. It is axiomatic therefore that we face the future of the ecumenical movement as people of faith and people in prayer.

Confessing our faith

For this reason and also for the fact that we are participating in a world conference on *Faith* and Order, I think it is appropriate to begin this presentation with a "confession" of faith, a personal testimony, if you will, about the ecumenical movement.

- I believe that Jesus Christ is calling his disciples to unity and that the current movement towards the visible unity of Christians, the ecumenical movement, is a great gift of God's grace, by which we respond to the prayer of Christ that his disciples be one (cf. John 17:21).

- I believe that, in face of the evil and catastrophe that often confront us — war, drug abuse, violence of every kind — God is calling Christians to be reconciled to one another so that they can then be reconcilers in society; I believe that the achievements of the ecumenical movement offer hope for society because they show that God's grace can heal divisions and help humanity to come towards reconciliation (cf. 2 Cor. 5:16-21).

- I believe that every tendency towards the division of Christians, or acquiescence in maintaining division, is against God's will, and that God calls us to rise above division, above every sinful tendency towards division, above every situation that prevents bonds of koinonia between Christians, and above every factor that prevents their pilgrimage towards full koinonia in Christ.

- Among the ecumenical advances that have been made over the decades and which have brought us to Santiago de Compostela, I wish to emphasize the following: those convergences and agreements in faith achieved through dialogue, that common witness in which we have together brought the values of the gospel to bear on social issues; the common prayer which has motivated us and reminded us of God's call to unity, the emergence of united and uniting churches and of ecumenical structures fostering our reconciliation. I believe that these advances are the gifts of grace of a loving God.

Edward Idris Cardinal Cassidy is president of the Pontifical Council for Promoting Christian Unity of the Roman Catholic Church.

• I believe that, while we have made significant progress *towards* koinonia in faith, life and witness, God is calling us further: to *full* koinonia in faith, life and witness, to visible unity.

• I believe that, in the words of the Decree on Ecumenism of the Second Vatican Council, this "holy task of reconciling all Christians in the unity of the one and only church of Christ transcends human energies and abilities". We therefore place our hope "entirely in the prayer of Christ for the Church, in the love of the Father for us, and the power of the Holy Spirit".[1]

At the same time, to reach this goal of visible unity I believe that God continually calls us to cooperate with grace, firstly through conversion of mind and heart and by remorse over divisions and the longing for unity, which, as the Decree on Ecumenism says, the Lord of the ages has begun to bestow more generously in our times on divided Christians,[2] and secondly by continued dialogue, common witness, prayer and the many ways in which reconciliation can be fostered.

Since the future depends on God, our participation in shaping the future will depend on the depth of our commitment rooted in faith. The pilgrimage towards koinonia in faith, life and witness must be an act of worship; it must be empassioned by prayer.

Giving an account of our hope

The pilgrimage towards unity must also be characterized by hope. Our faith requires that we give an account of the hope that is within us.

Through the ecumenical movement, "fostered by the grace of the Holy Spirit",[3] we are today *participants* in a transition, as God's grace draws us from separation to koinonia. The present time is therefore a time of hope, a time of looking forward in hope.

Christians have begun to replace walls of separation with *bonds of communion*, linking us more and more visibly as the brothers and sisters in Christ that we are. Insights from bilateral and multilateral dialogues are showing how much of the apostolic faith we actually share. The *Faith and Order* movement, guided by the Commission on Faith and Order of the World Council of Churches, has been a major participant in this transition, helping to dispel the darkness of separation and lighting the way for our pilgrimage towards unity.

Our hopes then are nourished by what has already been achieved. In the thirty years since the fourth world conference on Faith and Order at Montreal, we have witnessed many milestones in the ecumenical movement, some but not all relating directly to Faith and Order. These are a stimulus for our hope, and a basis upon which to build.

One thinks of the significant steps taken in recent years towards *overcoming differences in Christological formulations*, over which Christians have been divided for more than 1,500 years since the council of Chalcedon (451). This has been the case in our Roman Catholic dialogue with several Oriental Orthodox churches,[4] also in relations between Eastern Orthodox and Oriental Orthodox churches. I wish to recall in this connection the pioneering work done by the Faith and Order Commission through the study group on the council of Chalcedon.[5]

Milestones too were the historic meeting in 1964 in Jerusalem between Pope Paul VI and the Ecumenical Patriarch Athenagoras I and their common declaration in 1965

make the church what it is and which enables it to be an instrument in God's hands to bring the gospel of reconciliation to the world.

The Catholic church, secondly, offers a deep and renewed commitment to Faith and Order.

Much of the richness of the ecumenical spirit in the Catholic church comes from the stimulus of its contacts with ecumenical partners, with brothers and sisters in faith from other churches and ecclesial communities. Involvement with Faith and Order has contributed to the shaping of Catholic ecumenical conviction, because Faith and Order has kept before us — all of us — the conviction that the goal of the ecumenical movement is nothing less than visible unity of Christians. Have you ever noted just how much the positions taken in Faith and Order documents, and in the vision of visible unity as articulated in the Canberra statement of 1991, are in the same line as perspectives opened in the renewal undertaken by the Second Vatican Council and expressed in documents of that council, such as *Lumen Gentium* and *Unitatis Redintegratio*?

In making its formal response, in 1987, to the Faith and Order document *Baptism, Eucharist and Ministry*, the Catholic church expressed its happiness with the convergence on central issues of faith which BEM represented. It called BEM "a significant result and contribution to the ecumenical movement". It stated that BEM "demonstrates clearly that serious progress is being made in the quest for visible Christian unity".[25] Stating that "the Catholic church wants to encourage Faith and Order to continue its valuable work for seeking unity in faith as the basis for visible unity", the response ended with a pledge of renewed commitment:

> We recommit ourselves to the process with other churches and ecclesial communities in that serious task to which Christ calls all of us.[26]

I would like to repeat that pledge today. We consider the work of Faith and Order of seeking visible unity in the one apostolic faith, one sacramental life, as a basic aspect of the ecumenical movement. We recommit ourselves to working with Faith and Order towards the goal that it proclaims.

NOTES

[1] *Unitatis Redintegratio*, 24.

[2] *Ibid.*, 1.

[3] *Ibid.*

[4] In the joint declaration on Christology of Pope Shenouda of the Coptic Orthodox Church and Pope Paul VI in 1973 (in Pontifical Council for Promoting Christian Unity, Vatican City, *Information Service*, no. 76, 1991/I, p.9). (Information Service, hereafter = *IS* plus number and page). Joint Declaration of Pope John Paul II and Mar Ignatius Zakka I Iwas, Syrian Patriarch of Antioch and All the East (*IS*, 55, p.62). Report of dialogue between the Malankara Orthodox Syrian Church and the Roman Catholic Church, 1990 (*IS*, 73, p.39).

[5] Cf. reports in *New Directions in Faith and Order: Bristol 1967*, Faith and Order paper no. 50, Geneva, WCC, 1968, pp.49-58, 153-54.

[6] Common Declaration of Pope Paul VI and Patriarch Athenagoras 1, 7 December 1965, in Austin Flannery ed., *Documents of Vatican II*, Grand Rapids, MI, Eerdmans, 1975, pp.471-473.

[7] Johannes Cardinal Willebrands, "The Future of Ecumenism", *One in Christ*, 1975, no. 4, pp.310-23.

[8] *Ibid.*, p.323.

[9] For example, the Lutheran World Federation in 1990 changed its constitution so as to describe itself as a "communion of churches". The extraordinary synod of bishops of 1985 in the Catholic church recalled the importance of the notion of an ecclesiology of communion for the Second Vatican Council's reflections on the church.

[10] Many of the international bilateral dialogues involving the Catholic church have focused on the ecclesiology of communion. The final report of 1981 of the Anglican/Catholic International Commission (ARCIC) was based on an ecclesiology of communion, and ARCIC II developed this further with its statement "The Church as Communion" (1990). Our dialogue with the Orthodox has articulated an ecclesiology of communion which reinforces our common vision of apostolic faith, life and succession. Our dialogue with the Christian Church (Disciples of Christ) has just published its report of twelve years of work focusing on the "Church as Communion in Christ". A recent report of our international Roman Catholic/Pentecostal dialogue is entitled "Perspectives on *Koinonia*". Other examples could be cited.

[11] *Unitatis Redintegratio*, 3.

[12] See, for example, "Towards a Common Understanding of the Church", the report of the second phase of International Reformed/Catholic dialogue 1984-90, *IS*, 74, ch. 1, "Towards a Reconciliation of Memories". Also, Karl Lehmann & Wolfhart Pannenberg eds, *The Condemnations of the Reformation Era: Do They Still Divide?* Minneapolis, Fortress, 1989.

[13] For example, "Towards a Common Understanding of the Church", after finding convergences on the church, indicates in chapter 3 basic issues in ecclesiology that still need to be explored.

[14] See Thomas F. Stransky, CSP & John B. Sheerin, CSP, "Doing the Truth in Charity", *Ecumenical Documents* 1, New York, Ramsey Paulist, 1982, general introduction, p.3.

[15] Matthew 28:19-20.

[16] For example, see note 12. Also, "The Apostolic Tradition", report of the joint commission between the Roman Catholic Church and the World Methodist Council, 1986-91, fifth phase, 86-98, *IS*, 78, pp.223-25.

[17] *Baptism, Eucharist and Ministry 1982-1990: Report on the Process and Responses*, Faith and Order paper no. 149, Geneva, WCC, 1990, p.131.

[18] See notes 12 and 16. Also, "Summons to Witness to Christ in Today's World", a report on the Baptist/Roman Catholic international conversations 1984-88, 48, *IS*, 72, pp.11-12.

[19] *Baptism, Eucharist and Ministry 1982-1990*, *op. cit.*, p.148.

[20] *Ibid.*

[21] *Strategies for Reception: Perspectives on the Reception of Documents Emerging from the Lutheran-Catholic International Dialogue*, *IS*, 80, p.42.

[22] *Unitatis Redintegratio*, 24.

[23] "The Twenty Fifth Anniversary of the Secretariat for Promoting Christian Unity, Pope John Paul II's Address to the Roman Curia", 28 June 1985, *IS*, 59, p.5.

[24] *Ibid.*

[25] Catholic response to BEM, in Max Thurian ed., *Churches Respond to BEM*, vol. VI, Faith and Order paper no. 144, Geneva, WCC, 1988, p.40.

[26] *Ibid.*

MESSAGE TO THE WORLD CONFERENCE

ARCHBISHOP IAKOVOS

The World Council of Churches, in the words of the incomparable William Temple, Archbishop of Canterbury, entered the life of the church in 1947, in the manner of an epiphany of the Holy Spirit. It was "the Spirit himself interceding for us with sighs too deep for words" (Rom. 8:26), over the cumulative sufferings of two world wars.

Two dates will stand out in the history of the twentieth century: 1945, when the United Nations Organization was established; and 1948 when the World Council of Churches was founded. These two bodies filled the skies like rainbows, like meteors illuminating the entire world, inspiring hope for a better future.

Today, some 45-50 years later, both organizations continue to exist: the one, the United Nations, with its international peace-making influence enhanced; the other, World Council of Churches, with its prestige similarly increased in matters of conscience and social order.

In their evolution neither could overlook radical changes in the political and economic life of the world, nor the unbridled rise of nationalism with its attendant radical movement for social justice and equality. Both organizations took note of these phenomena, and heard in them a universal cry; both strove to respond to that cry.

The World Council of Churches laid great stress on political and human rights; it mobilized itself with zeal and applied itself vigorously to the task of making them issues of universal conscience, inspired always by holy scripture.

Offspring and product of this effort, giving it its validation in fact, was an unprecedented activism, as we have come to call that social mobilization and the pursuit of its goals.

The assemblies of the World Council of Churches in Uppsala, Nairobi, Vancouver and Canberra, while they renewed the will which this effort demands, neglected (perhaps unintentionally) to undergird it with the mind and spirit of the World Council, which is the collective quest to recover the oneness of Christendom.

I trust that what I am saying will be taken not as a reproach, but in its true spirit. I recognize that for many of us this is a painful admission, however compelling a duty it was for the World Council of Churches to address the socio-political shifts and changes of our times.

But it is not the first time in history that such social trends and conflicts have emerged. They have always required of the church that it rethink its prevailing

---

Archbishop Iakovos is the primate of the Greek Orthodox Archdiocese of North and South America (Ecumenical Patriarchate).

theological and philosophical positions, though always within the framework of Christian sociology.

In their haste to make Christian sociological principles the basis and starting point of the new order of things, agencies of the World Council of Churches were drawn into actions not very well thought out, such as the material as well as moral support of those among our fellow humans who took up arms in pursuit of their social liberation.

And if this had succeeded, there might be some justification for such aberrations of the ecumenical movement. But inequality and injustice persist, indeed grow more acute with the added factor of racism and unspeakable acts of violence, as in South Africa, even the United States.

We must escape this "ideological" vortex in which the World Council has been caught, and in which that vision has been lost which electrified peoples with expectations for a peaceful and unified Christian world. This is the most urgent need at the present time, indeed into the future I would add. The order of our priorities must, if we truly wish for the World Council to have a future, begin with the dynamic renewal of Faith and Order, of Life and Work, that is to say, its functioning mode. The clerics and laymen of 1927 and 1948 were "in touch with reality" when they imparted life and breath to the ecumenical idea through the organizations of Life and Work, Faith and Order and the International Missionary Council.

The thinking, the work and the decisions of those churchmen, the pillars of the World Council of Churches, were inspired by the Bible, by history, and the experience of two great wars. Their patrimony, and that of all its presidents and general secretaries, has been, and remains, that all programmes originate from the same premise, and all be implemented within that same framework, namely Faith and Order, Life and Work, and the International Missionary Council. Not outside them.

These three committees can still be the source of all Christian and humanistic agendas and ideological currents, watering the arid and thirsty soil, and soul, of our divided Christian world.

A call to authentic witness

The future of the World Council of Churches is unfolding just as is that of the Christian churches and confessions, since they too are experiencing a terrible crisis of values. Therefore, the question concerning the future must preoccupy the member churches themselves. But only if it becomes for them in fact a matter of conscience will they be able to see themselves within the Council as an authentic instrument of divine providence, bringing together all the fragmented forces of the Christian world in a world free of divisions and wars.

How soon we might be led to that blessed day: by repentance; by making common cause; by returning to our spiritual roots; by obedience to Christ and his will, that the gospel be preached to all creation; only through prayer, and by recasting ourselves within the unity ideal, will we come to know the answer.

For the moment we continue to rend Christ's robe with theological and ethical liberalism, ill-considered ordinations, heretofore unknown to the policy of the church, with scandals, both financial and sexual, with persistent discussions over the recognition of avowedly homosexual communities — all of which impede the way towards a genuinely new future.

That future will not be determined by optimistic forecasts, nor by "good faith" hand-wringing by ecumenists. It lies within itself. By its will to re-examine itself, to reframe its structure, to rediscover its course as an ecumenical ecclesiastical movement towards unity, and to place itself at the service of that idea — if it truly desires to pave the way into the twenty-first century.

Theological watchwords, of the kind that commonly open and close conferences, have failed to signal a challenge for a considered and coordinated charting of the way towards a reunion of the churches.

Many of us rested our hopes in the highly optimistic post-war notion that we had transcended the "middle ages" of Christian divisions and opposing camps. We hailed the ecumenical movement as the dawning of a new Christian era. Yet, in spite of all the interfaith conferences and the bilateral or multilateral dialogues, we proved ourselves unequal to God's command, and to the challenge of the times, "that we may be one", the reality being that we still speak of uniatism or re-evangelizing peoples who have been Christian for centuries, but have had the misfortune to live in the darkness of martyrdom during the seventy-year sway of communist atheism.

The World Council of Churches must have a future, lest it too turn out to have been a long and endless experiment of the churches without consequence or continuity. But to have a future, it must strive to unite all the Christian churches, without exception, in a truly ecumenical Christian dialogue; carefully delimiting its bounds, and disallowing the extremes, whether of liberalism or conservatism; also the rhetorical pyrotechnics that can in no way advance the great yearning of true Christians.

The World Council of Churches can still have a future, so long as insurmountable obstacles do not impede its course, deflecting it from its set course, or deviating from the essential purpose of its existence. If it believes in unity based on the one undivided, catholic and apostolic church, then let it signal the movement of all the particular Christian groups towards itself.

The vital presupposition for this first step is for Christendom to reform and restore itself. And is this not precisely the vocation of the World Council of Churches? It is called to remind the world that church unity is the "Lydian stone", the ultimate test of the claim that they truly desire it. It is the only — and therefore the anticipated — response to Christ's prayer when he said: "Sanctify them in the truth; thy word is truth... For thy sake I consecrate myself, that they also may be consecrated in the truth" (John 17:17-19).

My prayer to God, and my appeal at this moment, is that the World Council of Churches, strengthened through Faith and Order, and through our common obedience to the Lord's will, may give the answer to the aching hopes of our divided and disoriented world.

THE FUTURE OF THE ECUMENICAL MOVEMENT: FROM THE PERSPECTIVE OF A MEMBER OF A UNITED CHURCH

1. A note on the Church of North/South India

The ecumenical movement in the twentieth century grew out of the international missionary conference held at Edinburgh in 1910. The national Christian councils in India and other countries, and the World Council of Churches, were also formed as a result of the vision of its participants. The efforts towards unity of churches became more significant in India after a meeting of some church leaders at Tranquebar in 1919. A statement was issued at the conference which included the following words:

> We believe that the challenges of the present hour... call us to mourn our past divisions and turn to our Lord Jesus Christ to seek in him the unity of the body expressed in one visible church. We face together the titanic task of the winning of India for Christ — one fifth of the human race. Yet confronted by such an overwhelming responsibility, we find ourselves rendered weak and relatively impotent by our unhappy divisions — divisions for which we were not responsible, and which have been, as it were, imposed upon us from without.[1]

From the tenor of this statement it seems that there were three compelling factors which influenced and furthered the cause of the church union movement in India: first, that a divided church was a hindrance to the spread of the gospel; second, that the Christian denominations in India were foreign and accidental; and third, that Christians were a tiny minority in India and it was absolutely essential that they be together.

Although the problems of disunity were seen in these rather simple terms, it took us several conferences and several decades of negotiations to sort out the differences between the different denominations which negotiated for church union. The formation of the Church of South India in 1947 was a historic event for the church in India. It could be considered as the first fruit of ecumenism, bringing together different churches under one umbrella. The parties to the union were the South India United Church (the combined body of the Congregationalists and the Presbyterians), the Anglican dioceses in South India, and the South Indian districts of the Methodist communion. A union of such different traditions was no ordinary enterprise. From the first it was realized that the issues raised by the proposals for the union — aimed as they were at solving some of the most stubborn problems left behind by the Reformation — were of far more than local importance, and were bound to affect all parts of the Christian world where those problems were to be found. Whether in India or elsewhere, the great division of opinion was between those who thought that the proposals gave up too much of the catholic doctrine and practice for the sake of superficial union, and those who feared that they would lead too far in a "catholic" direction.

The Rt Rev. Dr Samuel B. Joshua is bishop of the Bombay diocese, Church of North India.

The Church of North India was formed in 1970 by bringing together six churches, namely the Anglican dioceses in North India, the United Church of Northern India, the Disciples of Christ, the Brethren, the Baptists, and the Methodist Church (British and Australian conference). The measure of agreement reached in the plan of church union in North India was achieved through great perseverence and painstaking negotiations. The difficulties chiefly centred on the following questions:
1) the place of the episcopate;
2) acceptance of the ministry of different churches;
3) the tradition of infant and believer's baptism.
The consensus reached on these crucial issues are as follows:

a) The episcopate: The episcopate of the Church of North India is both constitutional and historic. It is constitutional, because its bishops are appointed and they perform their functions in accordance with the constitution of the church. It is historic, because it has historic continuity with the early church. However, the Church of North India is not committed to any one particular theological interpretation of episcopacy.

b) The ministry: The Church of North India had a service of unification of the ministries of the uniting churches at the very outset. It was a representative act of unification of the ministry by the mutual laying on of hands and a prayer which clearly expressed and conveyed the intention of the act.

c) Baptism: In the Church of North India, both infant baptism and believer's baptism are accepted as alternative practices. The church has provision for the dedication of infants and the administration of baptism by immersion as the seal of faith. For those who are baptized at infancy, profession of faith is required before admission to full membership in full standing in the church.

2. The effects of union on congregations

a) Freedom from denominationalism: Each church which joined the union in 1970 has given up its old denominational name. There is an overall feeling that the Church of North India is a visible expression of our oneness in Christ.

b) Eucharistic fellowship: All parishes/pastorates within the Church of North India, whatever their past denominational affiliations may have been, are open to one another in the celebration of the Lord's supper.

c) Common ministry: Presbyters can interchange their places without any apprehension of having to encounter differing theological persuasions characteristic to the old denominations.

d) One structure: There is one administrative structure, one constitution, making for a uniform pattern of administration at diocesan and pastorate levels, with a certain amount of freedom to adapt to local situations. The Church of North India accepts the episcopal, presbyterian and congregational elements in church order, as the means through which the Lordship of Christ in his Church may be realized.

3. The emerging disappointments of the united church

a) Mission and evangelism: One of the arguments advanced in furthering the union of churches was that the united church could fulfil the mission of the church more effectively than a divided church. It was said that a divided church was a scandal to the preaching of the gospel. "We believe", said the uniting churches, "that the unity to which God is leading us will make the church in North India a more effective instrument for his work, more eager and powerful to proclaim by word and deed, the gospel of Christ." This assumption that the united church would be more effective in mission and evangelism has not proved right. In the twenty-two years of its history, the Church of North India has not had any serious agenda on mission and evangelism, except seminars and conferences on the subject by non-field workers. Neither the pastorates nor the dioceses, nor the synod reflect any indigenous budgetary provisions for mission and evangelism. The engagement in the field of mission and evangelism by the united church seems to be less than the sum total of what was being done by the various denominations before the union.

b) *Liturgy and worship:* Each of the six churches which united had certain distinctive forms of worship to which its members were strongly attached. At the time of the union it was agreed that the united church would seek to conserve "for the common benefit, whatever spiritual riches have been gained by the uniting churches in their separate experiences". This meant that all forms of worship which were in use in the different churches before the union were permitted in the united church. There was also the understanding that no form of worship will be imposed on the members of the congregation. It was envisaged at the time of the union that the Church of North India would "seek to adopt and develop new forms of service adapted to the needs and experience of the country". Experience, however, shows that the united church has not been able to preserve its past heritages, nor has it been able to exude its own aroma in acts of corporate worship.

There are obvious reasons for this failure. Liturgy and worship is rooted in the history of congregations and churches. They are nurtured and cultured within traditions which are alive. Further, they receive mutual enrichment and contemporary relevance by being part of a larger or universal organic body, even though it may be denominational in character, for example, Roman Catholic, Anglican, Orthodox, Lutheran, Methodist and so on. This liturgical koinonia is not a part of the united church. I say this without prejudice to need for development of indigenous forms of worship.

c) *An island church:* Each of the six churches which came into the union was part of its respective world communion. Each church was a physical and psychological part of the global church which that denomination represented. The united church, which has itself now become a denomination, has lost its intimacy and family ties with churches beyond its border. We have to be satisfied with "intercommunion" and a superficial relationship of being "partners in mission".

d) *Resources of the united church:* The united church started with an empty vessel, hoping that each of the uniting churches would pour its resources into the cauldron of the united church. This expectation has not materialized. Internecine quarrels and numerous litigations over properties and institutions have frustrated the purpose of the union.

e) *My personal opinion:* At the risk of being misunderstood by my church, I have expressed my personal feelings about the gains and the failures of our visible union. In my opinion, the gains have been superficial, while the new burdens of litigations, dissensions, and lack of accountability have become unbearable. Whether churches in Europe and America at any future date will produce results of a type other than experienced in India is yet to be seen.

4. World ecumenism

During the past 83 years or so, much time, energy and money have been spent in motivating and challenging the churches to the goal of visible unity in one faith and one eucharistic fellowship. However, the achievements in this respect have not been much, when weighed against the number of years that have been consumed in the exercise. One notable achievement in recent times has been the Faith and Order document on *Baptism, Eucharist and Ministry*. But then, that has not as yet resulted in any consequential action on the part of the participating churches. As the world conference discussion paper points out: "churches have failed to draw consequences for their life from the degree of communion they have already experienced and the agreements already achieved. They have remained satisfied to co-exist in division."[2]

A basic question which then arises is: Are we to go on like this for ever? Or can we give a "shake up" to the agenda of the WCC, and set new goals? Perhaps now is the time to ask whether the *visible* unity of churches that we are seeking is a misdirected goal? My foolish submissions in this regard are as follows:

a) Visible unity — a utopian concept: Visible unity of the church sought in terms of theological and doctrinal consensus and structural authority cannot be achieved as a practical goal. It is evident that any union arrived at on the basis of theological/doctrinal agreement today is open to division and disintegration tomorrow. No individual or class of people can claim finality in matters of faith and order. Hence to seek visible unity in these terms is to build the house upon the sands of time. The notion that there was visible unity in the "early church" is not supported by evidence. The assumption that at some point of time in the past "there was a universal framework of theological understanding acknowledged by the whole church" is a wrong assumption. As for the Nicene-Constantinopolitan Creed, all that we can say categorically is that that was an attempt by the churches of the day, in the context of the day, to give expression to the Christian faith in a few words which the faithful could recite, and to guard themselves against those whom the council considered to be heretics and schismatics.

b) Visible unity — a theocratic-political concept: Visible unity is a theocratic-political concept — a people of God, God's own people, a chosen race, a peculiar people, the household of God, etc. Implied in these concepts is the notion of *a people*, visible and identifiable and separated from the rest for a purpose. In the New Testament these concepts converge into the concept of the "body of Christ", the church. The theocratic-political connotation of the "people of God" has wittingly or unwittingly seeped into the concept of the church. The church as an institution has never been entirely rid of this theocratic-political sub-conscious. The striving after a *visible unity* of a people is a surge of this sub-conscious.

c) Visible unity — a monocracy: Experience shows that unity expressed in and through a single structure tends to concentrate power in the hierarchy. The hierarchy assumes unrestricted power and tries to enforce uniformity in matters of faith and order. Diversities of theological traditions, cultural, ethnic and historical contexts cannot thrive under one umbrella.

5. A fresh look at the unity of the church

Jesus by his intimate and calculated relationship with a few men over a period of time, manifested (opened) the Father to them: "I have manifested Thy name to them..." That they apprehended the manifestation was revealed by their response to Jesus: "[they] know in truth that I came from Thee; and they have believed that Thou didst send me" (John 17:8). This *knowing in truth* was absolutely essential to the mission of Christ. Without it the love of God would have been lost upon the world. This response of these immediate followers was as vitally significant to Jesus, as was Jesus' own obedience to the Father. Jesus glorified the Father; these followers glorified Jesus — "I am glorified in them". Through them the world would also come to believe that Jesus came from the Father. Jesus then prays for them intensely "that they may all be one; even as Thou, Father, art in Me, and I in Thee, that they also may be in us, so that the world may believe that Thou has sent me". Oneness amongst and between them meant that they would be in one another, even as the Father was in Jesus and Jesus in the Father. Such a oneness amongst them was possible because Jesus was in them — "I in them". And because Jesus was in them, they would also be in the Father-Son relationship — "that they also may be in us". Thus, if for a moment we can forget our doctrines and dogmas and church order and enter into a vision, what do we see? We see persons — the Father, the Son and the spirits of just men — and women — made perfect (Heb. 12:22-24). It is my humble submission that the unity of churches (Christians) must be seen and experienced and sought after in terms of *persons* and not in terms of doctrines and church order. All those who recognize Jesus know in truth that he came from the Father and in him we are in one another, a unity of persons. From this unity of persons flows theological perceptions, doctrinal agreements and disagreements, church order. All these activities find accommodation in the unity of persons and none of it need separate us from one another. This concept of unity is comprehensively expressed in the discussion paper as follows:

> Those who share in the life of grace are brought into communion with all who share in the same life of grace in each place and every time. The variety of gifts everywhere, working together, builds up the common life. Moreover, gifts of grace are bestowed in such a way that no one is self-sufficient. Thus the disciples are one, while being enriched by their differences. Diversity as well as unity is a gift of God. God calls the churches to be a koinonia that is empowered by the Holy Spirit to be at the same time fully united and entirely respectful of the diversity of persons, population groups and cultures. The church is to be catholic, that is, one in faith and diverse in expressions of this common faith and life: indeed this is God's design for the whole of humanity. This diversity must be encompassed by unity so that it does not lead to ecclesiastical, racial and other divisions; and unity must be enriched by diversity so that it does not degenerate into uniformity. In this way, the church is catholic. Catholicity is expressed at the local as well as the world-wide level since in each place the fullness of communion is offered and experienced.[3]

6. Structures of mutual accountability

If it is perceived that unity is the unity of persons, then we shift our emphasis from seeking visible unity of churches to what the document *Costly Unity* calls "structures of mutual accountability".[4] Past and present experiences show that we would like to keep our own way of life, church order, and to some extent our own theological perceptions and doctrinal emphasis. Our attempts to gather them together should be no more than gathering the fragments into one basket. Any attempt to make a pulp out of the fragments would be contrary to the very essence of our creatively diverse existence. The World Council of Churches for the time being is the basket in which the fragments can be gathered so that nothing is lost.

The document *Costly Unity* has, I believe, by a stroke of revelation indicated the future course open to the WCC. It says:

> Are the different communions ready to see that communion between them — koinonia — whether in matters of faith or ethical responsibility, calls for steps towards structures of mutual accountability? The fifth world conference on Faith and Order will ask if the churches can take further steps towards "conciliar communion". At the very least, this phrase means being responsible to one another in witnessing to faith in Jesus Christ, and to the implications of this faith for justice, peace, and the integrity of creation. How long will the communions refuse to be challenged by what unity really requires?[5]

The concept of "structures of mutual accountability" provides for diversity in unity, and at the same time, it will act as a mutual safeguard against ecclesiastical, racial and other divisions. The WCC will be the forum for ongoing theological pursuits, not for the goal of seeking visible unity, but as an end itself, in ever trying to fathom the mysteries of God revealed in his Son Jesus Christ our Lord. In this ongoing common exercise in faith, there is no question of anyone being "right" or "wrong". As Paul says: "For all things are yours, whether Paul or Apollos or Cephas or the world or life or death or the present or the future, all are yours; and you are Christ's; and Christ is God's" (1 Cor. 3:21).

7. Communion

A question that naturally arises, and one that has to be answered in this context, is: Why not take a plunge and open our *meals* to one another? Should we wait till we have all arrived at a consensus of doctrine? Till we all have agreed that there shall be no differences of opinion in the future? Till we have committed the blasphemy of assuming that we have uttered the ultimate in faith and order?

The ecclesiastical bureaucracy is keeping the faithful divided and literally stopping them from being in communion with one another. My experience of a united church is that as long as we were in our divided state, the bureaucracy of each church built up a mountain of theology about the Lord's supper (the eucharist) to justify their separateness. And therefore it took forty years to arrive at a consensus and to be united. After the union, looking back, the forty years of forced labour seems so unnecessary and prejudiced. The masses of believers who came into union continue to believe what they have always believed even before the union. The only difference that the union has made is that the bureaucratic interference has been eliminated.

I would plead with the member churches of the WCC that the time is ripe to welcome one another at the Lord's table. In fact we must acknowledge the fact that some of our faithful are already practising this communion out of conviction, without the consent of the bureaucracy. Is their participation invalid? Is excommunication of such people acceptable to the Lord? These are uncomfortable questions which cry out for answers.

8. Koinonia

Koinonia (in its meaning of fellowship rooted and grounded in Christ) of local congregations is the crying need of the hour. It is the koinonia at the grassroots that touches the masses and which is relevant to their immediate socio-political-religious context. This fact is constantly brought to the fore whenever there is communal violence, religious barbarism, poverty and hunger. In the apostolic community of the days of Peter, James and John, of Martha, Mary and Salome, what was convincing to the people and which acted as an advertisement of the good news was the koinonia of the believers, which included the breaking of bread together and the sharing of resources. There can be a return to such a koinonia if we shift our emphasis from visible unity of the church to the unity of persons, with an agenda of mutual accountability. The time is at hand, and the trumpet call is to move fast!

NOTES

[1] Ruth Rouse & Stephen Neill eds, *A History of the Eumenical Movement*, Geneva, WCC, vol. 1, 4th ed. 1993, p.473.

[2] *Towards Koinonia in Faith, Life and Witness: A Discussion Paper*, Faith and Order paper no. 161, Geneva, WCC, 1993, p.12.

[3] *Ibid.*, p.19.

[4] *Costly Unity: Koinonia and Justice, Peace and the Integrity of Creation*, Geneva, WCC, Units I and II, 1993, p.13.

[5] *Ibid.*, p.13.

THE FUTURE OF THE ECUMENICAL MOVEMENT: A PERSONAL REFLECTION

RENA WELLER KAREFA-SMART

Introduction

1. I often hum a popular song, happily accepting its description of my personal situation. "I've got plenty of nothing, and nothing's plenty for me." Precisely because I own nothing, manage nothing, lead nothing, I can go on my way, rejoicing! For I know that *nothing* (like a second defining reality, *blackness*) is more apparent than real. "Nothing" is plenitude — God's gift of being unencumbered in freedom. The other apparent reality, blackness, is really the place of many colours from many forebears (African, Caribbean, British, American) — colours that are in harmony, blended, true and beautiful! I am usually happy to have plenty of nothing... and to sing about it.

2. Then came the invitation to join the Faith and Order pilgrimage to Santiago, 1993. We say, "when in doubt, sing!" So I did. Loudly! "I've got plenty of nothing, and nothing's plenty for me"... Go to Faith and Order with only my nothing and my blackness? More loud singing! Then it came to me, over the sound of music, that the invitation to pilgrimage is a gracious offer to me to join with the ecumenical family who will recall God's merciful love and care. Many of us, with nothing much to offer, have found abundance of life on the ecumenical way, together. Now, remembering is an occasion for joyous reunion. We are to remember Christ's presence with us, before and after Montreal, 1963. Singing brought me here.

3. At Santiago, two hymns have set my mood and opened my heart. First, from Revelation (19:1): "Hallelujah! Salvation and glory and honour belong to our God!"[1] The second is a renewal hymn, a gift to the charismatic movement from the Holy Spirit:

> Give thanks with a grateful heart,
> Give thanks to the Holy One,
> Give thanks because He's given Jesus Christ, His Son —
>
> And now let the weak say I am strong,
> Let the poor say I am rich,
> Because of what the Lord has done for us, Give thanks![2]

4. I am here, in the communion of saints, in praise, giving thanks, remembering. Anamnesis is remembering that our Lord is present with all Christians who ask *and then find* a way out of separation and division. It is recalling how Christ suffers with us as we walk the way of deliverance from centuries of unfaith during which we are, all

---

The Rev. Dr Rena Weller Karefa-Smart is ecumenical officer of the Washington, DC, diocese of the Episcopal Church, USA.

of us, refusing to receive his body and blood as the one people of God. To remember is to see — to discern the truth, and by it to be set free to continue on the journey into the future.

5. After arriving here I discovered a single, uniting, haunting question that recurs in our morning liturgies. It is this question that is central to my reflections, and that is, I believe, a true measure of where many of us are as we remember. Daily, during our intercessory prayers we ask: "Where have we gone astray?"

> Tell us Lord, tell us, Lord.
> What has happened to us? What has happened to us?
> Where did we go astray? Where did we go astray?[3]

6. Through this prayer-hymn I am led to see a single, major source of misdirection in the journey of the last thirty years. I turn to this, praying that we will together hear whatever God is saying about the true condition of the ecumenical movement. To speak of the future, we must hear the word of God in judgment but, mercifully, also in love. We must be open to the word as we recall the past, in Christ's name. If there is a future, it will be a new way — one that departs from the places where we have gone astray.

> Stony the road we trod, Bitter the chastening rod
> Felt in the days when hope, unborn, had died.
> Yet with a steady beat,
> Did not our weary feet come to the place for which our Fathers died?[4]

Imperfect union

7. The theme of this conference convicts us of missing the mark. For, according to God's promises, the gift of koinonia is available to us now.

If received, this gift would reverse the direction of years lived in our common refusal of the gift of community in Christ. Divided, the ecumenical pioneers acknowledged the sin of separated churches. They challenged each other and their churches into church union. Lay, clergy, male, female, Reformed, Evangelical, Orthodox, Roman Catholic — Western, Eastern, Southern — their voices spoke in unison, prophetically. They called the churches to respond to God's call to union. Although some churches have responded, in India and in Canada and in other places, recovering unity through union, churches in the ecumenical movement have for the most part taken a different route. In doing so, they have left united churches to live attenuated lives in "union". Denominations and confessions, national and international councils, worldwide confessional bodies, and communions have all taken the way that moves "towards visible unity". We have gone astray, it seems, by losing the vision of radical change that was shared by Brent, and Mott, and Brilioth and Bell, and Ainslie and many others. We have wandered away from the goal of union — *koinonia now*.

8. The icons of *dis*-unity — conferences, studies, aborted agreements — constitute a mammoth retreat from earlier goals for ecumenical life. The road to koinonia is littered with the wreckage of lost dreams. In periods earlier and now, the documents tell the account of the betrayal of the hopes of many of those who started on the way to a whole church for a whole world. We have only to review the history of the Consultation on Church Union (COCU), of the Anglican-Roman Catholic International Commission (ARCIC), or of the Lutheran-Episcopal Agreement (the Concordat

process) to find recent examples of the patterns of evasion and delay that have shaped ecumenical life in our period of history. These are the delayed (possibly the failed) models for ecumenical life — that would, God willing, have made possible a lived koinonia now. Contemporary ecumenical partners contribute in another way to our distance from koinonia now. Ecumenical programmes, such as the WCC Programme to Combat Racism, are challenged on quite untenable grounds of "ideology", "lack of theological rigour", and so on. These exercises serve to weaken common united prophetic and pastoral ministries from Australia to Korea, the USA to Southern Africa. As to ideology, God is *never* without a witness — when Christian theologians have failed to create conceptual resources for social analysis *then* tools wherever found are utilized. If Faith and Order would go beyond cautionary words on "racism and heresy" to the problematic of equal justice, reparations and the reconstruction of community — extending its work on the theology of *power* — we would all be living closer to — if not *in* — union. This history is one of the sources for the view that an ecumenical winter is upon us. Similar developments earlier on occasioned a now-famous remark by the eminent ecumenist, Albert Outler. He asserted that the ecumenical movement is "... dead in the water". (As we shall see later in this reflection, this was not his last word on the matter.)

9. Where might the world be in its search for the unity of humankind had it not been for the many acts of resistance to the church union imperative? What deprivations might have been avoided had the one church become an institutional reality in this century? Where might the search for unity in the "global village" be now, had the vision of the pioneers been lived in a koinonia that holds together "all sorts and conditions of men"?[5] The world suffers: alienation, polarization, destruction and devastation — all have taken on demonic power in a divided world as the churches go their separated ways, impotent before massive suffering that is found among the people of all societies. Had the churches been in union, bringing together all Christian communities, apartheid, Christian and secular — and its analogues in other societies — would have been impossible. But because apartheid is "too strong for divided churches", it has spawned moral death.[6] Relatively ineffectual in the face of these conditions, churches continue to allow past schisms and contemporary intransigencies to delay the moment of union. We continue to be people of little faith, responding to our Lord's prayer for unity with acts of *dis*-unity. We deny our essential being as participants in *koinonia now*.

10. The history of contemporary ecumenism confirms the impression shared by many that the combination of doctrinal and non-doctrinal issues that divide the churches is a fatal one for any genuine appropriation of the gift of koinonia *now*. Ironically, the wider the circle of partner churches in unity conversations, the greater the distance still to be travelled in reaching church union goals such as those given classic statement in the Chicago/Lambeth quadrilateral of 1888. The four "pillars" of church unity contained in that document are scripture, faith, sacrament and common ministry.[7] How else to understand the debate on ordination of women? Had churches been in union the *whole* Tradition on ministry would have been given *full* expression, making quite unthinkable the exclusion from holy orders, on doctrinal or non-doctrinal grounds, of any one class of the faithful. Especially is this true if we accept the word that the exclusion of women is experienced as a mortal wound in the *being* that is the ground of life in the body of Christ.

Although Faith and Order has served the churches well in fulfilling its mandate to give direction to the ecumenical theological enterprise, producing an astonishing corpus of theological studies, interchurch agreements, and cross-disciplinary ecumenical texts, it has not been able to find the means for assisting the churches and confessions to commit themselves to *koinonia now*. This is one of the sources of the widespread apathy and disappointment that those who are not involved in the formal study of classical ecumenical theology feel. These are not simply the "grassroots". Many Christians in theological education, the universities, the professions and public affairs are ready for the work of ecumenical theologians to have a positive impact on the decision-making of their churches with respect to unity. (They may in their frustration with the ecumenical process be the victims of the inevitable, given the unresolved issues of authority, autonomy, representation and communication which are extremely complex, in part because of the structure of Faith and Order and World Council of Churches relationships. The ecumenical movement is much wider than Faith and Order. Although Faith and Order has a broader membership than the World Council of Churches, it is not a movement, nor does it have direct contact with many Christians for whom *koinonia now* is a faith imperative. It does not have, nor does it wish to have, authority over the decisions of the churches.)

I believe that the frustrated and the apathetic are part of an ecumenical minority that is profoundly disturbed by the way the ecumenical movement has taken. Sharing a common vision of a truly united body of Christ, they are reluctant supporters of the conciliarity that is the locus for a "communion of communions".

11. It could be argued that there is no future, ecumenically, for Protestant, Orthodox, and Catholic bodies represented here if effective action to achieve organic union is not taken now. For intentions stated ("we intend to stay together" — the WCC founding assembly at Amsterdam in 1948) by Protestants and Anglicans have not proved to be compelling with the other partners. Verbal protestations soon lose their force if they are not made operational.

If I were a member of the committee to plan the next ecumenical council I would interpret what the churches are saying today as indications of hesitancy, indecision and uncertainty! There is a lack of commitment locally, regionally and at the world level to *koinonia now*. Whereas in the early years of the ecumenical movement there was enthusiasm and openness to union, recent events show that the churches are now on a different road "towards visible unity".

Are not the churches frozen into a seemingly permanent pre-conciliar — and even pre-*ecumenical* — life of denominations, confessions, world communions, institutes of ecumenical studies, and world denominational bodies? "Towards visible unity" serves as a moving target, legitimating patterns of evasion, with the result that incremental gains, carefully chosen schedules, and imposing publications all add up to *churches still separated and divided in their "ecumenical" life*.

The loss of the founding, radical union-vision, the inability of the churches to live for the world, and problematic relations within the ecumenical movement all contribute to the present state of imperfect union.

12. Ecumenical realism must identify the two ecumenical options: either towards visible church unity, a very long-term goal, or church union, *koinonia now*. Everything is in working order for the first to be the organizing principle of ecumenism

today. Indeed, Santiago is a part of this set of goals, methods and resources. It is to the second goal that I now turn.

Koinonia in faith, life and work *now*

13. Professor Outler gave his ecumenical vision to the churches: a united Christian community *really* united in *communicatio in sacris* (in membership, ministry and sacraments), in which the distinctive witness of diverse denominations, functioning as *orders, societies or movements* under their own self-appointed heads, will be conserved within a wider catholic perimeter, organized constitutionally on some collegial and conciliar pattern.[8]

More than "reconciled diversity" is involved in this way of seeing church union. Outler comments:

> Who should know better than we [Methodists] that denominations may be justifed in their existence for this "time being" or that, but not forever?... We are, or ought to be prepared to risk our life as a separate church and to face death as a denomination in the sure and lively hope of our resurrection in the true community of the whole people of God... The price of true catholicity may very well be the death and resurrection of the churches that we know — in the faith that God has greater things in store for his people than we can remember or even imagine.[9]

14. One of the preconditions for church union is agreement among participating churches on the acceptance of the principle of ecclesiological provisionality. Formulated in relation to the dialogue within the Methodist family, the concept is also useful in other discussions. "Koinonia now" *does* mean finding new ideas and models that are created from within very specific situations. The orthopraxis of ecumenical relations is both the source and the demand for new forms of thinking and acting.

15. Bishop Stephen Neill in his review of Anglicanism addresses the issue of "visible and organic Christian unity" from an historical perspective. Anglican commitment to Christian unity goals has been both continuous and significant. Hard lessons have been learned.

> Any confession which takes seriously the possibility of visible and organic Christian unity must reckon with the possibility of its own disappearance, or of such modifications in its life and structure as would make it hardly recognizable as that which it had been in the time of separation. Denominations may be necessary, but they should never be regarded as a permanent feature of the Christian landscape. They justify their existence on the grounds of the maintenance of certain aspects of Christian truth which would otherwise be imperilled. But if Christian truth can be adequately safeguarded in a united church, is there any valid argument in favour of continuing in separation? Must not the denomination be prepared to lose its individual existence by becoming merged in a larger whole?[10]

16. The ecumenical minority that is encountered in every denomination, confession and communion understands that the option for *koinonia now* is appropriate, not only because of the imperative it gives but also because of the answers it provides for those seriously questioning the faithfulness of separated and divided churches. *Visible and organic Christian unity* is the union-vision of the ecumenical pioneers. Even in the more limited forms of union that have been achieved by families of denominations (for example in the USA among Presbyterians, among Lutherans, among Methodists), and

in united churches in several countries..., there is meaningful experience of a deeper
level of community than was true before union. The point is made negatively in
situations where ecumenical models have altered their original goals so radically that
they have shifted from *koinonia now* to "towards visible unity" models. Christians
continue to suffer, deprived of the life of koinonia in faith, life and witness as they
cooperate in tasks of mission, education and service.

17. The experience of the USA Consultation on Church Union (COCU) could
serve as a case study of the shift from "union now" to "unity gradually achieved".
A brief summary: when the original goal of a merger of nine denominations was
refused by the churches involved, a plan of "covenanting communion" was agreed
to by all of the partner churches. Gerald Moede, formerly the COCU executive, is
now a parish pastor. In this ministry he has discerned a need for sharing in the
eucharist by Christians of various denominations that are not yet in full communion.

> We do well in ecumenical organizations locally at common mission. But certain things
> you hardly get, the traditional things that mark the unity of the church: the eucharist shared
> together, the celebration of shared baptism, and ordination together. The consultation or
> some other format, or maybe a combination of them, is needed to work to reach agreement
> on the eucharist, or ordination.

The pain of such situations is addressed by Moede in other remarks:

> We (Christians united in mission in the community) could pray together but we could not
> receive the Lord's supper together. We could not be one together as Christians in that
> assembly.[11]

18. The Canberra (1991) WCC assembly accepted the interpretation of "The Unity
of the Church as Koinonia..." and claims:

> The purpose of the church is to unite people with Christ in the power of the Spirit, to
> manifest communion in prayer and action and thus to point to the fullness of communion
> with God, humanity and the whole creation in the glory of the kingdom.[12]

Two elements of lived koinonia are:

> a common sacramental life entered by the one baptism and celebrated together in one
> eucharistic fellowship; a common life in which members and ministries are mutually
> recognized and reconciled... The goal of the search for full communion is realized when all
> the churches are able to recognize in one another the one, holy, catholic, and apostolic
> church...[13]

What Canberra leaves open is the question of post-denominational ecumenism —
the import of the Outler and Neill insights referred to earlier. *Koinonia now* is not the
natural choice of these bodies, for this would end the period of their hegemonic,
separate, independent and competing histories.

19. While the opening for exciting, cooperative work in areas such as ecumenical
ethics is given by the Canberra framework — for example, one could ask: "Is the
moral imperative to realize *koinonia now* not only compelling, but one that over-rides
all other considerations?" — I will move on to the sacramental life of the churches to
questions that focus on the possibility for new ways to *be* in communion with God,
with one another and with the world.

The sacrament of union and the future of ecumenism

20. "Blessed be God, the Father of our Lord, Jesus Christ, by his great mercy we have been *born anew* to a living hope through the resurrection of Jesus Christ from the dead." (1 Pet. 1:3)[14]

The question of direction — "Have we gone astray?" — is linked, I believe, to the question of the preparation for the ecumenical journey. Clearly, we are in a threatened situation of declining churches, while the resources for ecumenical ministry at the local level are continuing to decrease. The counsel to undertake "an ecumenism of the possible" signals a present that does not point to a strong future. Yet there is the reality of convergence, and of increased participation, at some levels, of Evangelical churches, the Roman Catholic Church, and other bodies.

But churches are called to union — to be *in*, not *in search of*, union.

21. "Born anew to a living hope..." *Koinonia now* is the experience of new life, the gift of God to those who through repentance and forgiveness become sons and daughters and sisters and brothers in the people of God, sharing in the benefits of life in Christ. A change in the very *being* of the person (and of the community?) takes place, a qualitative difference in the faith life is apparent, and the spiritual power to be sustained in a holy life is clearly present. This is, essentially, the ontological dimension of spirituality, the *sine qua non* for living in relation to God and to neighbours. The human being is transformed, brought into a living relationship with the being of God who, in agapeic love, unites all repentant beings to God and to one another. The transformed person is in Christ an other-directed person, living, following *metanoia*, a penitential spirituality that links confession and restitution and walking in new ways.

22. Could it be that our enormous incapacity for lived church union, *koinonia now*, is rooted in an underdeveloped ecumenical spirituality? Could it be that we are all impoverished in the deepest recesses of our being? That the gift of God, the transformation of the being of each one of us and of the churches in which we live, is not being appropriated, with the result that we are, about church union, like babes? Could it be that the most radical and joyous and liberating change which is part of God's provision for life in faith is overlooked in our spiritual formation, and in the company of the faithful? That for many of our churches the phenomenology of *sanctification* must be more fully explored to arrive at the full truth of that in which personal and corporate transformation exists?

The church as the people of God is called to live in union in Christ through the power of the Holy Spirit. The transformation that makes this possible — for persons and for their churches — is, in truth, a new spirit of redeeming love, preparing the new being to live in expressions of Christ's love — the "community of equals", the non-racial community, the non-denominational society or order or group within the larger, catholic "perimeter" in which the Christian community is really united in membership, ministry and sacraments.

Could it be that the *sacraments* are the key to discovering resources not yet celebrated in the name of Christ? The sacramental life of the people of God is clearly foundational in most traditions. Differences arise over the number of sacraments but not, among those whose ecclesiologies are sacramental, over which ones are formative of Christian fellowship and community. Could it be that churches are overlooking in sacramental life the celebration of the *change of being, transformation, the experience* of the new life that is a miracle of God's grace? How is the experience of *union*, with its vertical and horizontal dimensions, made explicit in sacramental liturgies? It may be that there are aspects of these experiences that are distinctive, needing to be celebrated in a fuller way than is provided for now. Union is at the heart of the life of the people of God — union with Christ through the power of the Holy Spirit. This is the gift that empowers for the ministry of unity and of which the church is the custodian in history. Where it is not appropriated or where it is denied by the life of resistance to church union there may be the experience of "going astray" with which we began this reflection. Enormously complex issues of sacramental theology are raised by these questions, as are those of authority. Nevertheless I see in the problematic of ecumenical common life reason to pursue issues such as the one surrounding the sacramental life of the churches. To recover the gift of unity in union we may have to recover spiritual resources that God gives to all the faithful.

Conclusion

23. The future of the ecumenical movement is linked to the question of faithfulness to a vision of life in union, the gift of the Triune God to the people of God. The years of ecumenical pilgrimage have been a time for wandering, although by God's grace much has been planted for harvesting.

If the churches are to find a way into the future, it will be through re-visioning the ecumenical task, and recovering the full measure of the resources God makes available to the churches. The sacramental life of the church may be a source of additional grace and power.

God be praised for the gift of new birth, the foundation of the ministry of union in Christ.

24. A closing faith statement:

Come along, chillun, don'tcha get weary,
There's a great camp meetin' in the Promised Land!
                    American Negro Spiritual

Amen.

* * *

A final note: I have spoken out of my location in the North American ecumenical world, and in solidarity with the churches of West African countries in which I lived and worked. I believe that these reflections are relevant to the faith and order (and to the life and work and mission) of Christians no matter where we may be. The specifics of culture differ, but the nature of koinonia-acceptance or koinonia-refusal is the same wherever the churches may be. As the church of Christ is one, so is the essential experience of Christian ecumenism of one piece.

NOTES

[1] The translation used is the Revised Standard Version.

[2] *Hosanna! Music, Worship with Don Moen*, Mobile, Integrity Music, 1992.

[3] "Tell Us, Lord..." by Fr Milos Vesin, *Worship Book/Libro de Culto/Gottesdienstbuch/Recueil de prières et de services liturgiques*, fifth world conference on Faith and Order, Santiago de Compostela 1993, Geneva, Commission on Faith and Order, 1993, no. 41, p.95 (this song was written especially for worship at the world conference — ed.).

[4] James Weldon Johnson (1871-1938), words copyright by Edward B. Marks Music Corporation.

[5] *The Book of Common Prayer*, according to the use of the Episcopal church, 1979, "Prayers for the World", p.814.

[6] Most Rev. Desmond Tutu, Archbishop of Capetown, cf. p.96 above.

[7] Cf. Gillian R. Evans, "An Anglican Perspective", in *The Unity of the Church as Koinonia*, Günther Gassman and John Radano eds, Faith and Order paper no. 163, Geneva, WCC 1993, pp.10-13.

[8] A.C. Outler, *That the World May Believe: A Study of Christian Unity and What It Means for Methodists*, New York, Board of Missions of the Methodist Church, 1966, p.74, cited in Geoffrey Wainwright, *The Ecumenical Moment: Crisis and Opportunity for the Church*, Grand Rapids, MI, Eerdmans, 1983, p.220.

[9] *Ibid.*

[10] Stephen Neill, *Anglicanism*, New York, Oxford University Press, 4th ed., 1977, p.494.

[11] Gerald Moede, National Workshop on Christian Unity, Milwaukee, Wisconsin, USA, May 1993.

[12] "The Unity of the Church as Koinonia: Gift and Calling", statement of the WCC seventh assembly, Canberra, 1991, para. 1.1. Published in *Towards Koinonia in Faith, Life and Witness: A Discussion Paper*, Faith and Order paper no. 161, Geneva, WCC, 1993, p.11.

[13] *Ibid.*, para. 2.1, p.12.

[14] Revised Standard Version.

THE FUTURE OF THE ECUMENICAL MOVEMENT: REPORT OF THE YOUNGER THEOLOGIANS AND OTHER YOUNG PARTICIPANTS

1. Introduction

It is with great respect that we regard the considerable achievement of Faith and Order. We think of the long journey which already lies behind us. One could compare Faith and Order to a wise person, a loving grandmother. (We have learned that in the context of Europe to be old has negative connotations; in Africa old people are viewed with respect and treated as dignitaries!)

On the journey towards koinonia, the grandmother is now taking her grandchildren along with her and giving them the opportunity to ask her questions about her eighty years of life. Koinonia is becoming a conversation between the generations. For this marvellous opportunity for us younger theologians to accompany you on the journey towards koinonia, we should like to express our heartfelt thanks.

We are glad that the statement made by young theologians in Budapest has been translated into action.

However, we do not only harvest the fruits of the work already undertaken: we have also inherited the doctrinal differences. Is that a sign that we have correctly learned the lessons of unity in diversity?

We ask ourselves the questions: is koinonia too a *querelle des anciens* (argument between the old-timers)? And do we wish to continue this *querelle des anciens*, or find a new way forward? The divergences between us are not only of a doctrinal nature. There are also existential issues which concern us in our various contexts. Three groups have worked on the following issues: youth and younger theologians: their crises and expectations; Faith and Order working methods; issues. We shall now hear the findings of the work by the groups.

2. Subgroup on youth

2.1. Young people in the churches

As younger theologians we have the task to enable the gospel to bear fruit in our churches and societies by means of proclamation, the eucharist and social action. We are aware that young people in the countries we come from suffer severe disorientation. Changing idols of opinions in pluralist societies, and the impenetrable complex of political power relationships — all make it difficult for young people to find an identity. They so easily become a political football for agitators, so that neo-nationalist tendencies receive much support. We see in our societies an increasing readiness to resort to violence. The excessive secular emphasis on material values leads to consumerism, with its attendant exploitation, unemployment and poverty.

Hardly any alternative models of fulfilled life are being offered to counter the resulting purposelessness. On this whole context, the churches' preaching and sacramental life also lacks spiritual power and a convincing ethic.

This lack leads many into the hands of esoteric groups, or lays them open to being proselytized. Others turn completely away from the church and religion.

We see that for many the churches' proclamation has lost its credibility. We long for a convincing life-style on the part of believers in the churches.

- How can the ecumenical debate in Faith and Order contribute to a renewal of the proclamation of the Christian faith?

During the conference we have heard voices which take seriously the actual context of the churches and the practical witness of local churches in the process in which the various churches grow together in their belief and structures.

- How can Faith and Order contribute to the finding of solutions in the particular context of each local church?

2.2. Younger theologians in Faith and Order

We welcome the fact that the category of "younger theologians" has been acknowledged by realizing them as a working group in the Faith and Order conference in Santiago.

However, the time allocated for our meeting was so short that it was not possible to grow together as a group, nor to do effective work: we only had Friday from 22h. to 23h., without official interpretation.

We ourselves organized further meetings, and only that gave us the time to produce this joint presentation to the conference.

We propose that in subsequent conferences more time should be allocated for spontaneous meetings and that younger theologians should be invited to a preparatory meeting before the commencement of the official conference.

We have the impression that as "younger theologians" we are welcome in Faith and Order. The chosen description "younger theologians" indicates by age and role a different group from the WCC category "youth".

We would thus like to make the following proposals as to how younger theologians can more effectively cooperate in and with Faith and Order.

It seems meaningful to us to set up a network of "younger academic specialists" in Faith and Order. This would include theologians but also specialists from other disciplines. In this network we could develop our expectations for the future and integrate them into Faith and Order. For this to happen national encounters and international exchange would be necessary.

2.3. Towards an ecumenical approach

It is our strong desire to engage in common witness for the healing of society and the earth, and we view that as first and foremost a challenge to Christian ethics:

- How can we preach peace in societies in which even schoolchildren have pistols and in churches which condemn one another and fight one another?
- How can we baptize with water from rivers so polluted that the fish in them are dying?
- Destructive forces (in the form of drug abuse, lack of respect for life, and violence) are making aggressive onslaughts into our societies and we can only resist them by *common* action.

Now is the time for action, and our common witness will arise out of such action.

- What obstacles still stand in the way of ecumenical approach in koinonia?
- Is it our fear that we would lose power?
- As theologians, can we live in gospel simplicity, free from the need to define ourselves by titles or specialist knowledge?
- Can the testimony of the presence of the spirit of God in our meeting be so clearly expressed that a generation seeking a purpose in life will find fresh support in the church of Jesus Christ?

3. Subgroup on Faith and Order methods

Looking back on what has been accomplished since the last world conference on Faith and Order, it is clear that the Commission has played a very significant role in developing ecumenical relationships characterized by koinonia in faith, life and witness. Theology is where people are, and there are many countries where the majority of Christians are under thirty years old. It is apparent to some that a generational shift is taking place in the Faith and Order Commission, and we understand that we have been invited to attend partly as representing the future of the commission, within the ecumenical movement. This is a great responsibility. However, we are also part of its *present*, and the reality of that present is that we are a group characterized by diversity. Represented among us are many different theological approaches, and we ask the question: "How are we going to discover and develop a common framework of language and concept to carry on the ecumenical discourse?" There are new challenges for ecumenical theology as the increasing fragmentation of our cultural contexts is reflected in the variety of our methodological approaches. It is not only doctrine which divides us.

There is debate as to whether Faith and Order has reached a limit in the possibility for "mining" new ground using convergence methodology. We propose that Faith and Order extends its range of methodological approaches, initiating a new dialogue between contextual, convergence, consensus and comparative theologies. We suggest that Faith and Order undertake a study of how contextual theologies can be ecumenical theologies, and can be further integrated as a tool for the work of the Commission. How does one contextual theology speak to another? Theological reflection within the ecumenical movement finds its context both in the tradition of the faith of the church, and in the struggle of hungry people for daily bread.

We also recommend that there should be a re-examination of the possibilities offered by a comparative theological method, and in a context of developing ecumenical relationships, expecially an exploration of the experience of lived-relationships between the churches at all levels.

We suggest this re-evaluation of the comparative approach partly because we have begun to ask of one another: "Where do we find our own tradition within one another's churches?" Where do we find and affirm that which is common to us in our traditions, in spirituality and in the conceptual framework of our approach to the discussion? How can we prepare ourselves to begin to give and receive from the treasury of our traditions?

These differing methodological approaches are not opposing and mutually exclusive options: Faith and Order must embrace a rich variety of theological approaches if it is to continue its special task of creative theological reflection, in the service of the churches, in and for the future.

Recommendations

The group of younger theologians (which has included some stewards, co-opted staff, delegates and younger contributors attending under other categories) recommends:

1. That Faith and Order explore ways of continuing its relationship with those who are invited to participate at particular meetings as younger theologians, looking for ways in which younger theologians can be still more deeply drawn into the whole work of the Plenary and Standing Commissions. Would it be possible to appoint younger theologians to work as a part of those commissions?

2. That Faith and Order provide support for internships, to enable younger theologians to work within the WCC.

3. That Faith and Order prepare outline courses and background study materials to assist in the teaching of ecumenics, and to help those in theological education to share in the work of the Commission.

4. That Faith and Order develop new strategies for communicating its work to the churches at a variety of levels, and for renewing its agenda in dialogue with the creative questioning which could be the product of such a deeper process of reception.

5. Finally, we ask all those who are members of the Commission to see it as part of their role as members to share the work of Faith and Order with younger theologians in their church and region, and to encourage church structures to enable younger theologians to be part of the ecumenical movement.

4. Subgroup on issues

The following are some thoughts from Indoamerican youth.

Our understanding of koinonia leads us to reflect in favour of life in all its fullness, beginning from the present reality, from our faith and our witness.

Our reality is scarred by the visible and invisible forces that are against creation. The so-called "third-world" countries suffer the burden of an unpayable foreign debt; the intervention of the International Monetary Fund; national and international corruption; the production, consumption and exportation of drugs; injustice at all levels of society. For example, penal justice reflects moral degradation. Those guilty of crime and theft are so often "released" because of bribes. All this produces a total lack of confidence in all political leaders and even in the acceptance of authority.

As we face the present situation we are convinced of the need of koinonia, where we can bring together our faith, our life and our witness, all struggling towards a creative restoration.

The industrial world perceives human beings and our ecological environment in merely utilitarian terms, which deny the image of God in creation and human dignity.

We believe that the future of the ecumenical movement will consolidate when solutions are forged in solidarity with those who are already experiencing koinonia, specially among indigenous churches and communities.

In the light of all this we make the following recommendations:

1. That we encourage each other in the spirit of koinonia to search together for a Christian inculturation which will reflect an authentic organic image of Christ, which seriously considers the context of the people.

2. That the experience of koinonia of this conference inspire us to reinterpret the dogmas in the light of the diversity of our confessions, so as to be able to give an inclusive meaning to our Christian practice.
3. That we exhort each to reflect a koinonia in our daily life, in our faith and in our witness, specially in relation to the multitude of marginalized and oppressed peoples who are claiming desperately for koinonia.

We now call on God: the Father, the Son and the Holy Spirit that when we leave this conference, we go beyond the Inca moral code: Ama Sulla (don't steal); Ama Quella (don't lie); Ama Llulla (don't be lazy). Because koinonia is much more than only moral issues. Amen.

VI

The WCC
and Faith and Order:
A Common Future

☐ Introduction

The conference focused on the future of the World Council of Churches and of Faith and Order in plenary XIV, 13 August, 9h.15, vice-moderator the Rev. Araceli Rocchietti presiding; plenary XV, 13 August, 11h., Prof. Nicolas Lossky presiding; and plenary XVI, 13 August, 16h., moderator Dr Mary Tanner presiding.

At the request of the Rev. A. Rocchietti, Prof. MUNDUKU Ngamayamu-Dagoga opened plenary XIV with prayer. She then called upon the Rev. Dr Konrad Raiser and Archbishop Dr Aram Keshishian to deliver **papers** on the future of the World Council of Churches and the role of Faith and Order in the context of the ecumenical movement. Three further **papers** on this topic were delivered, two in plenary XV by the Rev. Dr YEMBA Kekumba and Dr Constance Tarasar and one in plenary XVI by the Rev. Prof. Jean-Marie Tillard, O.P.

THE FUTURE OF
THE WORLD COUNCIL OF CHURCHES
AND THE ROLE OF FAITH AND ORDER
WITHIN THE ECUMENICAL MOVEMENT

KONRAD RAISER

Dear friends, brothers and sisters in Christ,

It is a joy and a privilege for me to greet you as general secretary of the World Council of Churches. Obviously, this fifth world conference on Faith and Order is a very significant event in the life of the World Council of Churches which is expressed by the fact that all four officers of the WCC are present and have been actively involved. For me personally, it was also a welcome occasion to be involved afresh in the work of Faith and Order, which has been my ecumenical training ground. I remember the time when I joined the staff of Faith and Order in 1969. The impulses and reverberations of the fourth world conference at Montreal were still alive then throughout the Council. New directions had been opened up in Faith and Order and had attracted my attention as a young theologian.

Thirty years later, great expectations have been focused on this world conference in Santiago de Compostela. The results of our common work are now before us. It is my hope that they will not only provide orientation for Faith and Order in the years to come, but help to strengthen our common efforts in the World Council to articulate in a fresh and coherent way the ecumenical vision for our time.

* * *

1. The founding of the World Council of Churches in 1948 came about because of the far-sighted conviction on the part of the leading minds of the early ecumenical movement that the churches themselves had to take responsibility for this new start towards representing the visible unity of the church, bearing common witness to the gospel throughout the world, and assuming Christian responsibility for justice and peace. Nowhere is the feeling that the founding of the World Council through the coming together of the two world movements of Faith and Order and Life and Work was an act of genuine renewal and conversion expressed more clearly than in the message of the first assembly at Amsterdam, which states:

> We bless God our Father, and our Lord Jesus Christ, who gathers together in one the children of God that are scattered abroad. He has brought us here together at Amsterdam. We are one in acknowledging him as our God and Saviour. We are divided from one another not only in matters of faith, order and tradition, but also by pride of nation, class and race. But Christ has made us his own, and he is not divided. In seeking him we find one another. Here at Amsterdam we have committed ourselves afresh to him, and have covenanted with one another in constituting this World Council of Churches. We intend to stay together. We

The Rev. Dr Konrad Raiser, Evangelical Church in Germany, is general secretary of the World Council of Churches. This paper was translated from the German by the WCC Language Service.

call upon Christian congregations everywhere to endorse and fulfil this covenant in their relations with one another. In thankfulness to God we commit the future to him....

Our coming together to form a World Council will be vain unless Christians and Christian congregations everywhere commit themselves to the Lord of the church in a new effort to seek together, where they live, to be his witnesses and servants among their neighbours. We have to remind ourselves and all people that God has put down the mighty from their seats and exalted the humble and meek. We have to learn afresh together to speak boldly in Christ's name both to those in power and to the people, to oppose terror, cruelty and race discrimination, to stand by the outcast, the prisoner and the refugee. We have to make of the church in every place a voice for those who have no voice, and a home where everyone will be at home. We have to learn afresh together what is the duty of the Christian man or woman in industry, in agriculture, in politics, in the professions and in the home. We have to ask God to teach us together to say "no" and to say "yes" in truth. "No", to all that flouts the love of Christ, to every system, every programme and every person that treats any human being as though he/she were an irresponsible thing or a means of profit, to the defenders of injustice in the name of order, to those who sow the seeds of war or urge war as inevitable; "yes", to all that conforms to the love of Christ, to all who seek for justice, to the peace-makers, to all who hope, fight and suffer for the cause of man, to all who — even without knowing it — look for new heavens and a new earth wherein dwelleth righteousness.[1]

This vision of the early days still holds good today. Indeed, given the present "disorder" in the world and the quest for reassurance about "God's design", it is more topical than ever.

2. Today, 45 years on, the face of the World Council of Churches has changed. The churches involved in its founding were chiefly the historical Protestant and Orthodox churches of Europe and North America. Since then it has become a *World* Council of Churches in the full sense of the word, and the majority of its member churches are now to be found in the southern parts of the globe. This reflects the fact that the centre of gravity of the Christian world has shifted in our century. What is more, with the admission into membership of all the Eastern and Oriental Orthodox churches and the opening of regular relations with the Roman Catholic Church, the World Council of Churches has moved closer to its calling to be an instrument of the "one" ecumenical movement of all Christian churches, even though many Evangelical and Pentecostal churches still regard the Council with reserve or suspicion. The growth in membership coincides with the development of a new ecumenical tradition which has its inner continuity and coherence and constitutes a precious heritage on which we can build in the future.

But the world in which the member churches of the World Council committed themselves to "seek together to fulfil their calling"[2] has likewise changed. Today, all our societies are closely interlinked. But, for many people, the hopes of a new order of human community living together in justice and peace have dissolved into hopelessness and fear. The gap between rich and poor is deeper than ever. The end of the global arms race has not so far brought greater security, but rather an increase in tensions and conflicts. The destruction of the bases of human life continues unabated, and racism, violence and the violation of basic human rights are the reality of life for countless human beings.

The convictions that underlay the founding of the World Council of Churches in 1948 are as relevant today as they were then and there must be no falling back behind this foundational vision. If the World Council did not already exist, we would certainly have to create it today. Seldom before have the expectations of common witness and common action by the churches and of a credible manifestation of its much-invoked unity been so high as they are today. "That they may all be one... so that the world may believe." Credible fellowship, common work for justice and for the life of the whole creation striving for peace and reconciliation: this is the witness that the churches owe to the world today if they are to be messengers of the gospel.

3. What we actually find is something quite different. The very churches which brought the World Council of Churches into being have been gripped by deep uncertainty and spiritual paralysis. Despite the impressive results of the persistent efforts for convergence and agreement in central issues of doctrine, they lack the spiritual strength to slake off the confessional identities that have been shaped by mutual differentiation and exclusion. The continuing exodus from the church and the simultaneous growth of new religious movements in the traditionally Christian countries, the reawakening and spread of the major world religions, especially Islam and Hinduism, and the increasing mobility and mixing of traditionally homogenous population groups have created a situation of uncertainty. The reaction of the historical churches has been to retreat back into their tradition. Church unity for them means above all preserving continuity with their roots, holding the community together and resisting the forces of disintegration. Certainly, they do not want to jeopardize the agreement that has developed with churches of other traditions as a result of ecumenical endeavours; they adhere to the "goal of visible unity in the one faith and the one eucharistic fellowship";[3] but they are hesitant when it comes to taking steps that would lead to a real ecumenical breakthrough. Securing their own identity often takes precedence over ecumenical opening and renewal, with its unpredictable consequences.

A new ecumenical reality

4. At the same time it is becoming increasingly obvious that a new ecumenical reality has developed in the midst of and between the churches in the past 25 years, and this is now seeking to express itself and demanding insistently to be recognized. For more and more people in the North — especially among women and the younger generation — the inherited confessional traditions and identities do not command absolute loyalty any more. Being a Christian and active church membership are drifting apart. In the North and South new forms of Christian community life are emerging. Liturgies, prayers, songs expressing an ecumenical spirituality are shared with one another. Common translations of the Bible and theological collaboration, the experiences shared under persecution and in the common struggle for justice and respect for human rights as well as in the movements for peace and for the healing of God's creation — all these things have helped to create an awareness of solidarity and belonging together to which the old forms no longer correspond. Among the historical Protestant churches links are now so close that even without formal mutual recognition we can speak of a *de facto* church fellowship. The official statements of the churches often simply confirm what has long been established practice in the local churches.

5. It is somewhat difficult to relate the official bilateral and multilateral dialogues between delegated representatives of the big churches and this new ecumenical reality. The clarifications and the new common language offered by the dialogue reports are

based on a state of awareness that belongs to a former situation. And in any case, the fastest-growing form of Christianity, the Evangelical or Pentecostal communities with strong indigenous ties, which predominates in the churches of the South is scarcely involved in such dialogues. If the stalemate of the ecumenical process in the quest for visible unity is to be overcome, a new approach will have to be found. Instead of the separate bilateral dialogues and the multilateral conversations we will have to find a form that makes it possible to recognize the simultaneous existence of different Christian cultures, which are Eastern Byzantine, Western Roman, Western Protestant and predominantly Southern Evangelical or Pentecostal in character. The ecumenical dialogue of the future will then be a constructive dialogue among these different cultures — a dialogue which aims at increased understanding for the integrity of the other, the alien, and does not stand under the pressure of having to dissolve the differences into consensus. For this we need an ecumenical intercultural hermeneutic which will enable us to comprehend unity as a fellowship of those who continue to be different and to offer criteria for this. This does not mean to take for granted the sinful separations and divisions of the church or to be indifferent to the disintegration of the church universal. But a hermeneutic of this nature would have go beyond the much-discussed limits of diversity and consider also the limits of tolerable, acceptable unity, i.e. set criteria for "necessary and sufficient" unity. The hermeneutical discussions and studies carried out by Faith and Order in the sixties need to be taken up again with this perspective in mind.

6. When the World Council was founded in 1948, the constitution simply committed the Council to continuing the two world movements of Faith and Order and Life and Work. Since the revision of the article of the constitution concerning the functions of the WCC in 1975, the Council as a whole has adopted the more specific task of the Commission on Faith and Order, that is, "to call the churches to the goal of visible unity in one faith and one eucharistic fellowship expressed in worship and in common life in Christ, and to advance towards that unity in order that the world may believe".[4] This shows beyond all doubt that the work of Faith and Order is central among the tasks of the World Council of Churches. In this sense it is appropriate to affirm that the Council's noblest task, indeed its very raison d'etre, is to promote church unity — coupled with the warning that the Council must not neglect this task. However, a reminder then has to be given as well that in the description of the purpose of the Council unity, mission and witness, service and renewal belong inseparably together. There can be no priority or "hierarchy" of tasks here. This inclusive understanding of ecumenical commitment is incidentally also reflected in the by-laws of the Faith and Order Commission, in the programme of work done by the Commission over the past thirty years and, not least, in the theme of this world conference.

Unity and the one ecumenical movement

7. The unity of the church as gift and calling is indivisible. The same applies to the ecumenical movement, which represents the churches' effort to make visible their koinonia in faith, life and witness. It was therefore a decisive ecumenical breakthrough when the Second Vatican Council, with its Decree on Ecumenism, made it possible to speak of the "one and only ecumenical movement".[5] This movement involves all the churches which recognize that among those who believe in Christ and who are

baptized in his name there exists, despite all divisions, a real if as yet incomplete communion.

The WCC sees itself as the instrument of this one ecumenical movement, which is however wider than its official membership. For, despite the greatly expanded circle of its member churches the World Council still essentially embraces only the historical churches of the Orthodox and Protestant traditions. The Roman Catholic Church, after mature reflection, has so far declined to become a member of the World Council. The reasons are well-known and need not be elucidated here. It is therefore all the more important that the Roman Catholic Church was and is ready to participate officially in the work of the Commission on Faith and Order together with all other churches. This was made possible by the circumstance that the by-laws of the Faith and Order Commission expressly provide that "persons who are members of churches which do not belong to the Council but which confess Jesus Christ as God and Saviour are eligible for membership of the Commission".[6] This provision was applied not only with regard to Roman Catholic theologians but also from early on in relation to conservative Evangelical churches. This lends particular weight to the work of the Commission, as could be seen, for example, in the extent of the response to the convergence statements on baptism, eucharist and ministry. The special position of the Faith and Order Commission particularly because of the Roman Catholic Church's explicit involvement — which has a certain parallel in the special composition of the world conference on mission and evangelism — should not, however, be interpreted to mean that, by appealing to the earlier tradition of the Faith and Order movement, the Commission could be detached and differentiated from the Council. It is and remains a commission of the WCC which grew out of the merger of the Faith and Order movement and the Life and Work movement, which were subsequently joined by the International Missionary Council and the World Council of Christian Education. The WCC must certainly be open to future changes in its structure to enable it to fulfil its service to the one and indivisible ecumenical movement more convincingly and effectively, but it does little service to this task to call in question the convictions that underlay the founding of the World Council of Churches.

8. The WCC is beginning to prepare for its eighth assembly which will take place in 1998, in the fiftieth year since its founding. In anticipation of this date, all the member churches are invited to take part in a process of reflection on the common understanding of the WCC and the ecumenical vision that unites and binds them. In biblical terms the fiftieth year is the jubilee year following on seven sabbatical years, a year when remission from debts is granted and slaves are given their freedom, but also a year when the land is restored to its original distribution corresponding to God's will. For the land belongs to God.

This analogy could be an encouragement to us to approach the fiftieth year since the founding of the World Council as an ecumenical jubilee year — a year when the doctrinal anathemas of the past are lifted and the churches are expressly converted from separation to the koinonia which is God's gift and calling to them. In a great act of unity the churches, through their appointed delegates, could confirm that they are bound together in a real ecclesial communion grounded in the one baptism and in the common confession of Christ. This communion in the worldwide body of Christ is the gratuitous gift of God through the power of the Holy Spirit. It is thus indivisible and no church can lay claim to the privilege of owning it nor declare itself to be the centre of this koinonia.

Conversion and convergence

The new ecumenical reality which has developed between the churches in recent decades, and especially in the period since the Second Vatican Council, demands that we undergo such a conversion today — a fundamental change of orientation. Rather than analyzing what still divides us we should look instead at the already-existing communion and try to deepen and expand it and make it manifest. This involves an act of conversion as described in the latest remarkable text by the Groupe des Dombes,[7] a conversion in the sense of convergence towards the centre of koinonia, taking seriously the statement made by the third world conference on Faith and Order that

> ...as we seek to draw closer to Christ we come closer to one another. We need, therefore, to penetrate behind our divisions to a deeper and richer understanding of the mystery of the God-given union of Christ with his church. We need increasingly to realize that the separate histories of our churches find their full meaning only if seen in the perspective of God's dealings with his *whole* people.[8]

The same "word to the churches" from the third world conference goes on to say:

> The measure of unity which it has been given to the churches to experience together must now find clearer manifestation. A faith in the one church of Christ which is not implemented by *acts* of obedience is dead. There are truths about the nature of God and his church which will remain for ever closed to us unless we act together in obedience to the unity which is already ours. We would, therefore, earnestly request our churches to consider whether they are doing all they ought to do to manifest the oneness of the people of God. Should not our churches ask themselves whether they are showing sufficient eagerness to enter into conversation with other churches, and whether they should not act together in all matters except those in which deep differences of conviction compel them to act separately? Should they not acknowledge the fact that they often allow themselves to be separated from each other by secular forces and influences instead of witnessing together to the sole Lordship of Christ who gathers his people out of all nations, races and tongues?[9]

The future of the World Council of Churches will be decisively influenced by whether or not it succeeds in convincing the churches that the time has come for such an act of conversion in the sense of convergence towards the centre of their unity. The Commission on Faith and Order clearly has a specific task in shaping the future of the Council by preparing and laying the foundation for this step. In doing so it would at the same time fulfil its own special role in the context of the ecumenical movement today and would remain true to its own tradition as expressed by earlier world conferences on Faith and Order. Let us then resolutely work together for this renewal of the ecumenical vision.

NOTES

[1] W.A. Visser 't Hooft ed., *The First Assembly of the World Council of Churches*, London, SCM, 1949, pp.9-10.
[2] Cf. Constitution and Rules of the World Council of Churches, I. Basis, and III. Functions and Purposes, 1).
[3] *Ibid*, III. Functions and Purposes, 1).
[4] *Ibid*.
[5] See the "Second Official Report of the Joint Working Group between the World Council of Churches and the Roman Catholic Church" (1967).
[6] By-laws of the Faith and Order Commission, article 3(h).
[7] Groupe des Dombes, *For the Conversion of the Churches*, Geneva, WCC 1993.
[8] Oliver S. Tomkins ed., *The Third World Conference on Faith and Order*, London, SCM, 1953, p.15.
[9] *Ibid.*, p.16.

CHALLENGES FACING FAITH AND ORDER

ARCHBISHOP ARAM KESHISHIAN

The dramatic changes that are taking place in the life of the churches and societies, the new realities and concerns that are emerging in different parts of the world, challenge us all, partners in the one ecumenical movement, to a new awareness of our common ecumenical endeavours and lead us to new expressions of the ecumenical vision. The Faith and Order movement, which is called to take a leading part in determining the future course of the ecumenical movement, is also confronted with new situations and challenges. In fact, in the midst of changing norms, forms and priorities of the ecumenical movement, searching questions are being raised about the identity and vocation of Faith and Order and about how it will proceed. Hence this is not only a moment of celebration, harvesting and reappropriating the thirty years of work, but also a decisive moment of self-critical appraisal and looking forward with a clearer self-understanding and vision.

The new perspectives, priorities and guidelines established by this conference will undoubtedly shape the future agenda of Faith and Order and give it a new direction. I would like to identify a few challenges and concerns facing Faith and Order that must be wrestled with realistically and boldly as we embark on a new period in the history of the Faith and Order movement.

Refocusing the role of Faith and Order within the ecumenical movement

It is not possible to speak about Faith and Order and the ecumenical movement as separate entities. They belong to each other. They condition each other, being inseparably interwoven. In view of some prevailing misconceptions and ambiguities about Faith and Order, it is vitally important that its specific role within the ecumenical movement be reassessed and clearly redefined. Three major concerns deserve special attention.

De-institutionalization of Faith and Order

At this point, two important affirmations must be made. First, Faith and Order is not an institution. It seems to me that during the last few decades the movement character of Faith and Order has been considerably decreased to the extent of limiting Faith and Order to a programmatic entity in many councils of churches with its own specific agenda, function and commission. Irrespective of its institutional expressions, which are indispensable indeed, Faith and Order essentially is and should remain by its very nature and goal a *movement* of churches in search of Christian unity.

Archbishop Aram Keshishian, the Armenian Orthodox primate of Lebanon, is the moderator of the central committee of the World Council of Churches.

Second, Faith and Order is not just a unit of the WCC. I know that for some churches the close identification of Faith and Order with the WCC may raise questions about the future of Faith and Order. Faith and Order should continue to remain, with its specific agenda, methodology and style, structurally located in the WCC which is a "privileged instrument" and the most comprehensive and organic expression of the ecumenical movement. Yet, on the other hand, we have to be alert not to reduce it simply to a programmatic area of the WCC. Such a tendency may endanger the identity of Faith and Order and marginalize its priorities. We must constantly remind ourselves that many churches became involved in the ecumenical movement through the Faith and Order movement, and that for these churches the search for the unity of the church remains very much identified with Faith and Order. Therefore, Faith and Order should not be possessed or conditioned by any ecumenical body. As a movement of churches it is wider than any local, regional or global ecumenical structure.

A movement embracing the whole oikoumene

Faith and Order, as a movement within the ecumenical movement, is facing three major problems.

First, it is in the process of self-isolation in an ecumenical movement which is increasingly becoming grassroots and action-oriented. In other words, the growing pragmatism and activism in the ecumenical movement has led Faith and Order into the danger of a self-centred and self-contented existence. As I pointed out earlier, the Faith and Order movement is an integral and vital part of the ecumenical movement. The latter cannot be fully and authentically itself without Faith and Order. And Faith and Order has no raison d'etre apart from the wider ecumenical movement. It is in this context of interdependence and complementarity that the unique role of Faith and Order must be conceived and assessed and an attempt made to review and reshape it.

Second, participation in Faith and Order of new churches, groups and Christians from all regions has made it truly a pan-Christian movement. Faith and Order should avoid becoming, strictly speaking, a membership-based and -bound organization. As a movement of renewal and unity, it should transcend the institutional boundaries of the churches to embrace the entire oikoumene. However, it is essential that the "ecclesial" character of Faith and Order be preserved and deepened further against the secularistic trends within the ecumenical movement.

Third, Faith and Order still remains, to a large degree, a Euro-centred movement. Its widely representative membership has not brought substantial change in its language, methodology and orientation. Furthermore, due to its specialized agenda, Faith and Order has not been able to reach people at the grassroots level and has become a movement of selected persons. The churches, in their turn, did not respond seriously to many of the initiatives of Faith and Order, considering them largely irrelevant to their local situations. It is important, therefore, that a mutually challenging and enriching interaction be established between globalism, contextualism and confessionalism in the theological work of Faith and Order. Not only will such an approach provide a broader ecumenical perspective; it will also greatly help Faith and Order to relate itself more directly and meaningfully to the new realities and situations in which the churches are living and witnessing in different parts of the world.

A well-defined agenda with a holistic vision

For some years, there have been critical questions about the relevance of the Faith and Order agenda. Some people think that in an ecumenical movement which has considerably enlarged its agenda, Faith and Order, too, ought to go beyond its traditional agenda and grapple with those issues emanating from the present ecumenical "realities". I do not share such a view. For the sake of keeping pace with the changing ecumenical priorities and concerns, and for becoming more responsive to new situations, Faith and Order cannot make the entire agenda of the ecumenical movement its own. The mandate of Faith and Order is determined by its specific goal. On this point, however, I want to make the following observations.

First, the reflection processes of Faith and Order will remain isolated and unrelated to each other, and its studies will eventually be doomed to decorate the shelves of ecumenical offices and libraries, if its agenda is not conceived and implemented as a coherent whole. This implies inner continuity and dynamic interaction between the so-called "old" and "new" concerns and priorities of Faith and Order. In fact, the studies on the "Community of Women and Men" and "Church and World: the Unity of the Church and the Renewal of Human Community" and other similar initiatives are serious attempts, though of a limited nature, to deal with the agenda items of Faith and Order as a continuous and coherent whole. These efforts must continue with new impetus and in a more organized manner.

Second, in spite of some recent attempts, Faith and Order did not articulate sharply and efficiently enough the inter-relatedness of its agenda with the broader ecumenical agenda. Therefore, Faith and Order needs to broaden both the perspective of its approach and the scope of its reflection and identify the implications of emerging ecumenical concerns and issues to its priorities. For instance, the growing importance of dialogue in the pluralistic societies of today, the process of Justice, Peace and Integrity of Creation (JPIC), the search for participatory and inclusive community have significant bearing on Faith and Order issues. This is not a threat to the classical Faith and Order agenda and its proper focus, as some may think. It is aimed rather at locating more meaningfully the basic priorities of Faith and Order within the context of the ecumenical agenda, and at giving more visibility and urgency to its major goals.

Third, the stereotyped patterns of thinking, modes of expression and traditional methodologies still prevailing in Faith and Order, are no longer relevant in a rapidly and radically changing world. We need new languages, new approaches, new styles that are flexible, open and responsive to new situations. Those who think that Faith and Order should eventually aim at an "ecumenical" theology are mistaken. The task of Faith and Order is to transform the mere co-existence of theologies in the ecumenical movement into a dynamic and creative interaction, and to generate a more substantial, vital and coherent theological reflection in the ecumenical movement.

These necessary efforts aimed at a closer interconnectedness of concerns, inter-action of perspectives and integration of agenda items, should never be done at the expense of the identifiable task of Faith and Order within the ecumenical movement.

A broader vision of unity

The unity of the church is the primary goal of the whole ecumenical movement. Faith and Order from its very inception has been instrumental in the churches' search for unity. It has tackled the question of unity in different contexts and perspectives, and has proposed challenging "models" and "concepts" of unity. But the question is: Where are we now, and where are we going in our search for unity? Four major concerns claim our attention.

First, our discussion of unity has reached a crucial point. After so many years of extensive and arduous work, the absence of a major breakthrough may lead the churches to impatience, disappointment and stagnation. Furthermore, the growing horizontalism, secularism, activism and pragmatism in the ecumenical movement may bring a shift of emphasis from the question of unity to other ecumenical priorities. In view of this emerging tendency, the churches should re-commit themselves to the common search for unity, concretely expressing, particularly on the local level, the degree of unity that already exists among them, and identifying the practical implications of the theological agreements that they have reached through bilateral and multilateral dialogues.

Second, the brokenness of human community, namely, cultural, social and economic divisions and injustices, has deepened further the doctrinal and theological division of the churches. The growing nationalism, ethnicity and religiosity in the world of today have also become divisive factors. While Faith and Order is mainly concerned with the ecclesial dimension of unity, it cannot ignore the socio-political and economic dimension of it which is acquiring urgency in the life of present societies. In fact, according to its by-laws Faith and Order is urged "to examine such social, cultural, political, racial and other factors as affect the unity of the church".

Third, in spite of continuous efforts we have not yet been able to reach a common conception of unity, since we have a different understanding of the church. The pivotal question is not, therefore, what is the nature of the unity we seek, but what is the nature of the church? Clearly, our ecclesiological perceptions condition our vision of unity. For some, it is a goal that must be achieved. For others, it is a given reality which already exists in the church; it must be expressed. The concept of koinonia, which will acquire through this conference a deeper importance in the ecumenical movement as well as the newly established study process on "Ecumenical Perspectives on Ecclesiology", will significantly help the churches to embark on a more comprehensive ecclesiological reflection. I believe that this reflection process will, in turn, greatly advance the search for unity.

Fourth, unity has never been the only focus of the ecumenical movement. Renewal, common witness and service have also been essential dimensions of the ecumenical vision. This fact is well-articulated in the constitution of the WCC. The ecumenical vision may have different emphases and manifestations in different times and situations, but it is one and indivisible. In the context of this oneness, wholeness and inner integrity and coherence of the ecumenical vision the unity of the church must be located. In other words, unity needs to be dealt with in a holistic way as an integral part of other concerns. This is also true of other ecumenical issues that claim priority today. Such an approach on both sides does not undermine the top priority and crucial urgency of unity; rather it sharply spells out the inner interconnectedness of unity and its broader implications. Faith and Order has been able to establish in recent years a close interaction between the unity of the church and the renewal of human community, between the struggle for unity and commitment to justice. I consider this vital for the future work of Faith and Order on unity.

Baptism, eucharist and ministry: a crucial ecumenical test

BEM remains the most widely circulated and seriously treated ecumenical document in ecumenical history. Its ecumenical impact is profound and far-reaching. The churches' responses to it have revealed a considerable degree of convergence which may provide a solid ground for a common affirmation of the essentials of our common faith contained in BEM. The same responses have also indicated areas of divergence which need to be explored further.

After an initial worldwide enthusiasm, there is now, in my assessment, some weariness and indifference about BEM in church and ecumenical circles. The BEM process must continue with renewed awareness of its crucial importance for the whole of the ecumenical movement. With this view in mind, I would propose the following actions to be taken by Faith and Order.

First, Faith and Order should continue to give top priority and urgency to the BEM process, constantly reminding the churches that BEM is not just a convergence text offered for theological reflection, but a challenge, an invitation and an urgent call addressed to the churches for mutual recognition. The churches should realize that the BEM process presents a decisive turning-point in the history of the ecumenical movement and is a real test of their seriousness about the ecumenical movement in general, and the question of unity in particular. Therefore if the churches fail to commit themselves to, and involve themselves more responsibly in, the BEM process, thereby making it their own, the ecumenical movement may undergo a serious setback.

Second, for a variety of theological reasons it seems that a full and immediate reception of BEM is not yet possible for many churches. We have to be patient and realistic. I would propose that the "reception" process proceed step by step. As a first concrete step forward, I do not think that the churches will have any difficulty in declaring the common baptism as the basis of their unity. In my view, the question of eucharistic sharing needs deeper theological reflection and further ecumenical growth. I do not see much difficulty in achieving, in most cases, the mutual recognition of ministries which must follow the affirmation of common baptism. Therefore, Faith and Order must establish a new methodology, procedure and timetable to enhance the BEM process.

From dialogue to "reception"

The last thirty years of the history of the ecumenical movement have been marked by an intense theological dialogue on the bilateral level. A number of consensus statements and theological agreements were produced on major doctrinal and theological issues. It is now time to bring together and evaluate their results and future course. Let me mention some considerations for the evaluation process.

First, while assessing the results of these dialogues in a broader ecumenical perspective and context, Faith and Order must take into consideration the following factors: (a) the formal character and mainly doctrinal nature of these dialogues can immensely help Faith and Order to advance more surely on the way to unity; (b) most of the bilateral agreements remain isolated and unrelated to each other; they need to be reinterpreted and reappropriated vis-a-vis new ecumenical situations; (c) more effective interaction must be established between bilateral and multilateral dialogues, and their theological complementarity be given more meaningful expression.

Second, how can these theological agreements be implemented in the life of the churches? I believe that the churches should progressively move forward from the stage of being together, praying together and talking to each other to a continuous and dynamic process of "reception". I do not use the term in the sense of adoption of a given doctrinal or theological statement, but in terms of effective communication, dynamic interpretation and ecumenical conscientization. This process of "reception" basically implies ecumenical education and conversion as well as mutual accountability. Such a mutuality and the sense of inter-relatedness will make the churches experience koinonia existentially in faith, life and witness.

Third, in spite of the fact that bilateral dialogues have lost much of their theological significance and ecumenical impact and have become part of church politics, they still retain for many churches and world communions their validity and importance. There are also those who believe that a shift of emphasis should take place from bilateral to multilateral dialogue. Hence, parallelism between bilateral and multilateral dialogues will prevail at least for some time. But is it not time to think about new alternatives that generate new vitality, creativity and coherence in theological dialogues both on bilateral and multilateral levels? Is it not time to move the churches from dialogue to convergence and reception? Faith and Order should take this challenge seriously.

From convergence in faith to convergence in life

The work of Faith and Order has remained highly theological and academic in nature, methodology and scope. This has sometimes created a gap between reflection and action, theology and actual life, between Faith and Order and the churches, giving the impression to many that Faith and Order is a group of selected persons who work for theological consensus. Faith and Order must correct this impression. In its programmatic priorities, language and methodology, the wholeness and integrity of consensus in faith and communion in life should be articulated efficiently with the following considerations.

First, Christian faith and life form an indivisible whole. The WCC was brought into existence by the integration of the Faith and Order and Life and Work movements. Involvement in service and witness necessarily entails commitment to ecclesial unity, and commitment to ecclesial unity necessarily implies involvement in service and witness. Therefore, any dichotomy between Christian faith and political involvement, between unity of the church and struggle for justice, is an ecumenical heresy. The "common calling" of the churches, according to the basis of the WCC, is not only "to proclaim the oneness" of the church.[1] The "common calling" of the churches is also "to express the common concerns of the churches in the service of human need, the breaking down of barriers between people and the promotion of one human family in justice and peace".[2] This basic ecclesiological and missiological conviction ought to remain the sustaining power and driving force of the ecumenical movement.

Second, the twentieth century was a period of ecumenical dialogue and theological reflection. There are signs which indicate that the coming century will bring with it an ecumenism that is mainly preoccupied with concrete issues of church and society. Faith and Order must be ready, without moving from its basic focus and primary concerns, to relate itself more meaningfully to the existential realities of life and to the concrete struggles of the churches. The theme of this conference reminds us that the issues of faith, life and witness will continue to remain closely related to each other. In order to remain a credible instrument of the ecumenical movement, Faith and Order should constantly identify the relevance of its concerns and their implications for the local life of the churches. Convergence in faith has no meaning if it is not translated into convergence in life.

Faith and Order: an ecumenical challenger

The role of Faith and Order is one of listening, reminding, serving and facilitating. In an ecumenical movement that is exposed to internal and external threats of various nature and scope, Faith and Order should also assume the role of challenger.

- Faith and Order has a corrective role to play in an ecumenism that tends to relativize the Christocentric Trinitarianism as a way of dialogue with other faiths, and advocates syncretistic attitudes for the building of one human community.
- Faith and Order is called to stand firm against all sorts of ecumenical activism and pragmatism that consider Faith and Order issues and goals as being obsolete to modern Christian men and women.
- Faith and Order should strongly oppose all secular ecumenical trends that may overshadow the vertical dimension of the ecumenical movement and marginalize the question of unity.
- Vis-a-vis the growing confessionalism and parochialism, Faith and Order must also challenge the churches not to lose the urgency of their common struggle for Christian unity.

Faith and Order itself needs to be constantly challenged by an ecumenical movement which is in a process of transformation.

* * *

Any movement grows, endures and attains its objectives through committed and visionary people. The words of W.A. Visser 't Hooft are still challenging:

> We need the impatient people who call for boldness, imagination and forward-looking hope in action. But there is an impatience which gives up and an impatience which builds up. Merely to say no and to turn our backs on the existing ecumenical movement would be a desperate remedy and an act of sheer ingratitude. We have no right to throw away all that has been given to us in the movement in the past forty years. What we are free to do is to renew it, purify it, and adapt it to present tasks.[3]

The goals of the Faith and Order movement are not yet achieved. We are still "on the way" to Christian unity. The road is long and thorny. The pilgrimage is risky and costly. Lausanne (1927), Edinburgh (1937), Lund (1953) and Montreal (1963) were important stages of critical reflection and self-assessment. In Santiago de Compostela, in this ancient city of pilgrimage, let us, the old and new pilgrims of the Faith and Order movement, renew our commitment to move forward together in prayer, hope and action.

NOTES

[1] Cf. Constitution and Rules of the World Council of Churches, I. Basis, and III. Functions and Purposes, 1.
[2] *Ibid*, III, Function and Purposes, 4.
[3] W.A. Visser 't Hooft, *Has the Ecumenical Movement a Future?* Belfast, Christian Journals, 1974, pp.52-53.

THE FUTURE OF THE WCC
AND THE ROLE OF FAITH AND ORDER
WITHIN THE ECUMENICAL MOVEMENT:
REFLECTIONS

YEMBA KEKUMBA

Moderator, sisters and brothers,

1. I was asked to put some thoughts together as one of the reactions to the very important papers presented by the general secretary of the World Council of Churches, Konrad Raiser, and the moderator of the central committee of the same ecumenical body, Archbishop Aram Keshishian. They are among the papers which, by their content and as major conference materials, will certainly help this fifth world conference on Faith and Order to shape the task of the Faith and Order Commission at the eve of the new century. How is Faith and Order going to tackle this task as a continuing agenda and how is this agenda going to take into account the new challenges the churches and societies are facing at the end of this twentieth century? How does Faith and Order understand its mandate as one of the World Council of Churches commissions on the one hand, and as the heart of ecumenical movement on the other hand?

2. A simple observation on the life and history of Faith and Order in the last years leads to a general understanding of Faith and Order's challenging situation. Any public institution in the world today operates on the basis of its constitution, by-laws and regulations. This is true for secular institutions and we may say that it is also true for ecclesiastical organizations. The World Council of Churches, founded in 1948 in prayers, commitment and dedicated service of the member churches and countless Christians, was called and is still called to continue the two then existing movements, namely Faith and Order and Life and Work. Two more streams, the missionary movement, organized in the International Missionary Council, and Christian education, later on known under the name of World Council of Christian Education, joined the World Council of Churches in 1961 and 1971 respectively. The World Council of Churches became, therefore, the most visible international expression of the ecumenical movement in this century. How privileged we are to be witnesses of these events and to be servants in their development for the benefit of Christian generations to come.

3. The modern ecumenical movement is based on various understandings of the concept of oikoumene. By it and through it churches and Christians seek to promote "the whole task" of "the whole church" in "the whole world" as stated in the early history of the World Council of Churches. The basis of this Christian world organization, reformulated at the New Delhi assembly in 1961, specified that:

> The World Council of Churches is a fellowship of churches which confess the Lord Jesus Christ as God and Saviour according to the scriptures and therefore seek to fulfil together their common calling to the glory of the one God, Father, Son and Holy Spirit.[1]

The Rev. Dr YEMBA Kekumba (Methodist) is dean of the Faculty of Theology, Africa University, Mutare, Zimbabwe.

The history of the World Council of Churches and its basis show us that as an organization, this ecumenical body came into existence as the fruit of the ecumenical movement and remains an instrument of the churches to serve for the sake of the ecumenical movement. Confessing Jesus Christ as Lord, God and Saviour constitutes the requirement and the ground on which church membership is possible. Fulfilling the common calling to glorify the Triune God in word and deed must be the task that member churches have constantly before them. But this fellowship on which the churches agree must also help them to grow together towards visible unity. It is a demanding and exciting task with an enormous agenda, always in revision.

4. It is, therefore, within and beyond this framework of the World Council of Churches that Faith and Order received its commission and mandate as defined in the aim for which it exists:

> to proclaim the oneness of the church of Jesus Christ and to call the churches to the goal of visible unity in one faith and one eucharistic fellowship, expressed in worship and common life in Christ.[2]

The Faith and Order raison d'etre is therefore clearly defined, that is to say, to proclaim the oneness of the church of Jesus Christ with all that that proclamation implies, to call the churches wherever they live to the goal of visible unity, and to remind the churches constantly of the importance and necessity of mission work for the edification of their Christian life. Faith and Order, then, is an instrument to call the churches in their divided situation to the goal of unity, precisely because in its nature the name "church", which each claims, implies oneness, holiness, catholicity and apostolicity. All these characteristics of the church must be recognized in the one Spirit and confessed as one body of the one head, Jesus Christ. The unity of the church does not mean an additional sociological theory among many others. Rather, it must be understood as the manifestation of eucharistic fellowship in authentic worship rooted in the sharing and common life that only the Spirit can grant.

5. The history of the World Council of Churches and Faith and Order indicates in many ways just how considerable has been the amount of work accomplished since 1948. But the question one has to ask is what is then the impact of this work in the life of the churches that both ecumenical bodies are called to serve? In other words, how do the churches perceive today the state of ecumenical engagement Faith and Order and the World Council of Churches are called to facilitate? And how, given this state of affairs, are they preparing for the future of the oikoumene? In all cases the churches are the only ones to provide ecclesiological answers to these questions.

6. The traditional world conference on Faith and Order provides an opportunity for the churches to measure the temperature of their ecumenical health in a given period of time. In measuring the temperature of the human body, one presupposes, in most cases, a state of being uncomfortable or ill. The apostle Paul compares the church to the body. For him the church is the body of Christ (Eph. 1:22). Whatever interpretation given to this phrase or idiom today, whether as metaphor or reality, the function of the church as "body" seems well-established in the history of Christian theology. The fifth world conference on Faith and Order held in this memorable city of Santiago de Compostela has helped us, as delegates of our churches and representatives of Christian communions, to deepen our conversations around the fundamental question: Where are we and where are we going in the ecumenical movement? Of course we

have spent two weeks together enriched by intense listening, sharing, reflecting, arguing and reacting, but also worshipping, praying, singing and studying the Bible.

7. I would like to point out briefly three areas that I consider crucial in the coming years for the work of Faith and Order within the World Council of Churches and the whole ecumenical movement. In listening to presentations and discussions during all the days of our gathering here, it seems to me that it is vital for Faith and Order to play its role of instrument in the search for visible unity of the church in one faith and one eucharistic fellowship and therefore careful attention will once again be needed in the three following main areas: institutional structures, methodology and a selected agenda. Attention to these areas is a matter of faithfulness to its fundamental aim on the one hand and, on the other, effective service to meet the expectations of the churches and all those who are committed to the ecumenical movement.

Faith and Order and institutional structures

8. There is an uncertainty as to the function of Faith and Order as a commission within the World Council of Churches and its role in the ecumenical movement in general. The uncertainty becomes more relevant when one considers the founding of the World Council of Churches as a network of ecumenical movements which are still, each one of them, "wider and deeper than any one of its structured expressions, including the WCC fellowship of churches".[3] We have here a kind of tension, which is of course found in many churches. Any church is moved in its operations by the seemingly opposed demands of its calling as a movement for mission, on the one hand, and its institutional and organizational nature, on the other. I am not quite sure if this tension can be completely overcome in the life of an ecclesiastical organization. The tension between being an institution for better service in the world, and functioning as a movement, as event for the missionary nature of the church, has its own tradition in the history of the church. And this is also true for any church organization. But this tension is not only of an ecclesiastical nature, it is first of all a Christological tension. Since the council of Chalcedon the church maintains this Christological tension as the heritage and mystery of our faith. The very point here deals mainly with the specific orientation of Faith and Order work in the light of its objectives. Uncertainty of structures may considerably affect the efficacy of the work. It is true that in today's world institutions operate on the basis of their constitution and by-laws, as do the World Council of Churches and Faith and Order. But as ecclesiastical bodies it is vital for them to keep open to the wind of the Spirit and new inputs resulting from their own achievements. The role of Faith and Order in the search for the visible unity of the church goes beyond administrative structures of the World Council of Churches. The Faith and Order task involves the whole ecumenical constituency. Consequently there is necessity for flexible institutional structures both for the Faith and Order Commission and the World Council of Churches.

Theological methodology in Faith and Order work

9. This fifth world conference on Faith and Order takes place at a crucial epoch of world history. We live in a time of rapid and profound mutation in terms of politics, societies, communication, transport, health and economy. Therefore the issues of justice, peace and the environment are still at the top of world leaders' agendas.

The ecumenical situation has considerably changed also since the last world conference on Faith and Order held in Montreal in 1963. Contemporary ecumenism is mainly marked by a wider constituency, development of dialogue in bilateral and multilateral ways, substantial contributions of the united and uniting churches to the ecumenical movement as expressions of unity "in each place", and the emergence of important new approaches to theological reflection. In this regard Faith and Order has to take seriously into consideration the issue of methodology in the theological support that the churches need for their ecumenical pilgrimage towards visible unity. But one thing must be clear. The revision of the Faith and Order methodology does not mean, in any case, to sacrifice the rigour of theological reflection, nor does it mean that the foundation of the Christian faith should be negotiable. The point is that today in the ecumenical movement there are contextual theological reflections which have brought real support for the life of the church and these need to be integrated into the process of ecumenical theological reflection. The approach of regional consultations, initiated by Faith and Order, to discuss global issues at regional levels but also to include regional issues in global discussions, for example, must be encouraged. The Faith and Order methodology can also be enriched by joint studies with the other units within and outside the World Council of Churches in the light of its mandate. Revision of methodology should bring in a new style and language for the sake of ecumenism. The time has come to develop an ecumenical methodology for an authentic ecumenical ecclesiology.

The agenda of Faith and Order work
10. The mandate of Faith and Order remains to serve as an instrument to help the churches and Christians in their search for the visible unity of the church. The studies on "Church and World" and "Confessing the One Faith", along with the churches' responses to *Baptism, Eucharist and Ministry*, are still relevant for the coming years. There is a general feeling that Faith and Order has reached a stage where, with materials so far produced, a plan has to be shaped in order to tackle the issue of ecclesiology. This is especially feasible on the ground prepared by the Canberra statement on "The Unity of the Church as Koinonia: Gift and Calling" and the rich materials from this fifth world conference on Faith and Order under the inspiring theme "Towards Koinonia in Faith, Life and Witness".

The agenda of Faith and Order must be selective in the light of its mandate. Faith and Order cannot do and be identified with everything. Activities such as dialogue, theological study and research, worship and prayer are constitutive elements in promoting the visible unity of the church. Those activities must be performed from and in perspective of search for the oneness and the visible unity of the church.

NOTES

[1] Cf. Constitution and Rules of the World Council of Churches, I. Basis, and III. Functions and Purposes, 1).
[2] By-laws of the Faith and Order Commission, 2. Aims and functions.
[3] "World Council of Churches", in *Dictionary of the Ecumenical Movement*, Geneva, WCC, 1991, p.1083.

THE FUTURE OF THE WCC
AND THE ROLE OF FAITH AND ORDER
WITHIN THE ECUMENICAL MOVEMENT:
REFLECTIONS

CONSTANCE TARASAR

The historical survey and reflections presented to us by Dr Raiser and Archbishop Keshishian raise a multitude of issues and questions that could occupy the agenda of Faith and Order for many years. Although I might be tempted to respond to many of the points raised, I will focus only on two major themes that underlie several problems in ecumenical dialogue today.

Cultural diversity and the problem of language

Dr Raiser spoke of the need for an ecumenical intercultural hermeneutic to facilitate dialogue among persons of different cultures. It has long been recognized, even within cultures, that persons from varied backgrounds carry within them different ways of conceptualizing and speaking about reality.

Allow me to begin with a personal reflection on my first formal ecumenical experience. I was introduced to the ecumenical movement more than thirty years ago as a participant in a youth assembly held in Ann Arbor, Michigan. A young American-born Orthodox priest, who had attended the Evanston assembly, shepherded a group of eight young people through the complexities of that ecumenical event which included the normal activities of Bible study, plenaries, group work, reports and fellowship. It was our first discovery as Orthodox Christians, born and educated in America, that something stood in the way when we tried to articulate our experience of faith and life to those of Western Christian traditions. It seemed after we spoke that no one really cared about what we had said, or had even listened. Consequently, before the assembly had ended, our sometimes confused and frustrated little group had drafted its first Orthodox statement in response to the assembly. We identified only too easily — and somewhat presumptuously — with the words of the Bible study of 2 Corinthians: "We are afflicted in every way, but not crushed; perplexed, but not driven to despair; persecuted, but not forsaken; struck down, but not destroyed" (2 Cor. 4:8-9); but we also became conscious of a new vocation as we heard the words that "all this is from God, who reconciled us to himself through Christ and has given us the ministry of reconciliation... as ambassadors for Christ" (2 Cor. 5:18-20). For me, as for many others here, that experience has been repeated many times during the past three decades, but fortunately with a decrease in separate "statements".

The multi-cultural character of the ecumenical movement has multiplied considerably since that time, and the difficulties of bridging north-south, east-west, east-south, etc. differences in language and thought-forms have often been discussed but never seriously acted upon — perhaps because those in the dominant group never felt

Dr Constance Tarasar (Orthodox Church in America) is executive for ecumenical formation in the National Council of the Churches of Christ in the USA.

there was a problem. The only problem was the presence of some who never quite understood where they should be moving. Today, however, the problem is felt and recognized by all participants.

In the light of our theme, "Towards Koinonia in Faith, Life and Witness", it is clear that any movement *towards* koinonia must be accompanied by a new openness, willingness, true desire and effort to take the time to understand what the "other" person is saying, and to be able to repeat it in a way that confirms that communication really took place.

Too often in ecumenical gatherings we are only concerned about the points we want to make: how to communicate *my* thoughts, *my* concerns, *my* ways or conceptions of speaking and doing theology. We are like those of whom Christ spoke: "seeing, they do not perceive; and hearing, they do not listen, nor do they understand;... for this people's heart has grown dull" (Matt. 13:13,15). The desire and effort to truly understand one another is not mere communication process but an act of theology, for as we enable one another to articulate and confess faith in Christ, we begin to grow together in him and truly to know him.

True communication involves much more than articulation of the proper words or conceptions; it includes gestures and attitudes of openness or indifference, honesty, trust, humility and love. Communication requires us to be truly persons-in-relation with one another in Christ. After my five months at the graduate school in Bossey, I tried to find words to summarize what I had learned there. The words that said it best were "speaking the *truth* in *love*". Without truth, there is no integrity; without love, there is no spirit or soul. We must be transformed in the spirit of our minds for our multicultural dialogue to be genuine and effective. Perhaps the best guidelines for our dialogue are those from Galatians: "love, joy, peace, patience, kindness, generosity, faithfulness, gentleness, and self-control" (Gal. 5:22). Maybe then we can truly see and perceive, hear and understand.

Koinonia and ecclesiological ignorance

The second problem I wish to address is that of our ecclesiological ignorance of one another — ignorance in that we not only do not know one another as churches, but also that we perhaps do not really care about one another as churches. Aside from those who participate in bilateral dialogues, there are few opportunities in the ecumenical context for churches to truly engage one another as churches. For most representatives of churches, the primary ecumenical experience is a committee or board meeting, a legislative body that reviews administrative tasks, programmes, budgets and elects constituents for various tasks, or — at best — a study group or committee to draft a "common text". Rarely, even in Faith and Order, do we engage in a true person-to-person, church-to-church encounter on matters of faith that involves the kind of engagement that helps us to *enter into* the life of the other, to see, taste or assimilate something of the ethos of the faith, life and worship of another tradition in its wholeness or integrity.

How can the World Council of Churches and Faith and Order, particularly, help us to understand the faith, life and witness of each other's churches "from within"? I will comment briefly on several starting points.

First, the problem of worship. Since Vancouver, "ecumenical worship" emerged as a new phenomenon, consisting essentially of a rite based broadly on a Reformed model but incorporating elements of art and music across multicultural lines — an Orthodox "kyrie eleison" or "Holy God" here, and an African, Caribbean, Latin American or Asian hymn there, preferably with drums. The integrity of any one tradition of worship was given up to a mosaic of the many. What became clear to me here in Santiago as we also attended vespers and liturgies in the Roman Catholic tradition, in different styles and languages, was that the integrity of a given tradition that was represented here was what we had lost in our so-called "common" service. What we have lost in ecumenical worship is the opportunity to truly "enter into" the life of another church, to understand its theology through the expression of its worship, its spirituality, its commemoration of saints, arts, music and spiritual literature in its wholeness and integrity. Rather than a return to a form of comparative ecclesiology, the focus I am speaking of is a call to enter more deeply into another tradition, to increase our understanding and to allow ourselves in humility to appropriate something of the ethos of how persons in that tradition live in and with God.

The second example is related to the first. It is the model now being used by the Bossey institute in its annual Orthodox seminar. Held in 1992 in Moldavia, Romania, the seminar will be held in January 1994 at St Vladimir's Seminary in New York, and in spring 1994 in Thessalonica. It provides the opportunity for persons from other churches both to study and hear lectures on Orthodox faith, life and witness, and to immerse themselves in the life of worship in a local context. It would be my hope that non-Orthodox Christians in other cultures might have such opportunities in the future in places like Joensuu, Finland; Nairobi, Kenya; Tokyo, Japan; or Seoul, Korea. Similar seminars could be held, for example, in Atlanta, Georgia, to acquaint Christians with the particular African-American experience of the historic black churches, or an understanding of Pentecostalism in Latin America, or at Fuller Theological Seminary in California. These are only a few examples of the kind of programmes that would help persons and churches to know one another as churches. A final example is an extension of the team visit programme that took place before Vancouver, where (in addition to separate visits), a two- or three-day immersion programme was held prior to WCC-sponsored meetings. These programmes involved study and worship in a particular church tradition or traditions of that place where the meeting was being held. Faith and Order together with the Bossey institute should explore the variety of means possible to facilitate such in-depth encounters, as well as their own methodologies in existing programmes, to enable persons and churches to meet each other as churches. Guidelines could be developed to ensure necessary components in such programmes for implementation by any unit in the World Council.

The dynamic of how we approach, meet, and enter into dialogue with each other as we move "Towards Koinonia in Faith, Life and Witness" is critical to our future work together. As theologians, we cannot afford to dismiss or trivialize these issues by referring to them as "process" questions. Koinonia will not happen solely as a result of discussions and agreements "about" God, but only insofar as we also strive to grow together in our knowledge and experience "of" God and of each other.

THE FUTURE OF FAITH AND ORDER

J.-M. R. TILLARD

Will the discussions at this the fifth world conference on Faith and Order leave their mark on the future of the ecumenical movement? That will depend on our churches. Will *they* "receive" them?

As we have reflected together on the church of God in a remarkable spirit of fellowship, experiencing a profound unity in love and mutual respect which makes it impossible for us to engage in mutual denunciation, we have become more convinced than ever that it is impossible to separate the church's mission from the destiny of the whole of humanity. We have reaffirmed that the church is given to the world to be in it, inseparable from it, the anchor point and the leaven of the humankind which is God's will. Christ draws it along with him into a new humanity which, following him and *in him*, is passing from a night of many tragedies to the dawn of a new world. That is an irreversible gain. This conference has made that clear by setting it in the full breadth of the Christian faith, without separating it from all we can know of the will of God.

We must take note of the imperatives arising from this for the role Faith and Order is called to play in the future of the ecumenical movement.

Imperatives from the world conference

I. One initial point stands out. This conference has not presided over the death of Faith and Order. On the contrary, it has enabled us the better to understand and identify the urgency of the task which since Lausanne — and, for the Catholic church, since Vatican II — the churches recognize as that of the ecumenical movement and of the Commission. There are several reasons for this, but for lack of time, I shall only spell out the most essential one here.

At this time when thinking on economics, politics, the environment and sexuality has become of prime and urgent interest for our societies and for our churches themselves, talk about the faith has receded, sometimes hedging itself with so many qualifications that it offends the demand for truth which lies hidden in the depths of the human heart. Several speakers have pointed this out in the course of this conference. Now, in communion with the other ecumenical and ecclesial bodies, and acknowledging their specific role and strongly reaffirming the need for them, it belongs more than ever to Faith and Order to listen to theological research and to concentrate on this matter of the faith. By doing this, because truth is the bearer of meaning, Faith and Order will help the churches in what they have all hitherto acknowledged as the

The Rev. Prof. Jean-Marie Tillard, O.P. (Roman Catholic), is professor of dogmatic theology in Ottawa, Canada, and Fribourg, Switzerland, and a vice-moderator of the Commission on Faith and Order. This paper was translated from the French by the WCC Language Service.

specific contribution of Christianity to human history: hope, based on the God who saves and who restores meaning to human existence. Thus, in the *communion* of ecumenical service, together with other bodies working for unity, Faith and Order will be faithful to its task.

To concentrate on the faith is a demanding task. It is certainly not a matter of accommodating ourselves to all ideologies, of echoing every clamour, nor even of saying "yes" to all that the churches are doing and saying. The task of Faith and Order is to help the churches, amid the confused din of contemporary voices, to make heard as clearly as possible the voice of Christ and what it is saying. Now, that voice can only become audible to the extent that it is being spoken by disciples who in their service to humankind do not betray their Master and who bear witness to him by what they truly are. Proclamation, *martyria* and service are in constant osmosis. How then can the churches claim to pass on to a tragically-divided world the voice of him who has come to gather the scattered children of God by reconciling them, when they contradict that message by their own divisions, giving the impression that in their mouths that word is little more than a pious wish which can be taken lightly, or else that it is the message of some great personality whose plans have in any case gone wrong, because the churches are still divided. Proclamation of the faith and the communion of the churches thus belong together in the name of the lordship of Christ.

II. This leads me to my second point. The word "unity" must not be allowed to become a hollow word, drained of real meaning through constant misuse. The churches we represent thus stand before a choice that they have to make *before God*, and in which it is Faith and Order's mission to help them.

Since what is at stake is the truth of Christ, Christians would be betraying their faith if they were content to make do with a facile togetherness, a "kissy-kissy and smiling unity", based on compromise at the expense of truth. Unity can in no way evade what is probably for each Christian "confession" the most painful cross: a courageous re-examination of its doctrine in the light of the *katholon* of the apostolic faith. Does it recognize it in its entirety, and in its authenticity, in what it teaches and in what its members bear witness to? Here Faith and Order has, before God, an essential service to render. Throughout its history Faith and Order has been sustained by this conviction which is so to speak the fundamental consensus which explains its existence and guides its work.

Several requirements follow from this.

Implications for the future

1. The first concerns the place of Faith and Order in the World Council of Churches. It has become obvious that none of the WCC commissions can work in isolation. We have deliberately been using the word "communion". When you say "communion", you do not mean "take-over", or "absorption", or "mixture". In the communion of ecumenical service everyone does not do everything. Each group retains its specific task: not by isolating itself but by allowing its work to serve the common goal. And this conference has reaffirmed that this common goal is unity viewed as *koinonia in faith, life and martyria*.

2. In this context the following question arises: Do the churches wish to rest content with the unity which already exists? Or, on the contrary, building on that foundation, preserving and deepening what has been attained and the achievements in

the ethical and social fields, will they commit themselves to grow into a communion at the deepest level, rooting their solidarity and their work in the undivided faith, the common confession of the Triune God, a ministry in genuine communion, and, ultimately, one same eucharist? Is not that the full communion which God wills, not in opposition to service to the world, but as its focal point?

The discussions during these days have shown that many churches have been strengthened in the conviction which Faith and Order has helped to clarify in recent decades: the conviction that, in God's plan, the church should already constitute — in constant tension with the weakness, the *peirasmos* and the sins of its members — the fruit of what the New Testament puts at the centre of the work of Christ, i.e. communion between everyone in the grace of reconciliation. Real reconciliation: not a succession of initiatives blocked half-way by some obstacle which we refuse to remove because of an uncritical confessionalism or because we are entrenched in our own power, but reconciliation based on the identity given us by our common belonging to Christ in the koinonia of grace, reconciliation which cannot be extended to include humankind unless it has first been received and put into practice. In *effect* the church is not only *in* the world and *for* the world: it is *for* the world by being *in* the world the community which God wills, built on what is *not of* the world. In the symphony of all the ecumenical commissions and within the World Council of Churches itself, Faith and Order is committed to maintaining this balance between being *for*, *in* and *not of*. It must remain the memory and the servant of this for the sake of the whole of humanity in a reconciled creation. It is our relationship with God, as revealed in the truth of Christ, which is the foundation of koinonia. On it fellowship is woven. And service of humankind and of creation is rooted in it. It alone can transform the *desires* of a torn and divided humanity into *hope*, within a creation that is being attacked from all sides precisely because human desires have become distorted by being separated from God.

3. Several efforts are thus necessary to draw these threads together. The first is in my view urgent. In his sermon Mgr Torrella laid great stress on the real though imperfect unity existing between us, a unity to which Faith and Order has contributed. All of us have experienced this degree of koinonia. We *must* find the means to translate what has been achieved into action, to give it a concrete enduring form, and, I would venture to say, to embody it in institutions and structures. Otherwise it will evaporate. Just as the pilgrims to Santiago de Compostela need a Vézeley, a Moissac and a Conques as established staging posts along the way, with a "canonized" architecture, recognized by all pilgrims and used by them all, so too do those engaged on the journey of the visible koinonia. Otherwise, what has been achieved will evaporate or will run into the sand. As I see it, this is urgent. The question of unity by stages, or communion by steps, must find its way onto the Commission's agenda. That applies in particular to three major achievements at this world conference. They are:
— the incorporation of the Christological vision of the church into the Trinitarian vision, which is its foundation;
— the relation between koinonia in faith, baptism, the eucharist and the ministry and *diakonia* of the creation performed *before* God in faithfulness to his plan; and
— the fact that in practice we have got beyond the mutual condemnations of the past in the loving fellowship and mutual service which have been a feature of our prayers and debates, and have thus become a token of their success.

Alongside these three basic achievements, and inseparable from them, other important aspects of what constitutes the foundation of the church's commitment, before God and in the name of faith, in the turmoil of human history, have clearly emerged. It seems to me that Faith and Order should study them further and in the light of them re-examine several of its earlier findings. Chief among these must be that of leaving behind the dual concept of church/world and replacing it with the infinitely richer church/creation. The church/world concept always in effect carries with it a reference to the Johannine vision of a world which disciples must resist, for there lie hidden the powers of darkness which invade people's spirits and hearts, and make them unable to receive the light of God's word. In this sense world and Spirit are almost mutually exclusive. By contrast, creation involves a fundamental relationship with God, whose glory it sings, since he has made it and sustains it "with his two hands, the word and the Spirit" (Irenaeus). Several of the dead-ends hitherto encountered by church/world thinking — even in the Faith and Order document entitled *Church and World: The Unity of the Church and the Renewal of Human Community*[1] — would have been avoided if the category church/creation had been used. Studies in other areas of the ecumenical movement on the "integrity of creation" have contributed to this widening of horizons. But these studies themselves will simply come to a halt half-way if they are not grafted onto what the church of God carries in its memory, especially in its liturgy: the *cosmic* lordship of Christ and with it the inclusion of "worlds seen and unseen" in the glorification of the living God, whom the Book of Revelation shows us as deeply involved in history. Thus, the ethics of service become *leitourgia*, and *orthopraxis* is rooted in *doxologia*. The churches' opposition to the damage being done to creation is one aspect of their koinonia in God's activity and does not simply arise out of a wide ethical concern. It is the consequence of the gracious dynamic presence in them of the "two hands" of the Creator. Here again, the recovery of Trinitarian thinking, which I have mentioned earlier, enables us to surmount dangerous polarizations. Faith and Order should, in communion with all ecumenical commissions and agencies, remind people and help them to understand that commitment to serve the creation must not sink into blind activism. It must at all costs be given the "charismatic" dimension — in the true meaning of "charismatic" — which its relationship with the Triune God calls it to. Before God action is only of value if it is straining forward to *doxa*.

Unity and variety

In a completely different area, this world conference has re-examined the difficult issue of diversity. It seems to me that, without in any way calling in question the need for the inculturation and contextualization which bridge the gap between creation and catholicity, we have become more aware of the absolute necessity that diversity and differences should be kept within the sphere of unity. Unity is not a cluster of different elements, nor the sum total of them, nor a combination of them. It is rather what is expressed and revealed in them in all its rich variety. We are being challenged by this world where disintegration and division seem to be the work of diabolical powers, often latent in the guise of national and tribal loyalties, which they transform into masks of hate and war. That is why we have insisted on limits within which diversity is an enrichment and outside which it is not only unacceptable but also destructive. What is valid for humanity as such is obviously also valid for the church. Certainly differences have their place in koinonia. They are the material out of which the Spirit creates reconciliation marked by mutual respect and complementarity. But not all differences are reconcilable. A change, a conversion must take place. The Commission, in its study on ecclesiology, will have to tackle this sensitive and difficult issue. Is it not in fact the case that ecumenical responsibility and effectiveness have sometimes been somewhat blunted and obscured by decisions taken — and accepted by others, perhaps against their better judgment — out of a simple desire not to exclude?

It is the undeniable vocation of Faith and Order to call the churches to visible *unity* rather than invite them generously to accept all diversities and all differences. Faith and Order places diversity *within* unity and sees it *in terms of* unity. That is its specific contribution in the wide communion of workers in the ecumenical movement. We stand on the threshold of a new way of living for humankind, and thus our service to the unification — not simply the unity — of Christians, rejecting clever compromises and exposing irreconcilable differences, can help the churches to play their role as witnesses to the God and Father of our Lord Jesus Christ. For this God saves humanity by gathering us together, thereby rescuing us from the powers of sectarianism, of insensitive demands for more, and of imprisonment in our ego, which before our eyes are leading us to death. Differences can become the rich variety of koinonia only by passing through the crucible of a conversion in faith, hope and love. Otherwise they run the risk, for the slightest reason, of turning into hostility. This link made at this conference between koinonia and conversion is a fresh element.

It seems to me that this conference at Santiago has thrown light on the immense progress made in these areas and gone more deeply into them. It is now possible to build on them and to give them more concrete form by getting the churches to acknowledge and receive them.

This obviously demands an effort to translate the fruits of the study work done by Faith and Order, which is often specialized, into the language, ethos and culture of the local churches. But here again we meet the theme of communion. Faith and Order is, by its origin, a movement. That means that its work is not confined to the texts published by the Commission, or to the secretariat in Geneva. It is the task of national, regional and local commissions to do that translating, but never in isolation. One of the tasks of the Geneva office and of the Standing Commission is to clarify and coordinate this work so that all the national commissions may recognize in their own and one another's translations the one and the same truth in its *katholon*.

4. The second task was that mentioned in a very beautiful sentence by the metropolitan of Mount Lebanon, Mgr Georges Khodr. We must — but in the context of the first article of the Nicene-Constantinopolitan Creed and not in a syncretistic way — reflect on "Christ... as he journeys through the infinite spaces of other religions". At this time when our world is splitting into rival groups which tear one another apart and kill one another, is not faith in the one God one of the essential ingredients of hope? We must think seriously, theologically, on the relationship between the koinonia of Christ's disciples on the one hand and, on the other, the solidarity before God of all who base their lives on their relationship to the Creator God. It is clear that in this area, too, Faith and Order will have to work in symbiosis with other groups, being alert to remind everyone of the ecclesiological perspective according to which faith in the lordship of Christ is the guiding principle for any undertaking which goes

beyond the strict limits of the Christian koinonia. God's call for a "cosmic" unity should thus become an explicit item on the agenda of any study on the unity which is God's will, a specific aim in the mandate of Faith and Order. The contemporary situation demands this. The more humankind becomes fragmented, the more does the churches' faithfulness to the Christian demand for reconciliation become the necessary form for Christian charity to take.

Why not, drawing inspiration from that prophetic act of bringing together the leaders of all religions to Assisi — why not consider a gathering of all the major leaders in the churches — perhaps in Jerusalem — simply to sing the creed together? That would be a wonderful expression of the degree of unity already present and of its origin; the concrete *acknowledgment* and *reception* of what has been at the heart of this conference, in which the plan of the Triune God has never been forgotten.

NOTE

[1] Faith and Order paper no. 151, Geneva, WCC, 1990.

VII
Sermons

☐ Introduction

Sermons were preached on five special occasions within the official world conference programme: during the opening and closing worships on 4 and 13 August respectively; within the Orthodox and Roman Catholic vespers services on 5 and 7 August respectively; and in the eucharistic service offered by the Spanish Protestant churches on 10 August. In each case the biblical passages upon which the sermon is based have been indicated. The sermon delivered during the Spanish Protestant eucharistic service was composed entirely of biblical texts; these are listed at the end of the sermon.

During the morning worship each day a biblical exposition/meditation was offered. These texts, a systematic exploration of the ecumenical implications of the struggle for koinonia reflected in Paul's letter to the Galatians, have already been published as *All of You Are One in Christ Jesus*.[1]

---

[1] Frances M. Young, *All of You are One in Christ Jesus: Bible Studies, Fifth World Conference on Faith and Order*, Geneva, Commission on Faith and Order, World Council of Churches, 1993.

SERMON AT OPENING WORSHIP
KOINONIA
Genesis 12:1, Romans 11:1-13, John 17:18-21

RAMON TORRELLA CASCANTE

Introduction

Today we begin, in prayer, the fifth world conference on Faith and Order. We take a new step on the journey towards the unity to which Jesus Christ calls his disciples. At this conference we reflect on this saving call of Christ and our hopes in responding to it under the specific theme "Towards Koinonia in Faith, Life and Witness". We do this in the city of Santiago de Compostela, famous for pilgrimages, in the hope that our pilgrimage towards unity may be blessed.

We find ourselves in a restless world. Weapons of destruction continue to be heard here in Europe and elsewhere. The tragic conflicts into which human beings fall, or in which they can find themselves, continue to lead to bloodshed and to take lives in various parts of the world. These tragic events contrast sharply with the vision of blessedness seen by Abraham, when God called him and told him: "In you all the nations of the world shall be blessed" (Gen. 12:4).

To this world in conflict, Christians are called to bring the saving gospel of Christ, the peace of Christ which the world cannot bring. Christian ecumenists and the ecumenical movement in particular should be able to bring to it an even deeper witness and experience of reconciliation. For reconciliation is at the heart of the ecumenical endeavour.

The need for *metanoia*

In the Letter to the Romans, chapter 12, the apostle exhorts his readers to conversion, to *metanoia*: "Do not be conformed to this world, but be transformed by the renewing of your minds so that you may discern what is the will of God — what is good and acceptable and perfect" (Rom. 12:2).

These words are appropriate for us in this setting. I would like to suggest that one of the keys to the success of this fifth world conference on Faith and Order will be the degree to which it will engender a deeper sense of *metanoia*.

The conference will deal with theological matters, with the results of studies. It may rejoice over the progress that has been made in the decades since the fourth world conference on Faith and Order at Montreal in 1963 and lament the obstacles still preventing the unity of Christians. It will also discuss the future directions for the ecumenical movement.

But most of all, if this meeting is to be successful, it must be an experience in *metanoia*. During these days at Santiago de Compostela we need to have a spirit of prayer and of openness to the saving grace of God, an attitude of penance for our part

---

Mgr Ramon Torrella Cascante is Roman Catholic archbishop of Tarragona, Spain, and is a former vice-president of the Secretariat for Promoting Christian Unity.

in continuing the divisions among Christians or creating new obstacles; a spirit of *metanoia* that allows God to transform our minds and hearts, to correspond to Christ's will for the unity of his disciples. We need to be transformed "by the renewing of our minds", so that we may discern what steps towards unity must now be taken to respond to the prayer of our Lord who, before his passion and death, prayed for his disciples "that they may all be one... so that the world may believe..." (John 17:21). These sacred words from the gospel of John have become a classical ecumenical text, reminding us that the purpose of the ecumenical movement, inspired by the prayer of Christ himself, is to foster the unity of Christians for the sake of the gospel, "so that the world may believe".

The invitation to this world conference on Faith and Order, then, should be considered first of all as an invitation to *metanoia*, to the spiritual renewing of minds and hearts necessary for ecumenical progress.

A shared heritage of grace

But, secondly, the ecumenical movement which has drawn us here is a movement guided by grace. Our responsibility to seek Christian unity, therefore, comes from deep spiritual demands rooted in the grace of God. This is a profound heritage that we share.

The ecumenical movement is a development of modern history and a particular aspect of church history. More than that, it is the result of God's grace. The Decree on Ecumenism of the Second Vatican Council, for example, speaks about the ecumenical movement in terms of grace. "The Lord of the ages", it says, "wisely and patiently follows out the plan of his grace on behalf of us sinners. In recent times he has begun to bestow more generously upon divided Christians remorse over their divisions and a longing for unity".[1] The Decree describes the growing movement for the restoration of unity among all Christians as "fostered by the *grace* of the Holy Spirit".[2]

Those of us who are participating in this world conference share a common heritage of grace. This heritage takes its more proximate form through the modern ecumenical movement in which we struggle in joy and pain to respond to our Lord's prayer "that they all may be one" (John 17:21). But it has more remote and deep roots in the history of salvation itself. The significance of this fifth world conference relates to both aspects of this heritage of grace.

The theme of this conference "Towards Koinonia in Faith, Life and Witness", for example, reflects the achievements of the modern ecumenical movement. Decades of common prayer, ecumenical dialogue and common witness have led us to realize that for many reasons, but especially because of baptism, divided Christians already share a certain, though imperfect, communion.[3] Koinonia is always a gift received gratuitously from God. But our journey at Santiago de Compostela "Towards Koinonia in Faith, Life and Witness" is built on a real though imperfect koinonia already shared.

This has come about as a result of the many moments of ecumenical struggle to achieve reconciliation, especially during the twentieth century. Prayer, dialogue, common witness have encompassed moments of grace which have bound Christians together more and more in fellowship. Famous landmarks which have helped create bonds of communion among Christians are the Edinburgh world missionary conference of 1910, the world conferences on Life and Work in Stockholm, in 1925, and on Faith and Order at Lausanne, in 1927, the foundation of the World Council of

Churches in Amsterdam in 1948, and the Second Vatican Council (1962-65). They have been moments of grace. And all grace comes from God. "Every perfect gift", as St James reminds us, "is from above, coming down from the Father of lights..." (James 1:17).

The specific Faith and Order journey from Lausanne 1927 to Santiago de Compostela in 1993 has been marked by its own special moments of grace. While all authentic aspects and expressions of the ecumenical movement are important, Faith and Order especially has had the responsibility, in view of the aim of working towards visible unity, for providing divided Christians with the opportunities of exploring together the dimensions of God's revelation, which is the foundation for koinonia. Faith and Order's particular responsibility is to keep before the ecumenical movement this goal of unity. Its mandate, and that of the World Council of Churches, is:

> to call the churches to the goal of visible unity in one faith and in one eucharistic fellowship, expressed in worship and in common life in Christ, and to advance towards that unity in order that the world may believe.[4]

In the thirty years since the fourth world conference at Montreal in 1963, we have witnessed a flowering of the Faith and Order movement and, therefore, an enhancement of the ecumenical movement. Member churches of the WCC, as well as nonmembers, have taken part fully in its work, including, after 1968, Roman Catholics. Major studies, such as "Baptism, Eucharist and Ministry", have challenged the churches, in responding, to search their minds and hearts for the depth of ecumenical commitment. Other important studies such as "Towards the Common Expression of the Apostolic Faith Today" and "The Unity of the Church and the Renewal of Human Community" are contributing to the quest for visible unity "in one faith and one eucharistic fellowship expressed in worship and in common life in Christ".

These are ecumenical steps towards koinonia, efforts to respond to God's grace calling us to unity.

But we share a deeper heritage of grace as well. We know in faith that we participate together in salvation history, in the blessed journey towards God to which Abraham was called long ago. The scriptures today remind us of this.

God called Abraham to go from his country and kindred and his father's house "to the land that I will show you" (Gen. 12:1). God promised Abraham "I will make of you a great nation" (v.2) and "in you all the families of the earth shall be blessed" (Gen. 12:3). In this call and this promise to Abraham, in which we share, we see already that the goal to which God is calling us is that of koinonia/communion with God, and within a people formed by God. These great saving events can be traced through the books of the Old Testament, and reach an apex in the saving mysteries of Christ, the sending of the Spirit at Pentecost and the showering of gifts on the church.

In chapter 12 of the Letter to the Romans there is a reflection on the dimensions of koinonia which characterize the community of faith called together by God, and also on the graces given by God. "We have gifts that differ according to the grace given to us," says St Paul (Rom. 12:6). He exhorts his readers to live so as to reflect the koinonia they share: "Love one another with mutual affection; outdo one another in showing honour. Do not lag in zeal, be ardent in spirit, serve the Lord. Rejoice in hope, be patient in suffering, persevere in prayer. Contribute to the needs of the saints; extend hospitality to strangers" (Rom. 12:10-13).

Our contemporary ecumenical call "Towards Koinonia in Faith, Life and Witness", then, is more than a response to the results of recent ecumenical agreement or convergence, or of recent unity statements. At root it must be seen as a renewed response and expression of fidelity to God's saving call to koinonia/communion. Our efforts towards koinonia today must be a grateful engagement in the continuing drama of salvation history, which is rooted in God's revelation.

A common responsibility

Verses 10-21 of the seventeenth chapter of the gospel of John are familiar as a classical biblical text in the ecumenical movement. Perhaps even more basically, they reveal the *depth* of God's saving grace as it flows through history. They remind us of how deeply God's original call and promise to human beings involve God's own deep participation with us in the history of salvation. The heart of salvation history is koinonia with God. Jesus prayed for his disciples on the night before he died, "that they may all be one. As you, Father, are in me and I am in you, may *they also be in us*, so that the world may believe that you have sent me" (John 17:21).

Jesus' prayer for his disciples gives spiritual nourishment to our ecumenical endeavours. But it also reminds us of a great burden that we have. Just as we share a common heritage of grace, so too we share a great common responsibility. Ours is the responsibility to respond together to Our Lord's prayer for his disciples "that they may all be one".

God's grace is always primary. There would be no ecumenical achievements were it not for the benevolence of God, given to us continually, and gratuitously, allowing us to take steps forward. We have come together today in prayer, and we will continue to pray and to search the scriptures during this world conference. For we know that our hopes for its success depend on the grace of God.

But we know, too, that we must respond to the grace of God, and not set obstacles to it. *Because* our Lord prayed for the unity of his disciples, *therefore* we must work for the unity of his disciples. And this brings us back once again to our need for prayer, for conversion of mind and heart, for *metanoia*.

Over the centuries pilgrims have come to Santiago de Compostela in a spirit of penance and devotion and prayer. I pray that we too have come here in a spirit of *metanoia*, a spirit of repentance for the disunity that still exists. I pray that we face our work together at this fifth world conference on Faith and Order in a spirit of gratitude and devotion to God whose grace has inspired this ecumenical movement and led us towards reconciliation. I pray that we come in a spirit of generosity and openness to one another, in obedience to the Holy Spirit who leads us "Towards Koinonia in Faith, Life and Witness".

NOTES

[1] *Unitatis Redintegratio*, 1.
[2] *Ibid.*
[3] *Ibid.*, 3.
[4] Constitution and Rules of the WCC, III.

SERMON AT CLOSING WORSHIP
John 8:30-36

NÉLIDA RITCHIE

Dear Sisters and brothers,

I thank God for this opportunity to share with you these brief reflections on the word of life.

Some of the commentaries about the meaning of the "Way of Santiago" (which appear in the information leaflets of the Xunta de Galicia and which I had at my disposal) caught my attention. I wondered how many convergent and divergent aspects existed between them... and those which we can take from our own experience as participants in this conference.

I shall summarize these commentaries:

— "The Way of Santiago": this reference in the singular is "generic" since it refers to a plurality of ways...

— Amongst the pilgrims who followed this way were those who "made their pilgrimage as penitents, seeking the forgiveness of their sins, or those who expected the supernatural aid of the apostle for their warlike intents..."

— The majority wore suitable clothing for the arduous journey, strong footwear, took the minimum of belongings and water to drink.

— "On the way they used to form groups with others, to give each other mutual aid..."

Perhaps we can also say that the Way of Santiago is for us both singular and generic. We flow together on this road from diverse situations, from diverse experiences, contexts and realities.

There are those who have come along ways that are difficult, arduous, perilous and dangerous. Others have come along ways that are wider and more comfortable. Some of us come from contexts of inequality, injustice and lack of opportunity, from realities of poverty, hunger, uncaring and the crushing of human dignity. Others come from situations of the absence of liberty, violence, exclusion, racism and death. Others come from more dangerous paths, contexts where individualism, consumerism, success presented as the supreme value, or prestige at whatever cost impregnate daily life and confound minds, hearts and actions.

Perhaps we also have experienced this mingling of realities, this plural aspect and at the same time this search for the common way, which leads to a proposed goal. And we enter this common way, this common singular way, with what we are and what we have, with our baggage, and the recognition of our weaknesses. It is on the way that we discover what is necessary, and it is on the way that we begin to do without the superfluous.

The Rev. Nélida Ritchie (Methodist) is a pastor in Argentina, and a vice-moderator of the central committee of the World Council of Churches. This paper was translated from the Spanish by Joseph Fleming.

It is on the way that we recognize our needs and the need of others (perhaps like past pilgrims moved by the desire to give mutual aid). It is on the way that we discover our difficulties in matching our step to the pace of our brother and sister. It is on the way that communion is created, that faith is celebrated and that life is shared.

However, is it only a question of walking? Is it a question of just *any* way?

It is interesting to see how Jesus shows himself to us in the gospels as the eternal traveller and at the same time offers himself to us as the way, the truth and the life.

Luke especially narrates his gospel from the perspective of the journey of Jesus to the cross; his journey up to Jerusalem; the fulfilling of his redeeming mission in obedience to the saving will of the Father.

However, on this journey he is stopped by the cry of the sick, the excluded, the sinners, by the cries of those who have remained by the wayside and at the margins of history. And Jesus stops to hear, forgive, heal, restore, strengthen and reconcile. To give new life! To create new possibilities, to offer new alternatives! To open new horizons!

No, it is not just a question of walking. It is a question of following the way proposed by Jesus, with the same capacity to translate love into action. It is a question of following this way of obedience in fidelity to the good news of Jesus Christ with "one ear to the people and one ear to the gospel", as said a martyr of the Christian faith in my country (I refer to Mgr Enrique Argelelli, a Roman Catholic assassinated on 4 August 1976 by the military forces).

No, it is not question of just *any* way. The way that Jesus offers is that of the truth which liberates. "You will know the truth and the truth will set you free" (John 8:32).

We do not reach this freedom by our own efforts, nor from our own arrogance or self-sufficiency, but from the recognition of our need to be made free, and to be freed from the oppression of sin. "If the Son makes you free, you will be free indeed" (John 8:36). The discussion in which Jesus makes these two affirmations has to do with belonging to the true way to know the truth of God.

In the text quoted, the Jews are offended by the words of Jesus since they consider themselves free, never having been slaves and thus in no need of being freed. However, although descendants of Abraham, they do not live like the Father of faith since they try to eliminate the one who says and does the truth (cf. John 8:40).

They accept no truth other than their own and exclude all others, including Jesus. Their exalting the past and considering it the only valid reference point prevents them from seeing in the present that which is totally new: God made a human being. This is the sin which blinds them. This is the sin which enslaves them, the inability to be changed by the revealed truth! Jesus talks to them about the truth: not the truth which is decreed or imposed; but about the revealed truth, that which transforms people and realities so that they become real and present living witnesses of the redeeming power of Jesus "who makes us free".

Jesus talks of the truth which generates a genuine freedom which allows us to decide, choose, create, live together, share and be community (communion) because it is constructed on a firm foundation: Jesus himself — the revealed truth.

— Freedom — which from diversity looks and works for unity as announced in the prayer of our Lord, "that they may all be one as you, Father, are in me and I am in you, may they also be in us so that the world may believe that you have sent me" (John 17:21).

— Unity — that difficult common way at which we have arrived from our own private ways (our own tradition, history, culture, experience, etc.) with our riches and poverty.

— Unity — like a way to be followed in communion from our differences, similarities, agreements and disagreements, convergences and divergences. Knowing that He who is the way of truth and life is the author of communion, giver of faith, sower of abundant life.

A few weeks ago, in a local Argentinian newspaper, an interview was published with a Roman Catholic bishop. When the journalist asked if it were true that there were "two churches" (the question was aimed at clarifying certain public declarations), Mgr Hesayne answered:

> To understand what the church is, one must put oneself inside it. I always make this comparison: the church is like a stained-glass window. A stained-glass window seen from outside normally appears to be nothing special. But a stained-glass window isn't made to be seen from outside, but from inside and with sunlight. The church is a mystery, but since it is the mystery of the living God in a community of men and women, the church has an aspect of holiness and another aspect of sin... I have held as a principle in the face of public opinion, that which Leo XIII said: "The true church must not fear the truth."

Further on he affirmed:

> The church is like a people on the move, some go more slowly, some more quickly. Even bishops, priests, religious, the laity mark our pace according to our conversions!

A *stained-glass window*, with its multiform and multicoloured diversity, forms itself into a unity and can only be seen and admired from a full commitment to the call to be the people of God, and its diversity and unity can only be appreciated in the light of the Holy Spirit.

A *people on the move*, committed to give witness to the fact that God has given them his inheritance inviting many others to join this way of searching for the true communion in faith and life.

Our pilgrimage did not begin in Santiago de Compostela, nor does it culminate here. But this can be an important point in the new directions that we take, if this journey together has been a true space in which to discover each other; if from love and truth we have been able to discover new riches in others and we have been confronted with some of our limitations.

This Way of Santiago (generic and singular at the same time) rather than an arrival point can be a *starting* point for new pilgrimages in the continual search for this desired communion which is proposed by God himself. Thus faith can be celebrated, life can be abundantly lived, and witness given in the unity of words and actions.

Because this is not a human proposal, but rather a human response to the divine proposal, we have hope for the future and together with brothers and sisters from other parts of the world we can affirm: "Although the gravity of the world situation obliges a more coordinated action, a profounder understanding, and a more daring commitment by Christians in the fight for a more humane life for all... our hope does not fail. Our faith grows stronger. Discouragement does not conquer us. Because we trust in the God of Life, who triumphs just where death appears to reign."

May the Holy Spirit come upon us as we journey, healing our wounds, strengthening our journeying, illuminating each step, accompanying us in the formation of a true communion, in life, faith and witness.

SERMON AT ORTHODOX VESPERS
ON THE EVE OF THE FEAST OF THE TRANSFIGURATION

ARCHBISHOP STYLIANOS OF AUSTRALIA

Sisters and brothers,

The transfiguration of our Lord does not only signify a characteristic church feast of Orthodox spirituality, but rather the most solemn manifestation of a threefold principle which pervades the entire divine economy, and this again as an immediate reflection upon creation of the divine life of the Holy Trinity.

Accordingly transfiguration is:

1) a strictly *theological principle* betraying in manifold energies the inaccessible essence of the living God;

2) a strictly *anthropological principle* betraying the deeper ontological and moral demands of human nature;

3) a strictly *eschatological principle* working ceaselessly towards the final triumph of God's will in his creation.

For all these reasons I believe it to be a providential coincidence that the traditional calendar in relation to the feast of the Lord's transfiguration falls within the dates of our fifth world conference on Faith and Order with the very significant theme "Towards Koinonia in Faith, Life and Witness". I have to state this in advance because, as we shall further see, koinonia in the theological sense is no less and no more than another name for transfiguration.

1. Let us then briefly see what transfiguration signifies first of all as a strictly theological principle.

In order to capture the deeper meaning of the relevant narrative of St Matthew's text describing the transfiguration of our Lord, one should consider not only the passage as such which starts in the seventeenth chapter, but the entire context from the previous chapter (16:13) where we find the discussion of our Lord with his disciples at Caesarea of Philippi concerning his identity. St Peter, who correctly confessed that Jesus is the Son of the living God and was "blessed" for this by the Lord, is the same one who shortly afterwards was rebuked and characterized as a "scandal" and as "Satan" by the Lord again.

The reason for this rejection is the fact that Peter was not in a position to see that all the passions, of which Jesus spoke as his forthcoming *kenosis* in Jerusalem, constitute the very heart of his glorification. Precisely here lies the key to the mystery of the unchangeable essence of God expressed in permanent communion, which means transfiguration both in the inner Trinitarian life as well as in his manifold energies towards creation. If God could be understood, even for a moment, as not being in permanent communion, namely in transfiguration, this would mean that God is no longer the unchangeable almighty source of love and life. The dynamism of the inner

H.E. Archbishop Stylianos (Harkianakis) is primate of the Greek Orthodox archdiocese of Australia (Ecumenical Patriarchate).

Trinitarian life, which the church fathers characterize as eternal interpenetration of the three divine Persons, is accordingly reflected in numerous energies and graces upon the entire creation, and it is precisely this which is the specific difference between the God of the philosophers and the living God of *creation out of nothing* and the consequent *revelation*.

This dynamism of divine love which reveals its glory even in *kenosis* was solemnly manifested on Mount Tabor, so that "having contemplated these wonders, the disciples may not be afraid of the forthcoming passions", as we chant in a relevant Orthodox hymn. It is this same optimism in God which St Paul teaches in stating that "the sufferings of this present time are not worth comparing with the glory about to be revealed to us" (Rom. 8:18).

Concluding our analysis of the strictly theological principle expressed in permanent koinonia as transfiguration, we must admit that only through such a concept of the living God can one justify the major dogmas of the undivided Christian church concerning not only the Holy Trinity as such but also the incarnation, namely the hypostatic union in the person of our Lord and the consequent deification of the human person as the specific economy of the Holy Spirit.

2. The transfiguration as strictly anthropological principle is properly understood only in the light of what has already been said.

Given that man is created in God's *image* with the specific purpose to proceed by grace to God's *likeness*, it is clear that Christian anthropology has its normative measure and example only in Christology. This in other words means that, since the event of *kenosis* signifies already in the divine life the climax of glorification, all secular concepts of *progress* or *perfection* should by definition be excluded, if not even ridiculed in Christian morality. It is for this precise reason that the "fools for Christ" have always signified in church history the ultimate limit of human endurance and glory.

In such a perspective it becomes clear that the main good which needs to be achieved and retained is not any immanent value or benefit as such, but only the koinonia with God which enables the faithful individual to communicate freely with the rest of the entire creation, leading, through all possible stages of transfiguration, to the final deification.

3. The transfiguration as strictly eschatological principle pervading the whole creation is only a deep consequence of what has thus far been said concerning the human person communicating on the one hand in God's beatitude and on the other in the whole process of the rest of creation towards its final "metamorphosis". When the apostle John speaks in his revelation of "a new heaven and a new earth", it is obvious that he is referring to the broader context between the uncreated God and the entire creation as they are related in the spirit of the Chalcedonian terms of "unconfusedly" and "undividedly". The characteristic Byzantine spirituality, as expressed for example by Maximus the Confessor, in underlining the ontological solidarity of man as "microcosm" and the world as "macro-anthropos", is a confession of a final cosmic transfiguration as the ultimate manifestation of God's love and glory.

After all this, one has to admit that transfiguration is proved to be not only the most comprehensive notion of the "divine energies" but also the deepest moral and spiritual desire of the human person, which explains why the church feast of the transfiguration is so popular in the entire traditional Christian world. Needless to say that the

Orthodox church, having developed, especially in the fourteenth century, the well-known Hesychastic movement directly related to the event of the "uncreated light" as it was experienced on Mt Tabor and interpreted by St Gregory Palamas, has given to the transfiguration of our Lord the most eminent place in the entire spiritual life and theology of the Christian church.

However, since this characteristic Orthodox doctrine undoubtedly expresses the broadest possible capacity of divine love, embracing, through the uncreated divine energies, even the slightest particle of creation, it is our prayer that such a spirituality gains more and more territory in the thoughts, feelings and actions of all Christians in order that the name of God is indeed glorified through us in all nations.

SERMON AT ROMAN CATHOLIC VESPERS
Romans 12:10-12

PAUL-WERNER SCHEELE

The ecumenical movement often suffers from the fact that some people become obsessed by the things that are not yet possible and disregard the thousand possibilities that do exist, while others wait for all the problems to be fully clarified before they set about doing the things that can be done here and now without any problem. The apostle to the Gentiles shows us a way out of this dilemma. He presents us with an immediate-action programme which is topical, realistic, progressive and universal. It can be implemented forthwith, in all our churches and communities, in all the countries of the world. Whenever we allow ourselves to be guided by the call of St Paul, we move forward on the way to the full unity.

The three sentences of our reading confront us with no fewer than eight commands. The first is: "Love one another with mutual affection" (v.10). Whoever our partners may be in our immediate circle or farther afield, whether they are close to us or not, whether they come towards us or turn away from us, we owe them all affectionate love, love "in deed and in truth" (1 John 3:18).

Whatever the position in regard to the ecclesial being of others, there can be no doubt about their being *Christian*. Our unreserved respect is due to every one of our fellow Christians. "Outdo one another in showing honour!" says the apostle (v.10). Dostoevsky was convinced that we ought in fact to kneel before every human being: if he lives in grace, then the Lord lives in him; if he lives in sin — which ultimately is not for us to judge — there still remains his calling to a life with God. The Decree on Ecumenism rightly urges in regard to every Christian wherever he or she may live: "It is right and salutary to recognize the riches of Christ and virtuous works in the lives of others who are bearing witness to Christ."[1]

The Most Rev. Paul-Werner Scheele is Roman Catholic bishop of the diocese of Würzburg, Germany. This paper was translated from the German by the WCC Language Service.

The memory of the Second Vatican Council and earlier phases of the ecumenical movement makes some people feel despondent today. Is it not true that much of the dynamic of those days has gone, that the fire kindled in so many places has largely gone out? Whatever the answer to that question, the apostle's call is appropriate: "Never flag in zeal!" (v.11). These words of Paul's can help us to avoid getting bogged down in regrets over the whole situation and forgetting in the process that we are all responsible for it. Before we accuse others we should remind ourselves of the Lord's words: "Why do you see the speck that is in your neighbour's eye, but do not notice the log that is in your own eye?" (Matt. 7:3). How different many things would be if everyone who complains about the ecumenical shortcomings of others were to discover their own shortcomings and with renewed zeal set about doing all the things that *do* unite.

Instead of complaining about the cooling of the ecumenical climate, we should respond to the apostle's call: "Be aglow with the Spirit" (v.11). The Lord has not promised his Spirit to this or that chosen one but to all of us. With all his heart he longs to give that Spirit to us and to see it at work in us. Does he not say: "I came to cast fire upon the earth; and would that it were already kindled!" (Luke 12:49). Not until the fire of the Spirit has consumed all that divides us will full unity be possible.

Unity is realized step by step wherever people decide to be there wholly for the Lord. Therefore, the apostle exhorts us: "Serve the Lord!" (v.11). Every movement towards the Lord is by nature an ecumenical movement because it brings us closer to the One whose will is that all should be one. Serving, he is there for all; if we serve him we share in his unifying action.

Because no worldly power can prevent this service we can be full of hope in regard to unity. This is all the more important in that the exhaustion that comes from lack of hope has spread like an epidemic in the church and in the world. We Christians have the ability and the duty to provide the "oxygen" of hope without which all human endeavour is a hopeless cause. "Rejoice in your hope," Paul urges us. These are the opening words of the last chapter of the study document *Church and World*. This is not just a pleasant general conclusion. By assuring us that we can hope for the best, it challenges us to do our best. Because God's promise sets us free "we can begin our pilgrim way, setting out in the direction of the kingdom without utopian illusions, yet with joyful hope. God has the final word. The future belongs to God."[2] Knowledge in faith is therefore a condition of our salvation; it gives us the staying power to keep going on the waterless stretches and helps us to resist the dangers which will not be lacking on the way to unity.

Paul speaks of trials and tribulations. He does not by any means promise that the problems will gradually disappear and that with a bit of goodwill everything will be all right in the end. He knows the tribulations will be even greater in the time before the end. Realistically the *Church and World* document says: "Suffering is and remains one of the characteristic marks of the church of Jesus Christ, who himself suffered for our sake that we might share in the kingdom of God."[3] That is why the "endurance and faith of the saints" (Rev. 13:10) are needed or, in the words of the apostle, "be patient in tribulation" (v.12). Which of us has not been seized with impatience when we see that things are not moving forward as we would wish in the ecumenical movement? Understandable as it is, such impatience is unfruitful. The Lord's promise is not for impatience, but for patience, for the courageous acceptance of tribulations in loving endurance and devotion. Let us learn from the great Spanish Saint Teresa of Avila: "Patience achieves all... God alone suffices. Sólo Dios basta!"

All this is only possible in living contact with the Lord. Consequently in his last exhortation the apostle says: "Be constant in prayer!" (v.12). This means more than occasional praying. Those who are constant in prayer *live* prayerfully. We are "constant in prayer" when prayer infuses our whole life and our life thus becomes a prayer. Speaking of this vital fellowship the Second Vatican Council describes prayer, together with conversion of hearts and holiness of life, as "the soul of the whole ecumenical movement".[4] Without this soul all efforts for unity are in vain. Let us do all in our power to keep this soul strong! "Watch and pray!" (Matt. 26:41).

Amen.

NOTES

[1] *Unitatis Redintegratio*, 4.
[2] *Church and World*, Faith and Order paper no. 151, Geneva, WCC, VII, para. 5.
[3] *Ibid.*, VII, para. 9.
[4] *Unitatis Redintegratio*, 8.

SERMON AT
THE PROTESTANT EUCHARISTIC SERVICE
"I Believe in the Communion of Saints"

ALBERTO ARAUJO

Giving thanks to the Father, who hath made us meet to be partakers of the inheritance of the saints in light.

For God so loved the world, that he gave his only begotten Son, that whosoever believeth in him should not perish, but have everlasting life. For it became him, for whom are all things, in bringing many sons unto glory, to make the Captain of their salvation perfect through suffering. For both he that sanctifieth and they who are sanctified are all of one: for which cause he is not ashamed to call them brethren... Forasmuch then as the children are partakers of flesh and blood, he also himself likewise took part of the same; that through death he might destroy him that had the power of death, that is, the devil; and deliver them who through fear of death were all their lifetime subject to bondage.

Let this mind be in you, which was also in Christ Jesus. That I may know him, and the power of his resurrection, and the fellowship of his sufferings. But rejoice, inasmuch as ye are partakers of Christ's sufferings; that, when his glory shall be

The Rev. Alberto Araujo is a pastor in the Spanish Evangelical Church.

revealed, ye may be glad also with exceeding joy. For we are made partakers of Christ. The cup of blessing which we bless, is it not the communion of the blood of Christ? The bread which we break, is it not the communion of the body of Christ? For we being many are one bread, and one body: for we are all partakers of that one bread.

Then they that gladly received his word were baptized... And they continued steadfastly in the apostles' doctrine and fellowship, and in breaking of bread, and in prayers. And all that believed were together and had all things common. And in these days came prophets from Jerusalem unto Antioch. And there stood up one of them named Agabus, and signified by the Spirit that there should be great dearth throughout all the world: which came to pass in the days of Claudius Caesar. Then the disciples, every man according to his ability, determined to send relief unto the brethren which dwelt in Judea: which also they did... He that hath an ear, let him hear what the Spirit saith unto the churches. Moreover, brethren, we do you to wit of the grace of God bestowed on the churches of Macedonia; how that in a great trial of affliction the abundance of their joy and their deep poverty abounded unto the riches of their liberality.

Be kindly affectioned one to another with brotherly love... Distributing to the necessity of saints; given to hospitality. Ye have well done that ye did communicate with my affliction. And our hope of you is steadfast, knowing that as ye are partakers of the sufferings, so shall ye be also of the consolation. For as we have many members in one body... so we, being many, are one body in Christ, and every one members one of another.

God is light, and in him is no darkness at all. If we say that we have fellowship with him, and walk in darkness, we lie, and do not the truth: but if we walk in the light, as he is in the light, we have fellowship one with another, and the blood of Jesus Christ his Son cleanseth us from all sin. And truly our fellowship is with the Father, and with his Son Jesus Christ. Partakers of the Holy Ghost.

The grace of the Lord Jesus Christ, and the love of God, and the communion of the Holy Ghost, be with you all. Amen.

Scripture texts used (King James version):

Col. 1:12;	Heb. 3:14;	2 Cor. 8:1f.;	Rom. 12:4f.;
John 3:16;	1 Cor. 10:16f.;	Rom. 12:10,13;	1 John 1:5-7:3;
Heb. 2:10f.,14f.;	Acts 2:41f.,44;	Phil. 4:14;	Heb. 6:4;
Phil. 2:5, 3:10;	11:27-30;	2 Cor 1:7;	2 Cor. 13:14.
1 Pet. 4:13;	Rev. 2f.;		

VIII

Spain:
Its Faith,
People and Life

☐ Introduction

The land, people and churches of Spain were the subject of plenary VIII, 10 August, 9h15, vice-moderator the Rev. Araceli Rocchietti presiding.

The Rev. A. Rocchietti introduced five speakers who made **presentations** on various aspects of the history, culture and church situation in Spain. Two are printed below, that by the Rev. Julio R. Asensio, president of the permanent commission of the Spanish Evangelical Church, on the situation of Protestantism in Spain; and that by the Rev. Don Julián García Hernando, from the ecumenical center of missioners for unity in Madrid and director of the secretariat of the Episcopal commission on interconfessional relations, on "a new chapter in the short history of ecumenism in Spain" (that is to say, after the Second Vatican Council).

Brief summaries are offered of the other presentations (which have regrettably been unavailable for publication). That by the Rev. Don Eugenio Romero Pose, professor of theology at the Seminario Mayor in Santiago de Compostela, dealt with the origins and early history of the Christian faith in Spain. This paper presented evidence to support the "widely-held view" that the apostle Paul visited Spain, and that St James had accepted particular responsibility for seeing that the gospel came to Spain. There is evidence of a strong Christian community in northern Spain by the mid-third century; theologians in Spain were active in discussions of theological controversies in the fourth century; and the sixth century saw the first "golden century" of Christianity in Spain, marked by the council of Toledo.

The Rev. Don José Maria Diaz Fernandez, canon archivist of the cathedral of Santiago de Compostela and president of the diocesan liturgy commission, spoke on the origins of the pilgrim "Way of Santiago" and its importance not only for the city itself but for all of Europe. The city, he stated, had become a symbol of hope for all Europe and — as diverse pilgrims met along the "Way of Santiago" — a symbol of unity. He suggested that the topic of pilgrimage should be developed in ecumenical dialogue and that it could be an especially appropriate topic for dialogue with other faiths, particularly Islam.

Bishop Arturo Sanchez of the Spanish Episcopal Reformed Church spoke on the topic of Christian pluralism in Spain. He noted that the Spanish member churches of the World Council of Churches (the Spanish Reformed Episcopal Church and the Spanish Evangelical Church) are small in comparison with the Roman Catholic Church; the additional Protestant churches in Spain are, by and large, not inclined to ecumenical involvement. He emphasized the considerable degree of ecumenical cooperation among Protestants and Orthodox in Spain. Better relations have been fostered by the invitation, in 1976, from the Roman Catholic Bishops Conference for other Christians to be represented in its yearly meeting; and new constitutional provisions in Spain have encouraged work on a wider ecumenical agenda.

THE SITUATION
OF THE EVANGELICAL CHURCHES IN SPAIN

JULIO R. ASENSIO

The present

It is not possible to say much in seven minutes. So this is not really a presentation but rather a few "brush strokes" on the reality of Protestantism in Spain.

Every present has a past, a history with positive or negative causes. Spanish Protestantism is very young, with barely 125 years of "recognized" presence. This distinguishes it, at least, from the rest of European Protestantism, which in the majority of cases goes back to the Reformation of the sixteenth century.

In the sixteenth century there was no Protestant Reformation in Spain because the religious, political and social circumstances of the country made it totally impossible for such a thing to take place. Of course there were some well known Protestants who died in *auto-da-fés* (in Valladolid, Seville, etc.), who suffered the same fate as befell Jews, Moors, visionaries and others, since it was necessary not only to profess the Christian faith but also to adhere strictly to the Roman Catholic Church and its doctrines.

Those who had the privilege of emigrating to other, more tolerant countries had better luck — Juan de Valdés, Casiodoro de Reina, Cipriano de Valera and others. These last two translated the version of the Bible which bears their name. It is recognized as a jewel of Spanish literature, and is possibly the first direct translation from the Hebrew and the Greek into Spanish (Castilian) without going through the Vulgate.

The Rev. Julio R. Asensio is president of the Permanent Commission of the Spanish Evangelical Church. This paper was translated from the Spanish by Daphne Tischauser.

The nineteenth century

In the nineteenth century there is evidence of Spanish Protestants making themselves known in places such as France, Switzerland, America, England and particularly in Gibraltar, since in Spain it was still not possible to do so.

In the first half of the nineteenth century the work of the British and Foreign Bible Society, in particular of its agent George Barrow, was of great importance. Fourteen thousand copies of the holy scriptures and portions of several of its books were distributed in the different languagues spoken in Spain, including *caló*, the gypsy language. In 1848 the scholar and bibliophile Luis de Usoz y Río, together with the Englishman Benjamin Barron Wiffen, an enthusiastic hispanist, began publishing a series of volumes entitled *Reformistas antiguos españoles* (Ancient Spanish Reformers), covering figures mainly from the sixteenth century, and this was continued after his death by the German E. Böchmer. The year 1868 is a key date for Spanish Protestantism. Up until then everything had to be done in the strictest secrecy and was the object of persecution, mainly by the Catholic clergy, but with the support of the civil authorities. With the abolition of the Tribunal of the Holy Office (that is to say, the Inquisition), it became illegal to burn "heretics" or dissidents, but they continued to be persecuted and were sentenced to exile or condemned to the galleys.

> Typical of the situation was the commission formed of delegates from several European countries (Austria, Denmark, Germany, England, etc.) that arrived in Madrid in 1863 to intercede for the Spanish "evangelicals" who were being imprisoned, tried and sentenced to various forms of punishment that were never light. Heavy prison sentences were commuted to nine years' exile. (M. Gutiérrez Marín)

A notable trial was that of D. Manuel Matamoros, the dedicated organizer of clandestine Protestant communities.

With the triumph of the so-called *Gloriosa* (the revolution of 1868 in Spain) and the fall of Isabel II and her government, the existence of Protestants in Spain was recognized. The words spoken to a Protestant delegation by General Prim, one of the three leaders of the coup, were significant: "Now you can go the length and breadth of Spain with the Bible under your arm". Thus ended one of the "clandestine" periods for Spanish Protestants — they could now preach, witness and serve, though not without difficulty, for the Catholic clergy, encouraged by the fanaticism and ignorance of the times, continued its persecution.

In some cases the civil authorities would give protection to the Protestants, although in many others they went along with the persecution.

The twentieth century

A cursory study reveals that in 1900 some 66 percent of Spaniards were illiterate. Less well known is the fact that the Protestants felt the need to tackle the problem by founding schools in many places throughout Spain, so that wherever there was a Protestant church there was also a school.

> The Spanish Protestants owe their existence to the tenacity and strength of their faith in the face of countless difficulties; toleration of them was always more or less restrictive and was extended only during the second republic. (M. Gutiérrez Marín)

The civil war of 1936-39, which was tragic and painful for all Spaniards, was none the less so for Protestants. After the war began a new period of intolerance, during which both the Franco regime and national Catholicism did their best to ensure that "Spain is one and Catholic". The persecutions, imprisonments and exiles of this time are so recent that it is perhaps better not even to refer to them too explicitly. There were brief moments of respite such as in 1945 with the *Fuero de los españoles* (the Charter of the Spanish People) and, little by little, the clandestine or private worship of Protestants became relatively public.

The winds of Vatican II reached Spain and it was this, perhaps, that enabled the law regulating religious liberty to be approved in 1967, protecting the rights of Spaniards in this respect.

This protection continued until the advent of democracy, the adoption of the present Spanish constitution, the law on religious liberty (which was less prescriptive but broader than the 1967 law) and the approval, in November 1992, of the pact of cooperation between the Spanish state and the federation of religious bodies of Spain. The Federation groups together the different Evangelical or Protestant church families of Spain. Over the years this body has held various names which are indicative of the changing situation of Spanish Protestantism. First of all it was called the commission for Evangelical defence; for a short time it became the Evangelical legal assistance service and, finally, quite straightforwardly, the federation of religious bodies of Spain.

Thus we have arrived at an absolutely new situation of liberty in which we are called to make responsible use of the privileges which this brings, and to face new challenges. Our churches continue to be in a minority, which means they have serious financial difficulties inherited from the past and resulting from their dependence on the solidarity of sister churches and institutions abroad. At the same time they are determined not to renounce their vocation to be the Evangelical Protestant presence in Spain.

These notes refer in particular to the Reformed Episcopal Church of Spain and to the Spanish Evangelical Church, both members of the World Council of Churches since its foundation in 1948.

ECUMENISM IN SPAIN

JULIAN GARCIA HERNANDO

History

The history of ecumenism in Spain is comparatively short; its beginning coincides with the Second Vatican Council. Up until then the climate for interconfessional dialogue was not only unfavourable but frankly hostile. There were times when non-Catholics were totally ignored, others when they were openly combatted. The Protestants, on their side, maintained an identical attitude. Anti-Catholicism was one of the most notable features of Spanish Protestantism, just as anti-Protestantism was the normal key-note struck by Spanish Catholics.

It is clear that the religious-political history of Spain has not been favourable to interconfessional relations. While it is true that there were times when members of the three monotheistic religions — Christians, Jews and Muslims — lived together peacefully, and were able to make contributions to science and philosophy which later spread to the rest of Europe, it is no less true that already in the time of *los Reyes Católicos* the history of Spain bore the mark of intransigence. This, it must be added, was also a general feature of the times throughout Europe. As far as Spain is concerned, and for several different reasons, this intransigence became accentuated from the fifteenth century onwards. The spiritual interpretation given to the reconquest of the Iberian peninsula from Islam, the religious unification achieved by expelling the Jews and the Moors, the Spanish participation in the wars of religion in Europe, the influence of the counter-Reformation and the presence of the Inquisition, were all contributing factors which left a deep imprint on the religious history of Spain, one which has persisted almost until the present day.

Vatican II, with its doctrinal orientation, the Decree on Ecumenism and the Declaration on Religious Liberty, created a more favourable climate that helped melt the ice of indifference and hostility, removed the enemy's weapons, ignited people's desire to know more about their fellow human beings and fostered many genuinely fraternal relations between the different Christian churches.

Civil legislation, for its part, supported by the new political changes, enabled the passage from the confessional state to the legal recognition of non-Catholic churches and Christian confessions. This recognition began timidly with the "law regulating the exercise of the right to religious liberty" of 28 June 1967, and culminated in the constitution of 1978 and the later, more extensive law of religious liberty of 1980, followed finally by the agreement of cooperation between the Spanish state and the federation of evangelical religious bodies of Spain, signed in November of last year.

Concrete expressions of ecumenism

Ecumenism in Spain bears the stamp of several qualities which give it a special character. Because of the reduced numbers on one side it has to remain modest, since

---

The Rev. Don Julián García Hernando is director of the secretariat of the Episcopal commission on interconfessional relations of the Roman Catholic Church, Spain.

the numerical proportion of Catholics to Christians of other confessions is clearly unequal. And also many Spanish Protestants belong to bodies which are not members of the World Council of Churches, a fact which may suggest something about the degree of ecumenical awareness.

To describe ecumenism in Spain, one needs to consider the different levels at which ecumenical action can take place: the *institutional* level and the *individual* level. In fact there are three levels when one includes the activities of the interconfessional Christian committee which, due to its particular status — neither official nor private but semi-official — is situated between the two.

A. *Official ecumenism*

Institutional ecumenism is the concern of the secretariat of the Episcopal commission on interconfessional relations, established in July 1966, the diocesan delegations for ecumenism, the parish councils and similar church bodies that work in ecumenism, the Spanish Evangelical Church (IEE), the Spanish Reformed Episcopal Church (IERE), the Lutheran church and the Orthodox members of the Patriarchate of Constantinople and the Romanian Orthodox Church.

1) Spiritual ecumenism: We all know that the Week of Prayer for Christian Unity, held in January, is prepared at international level by a joint committee of members of the World Council of Churches and the Pontifical Council for the Promotion of Christian Unity. On two occasions this group has met in Spain under the patronage of the Episcopal commission on interconfessional relations: once in the monastery of Montserrat (Barcelona) and once, in October 1988, in Madrid. The work had been prepared in advance by a local joint committee comprising members of the Spanish Reformed Episcopal Church, the Spanish Evangelical Church, the Roman Catholics and the Orthodox.

The interconfessional Christian committee is responsible for producing relevant literature for the celebration of the week. This annual event has made a deep impact in Spanish Catholic circles and each year is followed by an enquiry to the diocesan delegations for ecumenism, to ascertain its effect on the population and results achieved. Very often the Week of Unity is celebrated interconfessionally, with exchanges of pulpits between pastors and priests. In many cities the Week of Unity is a privileged moment for in-depth interconfessional dialogue, at least at the level of prayer.

2) Doctrinal and pastoral ecumenism: For seventeen years the secretariat of the commission for interconfessional relations has been organizing the interconfessional gathering on the theology and ministry of ecumenism for diocesan delegates, directors of ecumenical publications and people in charge of ecumenical ministries. This event has always taken place in an interconfessional atmosphere, not only because of the people present but also because of the speakers and the themes presented. Since 1984 the event, and also its organization, has been fully interconfessional.

Under doctrinal ecumenism one must mention the meetings which take place for the study of the theological agreements reached in dialogue between the Catholic church and the World Council of Churches, the Orthodox churches and the world confessional bodies, such as "The Anglican-Catholic Declaration on Authority in the Church", the document on "The Presence of Christ in the Church and in the World", the joint document on ministry by the Catholic church and the World Alliance of

Reformed Churches, the study of BEM, including the appraisal made by the Spanish Episcopal Conference, and other similar studies undertaken jointly with Spanish Protestants and members of the Orthodox churches in Spain. Some of you here today are qualified witnesses to these meetings, having been invited to participate in them.

Among the most notable contributions of institutional ecumenism are the "Norms of the Episcopal Conference on Mixed Marriages in Spain" and the 1982 publication, "A Practical Guide to Ecumenism", to which can be added the studies undertaken together with the Spanish Evangelical Church and the Spanish Reformed Evangelical Church for the elaboration of a document on the mutual recognition of baptism.

3) Collaboration in the biblical field: There is extensive collaboration in the fields of translation and diffusion of interconfessional editions of the holy scriptures, in accordance with the joint norms approved for this work. All the linguistic areas of the Spanish population are being covered. There is an interconfessional translation of the New Testament in Castilian and work is in progress on the Old Testament. The translation of the entire Bible in Catalan is completed, with the help of the biblical association of Catalonia and the abbey of Montserrat on the Catholic side, and of the United Bible Societies and the Evangelical Bible foundation of Catalonia on the Protestant side. The interconfessional translation of the New Testament in Basque has been published, and in about a year's time the whole Bible will be ready in the same language. Work is in progress on other editions in Asturian and Galician.

Joint seminars have been held for the preparation of the interconfessional translations, which have been made according to the principles of translation known as "dynamic equivalence". There have also been interconfessional biblical gatherings in some dioceses (e.g. Murcia and Badajoz), the exchange of professors and ecumenical study circles.

4) Ecumenical worship centres: Several ecumenical worship centres exist, for example in Tenerife (Canary Islands), on the Costa Brava, the Costa del Sol and the Costa Blanca. The Catholic church frequently lends its buildings to sister churches which do not have their own, particularly in Madrid, Barcelona, Alicante and other towns.

B. Private ecumenical initiatives

In addition to what has been achieved at the official level, interconfessional relations in Spain have been actively promoted by private individuals and institutions. Such relations have been established throughout Spain as the result of demands coming from local ministries, and several ecumenical centres have come into being. While they share the same objectives concerning the desire to promote unity, each has its own recognizable features which are in tune with their local environment. I will forbear going into more detail about their activities at this point, due to lack of time.

There are interconfessional centres like the one in Barcelona, presently called the Catalonian centre, which is the pioneer of all such centres in Spain. That in Valencia is also interconfessional. The others are confessional, either Protestant like the one in Los Rubios (Malaga), or Catholic, but all are open to interconfessional collaboration.

To name a few, I would mention first the centre for Oriental and ecumenical studies of the Pontifical University of Salamanca, which has promoted many interconfessional conferences and seminars, mainly with the Lutheran Centre of Strasburg, and has set up the valuable ecumenical library of Salamanca, comprising many interesting books, among which are the two volumes, in Castilian, of *Enchiridion Oecumenicum*.

The Centre of the Missionary Sisters of Unity in Madrid fosters mainly pastoral and spiritual ecumenism. It holds ecumenical training courses, also by correspondence/extension. It has set up the interconfessional gatherings of religious sisters; they meet this summer in Toulouse for the twenty-third time.

Along with these centres I would add the Lux Mundi centre of Fuengirola on the Costa del Sol, which ministers mainly to tourists and in the social field; the centres of Toledo and the John XXIII ecumenical association of Salamanca, which publishes the review *Renovación Ecuménica* ("Ecumenical Renewal"). Other periodicals are *Diálogo Ecuménico* ("Ecumenical Dialogue") and *Pastoral Ecuménica* ("Ecumenical Ministry").

C. Semi-official/unofficial ecumenism

In addition to many other activities and tasks of ecumenical collaboration carried out in Spain by different associations and movements such as Agape, FUACE, YMCA, IEPALA, Justice and Peace and others, those implemented by the international Christian committee, a semi-official body which began in 1968, must be mentioned particularly. This committee is made up of members of many churches — Catholic, Orthodox, Spanish Reformed Evangelical, Spanish Evangelical, Anglican, Lutheran, Baptist, Pentecostal and Adventist — and deals with matters that cause friction between the different churches. Since its beginning it has studied a variety of socio-religious topics relevant to Spain, mainly in the field of human rights. Several times the committee has studied conscientious objection and its implications as well as the demands of religious liberty, at the time when this was not officially recognized in Spain. They strongly advocated the abolition of capital punishment as well as the right to life, including that of the unborn. They have studied the problems of north-south relations and of the poverty-ridden areas in the big cities of Spain, particularly in Madrid. They have raised the question of the present law on the status of aliens with the competent authorities, and have made many public statements on questions of peace, disarmament, etc.

To all that has been said so far I would like to add that the secretariats for ecumenism and for tourist ministry have organized ecumenical meetings in tourist regions such as the Costa del Sol and the Costa Blanca. It is in these regions that many churches are loaned, on a permanent or a temporary basis, to non-Catholic communities and groups. The cooperation between priests and pastors in this respect is extremely positive.

The same can be said about the ministries in hospitals and prisons, which have been discussed and planned with the specialists concerned in several interconfessional conferences and meetings.

From the ecumenical point of view the year 1992 was of special importance for Spain. It was the year of the international exhibition in Seville and the Olympic Games in Barcelona. In the exhibition there was a *Pabellón de la Promesa* ("Pavilion of the Promise") and the interconfessional Christian centre, where visitors could obtain spiritual help. In Barcelona for the Olympic Games there was the Abraham centre for 400 persons, with a permanent chapel for each of the five religious bodies with an "officially recognized" presence at the Games: Jewish, Islam, Buddhist, as well as Protestant and Catholic. The centre, which was converted into a Catholic parish after the Games, continues to be open for interconfessional and inter-religious gatherings.

Perspectives

To sum up, I would say that for the reasons given above and as far as the interconfessional dimension is concerned, our ecumenism remains modest; that from its beginnings until the present time, it has made remarkable progress towards a more open climate. Our present situation is partly reflected in the texts you have given us for the preparation of this Faith and Order conference. We feel a weakening of enthusiasm on the part of those fostering the cause of unity. We are very far from putting into practice the Lund recommendation to "do together all things which our own conscience does not compel us to do separately". New problems, too, have arisen among us that have to be confronted.

We are conscious that, as von Allmen said in his own time,

> in the perspective of an ecclesiology of pilgrimage — and in that pilgrimage style which can be captured perfectly in Compostela — the Protestants, Catholics and Orthodox are all companions along the way.

Because of this we have taken the fifth conference on Faith and Order very seriously and studied the Dublin preparatory document (the Stuttgart document reached us too late) in two of the most prestigious ecumenical fora of Spain, the ninth interconfessional gathering on the theology and pastoral aspects of ecumenism, held in Madrid, 13-14 April this year, and the fourth interconfessional encounter, which took place in El Espinar (Segovia) from 1 to 6 July.

We hope that the important event in which we are now taking part, and the appearance of the new ecumenical directory of the Catholic church, will stimulate us to discover and to live the unity which we already possess, and spur us along the way towards that full unity which is still lacking, until we reach a true koinonia in faith, life and witness.

IX

Closing the Fifth
World Conference

☐ Introduction

The fifth world conference on Faith and Order concluded with plenary XVI, 13 August, 16h., moderator Dr Mary Tanner presiding. The plenary opened with Dr Tanner welcoming our host, His Eminence Archbishop Rouco Varela of Santiago de Compostela, to the session. Following the presentation of the last of several papers on the World Council of Churches, Faith and Order, and the ecumenical future, and the adoption of the conference **Message**, a brief reflection and a long series of thanks brought the fifth world conference on Faith and Order to an end.

Dr Tanner delivered a **Closing Statement** expressing her gratitude for the many beautiful and positive things which had happened during the world conference, and her hope that it might provide a new inspiration for the ecumenical pilgrimage "towards koinonia in faith, life and witness".

Then followed a long series of thanks. Dr Tanner recognized the three working groups established by the Faith and Order Standing Commission to plan and carry out the world conference programme: the planning, organization and finance group, moderated by the Rev. Dr Paul A. Crow, Jr; the worship and Bible studies planning group, moderated by the Rev. Janet Crawford (along with the worship team, whose members were introduced as the conference expressed appreciation); and the theme group, originally moderated by Metropolitan Dr G. Yohanna Ibrahim and then, when he was unable to be present, by Bishop Barry Rogerson. She also expressed appreciation to Prof. Dr Turid Karlsen Seim as moderator of the section steering group.

The Rev. A. Rocchietti expressed appreciation to the people of Santiago de Compostela for their warm hospitality, noting especially the role of Archbishop Rouco Varela and the civil authorites, and thanked the leaders of the Spanish Reformed Episcopal Church and the Spanish Evangelical Church for their contribution. She listed each of the institutions which had housed conference participants and offered meeting facilities, and thanked their directors and staffs. The Rev. D. Elisardo Temperan was called forward to receive the special appreciation of the conference for his untiring help with local arrangements.

The Rev. Prof. Jean-Marie Tillard, O.P., asked the conference stewards to come forward to accept the enthusiastic appreciation of the conference for their work. Then the director of Faith and Order expressed gratitude to the translators (including volunteers from among conference participants) and to the interpreters. He thanked especially OKR Dr Reinhard Groscurth for managing the plenary hall, in which task he had been assisted by the Rev. Roberto Jordan. The director also expressed appreciation to Prof. Dr Anton Houtepen for his work in coordinating the sections, and to all others who helped in that area of the life of the conference. Finally he expressed thanks to the technical staff from Geneva.

Dr Tanner then expressed appreciation to Archbishop Aram Keshishian and the officers of the World Council of Churches for their participation in the meeting, and extended her thanks to WCC general secretary Konrad Raiser, who was present throughout the event. She thanked all those who read papers and who gave leadership in worship, including the biblical meditations. She further thanked all those who had served as moderators, secretaries and drafters within sections and groups, and she expressed appreciation for the journalists who had attended and reported on the world conference. Finally, she called forward the director and staff of the secretariat of the Commission on Faith and Order to receive the appreciation of the conference.

The Rev. Prof. Tillard, O.P., then expressed the gratitude of all present for Dr Tanner's leadership, both as moderator of the Faith and Order Commission and of the world conference. The conference rose to a standing ovation. After a reference to the closing worship still to come that afternoon, and having thanked the Commission vice-moderators Crow, Rochietti, Swai, Tillard and Clapsis (the last in his absence) as well as Prof. Lossky (acting in the place of vice-moderator Clapsis), moderator Dr Mary Tanner then formally closed the fifth world conference on Faith and Order with prayer.

CLOSING STATEMENT

MARY TANNER

It is too early to give account of what happened here in these days. I, at least, need distance to make sense of all of this, and a release from the bondage of words.

Of one thing I am sure: our experience in this unique and hauntingly beautiful city has had an authentic atmosphere of prayer and a real desire to discover together the depth of Christian truth and the nature of our life together in Christ. That is what has made the quality of this meeting — that must be, and is, the ground of our hope for the future.

Our theme of koinonia is a theme whose time has come, for it holds together the life and love of God, creation and the church. It expresses the fullness of the gift of the kingdom and provides a way for us to understand and express that which we already know we share. From our encounter here comes the conviction that what binds us together now is not of our human manufacturing: it is precious gift but fragile treasure in our human hands.

Dr Mary Tanner is general secretary of the Council for Christian Unity of the General Synod of the Church of England, and moderator of the Faith and Order Commission.

I received a postcard here on Sunday which read:

Dear Mary,

I went to the Atlantic coast today alone, and looked for scallop shells, hoping I might find some to give to friends made here as mementos of koinonia we have shared. However, in five hours I found only one that was not in broken pieces. So I give it to you (an Anglican) with a Presbyterian intention for koinonia. I am sorry it is not perfect, but maybe a fragile, and slightly broken shell is a better image of pre-eschatological ecumenism.

We have indeed experienced that fragility and brokenness here. Our continuing separation at the Lord's table; the hurts we inflict upon each other, not least of all because of our lack of knowing each other, our failures to come out of our corners to listen to the others, in such a way that we never see our positions in quite the same way again. The structure of our meeting, which seemed too tightly planned for our theme of koinonia, so often seemed to imprison us — preventing that growth of mutual exchange and understanding we had intended. For that, those of us who planned this conference bear our responsibility.

Nevertheless, we leave this place with a message and section reports for the churches which delegated us. In these we have harvested past work, seen new perspectives and sown again for another harvest. We must wait to see how our churches will respond. We leave here too with a list of recommendations and challenges to Faith and Order which asks for both essential continuity and newness of perspective. The Faith and Order Commission will need to consider carefully the implications for future work. While this world conference has not, as Fr Jean Tillard suggested, "presided over the death of Faith and Order", it has shown that it cannot simply be "business as usual". Among all the questions raised we in Faith and Order are challenged to ask questions of method. Can we find a coherent and workable method which does justice, with integrity, to the faith of the church through the ages while being, at the same time, open to the experience of an ever-widening community of reflection and interpretation and to the experience of the new configurations of the future now emerging?

Faith and Order began planning this world conference with the intention of being conversational and contextual, through the regional meetings. The need for regionalization of Faith and Order holds at least one of the keys to our search for right method. But we cannot simply hold Faith and Order meetings in the regions but rather seek to stimulate regional meetings where the agenda is not imposed or controlled. My hope is that the next world conference on Faith and Order, the sixth world conference, will not lie thirty years ahead but a decade from now and that it will be able to give good account of our response to this challenge.

Ten days ago I began with the image of pilgrimage. Let me end there, for that is the image given us by this place. Two friends of mine recently walked for three months from Vézelay in France to Santiago de Compostela. Day after day they packed their bags, took their staffs and walked, meeting up with other pilgrims on the way, telling stories and listening with the openness and intensity that pilgrims have on the road. Reaching Santiago was a moment of achievement and of refreshment in the stillness. For in their walking they had found a rhythm of life which was established deep within them and from which they could not escape. Santiago de Compostela has been our resting place. May the commitment and the rhythm of life that characterizes pilgrims be ours as we move daily towards koinonia in faith, life and witness — God's calling and God's gift.

B

Message,
Section Reports,
Discussion Paper,
Minutes

I

Message

Introduction

A special committee prepared the conference **Message** which was considered in three stages: in plenary X, 12 August, 9h.15, vice-moderator the Rev. Prof. Jean-Marie Tillard, O.P. presiding; plenary XV, 13 August, 11h., Prof. Nicolas Lossky presiding; and plenary XVI, 13 August, 16h., moderator Dr Mary Tanner presiding.

During plenary X the Rev. Prof. Duncan Forrester, moderator of the Message committee, introduced the first draft of the Message. Prof. Forrester explained that the text attempted to "harvest" the central insights, ideas and perspectives of the conference, to celebrate the koinonia already enjoyed, and to identify the "sowing" needed for the ecumenical harvest which would come in the future. The draft was read by Prof. Forrester and Message committee vice-moderator the Rev. Olivia Wesley. The conference considered the second draft of the message in plenary XV. Prof. Forrester and the Rev. Wesley in presenting the revised text noted that since the first reading the message committee "had carefully considered every comment made or written and had accommodated most of them".

Plenary discussion and action

In the initial consideration of the Message in plenary X, 24 participants voiced a very wide range of comments and proposals for improving the draft. These ranged from challenges to the supposed "waning commitment to Christian unity", to encouragement to view "mission, testimony and service together as manifestations of koinonia", to the call that the message take seriously "new tensions" which have arisen in the ecumenical movement.

In the discussion of the second draft in plenary XV 12 persons were recognized to speak. Several emphasized the link between "theological perceptions" of koinonia and our expression of koinonia through response to specific situations of human need. It was emphasized that the power of Christ to break down walls of separation was the theological basis for our hope in all particular situations. The drafters were encouraged to speak to the "concrete situation of 1993", and several specific areas of concern (for example, Eastern Europe, Africa and Asia) were suggested for inclusion. One speaker, loudly applauded, emphasized that "koinonia in faith and witness" must include acts of protest against the persecution of Christians under totalitarian regimes around the world. Another noted that the question of *which* specific situations should be addressed in the Message was sensitive and difficult; the conference as a whole, rather than the message committee, should decide on this.

One speaker emphasized that in the Message Faith and Order was moving "beyond Lund": Lund had called on the churches to work together in all things "except those in which deep differences of conviction compel them to act separately"; in Santiago de Compostela we were actually identifying — and challenging — the convictions which *make* us act separately. There was a call for the message to speak, "as the churches expect", about future interaction between Faith and Order and Justice, Peace and the Integrity of Creation. One participant urged attention to "ecumenical hermeneutics and methodology". An intervention spoke of the offence felt by some Orthodox at what they perceived as a lack of proper respect for the mystery of the church as God's sacramental presence in history. The view was also expressed that in the future, Bible study embodying a critical perspective should not be an integral part of worship services.

One delegate emphasized the importance of interfaith relations today — a point strengthened, they said, by the fact that we were meeting in Santiago de Compostela. It was noted that the phrase "ecumenical creeds" was inappropriate since the term applies, properly speaking, only to the Nicene-Constantinopolitan Creed. One speaker expressed dismay that the aim of Faith and Order had been abbreviated in the Message so as to omit the important phrase "that the world may believe".

The Message was presented in plenary XVI for adoption by the conference. The Rev. Prof. Forrester explained that an attempt had been made to respond sympathetically to comments made on the second draft. However the Message committee had not been able "to add details about situations which the conference had not discussed, and it also wanted to avoid an imbalance due to references to specific situations of oppression". Since printed copies of the final draft were not available the committee secretary, Prof. Dr Michael Root, read aloud to plenary the 15 changes which had been made in the text.

After a pause for reading the revised text, moderator Dr Mary Tanner invited the conference to adopt the message. One delegate raised an objection to a wording about which he had been unable to speak in the previous discussion; the moderator indicated that delegates had been encouraged to submit suggestions in writing and that, according to the agreed rules of the conference, the text was now being put for a vote and further discussion of it was no longer possible.

The moderator then put the following motion:

The fifth world conference on Faith and Order adopts "The Conference Message" and instructs the director immediately to circulate it to all member churches.

This was adopted by the delegates with 159 voting in favour, 9 against and 6 abstaining.

The moderator then expressed gratitude to the Message committee.

[In conversations after the Message had been adopted, it became clear that negative votes and abstentions could have been avoided if there had been sufficient time for making a few changes in the text of the Message sensitive to the position of all traditions. The Faith and Order Plenary Commission, meeting on 14 August 1993, agreed that this fact should be explicitly mentioned when the Message was published.]

ON THE WAY TO FULLER KOINONIA: THE MESSAGE OF THE WORLD CONFERENCE

1. "The grace of our Lord Jesus Christ and the love of God and the koinonia of the Holy Spirit be with you all" (2 Cor. 13:13).

2. God, who calls all to unity and makes us one in Christ and the Spirit, has drawn us to Santiago de Compostela from around the world. We are a more comprehensive gathering than came together thirty years ago in Montreal at the last world conference on Faith and Order. Far more of us come from Asia, Africa, Latin America, the Caribbean, and the Pacific region. There are more women participants than ever before. The group of younger theologians has eagerly participated in the work. For the first time, the Roman Catholic Church has sent official delegates to a world conference. There is a significant presence of Pentecostal Christians. We have come together, sent by our churches, to further the work of the Faith and Order movement "to proclaim the oneness of the Church of Jesus Christ and to call the churches to the goal of visible unity" (Faith and Order Commission, by-law 2).

3. We come in joy, giving thanks for the great strides forward that have been made in recent years and for the eagerness of many Christians for a fuller koinonia, but also come in concern for waning commitments to Christian unity. We come in thankfulness for the breakthroughs to freedom that have occurred, for example, in Eastern Europe and Southern Africa. But we also come in concern for a world torn by injustice and strife in such locations as the former Yugoslavia, Somalia and so many other places. We come in pain when we remember what our sin does to humanity and the groaning creation. Our concern and pain become penitence when we think of our failure to do all that is already ecumenically possible and of our silence in the face of hatred and evil, or even worse, our participation in them. We come in hope for the ecumenical future, for the Church, and for the world. We now leave Santiago with renewed commitment and enthusiasm for the ecumenical vision. We say to the churches: *there is no turning back*, either from the goal of visible unity or from the single ecumenical movement that unites concern for the unity of the Church and concern for engagement in the struggles of the world.

4. *Koinonia* has been the focus of our discussions. This word from the Greek New Testament describes the richness of our life together in Christ: community, communion, sharing, fellowship, participation, solidarity. The koinonia we seek and which we have experienced is more than words. It springs from the word of life, "what we have seen with our eyes, what we have touched with our hands" (1 John 1:1), especially where koinonia is being realized daily in such forms as local ecumenical projects and base communities. This koinonia which we share is nothing less than the reconciling

presence of the love of God. God wills unity for the Church, for humanity, and for creation because God is a koinonia of love, the unity of the Father, Son and Holy Spirit. This koinonia comes to us as a gift we can only accept in gratitude. Gratitude, however, is not passivity. Our koinonia is in the Holy Spirit who moves us to action. The koinonia we experience drives us to seek that visible unity which can adequately embody our koinonia with God and one another.

5. The deeper koinonia which is our goal is for the glory of God and for the sake of the world. The Church is called to be a sign and instrument of this all-encompassing will of God, the summing up of all things in Christ. Jesus broke down walls of division in his identification with women and with the poor, the outcast, and the oppressed. A deeper koinonia will be a sign of hope for all or it will not be a true koinonia in the love of God. Only a Church itself being healed can convincingly proclaim healing to the world. Only a Church that overcomes ethnic, racial, and national hatreds in a common Christian and human identity can be a credible sign of freedom and reconciliation. While our particular focus at this conference has been the visible unity of the Church, the horizon of our work has been the wider reach of God's love.

6. One of our tasks in Santiago has been to examine the concrete ecumenical achievements over the past thirty years of the Faith and Order movement, including the bilateral dialogues. We have particularly noted and affirmed the importance of all convergences towards a common understanding and practice of baptism, eucharist, and ministry; towards a common confession of the one faith witnessed to in the Nicene-Constantinopolitan Creed; and towards a shared mission and service. The task before the churches now is to receive these convergences into their life. What steps is God leading the churches to take together *now*?

7. The ecumenical movement has changed over the past thirty years. The voices of women and of those from beyond Europe and North America have joined the ecumenical conversation in strength, bringing new insights, new experiences, new diversities. The significance for koinonia of common ethical commitment and action has been firmly placed on the Faith and Order agenda. The many positive movements of evangelical and charismatic renewal still need to be drawn into ecumenical partnership. The transformation is still going on and is at times difficult and controversial. Differences over the goals and methods of ecumenical work and theology have led to intense debates. In these debates, conflicting perspectives often each express significant elements of truth. We are confident we are being led through such tensions into a deeper and broader koinonia in the Spirit. A test of our koinonia is how we live with those with whom we disagree.

8. The ecumenical goal has not yet been reached. The churches still have not come to a full mutual recognition of baptism. There are still obstacles that prevent the sharing together of Christians from all churches at the Lord's table. The obstacles that stand in the way of a fuller koinonia must be felt in all their painfulness and honestly faced in penitence. The way forward will come by new ventures and insights in the faith that unites us, not by compromises that merely obscure the problems. Addressing these obstacles is the specific task of Faith and Order work. This task is more than ever essential to the ecumenical movement. The churches are challenged to an active partnership within the Faith and Order movement in addressing what still divides them.

9. At Santiago, we have again sensed the urgency of our need for greater koinonia in faith, life, and witness. The churches have made some progress in implementing the 1952 Lund principle that they should "act together in all matters except those in which deep differences of conviction compel them to act separately". But they must go further. Unity today calls for structures of mutual accountability.

10. Concrete challenges stand before the churches. In relation to *faith*, the churches must continue to explore how to confess our common faith in the context of the many cultures and religions, the many social and national conflicts in which we live. Such confession emphasizes the need for a deeper understanding of the Church and its apostolic character in the light of the holy scriptures. In relation to *life*, the churches must dare concrete steps towards fuller koinonia, in particular doing all that is possible to achieve a common recognition of baptism, agreement on a common participation in the eucharist, and a mutually recognized ministry. In relation to *witness*, the churches must consider the implications of koinonia for a responsible care for creation, for a just sharing of the world's resources, for a special concern for the poor and outcast, and for a common and mutually respectful evangelism that invites everyone into communion with God in Christ. But beyond all particular challenges, the churches and the ecumenical movement itself are called to the conversion to Christ that true koinonia in our time demands.

11. The world was made for this koinonia in God, a koinonia that has been won by the life, death, and resurrection of Jesus Christ. We stand before God and our final words must be prayer:

Holy and loving Trinity:
— we come to you in thanksgiving,
    for your gift of koinonia which we now receive as a
    foretaste of your kingdom.
— we come to you in penitence,
    for our failures to show forth koinonia where there is
    division, hostility and death;
— we come to you in expectation,
    that we may enter more deeply into the joy of koinonia;
— we come to you in confidence,
    to commit ourselves anew to your purposes of love;
    justice, and koinonia;
— we come to you in hope,
    that the unity of your Church, in all its rich diversity,
    may be ever more clearly manifest as a sign of your love.

Kindle our hearts. Direct our wills. Deepen our understanding. Strengthen our resolve. Help us to be open to you and to our sisters and brothers, that we may together witness to the perfect unity of your love. Amen.

II

Reports
of the Sections

☐ Introduction

The work in the sections began from, and was often centred around, the discussion paper (it drew also upon other sources, particularly the papers and discussions in plenary). The section reports grew out of initial discussions in the four sections, with more detailed work being done in a total of 17 small groups. The section reports were drafted on the basis of reports produced by these groups. Each section revised, and then adopted, its own report after discussion. The section reports were discussed in plenary XII, 12 August, 16h., vice-moderator the Rev. Dr Paul A. Crow, Jr, presiding; and plenary XIII, 12 August, 18h., vice-moderator the Rev. Dr Paul A. Crow, Jr, presiding.

Dr Crow introduced plenary XII by remarking on the "miracle" by which the section reports had been produced by the scheduled hour. He emphasized that the purpose of the ensuing discussion was not to amend the section reports: delegates would be asked only to "commend" the texts to the churches for study and action, and to Faith and Order as an indication of directions for further work. However a careful record would be kept of the plenary discussion of the four texts for use in that "further work". Those unable to speak in plenary due to lack of time could hand in their comments in written form, and account would also be taken of these in later work.

The **Report** of section I was presented by Most Rev. John Onaiyekan, who expressed thanks to his section co-moderator, the Rev. Raquel Rodriguez, and to the drafters of the text, the Rev. Alan Falconer and Prof. Dr Kyriaki Fitzgerald. After plenary discussion of this report Dr Melanie May presented that of section II, likewise expressing thanks to her section co-moderator, Prof. Nicolas Lossky, and the drafters, Ms Elisabeth Parmentier and the Rev. Prof. William Henn.

In plenary XIII Dr Crow invited the Rt Rev. Barry Rogerson to present the **Report** from section III; he extended thanks to his section co-moderator, the Rev. Christobella Bagh, and to the drafters, Sister Dr Margaret Jenkins, CSB and the Rev. Prof. Geoffrey Wainwright. Following discussion of this report Prof. Dr Turid Karlsen Seim presented that of section IV, thanking her section co-moderator, the Rev. Dr Yemba Kekumba, as well as the drafters of the text, the Rev. Dr Michael Kinnamon and the Rev. Lorna Khoo.

After the discussions of the section reports the following motion was put to the conference:

The reports of sections I, II, III and IV are commended to the churches for their study and action and to the Plenary Commission on Faith and Order for its future work.

This was approved unanimously.

☐   **Plenary discussion and action: Section I Report**

In presenting the report Bishop Onaiyekan noted that, since much had already been presented to the conference "on the theological aspects" of its topic, the section had focused on particular examples and experiences of koinonia.

In the discussion 13 persons spoke. In an initial exchange, the plenary moderator explained that the various recommendations included in the section reports would not be presented to plenary for adoption, but referred to Faith and Order "for consideration and implementation". One speaker welcomed the call for a study on ecclesiology. Another missed in paragraph 4 "something vital to the Reformation", namely the insight that the church is a community which lives by justification and reconciliation, and is in need of forgiveness. Another, noting that paragraph 5 mentioned Israel only briefly, regretted that Faith and Order speaks so rarely, and then negatively, in this area. A caution was issued against suggesting a dichotomy between the ministry and teaching of Jesus, and his death and resurrection (e.g. "above all", para. 6, first sentence). Another regretted the absence of the notion of incarnation in paragraphs 7 and 12, and argued that the incarnation is crucial for koinonia. Another said that paragraph 12 would be clearer if the words "word and" were added before "sacrament". Yet another, referring to paragraphs 17 and 18, warned against the frequent understanding of the term "universal" as equivalent to "catholic"; there is an important distinction between these terms which must be guarded.

Dismay was expressed at the grouping in paragraph 22 of such disparate issues as exclusion from the eucharist and acts of proselytism; with regard to the eucharist, such an approach "fails to appreciate the good faith of those with whom we may disagree". Two speakers continued the discussion of limits to "table fellowship" with reference to paragraph 33. One insisted that the phrase "eucharistic hospitality" was presumptuous, as the elements were not "ours" to dispense or withhold; another noted the danger of using words to mask continuing differences of conviction. Strong approval was expressed of paragraph 29's call for work to overcome past divisions and condemnations.

Calling attention to paragraph 23, one delegate emphasized the importance of koinonia in relation to human suffering. While there was agreement on the urgent need for collaboration between Faith and Order and JPIC, two speakers questioned the recommendation in paragraph 32 that *Costly Unity* be sent to the churches along with the publication of the Santiago results: this might be misleading, they felt, since the Commission had not yet studied the text fully, nor had the conference as a whole commented on it.

REPORT OF SECTION I:
THE UNDERSTANDING OF KOINONIA AND ITS IMPLICATIONS

Introduction

1. As Christians from every continent and diverse ecclesial traditions, we have gathered to reflect on the theme "Towards Koinonia in Faith, Life and Witness". "Koinonia" has been a key notion in the understanding of the Church and the experience of Christians through the ages. The theme is a prominent one in the Bible, and in the theology of the Eastern and Western Fathers of the Church and the writings of the Reformers.

2. The concept of koinonia has also been a prominent one in the history of the ecumenical movement. Indeed, the First World Conference on Faith and Order examined the theme explicitly, while the Second World Conference reads like a treatise on "koinonia", even though the language of koinonia is only implicit. Subsequent Faith and Order Conferences and the Assemblies of the World Council of Churches have deepened the awareness that koinonia is the experience and reality of the Triune God drawing Christians together. Since the Fourth World Conference on Faith and Order at Montreal (1963), there has been a whole series of bilateral dialogues in which the theme of koinonia has been the central focus, indeed, koinonia is central in articulating the visible unity of the Church.

3. The Fifth World Conference, therefore, examining the theme of "Towards Koinonia in Faith, Life and Witness" has sought to clarify the concept and its implications as a contribution to the search for the unity of the Church.

Koinonia as gift

4. "Koinonia" is above all a gracious fellowship in Christ expressing the richness of the gift received by creation and humankind from God. It is a many-dimensional dynamic in the faith, life and witness of those who worship the Triune God, confess the apostolic faith, share the Gospel and sacramental living and seek to be faithful to God in Church and world.

5. This gift of God is extended to all creation and humankind and to those who respond in faith to Jesus Christ. As human beings created in God's image, we have been created to live in the atmosphere of divine life, to love one another as God is love, and to act as responsible stewards of creation. In creation, persons are created to be in relationship with God and each other so that their very identity is shaped through the encounter with others, as gift and calling. This dynamic impulse to communion through the activity of God is evident throughout the story of the people of Israel, even when the community breaks koinonia. God's gracious gift of koinonia is an orientation to openness to a consciousness of the calling to justice and truth.

6. In the light of the ministry, teaching and, above all, the death and resurrection of Jesus, the Christian community believes that God sent his Son to bring the possibility of communion for each person with others and with God. His parables, miracles, ministry of forgiveness and self-giving to others and the incorporation into the people of God of those who were shunned and excluded offered koinonia to all people.

7. In the life, ministry, death and resurrection, Jesus Christ revealed the intimate relationship between himself and his Father in whom he abides (John 15:10), and the

power of the Holy Spirit working in him. The mysterious life of divine communion between Jesus Christ and his Father and the Spirit is personal and relational — a life of giving and receiving love flowing between them. It is a life of communion at the heart of which is a cross, and a communion which is always stretching out beyond itself to embrace and enfold all within its own life.

8. Through the power of the Holy Spirit, Christians die with Christ and rise to new life in him, and are thus joined to the Father (cf. Rom. 6:4-5). Koinonia signifies this dynamic relationship based on participation in the reality of God's grace. No one is untouched by God's gifts and call to service.

9. The many images of the Church in the New Testament point to the relationship of the community with God and to the relationship in space and time among members of the community. Our shared life, in which unity and diversity are inseparable, is grounded in the economy of the Triune God. It is in the Church that the Holy Spirit realizes this communion. The Church seeks to be a community, being faithful as disciples of Christ, living in continuity with the apostolic community established by a baptism inseparable from faith and metanoia, called to a common life in Christ, manifested and sustained by the Lord's Supper under the care of a ministry at the same time personal and communal and having as its mission the proclamation in word and witness of the Gospel. These disciples are one while enriched by their differences. Diversity as well as unity is a gift of God.

10. The interdependence of unity and diversity which is the essence of the Church's koinonia is rooted in the Triune God revealed in Jesus Christ. The Father, Son and Holy Spirit is the perfect expression of unity and diversity and the ultimate reality of relational life. In the Holy Spirit he makes human beings partakers of this relational life which is his own.

11. Such divine gift is not easily expressed or defined. What language is appropriate to evince the meaning of koinonia's rootedness in the divine Trinity? All attempts to express this experience are inadequate. This is truly a mystery of faith, yet koinonia for all its limitations has a plethora of meanings transcending its translations into any one vernacular. It is a searching term pointing us towards the fullness of life in God and shared life with others.

12. For most churches the Church is understood as the community of believers who celebrate "this is my body". For these churches it is above all in the celebration of the sacrament of the Lord's Supper that the Body of Christ is manifest. The members of the body celebrating the presence of God are united with the life, ministry, death and resurrection of the Lord Jesus who offers himself for the establishing of koinonia. This is both the event of the Church and a foretaste of the Kingdom. It feeds the impulse to engage in the task of standing in solidarity with the hungry, the dispossessed and the marginalized through costly acts of empowering as a sign of God's love for all humankind.

13. Just as God has been revealed to us as a Trinity of persons who abide in an eternal relationship of love, so we, too, are called to live likewise. As the Church, we are called to begin enjoying membership in the Kingdom with fellow believers from our very baptism and to grow to become partakers of the divine nature (2 Pet. 1:4). As the Church we are called to relate with each other as respectful persons and as members of the human community. As the Church we are called to care for God's creation.

14. The very structure of the Church is relational. It is expressed both locally and universally. Both expressions witness to each other in a living and intimate way. No Christian can exist as an isolated individual exercising a privileged and direct communion with God. The ancient Latin Christian saying, *Unus Christianus nullus Christianus* (that a single Christian is not a Christian at all) affirms the reality that human beings are called to help each other in the process of salvation.

15. Unity and diversity are safeguarded within the structure of the Church. Both unity and diversity are expressive of koinonia. There are two characteristics of koinonia which bear witness to each other. On the one hand, unity must be safeguarded. No one can say to another member, "I need you not" (1 Cor. 12). As there is absolute interdependence among all members of the community, there is also diversity within the Church. Every member is indispensable and offers his or her gifts to the one body.

16. All members belong but not all are the same; they are given to each other with their differences of personality, race, gender, physical abilities, social and economic status. Thus difference is not a factor to exclude anyone from the koinonia of the Church, especially when such differences are expressive of weakness or vulnerability. We recall examples from the stories of the life of the Lord Jesus Christ who incorporated into the people of God those who were shunned or excluded, the poor, the infirm and the broken, as their acceptance is a sign of the Kingdom (Luke 5:27-32, 19:1-10).

17. The koinonia of the Church is also universal. One community cannot be isolated from the rest. Again, the principle of authentic relationship is what binds particular communities within the universal. There is one Church while there are many local churches at the same time.

18. The relational dynamic of catholicity within each local church to the universal (the "one" and the "many"), echoes the relationship of the Trinity. The Holy Trinity actualizes the one Body of Christ by making each local church a full and "catholic" church. For the fullness of catholicity to be safeguarded within the life of the local church, both equally strong pneumatological and Christological emphases are needed.

Koinonia as calling

19. The divine gift of koinonia is both a gift and a calling. The dynamic activity of God drawing us into communion also entails the calling of Christians and Christian communities to manifest koinonia as a sign and foretaste of God's intention for humankind. Yet from the beginning of the Church, Christians have failed to realize the koinonia given to them by God. Both the Hebrew Scriptures and the New Testament recount numerous occasions when members of the people of God have perceived others as a threat rather than a gift. Yet God continues to call the Christian community to correction and transformation from beyond its boundaries. This call invites an openness to God's whole divine economy (activity), even when we do not expect it or resist it.

20. The dynamic process of koinonia involves the recognition of the complementarity of human beings. As individuals and as communities, we are confronted by the others in their otherness e. g., theologically, ethnically, culturally. Koinonia requires respect for the other and a willingness to listen to the other and to seek to understand them. In this process of dialogue, where each is changed in the encounter, there takes

place the appropriation of the stories of action, reaction and separation whereby each has defined himself or herself in opposition to the other. The search for establishing koinonia involves appropriating the pain and hurt of the other and through a process of individual and collective repentance, forgiveness and renewal, taking responsibility for that suffering. Confrontation with the other, individually and collectively, is always a painful process, challenging as it does our own lifestyle, convictions, piety and way of thinking. The encounter with the other in the search to establish the koinonia, grounded in God's gift, calls for a kenosis — a self-giving and a self-emptying. Such a kenosis arouses fear of loss of identity, and invites us to be vulnerable, yet such is no more than faithfulness to the ministry of vulnerability and death of Jesus as he sought to draw human beings into communion with God and each other. He is the pattern and patron of reconciliation which leads to koinonia. As individuals and communities, we are called to establish koinonia through a ministry of kenosis.

21. The Church as koinonia is called to share not only in the suffering of its own community but in the suffering of all; by advocacy and care for the poor, needy, and marginalized; by joining in all efforts for justice and peace within human societies; by exercising and promoting responsible stewardship of creation and by keeping alive hope in the heart of humanity. *Diakonia* to the whole world and *koinonia* cannot be separated.

22. As Christians and Christian communities we have to confess to a lack of koinonia. This calls us to repentance and renewed commitment to re-establish communion and community through a self-critical attitude of humility. The pain of the brokenness in the Christian communities is evident in the non-recognition of the ministry and members by a number of churches, in exclusion from the eucharist, in the re-baptism by Christian communities of former members of other churches, by acts of proselytism, in the treatment of women in the Church and in the attempt to impose uniformity.

23. The Spirit of God leads us to discover the imperfections of our visible koinonia. We are called to self-critical reflection on our relationship of interdependence with creation and the whole of humankind. Is it possible for us to serve the table of the world when we are divided at the table of the Lord? We must work on the issues which divide us, but recognize, too, that perhaps only a penitent brokenness can help us avoid the triumphalism of the past, and offer in weakness a diakonia to match the world's need. Do we listen to the cry of the poor and to the cry of the earth? Koinonia with humanity and the whole creation is broken when gifts of the earth are not shared. Do we make space to hear the voice of the voiceless, and to take sacrificial steps towards justice, peace and care of creation? Do we listen in humility to those who have knowledge and can guide us in practical ways? Do we celebrate the eucharist without living out its implications?

24. Yet we also experience anticipations of the fullness of koinonia. There is much that unites us as we pray together the Lord's prayer since we are brought again into the family of God, the community of forgiveness and sharing where we seek together the will of God and commit ourselves to faithfulness to God's dynamic activity.

25. Koinonia as the all-encompassing goal of reflecting God's intention for humankind lies ahead of the churches. This communion with Christ and with one another entails:

a) being rooted together in faith which is complete trust in the Triune God, changing life from within (e.g. Rom. 4);

b) receiving and sharing the apostolic teaching, communion in prayer and breaking of bread in koinonia (Acts 2:42);

c) authentic discipleship partaking in the sufferings of Christ and modelled upon his example, which never forgets the self-giving of Christ (Phil. 3:10; 2 Cor. 4:7-11; 1 Pet. 4:13, 5:1);

d) a sense of justice and compassion, a sharing in one another's joys, sorrows and sufferings (2 Cor. 1:6-7; Heb. 10:33);

e) the courage to struggle for truth when necessary even at the expense of comfort and peaceful unanimity (Gal. 2:5);

f) serving one another in love and mutual receiving and giving of material and spiritual gifts (Rom. 15:26-27; 2 Cor. 8:1-15; Gal. 5:13);

g) the preaching of the Gospel to the whole humanity (Matt. 28:19-20; Acts 2:14ff.);

h) care for the harmony of God's creation (Col. 1:14-18; Rom. 8:19-21);

i) looking forward towards sharing in a glory that will come when all things will be brought to ultimate koinonia (Rom. 8:7; 1 Cor. 15:27f.; Eph. 1:10; Col. 1:19-20).

26. We refuse to be satisfied with our partial experience of koinonia. We are impelled to seek to manifest that koinonia which is God's gift and his urgent calling to the Church as a sign of God's intention for humankind in the context of a world which knows the pain of the brokenness of community.

Steps on the way

27. Spiritual ecumenism should undergird all endeavours to foster koinonia. There is a need for a continuing emphasis in Faith and Order work that prayer and theology go hand in hand, and that Christian spirituality — growth towards holiness in heart and mind — is a means of preparing people to receive the koinonia which God wants to give to the Church. The importance of the place of prayer, penitence and humility should not be underestimated. As churches come together to manifest the unity which is sincerely sought, attitudes to God and to each other must be changed. This is the call to metanoia and kenosis. Many have spoken of the significance of locating this conference at Santiago de Compostela, the place for penitent pilgrims. As we strip ourselves of false securities, finding in God our true and only identity, daring to be open and vulnerable to each other, we will begin to live as pilgrims on a journey, discovering the God of surprises who leads us into roads which we have not travelled, and we will find in each other true companions on the way.

28. As we travel the way of pilgrimage, we will need to be able to understand each other's theological language and cultural ethos. We would be assisted in our journeying by intercontextual dialogues appropriately sponsored by regional ecumenical organizations, and in our interconfessional dialogues by a renewed Faith and Order study on hermeneutics, and new ways of doing theology which provide more adequate tools to express community on the way to the goal of visible unity.

29. On the journey, the different Christian traditions through the Faith and Order Commission will need to dialogue on those issues which make fuller companionship difficult. Mutual condemnations exist. These occurred partially due to a lack of clarity in understanding the other's true position, while others arose because the opportunity for dialogue ceased to exist. Many positions have been modified through time. We

invite the churches to work towards the mutual lifting of these anathemas and to begin the work of healing the memories of the past. "A common understanding of the relationship between, on the one hand, human gender, and on the other hand, both ordained ministries and the ministry of the whole people of God" has become a contemporary difficulty on our common journey. It is important that this issue — the subject of substantial discussions undertaken by the Faith and Order movement — be a continuing subject of dialogue.

30. The invitation to participate in the pilgrimage provides an opportunity to invite others who have been hesitant hitherto to engage in dialogue. Our fellowship is impaired without the presence of the members of Independent and Pentecostal Churches as well as representatives from evangelical traditions as sojourners on the way. We re-echo the call of the Canberra Assembly to the Faith and Order Commission and the member churches to explore ways of including these traditions as partners in dialogue.

31. As we have shared our experiences of working to make more evident the unity of the Church at Santiago de Compostela we have learned of numerous ways whereby koinonia has been fostered. We have recognized especially the many ways in which churches are already together in local, national and regional ecumenical structures some of which constitute structures of decision-making, and in innumerable spontaneous initiatives as well as in United and Uniting Churches. We recognize the ministry of the whole people of God and rejoice in those initiatives which have brought local congregations of different traditions and nations together through twinning arrangements. We rejoice in the expression of koinonia evident in Christian families, interchurch marriages, religious and monastic communities and ecumenical centres and intentional groups. We invite the churches to share their stories of koinonia in forums, publications and presentations which can inform and encourage all members to increase their commitment to the search for the visible unity of the Church.

32. The pilgrimage is both a shared conversation and a shared journey of witness. The work of Faith and Order and that of Church and Society are inextricably linked as we seek to be faithful to God's grace. We have been helped to see the importance of this relationship linking koinonia to justice, peace and the integrity of creation through the report *Costly Unity* (WCC, 1993). We recommend that this be sent to all member churches alongside the publication of this conference and its discussion paper as an encouragement to the churches. In particular we have been challenged by paragraphs 31-34 on conciliar fellowship which well expresses our interdependence and calls for the development of ecumenical accountability.

33. As we journey together, it is not possible yet to manifest table fellowship. We appeal to the churches "on the basis of convergence in faith in baptism, eucharist and ministry to consider, wherever appropriate, forms of eucharistic hospitality; we gladly acknowledge that some who do not observe these rites share in the spiritual experience of life in Christ" (Canberra Statement on the Unity of the Church, para. 3.2).

34. Learning from each other about our different ecclesiologies, implicit and explicit, we perceive the need for a substantial study to be undertaken by the Faith and Order Commission on the Nature of the Church and the Unity We Seek in the light of koinonia. An aspect of this might be a comparative study of the ecclesiologies that lift up the lives of our churches to make explicit their convergences and the differences that can become barriers for the achievement of unity. Another area which the concept

of koinonia appears to have considerable potential for ecumenical progress is that of tackling questions of church structure, ministry, authority, etc. The concept of communion can help us overcome traditional dichotomies between the institutional and the charismatic, the local and the universal, conciliarity and primacy, etc. This concept, if it is used creatively in ecclesiology, would also help to overcome any views of ministry, authority and structure in the Church, which hinder progress towards unity.

By these and other stages on the way, God's dynamic gift of koinonia is celebrated as we journey towards the visible unity which is his gift and his will for the Church.

Recommendations

1. That Faith and Order will engage in renewed studies on hermeneutics, and new ways of doing theology which provide more adequate tools to express community on the way to the goal of visible unity (para. 28).

2. That Faith and Order make possible the dialogue of different Christian traditions on those issues which make fuller companionship difficult (para. 28).

3. We invite the churches to work towards the healing of memories of the past that have resulted in mutual condemnations (para. 29).

4. That Faith and Order continue with the study of the Community of Women and Men in the Church (para. 29).

5. That Faith and Order along with the member churches explore ways of including the Independent and the Pentecostal Churches as partners in dialogue (para. 30).

6. We invite the churches to share their stories of koinonia in forums, publications and presentations which can inform and encourage all members to increase their commitment to the search for the visible unity of the Church (para.31).

7. That the report *Costly Unity* be sent to all member churches alongside the publications of this conference as an encouragement to the churches (para. 32).

8. That Faith and Order undertake a study on our different ecclesiologies (para. 34).

Cf. also the recommendation in paragraph 33.

□   **Plenary discussion and action: Section II Report**

After the presentation of the report by Dr Melanie May, 11 persons were recognized to speak. Noting that paragraph 3 underlines "the importance of mutual recognition of baptism", one speaker asked the Faith and Order Standing Commission "to consider procedures to facilitate action by the churches" in this area. Referring to the final sentence of paragraph 3, another speaker emphasized the importance of work on an "adequate ecumenical hermeneutics". The recommendations in paragraph 5, it was said, needed clarification in relation to the preceding paragraphs.

Acts 1:13-14 was commended for further study, as the phrase "together with certain women" in verse 14 raised the issue of the role of women in relation to the apostles named in verse 13. Future studies on ecclesiology, it was noted, should include work on the importance of Mary "as mother of Jesus and mother of God". Another speaker, referring to paragraph 6, asked for greater precision in the use of the term "Christian tradition": did this refer, in fact, to a Western church father?

Several speakers addressed the question of apostolicity. Again regarding paragraph 6, one stressed the importance of the "continuing testimony of the apostles" in the life of the community. Another expressed appreciation for the recommendation in paragraph 12 for a study "on the criteria for discerning apostolicity"; this should, it was said, pay careful attention to non-theological factors. In related comments caution was urged in speaking of "legitimate" and "illegitimate" diversity (as in paras 16 and 17), since there are so many complex issues relating to culture and the context in which the faith is lived out. Another participant welcomed the recognition of the importance of ecumenical sharing in ministerial formation (para. 12.2): such sharing, which should encompass a "wide circle" of inter-regional contacts, could greatly enhance mutual understanding.

Several speakers addressed points of language. One expressed concern at the appearance of "certain new terms" in Faith and Order discussions: for example, what is the precise meaning of "holistic" in paragraph 11? Another urged another wording for "Sunday worship services" (para. 31.5), so as not to exclude the Seventh Day churches.

Suggestions regarding further work included support for continuation of the apostolic faith study, and approval of the reference in paragraph 31.4 about dialogue with JPIC. The latter, it was said, should include study of the teachings of the church fathers in this area.

REPORT OF SECTION II:
CONFESSING THE ONE FAITH TO GOD'S GLORY

I. Koinonia in confessing the faith

1. "That which was from the beginning, which we have heard, which we have seen with our eyes, which we have looked upon and touched with our hands, concerning the word of life — the life was made manifest, and we saw it, and testify to it, and proclaim to you the eternal life which was with the Father and was made manifest to us — that which we have seen and heard we proclaim also to you, so that you may have koinonia with us; and our koinonia is with the Father and with his Son Jesus Christ." (1 John 1:1-3)

2. The proclamation of the good news about Jesus Christ gave birth to the common confession of faith by the earliest Christian community. From its very beginning, a principal aim of Faith and Order has been to assist divided Christian communities in a process leading to a common confession of the one apostolic faith. We rejoice that, through the efforts of many multilateral as well as bilateral dialogues, much has been accomplished. Among these achievements is the Faith and Order study "Confessing the One Faith" (WCC, 1991), which elaborates our koinonia in faith through the explication of the Nicene-Constantinopolitan Creed. This study can serve as a solid ecumenical instrument of understanding which calls us to mutual recognition. As such

it can help us maintain fidelity to the common faith, seek repentance where we have distorted that faith, and recognize our already existing communion in diversity. Nevertheless, this goal of arriving at complete koinonia in faith awaits full realization.

3. Many communities, according to their understanding of the deep interrelation between baptism and faith, already recognize one another's baptism by water and in the name of the Holy Trinity. They suggest that this be pursued among all communities and that the practice of rebaptism be abandoned. Others hold that the same interrelation between faith and baptism requires a larger area of theological agreement on faith for the recognition of baptism. At times different practices of baptism have arisen from different understandings of the Church, a fact which calls for further study of ecclesiology. Moreover, different understandings of "baptism", "faith" and "church" reveal the lack of an adequate ecumenical hermeneutics, for which deeper exploration is needed.

4. Confession of faith is not only a matter of theological articulation, but must be lived from day to day, not only liturgically but also in each given situation, some of them more conflicting ones, such as state oppression, economic exploitation and civil conflict. In responding to these situations, Christians are called upon to make a profession of their faith. While it is the churches in the local setting who are in a position to confess their faith in that context, their testimony should be shared with the wider ecumenical community so that koinonia in prayer and active solidarity can uphold Christians in times of testing and bring relief and healing. In this way it will become clearer that holiness includes not only such important aspects as prayer, the spiritual life and growth in virtue, but also being disciples in the world of today. The traditional expression *communio sanctorum* is congenial with a theology of koinonia. It refers not only to our unity with the saints who have gone before us and with the heavenly Jerusalem (our catholicity through time as well as space), but also to our eschatological hope for unity in the coming reign of God. It is this hope which urges us to take responsibility for our world as people who partake of the holy gifts and promises of God.

5.1. In light of the importance of our common confession of the one apostolic faith, we reaffirm the challenge of *Towards Koinonia in Faith, Life and Witness: A Discussion Paper*, paragraph 54, that "all churches find ways to recognize in each other the apostolic faith. Those churches which do not use the Ecumenical Creed are challenged to recognize it as a central expression of the apostolic faith and thus to use it on occasion. Those churches which use the Ecumenical Creed are challenged to recognize the apostolic faith as expressed by churches in other than credal forms." For reasons of ecumenical community, we further suggest that they return to the original text of the Creed without later additions that were unilaterally introduced.

5.2. We ask the churches to take advantage of the ecumenically elaborated explication, *Confessing the One Faith*, as an appropriate instrument for the process of better understanding of our common faith, within and among the churches. They are also invited to concretize the explication within their own contexts.

5.3. We recommend that the Standing Commission of Faith and Order take responsibility for producing a *Study Guide* of this explication. It should also facilitate access to the document for congregations, clearly mark the points of ecumenical convergence, as well as those questions still remaining open, and encourage local adaptation.

5.4. Those local churches which mutually recognize one another's baptism on the basis of the one apostolic faith should search for appropriate concrete ways and means of expressing their real, though imperfect, communion.

II. Recognizing apostolicity

6. Apostolicity is a quality of the faith of the Church which is confessed in the Creed to be one, holy, catholic and apostolic. Apostolicity characterizes the whole Church: it involves not only ordained ministry but also the way in which an entire community — clergy and laity, women and men, etc. — is maintained in truth by God's grace. To be an apostolic community is to be a community contemporary with Jesus, a community that is found where Jesus is. Thus it is a community witnessing to and worshipping the risen Christ. In the gospels, Mary Magdalene (John 20:16-18) — called *apostola apostolorum* in the Christian tradition — and the myrrh-bearing women (Mark 16:1-8) proclaim to the apostles the good news of the resurrection. The passing on of this good news is inclusively entrusted to the whole community, where the twelve apostles had a central and decisive role.

7. "Apostolic" means the authentic, original faith as witnessed normatively in the Holy Scripture, as summarized in the Confession of the Church, and which has found manifold expression in the history of the Church (cf. the description of "apostolic" in *Confessing the One Faith*, para. 241). "Apostolic" is further a predicate of the Church which describes its permanent authentic marks: witness to the faith and proclamation of the Gospel as the task for all Christians, the celebration of the liturgy, the transmission of ministerial responsibility, and also the living community of Christians and service of the Church in the world (cf. *Baptism, Eucharist and Ministry* (BEM), Ministry, para. 34). The concept "apostolic" thus also includes the Church's advocacy for Justice, Peace and the Integrity of Creation in all parts of the world.

8. The faith and life of the Church are thus brought together under the term "apostolic tradition" which, as a comprehensive process, is to be distinguished from the "orderly transmission of the ordained ministry" which is its sign and instrument (cf. *BEM,* Ministry, paras 34 and 35). The concept "apostolic" is a critical concept, in reference to which the faith, life and structure of the Church are to be repeatedly measured and oriented. This critical function operates in the Church as a unifying principle *(regula fidei)* energized by the Holy Spirit.

9. Our divided communities have not yet succeeded in recognizing full apostolicity in one another. The question of how we *recognize* apostolicity in each other's communities is never only a question of recognizing ministries, though this is significant and necessary for all churches if they wish to reach unity among themselves and koinonia in sacraments. For many of the churches, this involves also recognizing the apostolic succession as a sign of the validity of episcopacy in the churches and as essential to apostolic faith, insofar as it is understood as the means by which the risen Christ guarantees the unity, integrity and continuity of the Church. It is a question of recognizing whether the risen Christ *we* know is present in the life of others, and whether another church has means for opening itself to the reality of this same Christ.

10. Some of the criteria for recognizing the apostolicity of the Church in its continuity were summarized by BEM: "witness to the apostolic faith, proclamation and fresh interpretation of the Gospel, celebration of baptism and the eucharist, the transmission of ministerial responsibilities, communion in prayer, love, joy and

suffering, service to the sick and the needy, unity among the local churches and sharing the gifts which the Lord has given to each" (cf. Ministry, para. 34).

11. We must reflect further on the fact that our different traditions give differing levels of *priority* to various criteria; but if we can arrive at recognition of the same ensemble of criteria, even if they are being *used* in different ways, we shall have taken a step forward. We may expect the criteria and practice of another tradition at times to judge and convert us, and to send us back to the heart of our own tradition and discover it afresh. We must reflect further on the way in which we are all *called to call* each other to Christ who is always on the road ahead of us. We need to explore further the holistic model of apostolicity we have tried to outline, and what this implies for the recognition in each other's churches of diverse ways of applying similar or related criteria of faithfulness.

12.1. We recommend that Faith and Order undertake a study listing the criteria for discerning apostolicity which have been discussed in the bilateral dialogues, as well as a reflection upon the compatibility of these criteria.

12.2. In order to gain a more complete view of the apostolicity of the various churches, Faith and Order should continue to encourage ecumenical sharing in ministerial formation, in the broadest sense, and in the spiritual formation of all our people, so as to recognize our common calling to holiness. In this connection, we underline the importance of sharing between religious communities of different Christian traditions as a path to the recognition in each other of spiritual integrity.

III. Multiplicity of expression of the one faith

13. "For the glory of God and for the sake of the world God so loves, we are called to become a confessing communion of the one faith in many and diverse social, cultural and religious contexts. We rejoice in the ecumenical convergence that the One Apostolic Church is also catholic. The need to interpret, live, confess and celebrate the one faith in many contexts and diverse forms of expression is not to be regarded as a threat to unity but as the necessary consequence of the incarnational character of the Christian faith" (*Towards Koinonia in Faith, Life and Witness: A Discussion Paper*, para. 55).

14. Thus koinonia in faith does not imply a uniformity which eliminates diversity of expression. The fact that God's revelation in Christ is addressed to all human beings of every time and place requires that it find expression in a variety of linguistic, cultural and theological forms. The diversity of expression should be considered as a rich blessing upon the Church, bestowed by the Holy Spirit who leads into all truth (John 16:13).

15. Unity and diversity are related differently in the life of the Trinity and in the life of the Church. The Holy Trinity is the most sublime instance of unity in diversity, where there is diversity of the persons but complete unity of essence, knowledge and will. Our call to share in the unity given by God will be completely realized only in the Kingdom of heaven. In the life of the Church on earth, diversity is legitimate insofar as it serves and witnesses to the interrelated unity and coherence of the divine action.

16. However, diversity can obscure or threaten the Church's koinonia in faith. On the one hand, some diverse expressions may appear to be irreconcilable without actually being so. On the other hand, some attempts to express the apostolic faith prove to be inconsistent with "the truth of the Gospel" (Gal. 2:5-14). An important

aspect of maturing into "the unity of the faith" (Eph. 4:13) is the complex process of discernment by which legitimate diversities are reconciled and illegitimate expressions rejected.

17. "Diversity is illegitimate when, for instance, it makes impossible the common confession of Jesus Christ as God and Saviour, the same yesterday, today and forever (Heb. 13:8), and of salvation and the final destiny of humanity as proclaimed in Holy Scripture and preached by the apostolic community." (Canberra Statement, 2.2)

18. The canon of Scripture grounds the God-given unity of the Church especially in the truth of the Gospel (Gal. 2:5,14) and teachings which were later set forth and extended in the Nicene-Constantinopolitan Creed. To deny this unity and these teachings is to place oneself outside Christianity. The canon of Scripture also grounds diversity in the Church, not only because of variety in Scripture and the various situations in which Scripture was written, but also because of variety in approaches and interpretations (there is a long history of finding multiple meanings in a passage), and in one's standpoint or that of the community. Churches need to make clear their criteriological principles for the interpretation of Scripture (e.g. tradition, liturgical-sacramental context, justification by faith, experience, etc.). Because the one canon of Scripture exhibits such a wealth of theological diversity, it challenges the churches to grow in catholicity by assimilating the totality of the biblical witness.

19. As summaries of the apostolic faith, elements of tradition such as the Nicene-Constantinopolitan Creed have served as a means for discerning unity of faith among a diversity of expressions. Examinations of these symbolic confessions by churches in dialogue have led to reconsideration of their value by some who first opposed them. (For example, the Eastern Orthodox and Oriental Orthodox have come to see that their different Christological expressions are not impediments to unity.)

20. All language, even that in Scripture and creed, is inculturated. The Greek term koinonia itself represents an inculturation of the Gospel into a language and setting when Christianity was moving from Jerusalem into the broader world. Although God is most fully revealed in Christ (Col. 2:9), the very notion of koinonia — what is held in common (koinon) "having a part" and "sharing a part" (koinonein and metechein) — suggests that not all of what God is and the divine blessings may be received in its fullness by us until the end. God remains greater than our comprehension. But the revelation in Christ and the work of the Spirit may challenge some of our culture and concepts.

21. In overcoming divisions within the Church in many parts of the world, common confession of faith would involve much more than agreement on creeds and church orders. It would involve dealing with divisions arising out of non-theological factors, such as cultural and socio-political circumstances. Therefore it would mean an understanding of the relationship between Gospel and culture as well as between Gospel and power structures. What is involved is transformation of culture and power structures in accordance with the spirit of the Gospel. Since in many of the third-world countries the Church is a minority, this search has to be done along with the people of other faiths and non-believers. We encourage Faith and Order, as well as the churches in these countries, to take these issues seriously so that the churches may become true leaven in these contexts and may also discover unity in the process.

22. In relation to inculturation and its importance for understanding diversity in the expression of the faith, we wish to recommend to the churches the Gospel and culture study of Unit II, and urge Faith and Order to be directly involved in this study.

IV. Structures serving unity

23. Discerning our unity in faith requires structures for common decision-making and teaching. Such structures will have to correspond to the pneumatological dimension of the Church. If the churches are to find such common structures, it is necessary to come to an understanding of the concept "apostolic" in the context of the relationship between Scripture, Tradition and Church. Faith and Order has already made substantial progress on this topic at its Fourth World Conference (Montreal 1963) and in several subsequent studies, although there is need for yet further exploration of this theme (cf. *Baptism, Eucharist and Ministry 1982-1990*, WCC, 1990, pp.131-42). The context for the following remarks on structure is presented in the description of apostolicity given above in paragraph 7.

24. A fundamental structure of the Church is the ordained ministry of proclamation and teaching, so as to maintain unity in the apostolic faith. Correspondingly, this is also a liturgical ministry of presiding at the eucharist. Alongside this, other services and ministries form part of church life. The question of the ordination of women remains controversial and a cause of pain among the churches. Together we recognize the claims on us of the Bible and of the whole apostolic Tradition. But as we have sought to discern what that dynamic Tradition implies, we have come to different understandings. In continuing our study of this important issue, our more fundamental theological differences may be brought to light and eventually reconciled. Where our practice still differs we can at once seek deeper understanding and challenge each other to more faithful appropriation of our common faith (cf. *The Ordination of Women in Ecumenical Perspective: Workbook for the Church's Future*, Klingenthal 1978, WCC, 1980). We hope that churches coming to different conclusions and policies in this matter will be able to recognize in each other the desire to be faithful and obedient to the revelation of God in Christ.

25. The origin of a ministry of bishops rightly includes both historical research and theological interpretation. The different emphases of the churches have led to differing understandings about these origins. Some churches hold that the episcopacy is founded directly upon Jesus' action of choosing and appointing the twelve (Mark 3:13-19; Matt. 10:1-4; Luke 6:12-16). Other churches have a more differentiated understanding of the origins. What follows in the text does not deny any of the various theological positions, but rather seeks to open discussion of the structures for joint decision-making and teaching.

26. Some argue that, historically, the emergence of bishops in the early church, including the role of teaching (stressed in the pastoral epistles), arose from a transfer of the function of leader of a house church to leader of the entire community in a particular locality (ha kat'oikon... ekklesia, Philemon 2; *episkopoi*, Phil. 1:1). While some hold this understanding, we recall that some others see the origin of the episcopate in local churches more directly related to Christ through the apostles. Whatever the case, all agree that the preservation of the continuing faithfulness of the Church to its origin in the apostolic Gospel and the unity based upon that origin (1 Tim. 4:6; Titus 1:5,9) was the purpose of these developments. In this way the

ministry of a regional bishop became more common as a result of the continual growth of the Church.

27. Alongside this, some of the Councils of the Ancient Church became a reliable means of preserving the authentic faith of the Church. Today in synods and other ecclesial gatherings such as women's and advocacy groups, the responsibility of all Christians for the truth and unity of the Church is expressed. Here features of communal decision-making are entirely appropriate. Along with this, the gifts (charisms) of individual members of the Church — e.g. prophetic gifts — play a role in keeping the Church in the truth. All these different elements participate in a process of mutual reception, which is a process of koinonia energized by the Holy Spirit.

28. The connection of personal, collegial and synodical responsibility concerning teaching and unity of the Church is of fundamental importance also for Church structures on the universal level. Here we recall once more the Ecumenical Councils of the Ancient Church, in which, in principle, representatives of all churches participated. Today, ecumenical dialogues should take up once again the topic of a service to the universal unity of the Church on the basis of the truth of the Gospel. Such service should be carried out in a pastoral way — that is, as "presiding in love". It should also have the function of speaking for Christianity to the world at large, under conditions which need to be more precisely defined. This ministry must be bound to the community of all the churches and their leaders and is in service to the whole people of God.

29. One can rightly affirm that each local church is a concrete manifestation of the catholic Church, insofar as it is in communion with all the other churches. This affirmation raises the question of the presidency of this communion of churches. Accordingly, to such church structures on the universal level there must correspond the communion of all local churches and church communities. By means of mutual communication, a universal participation in the manifold efforts for the inculturation of the Gospel takes place. Without such living communion, the structure of the universal Church would not be credible.

30. Important for such a real worldwide communion of churches would also be interchurch communication by exchanging letters as was a custom among the ancient Church, as well as by other forms of accountability to each other.

31.1. We recommend that the Faith and Order Commission take up again the study *How does the Church teach authoritatively today?*, in particular with regard to the relationship between charism and ministry. Thus the challenges to the historical churches by charismatic renewal movements and Pentecostal churches should be especially considered, and participation by them in such study should be encouraged.

31.2. We recommend that the Faith and Order Commission begin a new study concerning the question of a universal ministry of Christian unity. Earlier bilateral and multilateral dialogues, which in general should be more interrelated because of their necessary complementarity, can form a valuable point of departure for this new study.

31.3. We ask the World Council of Churches in Geneva and the Pontifical Council for Promoting Christian Unity in Rome to call for and prepare together an Ecumenical Assembly in the jubilee year 1998 as a step further on the way towards conciliar fellowship of churches. It should express in appropriate ways the measure and quality of koinonia which will have been reached at that time.

31.4. We appreciate the recent emphasis of those concerned with issues of justice, peace and the integrity of creation (JPIC) that the Church's involvement in such areas be carried on within the framework of a common faith and facilitated by structures of mutual accountability. Since these are also major concerns of Faith and Order, we recommend that Faith and Order seriously consider dialogue with those involved in JPIC, concerning the continuing questions as to how the Church's social ministries are rooted in and shaped by the apostolic faith.

31.5. We ask all churches and local congregations to pray in their Sunday worship services for the unity of the Church, that the Holy Spirit illuminate and strengthen the leaders of the churches and all the faithful to search together for ways to overcome the separation between the churches.

Cf. also the recommendations in paragraphs 5, 12 and 22.

□   **Plenary discussion and action: Section III Report**

The Rt Rev. Barry Rogerson in presenting the report emphasized that it named convergences in baptism, eucharist and ministry, although these have not yet been fully received by the churches, nor are they reflected sufficiently in our common life. He emphasized the need to develop a new methodology "through which to receive and share insights from one another", and for work on an ecumenical hermeneutic.

In the ensuing discussion ten persons spoke. One asked that the issue of apostolic succession be addressed directly, emphasizing the need to build on what had been achieved in *Baptism, Eucharist and Ministry*. One speaker protested against the lack of reference to the notion of "*Word* and sacrament". Objecting to the term "younger churches", one speaker asked that "the continuing struggles of the united and uniting churches should not be forgotten". In addition, we should beware of the assumption that churches would "never" change their positions - this was not necessarily the case, even for positions considered "unchangeable" at the present time.

Several speakers addressed issues of sacramental practice. One appealed for clarity about our continuing differences over the sacraments, and rejected any effort to "cover up" these differences. Another questioned the removal of a reference which had appeared in an earlier draft to "unlimited sharing of the sacraments". Another asked for a list to be prepared of churches "which recognize one another's baptisms or offer eucharistic hospitality", as this would be useful for understanding the ecumenical situation today. Another called for further work on the "actual practise of 'eucharistic hospitality' and its consequences". Yet another asked for consideration of *who* administers baptism, noting that in some cases this includes both men and women, and ordained and non-ordained persons. One suggested that we should speak about the ordination of women to "sacramental ministry" rather than to the priesthood, saying this would show that it is not an issue only for Anglicans, Lutherans, Orthodox and Roman Catholics.

One speaker contrasted "continuity and unanimity" in faith and practice with "change brought about by a majority", saying that this "squeezes out" the

Orthodox perception of the church which has existed in continuity from the beginning. For ecumenical dialogue to take place, it was said, it is necessary that "the agenda and methodology of others" not be imposed on the Orthodox.

REPORT OF SECTION III:
SHARING A COMMON LIFE IN CHRIST

1. In 1982 the Faith and Order Commission, after several decades of interaction with the member churches, published a convergence document on *Baptism, Eucharist and Ministry* (BEM). The overwhelmingly positive response of the churches to this Lima text offers strong encouragement to the pursuit of these themes on the way "towards koinonia in faith, life and witness". Common life in Christ finds a measure and expression in sacramental practice. It will be profitable: to register the extent of the agreement which already exists in practice among the churches; to discern those agreements in understanding which have not yet produced their full practical fruit; and to identify those obstacles in understanding or practice which still block progress to fuller koinonia of life among the churches.

2. In their replies to the Lima text, the churches observed that existing convergences in the matters of baptism, eucharist and ministry already implied a certain common understanding of the nature of sacrament, and they called for further study of sacramentality as a help towards the overcoming of remaining differences. The churches also judged that further work on the ecclesiology underlying BEM might help to consolidate the progress made on the particular themes and set the convergences in the broader context which will have to be respected if the full benefits of BEM are to be drawn and a deepening and extension of the common life in Christ are to be achieved.

3. It is not only different understandings and practices concerning the nature and place of the sacraments that have divided the Church and Christians. In its historical journey, the Church is also affected by the tensions of the world in which it lives. Diverse social and cultural situations shape us not only in a positive way but also place a stamp of sin and injustice upon us. Isolation, social fragmentation and the struggle for individual and communal dignity impinge on the brotherly and sisterly character of the Church. Church unity will therefore be built up as Christians meet in solidarity in service of the suffering and in the struggle for a fuller justice among men and women.

4. The Fifth World Conference on Faith and Order senses the desire for greater koinonia among churches all over the world. This desire requires a deeper encounter between members of worshipping communities of different traditions and cultures. Continued efforts must be made to develop an ecumenical hermeneutic and methodology, particularly in the relations between the so-called younger churches and churches with a longer history. The consequence of both older and newer divisions must be acknowledged in a spirit of repentance. Koinonia also includes acceptance of the other, whose culture may be different from ours. From their own experience with the Bible and from the praxis in their own context, the younger churches are in a position to rejuvenate the Tradition in worship, theology, spirituality and Christian ways of

life. The younger churches must have the possibility to appropriate in an accessible form the qualitative deposit of the older Tradition without having to repeat the controversies and struggles which clarified some issues but also regrettably led and still lead to divisions.

Sacrament and sacramentality

5. The relation which is emerging in ecumenical discussion between the particular sacraments and a broader conception of sacramentality may be helpful for different churches and Christian communities in understanding more fully how common life in Christ and the celebration of sacraments are related to each other. A broader description which would meet with wide agreement is found in *Baptism, Eucharist and Ministry 1982-1990: Report on the Process and Responses* (WCC, 1990):

> In the incarnation, life, death and resurrection of Jesus Christ, God has communicated effectively the mystery of his saving love to the world. Through the power of the Holy Spirit, the risen Christ continues this saving action of God by being present and active in our midst. For this purpose God continues to act through human persons, through their words, signs and actions, together with elements of creation. Thus God communicates to the faithful, and through their witness to the world, his saving promise and grace. Those who hear and receive in faith and trust this gracious action of God are thereby liberated from their captivity to sin and transformed in their lives. Those who receive this gift, respond to it in thanksgiving and praise and are brought into a *koinonia* with the Holy Trinity and with each other and are sent to proclaim the Gospel to the whole world. Through this sacramental action, communicated through words, signs and actions, this community, the church, is called, equipped and sent, empowered and guided by the Holy Spirit to witness to God's reconciling and recreating love in a sinful and broken world. And so all who in faith long for fullness of life in Christ may experience the first-fruits of God's kingdom — present and yet to be fully accomplished in a new heaven and earth. (pp.143-44)

6. The broader notion of sacramentality helps to conceive the relation between the particular sacraments and life in its entirety. While all creation and the whole of human life may by God's grace be open to the saving presence of God, the particular sacraments indicate and embody the redemption which is necessary on account of sin before life can be lived in the koinonia with God and among humans which is God's purpose for humankind and the creation.

7. Situating the particular sacraments within the broader context of sacramentality also allows the churches to face again certain questions which have been controversial among them, as, for example, the number of the sacraments and the question of their institution by the Lord himself. In this connection the suggestion could be examined that an act of the Church may be a sacrament when it derives from the saving action of God in history, whether this be through the earthly Jesus, the risen Christ, or the exalted Lord in the Spirit.

8. Again, a broader understanding of sacrament helps in the question of authenticity. The liturgical and ritual action of a particular sacramental celebration both presupposes and enables a life in koinonia with God, with fellow Christians, and in solidarity with the neighbour, especially the poor and oppressed. If the daily life of Christians and of Christian communities does not correspond to the sacrament, the authenticity of their professed koinonia is called into question.

9. To set the particular sacraments in the context of a broader sacramentality also allows a clarification of the theological questions raised by the designation of the sacraments, in several traditions, as signs. By God's grace, the sacraments effectively signify — that is, both portray and accomplish — the history and reality of salvation of which they are themselves a part. Life truly and faithfully lived in and by the sacraments is dynamic and transformational.

10. Different churches may articulate somewhat differently the relationship between sacramentality in the broader sense and the particular sacraments, but respect for diversity in this matter is not precluded. Rather, sensitivity to the various nuances of understanding and practice can help manifest the richness of the divine mystery of God's saving approach to the human creatures. Some of us recognize that certain Christian traditions understand and experience baptism and communion in individual and corporate ways that are non-liturgical and non-ritual.

Baptism

11. The responses of the churches to BEM demonstrated a large measure of agreement on the meaning of baptism. The agreement extended to the efficacy of baptism, provided it was always recognized as God's work which can be received and appropriated only in faith.

12. Agreement in understanding, performance and practice is reflected in the fact that fewer and fewer churches and ministers repeat the rite when receiving members from other Christian families (even though the admonition in BEM against what might be interpreted as rebaptism sometimes still needs more effective implementation). This very fact invites closer investigation of the conditions on which at least such a minimum of "mutual recognition" takes place, and of the possibility that it suggests of even further consequences to be drawn. If the baptism celebrated by a community is recognized, then what else in the life of that community may already be recognized as ecclesial? Insofar as they recognize each other's baptisms, the churches may be at the start of developing a baptismal ecclesiology in which to locate other elements of shared belief and life. Meantime, mutual recognition of baptism may be attested, as is happening in some regions and among some churches, by the issuance of a common certificate of baptism and by presence and participation in each other's baptismal celebrations. Recommendations in this regard are made at the end of this section report.

13. A common baptism among the churches highlights the place of the sacrament in the appropriation of salvation. While all human creatures have in common their creation at God's hand, God's providential care for them, and certain social and cultural institutions which preserve human life, it is as they hear the Gospel and respond in faith that they are baptized and enter into the koinonia of Christ's Body (1 Cor. 12:13), receive that share of the Holy Spirit which is the privilege of God's adopted children (Rom. 8:15f.), and so enjoy by anticipation that participation in the divine life which God promises and proposes for humankind (2 Pet. 1:4). For the present, the solidarity of Christians with the joys and sorrows of their neighbours, their engagement in the struggle for the dignity of all who suffer and of the excluded and the poor, brings us face to face with Christ himself in his identification with the victimized and outcast.

14. When Christians themselves suffer at the hands of their neighbours on account of Christ and the Gospel, their martyrdom testifies also to the reality of their

incorporation into Christ and invites other Christian communities to recognize the authenticity of their baptism and the divine life that is being lived within that baptismal community.

15. A common baptism also expresses the paradigmatic nature of the Church in the world as an inclusive community, where men, women and children of different cultures and races can participate freely on an equal basis, where social and economic inequality can be surmounted, and where there is respect for different traditions and capacities, confirmed by the bonds of love for brothers and sisters and in fidelity to the Triune God.

Eucharist

16. The churches acknowledge the large measure of convergence in their understanding of the eucharist. The eucharist is generally recognized as an essential manifestation of the communion we seek. The eucharist completes what is begun in baptism, and both sacraments are intimately connected with the life of the Church. Gathered together as a reconciled and reconciling community, Christians celebrate the death and resurrection of Christ, who is present among us and with whom we are united. We proclaim the word, offer thanksgiving to God for God's marvellous deeds, pray for the gift of the Holy Spirit and in this meal anticipate the coming of a new heaven and a new earth. In the continuing effort of reconciling our different approaches to the sacrificial character of the eucharist and our different understandings of the nature of Christ's presence, great help has been found in the incorporation into eucharistic theology of the biblical understanding of *anamnesis* and with it the notion of *epiclesis*.

17. Growing theological convergence with regard to the eucharist, as well as in other important aspects of our Christian faith, has not yet reached a stage that allows for eucharistic sharing among all churches. This is a matter of grave concern for all Christians. There are, nevertheless, people in many of our churches who, out of deep conviction and on the basis of their common baptism, knowingly engage in eucharistic hospitality, both in inviting and in receiving. Many who do this do not lightly transgress the boundaries of the communities, but do so out of an obedience to a different understanding of eucharist that allows it to be a means of grace on the road to that fuller unity which it signifies. There are serious ecclesiological issues at stake here. Since, for some churches, the eucharist is and can only be the ultimate expression of the visible unity of the Church and not only a means to that unity, full participation in the eucharist of another church is possible only when one's own church is in communion with the celebrating church. The effects of unofficial eucharistic sharing remain to be seen. But the churches are increasingly obliged to reckon with this phenomenon and respond effectively. We suggest that the churches, while respecting the eucharistic doctrine, practice and discipline of one another, encourage frequent attendance at each other's eucharistic worship. Thus we all will experience the measure of communion we already share and witness to the pain of continued separation. Furthermore, those various expressions of ordinary hospitality which do form part of our liturgies must not be perfunctory gestures, but genuine expressions of Christian affection for each other.

18. One question that needs to be faced in the development towards full eucharistic fellowship concerns presidency at the service of word and sacrament. It is important

that the president at the eucharist be as widely recognized as possible, not only within the celebrating community but also by other eucharistic communities with whom koinonia is sought. All churches in fact have procedures for authorizing persons to preside at the eucharist: most churches reserve this function to an ordained minister; others agree with this principle in general but allow that, in circumstances of pastoral need, a non-ordained person may act as presiding minister; still others are happy to extend the role of presidency to those who are not ordained ministers. No full Faith and Order study has yet been devoted to this question. In the common theological exploration which is required, it could be of benefit to emphasize the fact that those persons who act as president do so not in their own right but in the name of Christ and in full communion with the whole community which they also represent.

Ministry

19. With regard to Christian ministry, the principal issues that need to be raised include:
a) the baptismal basis of all Christian ministry;
b) the nature and function of ordained ministry;
c) the question of the ordination of women;
d) the ministry of oversight;
e) primatial office.

20. In our ecumenical journey, significant convergences have been reached concerning ministry in the years since Montreal. With regard to ministry in general, all our churches now recognize that, insofar as we share a common baptism, we are all challenged to be witnesses to Jesus Christ and his saving work. Baptism is therefore the basis of all Christian ministry. At the same time, churches have grown to the perception of a differentiation between baptismal vocation and the more specific vocations of those who are ordained. It is acknowledged by all the churches that they have, over history, developed various forms and processes of authorization for the ordained ministry. Each church therefore exercises some organizing principle for the order of its life.

21. While these convergences are encouraging, there are still areas requiring further reflection and elucidation. For example, some churches consider the word "minister" in BEM to be used too ambiguously. They would advocate that a distinction be made between the concepts of particular ministry and general service. Furthermore, in our approach to ordained ministry we are divided over the type and structure of ordering. There is lack of agreement in the churches' criteria for admission to ordained ministry, and the goal of mutual recognition of ministries is still to be achieved. There are differences among the churches concerning the relationship between ordained ministry and presidency of the eucharist (cf. para. 18).

22. We therefore recommend that further work be done by Faith and Order and in the churches along these lines:
i) the discernment of how the gifts of baptism relate to the functions of ministry, so that questions regarding criteria for inclusion in or exclusion from ordained ministry may be resolved;
ii) the participation by churches in each other's ordinations, in the measure which is now possible — whether by simple attendance or by common prayer, or even in the imposition of hands;

iii) examination of the processes by which the churches authorize ordained ministry and the presidency of the eucharist;

iv) consideration of the role and significance of the diaconate. This could enrich our understanding and practice of ministry in general, as well as opening a new path in our dialogue.

23. The issue of the ordination of women to the priesthood continues to be controversial within and among churches, but there is an increasing willingness to discuss the issue amongst churches which have divergent practices in this regard. A clarification of the parameters of the debate shows that the fact of not permitting the ordination of women does not imply a rejection of women themselves since churches which do not ordain women nevertheless frequently appoint them to positions of considerable responsibility and influence. However, important as other ministries may be, the inability to be ordained to the priesthood is experienced by many women, who are convinced of their call, as a denial of their being and worth.

24. A continuing way forward will be marked by mutual respect and openness to the guidance of the Holy Spirit. We recommend that further discussion on the ordination of women take place within the context of the koinonia of women and men in the church, and their call to ministries. We suggest that this question be explored from the following perspectives: (a) theology and theological anthropology, (b) Tradition, (c) practice, (d) study of the churches' ordination liturgies, (e) processes of decision-making regarding this issue both by churches that do not and those that do ordain women to the presidency of the eucharist.

We also recommend that both churches which practice ordination of women and those which do not be invited to analyze and to share the reasons for their particular stance, as well as the factors contributing to the process that led them to it. Specifically, they might point to whether their stance is based on cultural considerations, or on issues of discipline, or on loyalty to tradition, or on obedience to the substance of the faith, or on the sacramental nature of ordination, or on other factors or combinations of factors. They might also explain the theological methodologies they have used in reaching their position. It would be helpful if churches would refrain from negative judgments on decisions either to ordain women or to continue a practice of not ordaining them, in order that, for the sake of the churches' unity, a constructive atmosphere for further study and discussion be created.

25. There is growing convergence amongst the churches regarding the need for a ministry of oversight (episkope) at all levels in the life of the Church. However, a tendency to identify this with the personal ministry of bishops and, in particular, with the historic episcopate, is problematic for churches which have a clear ministry of oversight but do not have personal bishops or stand within the historic episcopate.

26. The churches would benefit from joint theological and historical research into the exercise of episkope. This would be enhanced if carried out within the broader study of ministry in general. Such a study would include: the identification of different forms of exercising oversight and ensuring order and unity, questions of succession in time and place, the accountability of ministers of oversight (episkope) to a particular community, and their relationship to the whole Church. This latter factor is closely related to the notion of the eucharist as sacrament of unity, for, traditionally, it is the one who exercises oversight at the local level who also presides at the eucharist. Mutual recognition of the churches' ministry of oversight ensures the mutual recogni-

tion of their eucharist, for the Church of God fully united is manifested in the communion of all the local communities gathered around the eucharistic table presided by ministers in communion.

27. As we move towards this mutual recognition, we recommend that those who exercise the ministry of oversight or leadership promote in a special way the Christian task of creating public opportunities to display, through acts of mutual goodwill, their koinonia in Christ and to make explicit, when joining in public social witness, that their cause has a common origin in their one baptism into Christ.

28. At this stage in our journey into koinonia, the issue of the necessity or desirability of a primatial office and its nature can be only briefly touched upon. Churches from different traditions adopt very different positions with regard to such an office. Before taking up this matter, some will have to deal with the prior question of personal episkope as a focus of unity. Others have already reached a measure of agreement which allows them to discuss it. This issue should be on the agenda in any future ecumenical study of ecclesiology.

Ecclesiology

29. The responses of the churches to BEM perceived the need for further work on the ecclesiology which underlies and surrounds the understanding and practice of baptism, eucharist and ministry; and subsequent reflection has suggested that the notion and reality of koinonia furnishes a suitable leading category for this deeper study. The terminology of koinonia figures prominently in the vocabulary of the New Testament, and the same idea is enriched by associated images of the Church (e.g. the Body of Christ; the spiritual building; the vine and the branches). Ecclesiology as a special theme needs to be set in the wider dogmatic context represented by the ongoing study of Faith and Order on "The Apostolic Faith", while dogmatic reflection in turn must always be in the service of the living reality of the Church and, in particular, the extension and deepening of koinonia with God and God's people as instruments for the fulfilment of God's purpose now and in the completed reign of God.

30. Baptism, eucharist and ministry all need to be examined again in relation to the koinonia which they signify, express and create. The present achievements and continuing challenges are well stated in paragraph 6 and commentary of the baptismal section of BEM, and paragraphs 19-21 of the eucharistic section. With regard to ministry, a crucial question remains that of preservation and extension of the Church's continuity (temporal succession) and unity (spatial bonds) which most Christians see focused in the person and office of the episcopate.

31. The exercise and achievement of fuller churchly koinonia require that several other issues be addressed:
— Structures of mutual accountability and, where possible, common decision-making and action need to be discerned and developed (there are biblical models for this which ought to be explored, e. g. John 12:24-26, 13:13-16; Matt. 5:21-26, 18:15-20; Acts 6 and 15). In considering the structures of the common life, the experiences and witness of Anglican, Catholic, Orthodox and Protestant religious communities (orders, congregations) and of Protestant diaconal brotherhoods and sisterhoods should be harvested; some of these have developed an ecumenical common life.

— Further attention is needed to the meaning and forms of the "local churches truly united" which the 1975 Nairobi Assembly and the 1991 Canberra Assembly of the WCC envisaged as the components in a "conciliar fellowship".
— Churches need to find and display a justified confidence in the ecclesiality of other Christian communities with whom they are seeking a deepened koinonia, while encouraging shared worship across communions and traditions and more adequately equipping members to give a reason for the faith they adhere to. The destructive effects of intra-Christian proselytism upon churchly koinonia need to be observed and deplored.
— Continued efforts should be made to provide a joint theological education and ecumenical formation within our churches for mutual enrichment by our experiences with the Bible in our respective life-contexts.
— Further attention generally must be given to develop in all ecumenical publications a hermeneutic and language which might be understood easily by those whom we want to address but who are not familiar with our somewhat esoteric language.

32. All these theological and practical tasks can only be accomplished in an appropriate pastoral and spiritual framework. There is urgent need for the reconciliation and healing of memories. Inherited grievances and hurtful wounds can be overcome and transfigured by sometimes costly acts of koinonia that establish a new perspective and start to create new and better memories. The Fifth World Conference on Faith and Order, through common worship of the Triune God and through speaking the truth in love, experienced in a significant way the beginnings of such a healing.

Recommendations

1. We recommend:
— that Faith and Order put in process for consideration by the churches a way for the mutual recognition of each other's *baptism* by the churches;
— that, where this is possible but not already done, the churches develop a common baptismal certificate;
— that the churches invite neighbour churches to participate in baptism in appropriate ways (cf. para. 12 above).

2. We recommend that Faith and Order, as part of its work on ecclesiology and the development of koinonia, devote sustained attention and study to the question of *presidency at the eucharist* (cf. para. 18 above).

3. We recommend that further work by Faith and Order and in the churches on the doctrine and practice of *ministry* include the themes enumerated in paragraph 22 above.

4. We recommend that continuing work on the *issue of the ordination of women* be conducted along the lines indicated in paragraph 24 above.

5. We recommend a study of the ministry of *oversight* (episkope) in the terms outlined in paragraph 26 above.

6. We recommend that the Fifth World Conference on Faith and Order transmit to the churches, together with the report of the sections, the discussion paper entitled *Towards Koinonia in Faith, Life and Witness*.

7. We recommend that the Faith and Order Commission promote study and work on ecumenical hermeneutics and methodology.

Cf. also the suggestions in paragraph 31.

☐ **Plenary discussion and action: Section IV report**

Prof. Dr Turid Karlsen Seim in presenting the report emphasized its strong conviction that unity in faith, in witness and in action are not competing priorities but must be held together. In concluding she referred to the recommendations made in the report, including the call for development of a "new methodology" drawing from "faith experiences of participants in struggles with... issues", and for new strategies to promote the reception of agreements.

In the discussion nine persons spoke. One asked for the greater involvement of Evangelicals in the Faith and Order Plenary Commission, and at the national level. It was urged that the "proposed 1998 jubilee" [the WCC's eighth assembly, marking its fiftieth anniversary] should include perspectives from a wide variety of Christian communions: in this connection one should note that Pope John Paul II's "identification of the spiritual crisis and void" resulting from consumerism had been widely received, more so than some "WCC comments on society". Another speaker noted the foreignness of Christianity to *all* cultures, and insisted on the need for non-European cultures to begin hearing the faith articulated by "fresh voices" from within their own situation, rather than using language and thought-forms imported from outside.

Questions were raised about the formulation of statements concerning interfaith dialogue: in what *way* might we speak of the presence of God in other faith communities (para. 24)? One speaker regretted the absence of an explicit reference to Uniatism. Several referred to proselytism and related issues; one objected to the intensive use of "financial resources" to win converts for religious groups from outside, rather than for "work for koinonia" among the already-existing churches. Another questioned the wording of paragraph 16: did we mean to say that proselytism resulted from the failure of some churches to be concerned about salvation? Two speakers addressed issues of religious freedom. One expressed the need felt by their church for a discussion of this in relation to the problem of cults; the other appealed for understanding of the struggles of Christians who (as in Poland) had had to live under totalitarian regimes, insisting that those "from outside" were unable to judge their actions. A third urged greater consideration for minority languages in ecumenical work.

The situation of the China Christian Council as a "post-denominational" church was described in a moving and warmly-received intervention by the Rev. Gao Ying, the first representative of the China Christian Council to attend a Faith and Order meeting. The Council has experienced "a koinonia which has transcended denominational barriers", bringing Christians together "to face the task of being Christians in China". Faith and Order has not responded to this situation; to do so it needed to adopt "a more regionalized approach to unity", as called for at the Asian and Pacific preparatory meeting. Participants were reminded of Chinese theologian the Rev. Prof. Timothy Tingfang Lew's appeal at the first world conference on Faith and Order in Lausanne in 1927 for Christian unity in China: unity is necessary, he had then said, in responding to the challenges of today.[1]

---

[1] See *Faith and Order: Proceedings of the World Conference, Lausanne, August 3-21, 1927*, ed. H.N. Bates, London, SCM, 1927, pp.495-499.

REPORT OF SECTION IV:
CALLED TO COMMON WITNESS FOR A RENEWED WORLD

Introduction

1. Witness to God the Holy Trinity is an integral part of authentic Christian living. As such, common witness is an integral part of Christian communion, inseparable from koinonia in apostolic faith, sacraments and shared life.

2. The ecumenical movement has always insisted that the division of the Church is an obstacle to effective mission; the message is continually undercut by the disunity of those who bear the message. Thus, the experience of koinonia among those who have responded to the call of Christ is a sign to the world of God's reconciling intention for all creation.

3. It is also true, however, that common witness fosters koinonia. Sharing in struggles for justice or in acts of service or in moments of proclamation builds up and expresses our common life in Christ. Christian witness needs always to be deepened by theological reflection as we seek common understanding of the grounds for our convictions; but, in the same way, our theological confessions need to be tested by the experience of common witness for a renewed world.

4. The wholeness of this ecumenical vision can be seen in Faith and Order studies. In *Baptism, Eucharist and Ministry*, for example, the eucharist is understood as "precious food for missionaries" (Eucharist, para. 26), strengthening Christians for their work of witness. But the text also affirms that our eucharistic celebrations are incomplete apart from their extension in mission, what some have called "the liturgy after the liturgy". The memorial *(anamnesis)* we celebrate is precisely of One whose life was total self-giving; it is not only a remembrance but an anticipation of God's reign of justice, peace, and the restoration of creation. Common witness may, thus, be thought of as a "eucharistic vision of life" which gives thanks for what God has done, is doing, and will do for the salvation of the world through acts of joyous self-offering. In the eucharist God comes to meet us in Christ through the power of the Holy Spirit. Part of our response is the offering up the fruits of our cooperation with God's creation.

5. The current state of our world makes this discussion of unity and witness not just important but urgent. Christian koinonia, which is a gift and calling of God "that the world may believe", can also be seen as a form of resistance against those forces bent on fragmentation and destruction of the wider human community. As Archbishop Desmond Tutu said to us at this conference: "Apartheid is too strong for a divided Church." Such a statement is intensely theological. By denying the truth that human beings are created in the image of God, and by denying the unity Christians have through baptism, apartheid confronts us not only with an issue of human rights or social justice but of Christian faith. This integration of ethics and ecclesiology, and this insistence on the interrelation of Christian koinonia and wider human community, have marked our discussions in this conference.

6. Our experience confirms that common witness can help determine criteria for authentic Christian living. We believe that koinonia, which is a gift of God,
— will have as its purpose participation in God's trinitarian life and in God's mission for a world crying out for renewal;

— will help us experience and look forward to the fullness of the reign of God with its promise of salvation, reconciliation and renewal for the whole of humanity and creation;

— will be marked by diversity in its forms of witness. Some within the Body of Christ emphasize proclamation and invitation; others stress service or actions aimed at the transformation of unjust structures; still others give priority to lives of personal discipline and holiness. All three are responses to the gracious initiative of God and all three are needed if the Church's witness is to be complete. Evangelism is a witness to God's mercy; justice-seeking is a witness to God's righteousness; service is a witness to God's compassion;

— will be characterized by engagement in God's work for justice and by just relationships in its own life. Koinonia is compromised by continuing inequality between rich and poor, women and men, and Christians of different races and cultures;

— will be marked by an attitude of repentance;

— will be expressed through giving special preference to those who have been marginalized in our societies;

— will be marked by a lifestyle of respect for creation;

— will be marked by a lifestyle of dialogue, including that with neighbours of living faiths;

— will be marked by respectful appreciation of the integrity of other Christian communities;

— will not reflect the human addiction to dominating power;

— will be expressed in local settings where Christians live and witness;

— will be costly. There is a cheap unity which avoids contested issues because they disturb the peace of the Church. Costly unity will not be afraid of legitimate conflict.

7. Witness should remain a major concern on the Faith and Order agenda. Faith and Order's integration in the WCC underlines the conviction that unity in faith, active engagement for justice, and joyful proclamation of Christ are not competing priorities but complementary responses to the one Gospel.

Section IV pursued these, and other, themes under five headings:

A. Church and humanity in the perspective of the Kingdom

8. The Church understands itself as both foretaste and expectation of the koinonia of the entire creation with the trinitarian God, through the Body of Christ in the Holy Spirit. Therefore, it is vital that Church, humanity and kosmos be looked at holistically and in the perspective of the Kingdom. The Kingdom is a gift; its full realization is the very work of God. As partakers of the trinitarian life, however, the members of the Church are called to be co-workers with God (1 Cor. 3:9) for the implementation of the values of the Kingdom in the world.

9. History, and the current state of the world, prove that the word "progress" should be avoided when speaking of the way towards full realization of the Kingdom. Realization of the Kingdom cannot be based on human endeavour alone since such endeavour is very often dominated by sin and marked by alienation from its true, God-given vocation. It is widely recognized in our day that the ideology of progress has become, in many ways, destructive. This ideology contributes to the brokenness of

koinonia and community — within the Church, among members of the human family, and between humanity and creation.

10. The failure to live out the apostolic faith in the world also contributes to divisions among Christians and is a hindrance to the mission and credibility of the Church. Growth in our common confession of the apostolic faith, as expressed in life and witness, is part of the Church's cooperation in God's work of healing and renewal.

11. Renewal of church and world, in response to the initiative of God, will require a new quality and style of life. The implementation of such a new quality and style of life is conditioned, in turn, by the rediscovery of a fervent, all-embracing spirituality. Genuine spirituality is related to perpetual repentance. Through repentance, people open themselves freely and completely to the work and presence of God in their lives and, in humility, become aware of their own failures. The history of the Church makes clear that such lives of repentance and spiritual depth have been the source of Christianity's real missionary power. It is through such lives that God works to transform and renew the world. The rediscovery of authentic Christian life and witness, rooted in the one apostolic faith, is both a means by which Christians grow together into fuller koinonia and an answer to the increasing number of people who, in their desire for deeper and fresher spiritual experience, become disillusioned with their churches.

12. Faith and Order studies have, in recent years, used the language of "mystery" and "prophetic sign" when describing the relationship between Church, world and Kingdom (cf. *Church and World: The Unity of the Church and the Renewal of Human Community*, WCC, 1990, ch. 3 and *Confessing the One Faith*, WCC, 1991, part III). These terms, while not familiar to some Christian traditions, may be used to express (a) that the Church is a reality which transcends its empirical, historical expression, and (b) that the Church, moved by the Holy Spirit, points not to itself but beyond itself to the reign of God.

B. Common witness in mission and evangelism

13. To move towards true koinonia, two things are simultaneously necessary. First, we must continue to struggle towards a clearer understanding of the missionary nature of the Church. Second, we must seek new ways to cooperate in shared service, proclamation and action for justice. Indeed, our churches should challenge themselves to seek common witness in all situations except those in which deep differences of conviction compel them to witness separately. The participants at this conference have identified three issues which can be barriers to common witness in mission and evangelism and which we, therefore, urge Faith and Order to explore more fully.

14. *Proselytism among churches.* The use of coercive or manipulative methods in evangelism distorts koinonia. The evangelization or proselytizing of one another's active members violates the real though imperfect koinonia Christians already share. Such activities undermine the credibility of the Church's witness to the reconciling love and transforming power of God. While we are appreciative of previous studies in this area, we urge Faith and Order to undertake, in cooperation with Unit II of the WCC, a new and broader study of mission, evangelism and proselytism. Such a study will be incomplete and inadequate unless it includes the significant participation of Christians both within and outside the WCC circle of influence — including those who

are most frequently accused of these practices *and* those who have changed church affiliation through the efforts of another church.

15. Such a study should include a theological basis for mission and evangelism, clarification of terms, assessment of evangelistic and proselytistic practices and their effectiveness, and analysis of why those who have responded to them have done so. It should also provide opportunity for the churches to engage in self-assessment by considering the criticisms of those who have left their ranks.

16. We believe that most groups and persons who are engaged in such activities do so out of a genuine concern for the salvation of those whom they address, but they need to be engaged in dialogue and their methods and intentions still need to be challenged. We note that, for a variety of reasons, there is considerable movement of people between churches. Wherever churches show spiritual vitality in faith, life and witness, it seems that coercion, manipulation and proselytism generally fail.

17. Public allegations by Christians against other Christians who may be guilty of illegitimate practices in evangelism, acts of proselytism, or practices and legislation which are perceived to be oppressive, communicate a message which runs counter to that of the Gospel. These allegations often result from the failure of churches to address one another meaningfully and directly according to Jesus' instruction in Matthew 18. We, therefore, urge Faith and Order, in cooperation with Unit II, to take initiative towards facilitating reconciliation between WCC member churches, and between WCC member churches and those churches which are not WCC members, whose relations have been damaged by acts and allegations of proselytism.

18. *Religious Liberty*. The issue of proselytism itself raises questions, not only about our freedom in the Gospel (though that is primary), but also about our temporal freedoms. While there are no limits on liberty of conscience, which should be a value universally affirmed by Christians, it is important to recognize that absolute freedom of action has consequences which, at times, cannot be permitted — for example, when religious practices violate or threaten human life and basic human rights. What is the role of the state vis-a-vis the Church? How are we to avoid facile accusations of "manipulation" and "mind control", while acknowledging that clearly fraudulent and coercive religious practices should be restrained? Today, when new religious movements and older Christian bodies and movements challenge one another across international boundaries, there is need for a fresh examination of the nature and limits of religious liberty. We call on the WCC to undertake this examination, with the goal of formulating a statement of principles for reception by the churches.

19. *Gospel and Culture*. Despite much previous work in this area through the WCC, the churches' understanding of the relationship between Gospel and culture remains inadequate. Although Western Christians, in particular, have recently become more aware of the ways in which their cultural values and habits have falsely been proclaimed as Gospel truth, numerous unresolved questions remain. These are critical not only for the task of faithful and responsible evangelism, but for ecumenical conversation itself. What is the relationship, for example, between our identity as Christians and our identity as representatives of a particular culture? Can cultures themselves, as part of God's good creation, be bearers and revealers of God's truth *in their very particularity*? To what extent is the Word, the one who "was in the beginning", actively present among those who have not yet heard the Gospel

proclaimed? Increasingly, some argue that God has indeed been present in their cultures, divine gifts offered and divine goodness revealed, even before missionaries arrived with formal teaching and preaching. To take this claim seriously is not only potentially to rethink our theological methodology, but also to rethink the meaning and nature of the tasks of mission and evangelism.

C. Common witness in dialogue with people of other living faiths

20. Christians' approach to other persons, including persons of other living faiths, is grounded in the experience of God's love in Jesus Christ revealed in the Holy Spirit, which calls us to reach out to others in love.

21. The churches are part of a global community marked by religious pluralism, though they experience the urgency and quality of interfaith relations in different ways in their various contexts. This situation of dramatic diversity can be both positive and negative. On the one hand, dialogue among persons of different religious convictions can be enormously enriching. But, on the other, religion is an element in conflict and division in many parts of the world. Both of these realities need to be kept in mind when approaching the topic of interfaith dialogue.

22. It is important to acknowledge that dialogue among Christians and dialogue between Christians and people of other living faiths have different goals. Dialogue among Christians aims at full visible unity. By contrast, we understand interfaith dialogue to mean an ongoing conversation and encounter aimed at fostering mutual understanding, cooperation in response to human need, mutual witness and the shared pursuit of truth.

23. Such dialogue, like all Christian witness, follows Jesus Christ in respecting and affirming the uniqueness and freedom of others. Christians should allow their partners in dialogue to witness to their faith in their own terms. "Such an attitude springs from the assurance that God is the Creator of the whole universe and that he has not left himself without witness at any time or any place (Acts 14:17). The Spirit of God is constantly at work in ways that pass human understanding and in places that to us are least expected. In entering into a relationship of dialogue with others, therefore, Christians seek to discern the unsearchable riches of God and the way he deals with humanity" (*Mission and Evangelism: An Ecumenical Affirmation*, 1982, para. 43). It is from this perspective that Christians should pursue their mandate to share the message of God's salvation in Jesus Christ with every person and every people (cf. Matt. 28:19).

24. Through our discussions we have been able together to affirm:
— That conversations aimed at promoting the visible unity of the Church (the proper mandate of Faith and Order) need to take the interfaith context in which we live fully into account. This include traditional religions as well as the major world religions.
— That Christian koinonia has been and is diminished by mutual rejection among Christians because of different theological understandings of dialogue. Some speak of the presence and action of God, through the Holy Spirit, in other faith communities. Those who take this approach believe that work for tolerance and interfaith cooperation is a crucial part of the Church's mission. Others emphasize witness to the uniqueness of God's saving work in Christ, and thus believe that dialogue is primarily "pre-evangelism". Christians generally agree that witness and

cooperation for the good of the human community are integral to authentic Christian living.

— That Christian koinonia can be enriched by interfaith encounter. In dialogue, Christians learn to present their faith with humility and experience the wondrous variety of God's presence in creation.

— That the search for koinonia, based on a common confession of the apostolic faith and sacramental sharing, enhances our sense of Christian identity and, thus, contributes to the quality of our dialogue with people of living faiths.

D. Common witness: discipleship as corporate moral commitment

25. The Church is the community of people called by God who, through the Holy Spirit, are united with Jesus Christ and sent as his disciples to witness to and participate in God's reconciliation, healing and transformation of creation. The Church's relation to Christ means that faith and community are matters of discipleship in the sense of moral commitment. The being and mission of the Church, therefore, are at stake in witness through proclamation and concrete actions for justice, peace and integrity of creation. This is a defining mark of koinonia and central to our understanding of ecclesiology. The urgency of these issues makes it manifest that our theological reflection on the proper unity of Christ's Church is inevitably related to ethics.

26. Models of discipleship are based on the life and teaching of Jesus of Nazareth, and on the Scriptures. We are called to discipleship in response to the living word of God by obeying God rather than human beings, repenting of our own sinful actions, forgiving others and living sacrificial lives of service.

27. In the world in which we live, we are faced with urgent moral issues. Koinonia is both generated and shaped by our engagement in them. These issues are part of the life of the members of the Church and forge the way faith is lived out and reflected upon. In facing them the Church will often need to work with other communities of good-will, sharing in their expertise and commitment. Christians can frequently be motivated and challenged by the dedication and urgency that others bring to this task.

28. Christians, however, can contribute a particular dimension to their engagement in ethical and social matters. The source of their passion for the transformation of the world lies in their relation to God in Jesus Christ. They believe that God — who is absolute love, mercy and justice — is by the Holy Spirit working through them. The Christian community always lives within the ambient of divine grace and forgiveness. This not only allows its members to repent constantly of their own weakness and failure but also to be agents of reconciliation and forgiveness in our world.

29. Christian discipleship can raise complex ethical questions which need serious consideration within the community of faith. There are occasions when moral issues challenge the integrity of the Christian community itself and make it necessary to take a corporate stance to preserve its authenticity and credibility. To arrive at such a corporate stance, we urgently need structures of the type of the council described in Acts 15 which can generate koinonia. Coming to a common mind on divisive issues is always costly for Christians, but is an integral part of the call to discipleship and koinonia.

30. Koinonia in relation to ethics does not mean in the first instance that the Christian community designs codes and rules; rather, it means that the Church is a

place where, along with the confession of faith and the celebration of the sacraments (and as an inseparable part of these), the Gospel tradition is probed constantly for moral inspiration and insight. It is also a source which enables us to keep the issues of humanity and world ever alive in the light of the Gospel (cf. *Costly Unity*, WCC, 1993, para. 19).

31. While corporate witness is desirable, however, there are times when an individual or group of Christians may be called to take an alternative position, depending both on their interpretation of the Gospel and their perception and experience of social, political, cultural and economic reality. In situations where Christians or churches do not agree on an ethical position, they need to continue to dialogue with one another in an effort to discover whether such differences can ultimately be overcome, and if not, whether they are truly church-dividing. The ecumenical task is continually to seek obedience in relation to the great questions of the day. It is essential that the churches commit themselves to stay together within ecumenical structures and to realize mutual accountability within them as they pursue these answers.

32. We affirm that, in many places and at different levels, koinonia-generating involvement in the struggles of humanity is taking place. We recognize in these common involvements an urgent, real, but imperfect koinonia, and urge the Faith and Order Commission to give priority to lifting up and clarifying their ecclesiological implications.

E. Common witness in the care of creation

33. The Triune God who acts in human history also upholds all creation. Any discussion of koinonia, therefore, should include not only issues of human community but of the communion between humanity and the whole of creation. This is especially so since human rebellion and sin break this communion in ways which, today, threaten the very foundations of life on earth.

34. It is essential for the churches to recognize that the threats to human survival on this planet are real and that the tasks before us, in response to God's sustaining and redeeming work, are urgent. The human addiction to power and the selfish accumulation of wealth both degrade the earth and undermine our present existence and the lives of generations to come. The urgency of the hour demands a renewed Christian anthropology as well as a renewed emphasis on the call that Christians have to participate in God's healing of the broken relationship between creation and humankind. We must act now to arrest any further destruction of the earth's capacity to sustain life and enable justice. Indeed, we must be converted through the power of God, manifesting a new style of living in relation to our neighbours and the earth. We need an inclusive spirituality which recognizes that human beings are but a part of God's astonishing creation.

35. Discussion of this theme should always take full account of biblical perspectives. A biblical understanding of care for environment will include:
— the goodness of creation (Gen. 1-2);
— worship to the glory of God as the crowning response of creation (Gen. 1) and the refusal to deify or worship anything in nature (Rom. 1:23; Deut. 4:16; Jer. 10:15);
— creation of humans out of the dust of the earth in the image of God, a reminder of the interrelatedness of humanity and creation;

— the wisdom tradition in Scripture (e. g., Ps. 8 and 24);
— the reality of sin and the resulting exploitation of the earth and other human beings;
— the demand for justice in response to the justice of God;
— the God-given responsibility of humanity to tend the earth rather than to dominate it (Gen. 1:27f. and 2:15);
— the call Christians have to be "priests" as well as "stewards" — that is, offering back to God that which already belongs to God (Heb. 5:1ff; 1 Pet. 2:9).

36. It is important that churches within the ecumenical movement continue their discussion of the relationship between issues of justice and issues of ecology. What are the connections between economic justice and ecological preservation? How can all voices be heard in this conversation?

37. Another important dimension of this discussion is the question of power, the power of the reign of God as distinguished from the powers of this world. The power of the reign of God is displayed in self-giving love and in living the truth in word and deed. Such sacrificial love leads to the cross; yet, the power of the resurrection makes possible courageous truth-telling and committed action on behalf of the poor and for the sake of creation.

Recommendations

38. That a significant proportion of Faith and Order's time and energy be directed to collaboration with other units of the WCC on the following themes:

• *Proselytism and religious freedom* (see paras 14-18 above). This study should be done in cooperation with Unit II and should be carried out within the wider framework of mission and evangelism. It should also take into account previous and ongoing work in this area undertaken by the WCC and its Joint Working Group with the Roman Catholic Church and should involve both member churches of the WCC and non-member churches. Its particular aims, however, would be:
— to clarify such terms as "proselytism";
— to assess proselytizing practices in emerging pluralistic societies;
— to analyze the reason why such practices are effective in various places; and
— to propose concrete ways in which tension arising from such practices may be resolved.

• *Gospel and culture* (see para. 19 above). This study should explore ways in which the Gospel both critiques and affirms culture and context. As part of Faith and Order's mandate to promote visible unity, this study might explore:
a) ways of making decisions in different local contexts and their relationship to wider authorities;
b) the expression given to the apostolic faith of the Nicene-Constantinopolitan Creed as it is freshly discovered and transmitted in the different languages of humanity; and
c) the possibility of celebrating the universal gift of Christ's body and blood in the eucharist with elements taken from the many different forms of food and drink around the world.

• *Ethics and ecclesiology* (see paras 25-32 above). This study should be directly linked to local experiences of the interconnectedness of faith and action and move between an investigation of the moral substance of traditions and the moral experience of the people of God today. We recommend that a concrete plan for such work be brought to the WCC central committee in January 1994. We further recommend that Faith and Order encourage the Joint Working Group between the WCC and the Roman Catholic Church, as well as various bilateral dialogues, to seek clarity on whether contentious ethical issues need be church-dividing.

- *Anthropology and the theology of creation* (see para. 34 above).

39. That Faith and Order, alongside its other methods of study and reflection, employ more frequently a method which (a) begins by drawing upon the faith experience of the participants as developed in their struggle with social, cultural, political and economic issues, and (b) continues by reflecting theologically upon this experience and by bringing this experience into interaction with other contexts and with the other work of Faith and Order.

40. That Faith and Order develop strategies and initiatives for promoting the reception on local and national levels of ecumenical agreements, being aware that reception has also a spiritual dimension. This may include:
— inviting churches to analyze their own situations in the light of the call to unity;
— encouraging churches to respond to the agreements reached by Faith and Order and other ecumenical conversations;
— encouraging churches to employ these agreements, wherever appropriate, in prayer life and worship as well as in programmes of lay and clergy formation;
— offering theological support for the implementation of ecumenical agreements on regional levels to continue the conciliar process for justice, peace, and the integrity of creation;
— urging churches to find appropriate expressions of unity — locally, regionally, and globally — and, thus, to make visible the imperfect koinonia that already exists between and among them.

This focus on reception may involve the preparation of a working book containing major convergence statements and suggestions of models for facilitating conversations between churches.

III
Discussion Paper

☐ Introduction

Drafts of a "working document" on the theme and sub-themes of the world conference were prepared by the Faith and Order Standing Commission and shared in a two-year process with many ecumenical commissions and individuals, with participants at nine regional consultations around the world, and with a joint consultation on koinonia and JPIC with Unit III of the WCC. The text was revised in light of these experiences, and adopted as the discussion paper for the world conference.

The section reports and the discussion paper belong together and complement each other. Accordingly the Faith and Order Standing Commission, at its meeting immediately following the world conference, decided that the discussion paper should be included in the report of the world conference.

TOWARDS KOINONIA IN FAITH, LIFE AND WITNESS:
A DISCUSSION PAPER

PREFACE: THE PURPOSE OF THE WORLD CONFERENCE
AND OF THIS DISCUSSION PAPER

The last World Conference on Faith and Order took place in Montreal, Canada, in 1963. We believe that after thirty years the time has come for another representative gathering of the churches. So many things have happened in the ecumenical movement since 1963. So many new questions about the future course of this movement have arisen. With the help of its theme "Towards Koinonia/Communion in Faith, Life and Witness" the Fifth World Conference in Santiago de Compostela, Spain, in 1993 could thus provide a unique opportunity:

— to take stock of what has been achieved through ecumenical dialogue in Faith and Order and beyond on the way towards visible unity;
— to challenge the churches to receive these achievements more fully into their thinking, life and ecumenical relations;

— to encourage the churches to affirm and live the already existing, though partial, communion with each other and to resist all tendencies to move backwards;

— to identify and struggle with those issues, old and new, which still remain barriers to full communion and to indicate ways towards overcoming them;

— to reflect together on the future direction and priorities of the ecumenical movement, the World Council of Churches and especially its Commission on Faith and Order.

In preparing for the Fifth World Conference, the Faith and Order Commission has sought to engage the churches in conversation around the question: "Where are we and where are we going in the ecumenical movement?" Nine regional consultations in different parts of the world, a joint consultation with Programme Unit III of the WCC on "Koinonia and Justice, Peace and Creation" and over seventy responses from churches, ecumenical groups, theological faculties and individuals, have commented on the first draft of a working document on the theme and sub-themes of the world conference. In addition, a wealth of ecumenical concerns and hopes has emerged from these consultations. Many of the concrete suggestions have been taken up in the revision of the working document which was undertaken by a sub-committee of the Faith and Order Standing Commission between January and April 1993.

The Standing Commission has decided to call the former working document, in its present revised form, a "Discussion Paper". With this change of title we want to underline that there is no intention to refine this paper at the world conference into a convergence text. But we hope that it will prove to be a useful tool in stimulating and orienting conversation and also a potential quarry for the work of the sections and groups at the World Conference.

In this paper we have summarized the fruits of past Faith and Order work, insights of bilateral dialogues, results from other areas of work in the World Council as well as our experiences of a growing life together. In explaining the three elements in the theme "Communion in Faith, in Life and in Witness" the basic Faith and Order documents from the last period need to be used:

— *Confessing the One Faith. An Ecumenical Explication of the Apostolic Faith as it is Confessed in the Nicene-Constantinopolitan Creed (381)* (1991);

— *Baptism, Eucharist and Ministry* (1982) and *Baptism, Eucharist and Ministry 1982-1990: Report on the Process and Responses* (1990);

— *Church and World: The Unity of the Church and the Renewal of Human Community* (1990) and the renewal studies, including those on the community of women and men.

Our intention in preparing this Discussion Paper was that it will provide, despite its limitations in content and language, not only a useful basis for discussions at the world conference in August 1993, but also serve as an impetus and resource for continuing ecumenical reflection and efforts within the churches.

Our hope is that as the World Conference engages in a biblical and theological conversation around its theme and meditates in worship and prayer on the will and guidance of the Triune God, we shall claim and celebrate what has already happened in our growth in communion. We hope also that in a fresh way the churches are challenged and encouraged to take bolder steps towards koinonia in faith, life and witness so that they might become credible instruments of God's reconciling and transforming purpose for all humanity and creation. We also look to the World Conference to give to the Faith and Order Commission and the Faith and Order movement new challenges and directions for the next stages of their work of serving the churches in their ecumenical pilgrimage.

Commission on Faith and Order   Mary Tanner, moderator
Bernhäuser Forst   Günther Gassmann, director
Stuttgart, Germany, April 1993

INTRODUCTION: THE SEARCH FOR COMMUNION
IN A TIME OF CHANGE

The pilgrimage towards koinonia in faith, life and witness takes place in an ever-changing world and ecumenical situation. We have been made more aware of the complexity of this situation by the regional consultations which have formed a part of the preparatory process for the world conference. Meetings in Africa, Asia and the Pacific, the Caribbean, Europe, Latin America, the Middle East, North America, as well as the consultation on justice, peace and the integrity of creation, have brought together Christians from many traditions in these regions. They have highlighted the difficulty of describing the changing world and ecumenical situations in a few general references. They have also made us keenly aware of our interdependence in the Church and in the world. It is impossible to make sense of the call to become a communion in faith, life and witness without relating our vision of that communion to the changing world and ecumenical scene.

A. A changing world situation

1. The Fifth World Conference in 1993 has as its context a radically changed world situation from that of the Fourth World Conference in Montreal in 1963. Some believe the real global revolution of our epoch is only just beginning. In various places oppressive political systems are being challenged or changed. Democratic and/or capitalist systems often seem unable to deal constructively with their internal social and economic difficulties. The economic and social divide is growing between the northern and southern hemispheres, Western and Eastern Europe, and within many countries. We are witnesses of national disintegration and also of conflicting nationalistic tendencies, unjust distribution of resources, increasing numbers of political refugees, the misuse of science and technology, the proliferation of weapons, the epidemic of violence against women and children, the resurgence of racist practices, the spread of AIDS, etc.

2. We live in a world where four to five billion people are excluded from economic opportunities, where there persists an unfair transfer of wealth from poor to rich countries, where millions of children die every year, and where the favelas of the forgotten surround glittering enclaves of affluence. Human rights are violated in many places. Minorities are rarely protected, particularly the millions who become refugees of wars and poverty and as strangers in strange lands risk becoming targets of racist

violence. When human beings are thus regarded and used as mere commodities and denied their God-given dignity, women, children and older people are the most exposed victims.

3. Christians and churches have no simple solutions for the vast and complex problems of our time. But they are called to be engaged rather than retreat into a mood of powerlessness and a concentration on merely spiritual tasks. International institutions, non-governmental organizations, governments, voluntary movements and groups, churches and their agencies and ecumenical instruments seek to respond to these problems and situations. In many places and worldwide the churches together have a special charge and opportunity to join people of other faiths and convictions in confronting the problems and challenges of our world.

4. This engagement includes joining peoples' efforts to liberate themselves from dehumanizing poverty by sustainable development, through their own enterprise and skilled work backed by fair and representative government. This engagement includes helping people to keep up hope and confidence in the midst of their daily struggle for survival. People search for a sense of community and respect for moral values when they are confronted with the individualistic pressures for recognition and success in affluent societies. People yearn for a sense of purpose and meaning for life when ideological concepts and the optimism of unlimited progress have lost their fascination.

5. The ecumenical community must join other international organizations and movements in advocating for respect of human rights, for protection of all peoples and for a just world economic order. The ecumenical community must support the strengthening of international agencies for peace-keeping, joint environmental action and all efforts for reductions in armaments and in arms trade, and for the use of immense sums thus saved for worldwide reinvestment in human potential, in education, health care, job creation and land reform, giving special priority to the most marginalized. In an increasingly interdependent and pluralistic world, Christians are asked to develop a fresh awareness of the dignity and contribution of the different cultures and thus of the interrelation between diversity and globalism.

B. A changing ecumenical situation

6. The World Conference in 1993 will take place in a very different ecumenical situation from that of Montreal in 1963: it is a situation marked by both continuity and change. We have experienced the continuing transformation of relationships between many churches from isolation and estrangement to mutual understanding, cooperation and a sense of solidarity and common commitment. There has been an immense growth of ecumenical structures on local, national and regional levels. Through dialogue, spiritual sharing and joint activities in innumerable local situations the ecumenical movement has been "earthed" in the life of the churches.

7. Of historic significance was the entry of the Roman Catholic Church into the ecumenical movement during the period when the Montreal World Conference took place. Remarkable ecumenical perspectives have been opened by such official statements as the Decree on Ecumenism of Vatican II. A further broadening of the ecumenical movement was brought about by the increased presence and participation of churches from the southern hemisphere, historic black churches, evangelical and

charismatic/pentecostal churches. As a result of these developments we find today in many Christian communities a deepened awareness of the catholicity of the Church.

8. The emergence of bilateral dialogues after the Second Vatican Council has profoundly influenced the progress of ecumenical dialogue. Important theological convergences and agreements have been achieved in multilateral and bilateral statements since 1963. These dialogues, which have enriched each other with their insights and results, have, to a large degree, confirmed the expectation that they are complementary within the one ecumenical movement. The Faith and Order document *Baptism, Eucharist and Ministry* (1982) has become the most widely distributed and discussed text — receiving both affirmation and critical questions — in the history of the ecumenical movement. To this can be added the more recent Faith and Order study documents on *Church and World* (1990) and *Confessing the One Faith* (1991).

9. These theological advances have enabled a number of churches to formalize relationships with each other, including eucharistic hospitality or sharing (e.g. the Meissen agreement between the Church of England and the Evangelical Church in Germany (EKD), the agreement between the EKD and the Old Catholics in Germany, the interim eucharistic sharing between Lutherans and Anglicans in the USA, the formation of united/uniting churches). But even where such steps towards full eucharistic communion have not yet been possible, there is a recognition of an already-existing real, though imperfect, communion between the churches. This recognition itself makes us painfully aware of the remaining barriers and of our unfinished ecumenical tasks.

10. There are new opportunities and problems on the ecumenical pilgrimage. Among new opportunities since 1963 there is the emergence of new independent churches, especially in Africa but also in other continents, as well as the continuing growth of some evangelical and charismatic/pentecostal movements. Efforts towards a rapprochement between these and the traditional ecumenical movement have led to positive results and should be pursued. The process on justice, peace and the integrity of creation (JPIC) has helped Christians and churches to recognize their common responsibility in and for the contemporary world. The Ecumenical Decade: Churches in Solidarity with Women (1988-1998) seeks to help the churches to become truly inclusive communities.

11. Among new problems we observe in certain situations a decrease of enthusiasm and commitment to the goal of visible unity. Sometimes this decrease is the result of ecumenical achievements which are seen by many as a sufficient expression of positive and friendly relations between churches. In many places there is still a reluctance to do together what is ecumenically possible. Within the ecumenical community there are theological conflicts, across confessional boundaries, among those who have different approaches to relations with people of other faiths. There are churches now facing new barriers to their growing communion (e.g. the problems between churches in Eastern Europe, differences on social and ethical issues and the different practices concerning the ordination of women to the priesthood and episcopate).

12. More attention needs to be given to communication and interpretation in order to foster the reception of ecumenical achievements by the churches. The churches often appear to be reluctant to receive such advances into their life or to translate theological

convergences into changed relationships. At the same time ecumenical bodies are called to be open to the critical and creative voices in the churches relative to the search for visible unity. Demands to provide a full theological agreement on all points should not prevent the taking of provisional steps which are now possible on the way towards greater koinonia. Finally, a crisis of authority as well as the different structures of authority affect ecumenical relations and dialogue. This challenges the churches to reflect together on the sources of authority, structures of decision-making and ways of teaching authoritatively so that increasingly the churches will be able to decide and act together.

13. For a number of years there has been a growing proliferation of narrowly particularistic concerns within churches or regions. This is even more serious when it is linked to a resurgence of exclusivistic and militant nationalism or ethnicity as indeed seems to be the case in some parts of the world. The response of the ecumenical movement to these and other critical developments has failed to provide ecumenical initiatives or programmes with an overall framework of clear ecumenical perspectives. Today many WCC programmes find less public attention than certain secular voluntary initiatives with a clearer public profile in which Christians participate. To refocus the ecumenical movement around a renewed ecumenical vision and to concentrate the ecumenical tasks would enable a more effective response to be made to the cries of the present-day world. This would be most consistent with the mission of the Church.

C. The call to move towards koinonia in faith, life and witness

14. It is within this changing world and ecumenical situation that the churches are called to move towards visible unity in order to proclaim the gospel of hope and reconciliation for all people and to show a credible model of that life which God offers to all.

15. The calling of the churches to visible unity has been described in important statements of WCC Assemblies at New Delhi 1961, Uppsala 1968 and Nairobi 1975. A further attempt was undertaken by the WCC Assembly at Canberra in 1991 to describe the vision of unity of the Church today. *The Canberra Statement* used the notion of koinonia, communion, to set the unity of the Church in the broader context of God's design. The statement *The Unity of the Church as Koinonia: Gift and Calling* (cf. *Signs of the Spirit*, ed. Michael Kinnamon, Geneva, WCC, and Grand Rapids, Wm. B. Eerdmans, 1991, pp.172-174) starts with the saving purpose of the Trinitarian God for creation and humanity and the place and role of the Church as foretaste, sign and servant for this reconciling and uniting action of God. The central affirmations on the unity of the Church are introduced by references to ecumenical reality with its achievements and failures.

16. The central paragraphs of the statement (2.1 and 2.2) are informed by the notion of koinonia. They enumerate the characteristics of visible koinonia/unity in continuity with earlier Assembly statements. They also describe the goal of the process towards the fullness of koinonia in a new way: "when all the churches are able to recognize in one another the one, holy, catholic and apostolic Church in its fullness". This communion finds its local and universal expression in conciliar forms of life and action. An essential element of such a communion is its diversity, held together by the fundamental bonds of its unity. A new aspect of this statement is its direct challenge

addressed to all churches to undertake concrete steps towards the fullness of koinonia and to relate their efforts more closely to the concerns for justice, peace and the integrity of creation.

17. The statement concludes with the affirmation that it is the Holy Spirit who disturbs the churches in their complacency with the scandal of division, and makes them restless in their predicament, leads them to repentance and to hunger and thirst for full communion.

18. *The Unity of the Church as Koinonia: Gift and Calling (Canberra 1991)*

1.1. The purpose of God according to Holy Scripture is to gather the whole of creation under the Lordship of Christ Jesus in whom, by the power of the Holy Spirit, all are brought into communion with God (Eph. 1). The Church is the foretaste of this communion with God and with one another. The grace of our Lord Jesus Christ, the love of God and the communion of the Holy Spirit enable the one Church to live as sign of the reign of God and servant of the reconciliation with God, promised and provided for the whole creation. The purpose of the Church is to unite people with Christ in the power of the Spirit, to manifest communion in prayer and action and thus to point to the fullness of communion with God, humanity and the whole creation in the glory of the kingdom.

1.2. The calling of the Church is to proclaim reconciliation and provide healing, to overcome divisions based on race, gender, age, culture, colour and to bring all people into communion with God. Because of sin and the misunderstanding of the diverse gifts of the Spirit, the churches are painfully divided within themselves and among each other. The scandalous divisions damage the credibility of their witness to the world in worship and service. Moreover, they contradict not only the Church's witness but also its very nature.

1.3. We acknowledge with gratitude to God that in the ecumenical movement the churches walk together in mutual understanding, theological convergence, common suffering and common prayer, shared witness and service, and they draw close to one another. This has allowed them to recognize a certain degree of communion already existing between them. This is indeed the fruit of the active presence of the Holy Spirit in the midst of all who believe in Christ Jesus and who struggle for visible unity now. Nevertheless, churches have failed to draw the consequences for their life from the degree of communion they have already experienced and the agreements already achieved. They have remained satisfied to co-exist in division.

2.1. The unity of the Church to which we are called is a koinonia given and expressed in the common confession of apostolic faith; a common sacramental life entered by the one baptism and celebrated together in one eucharistic fellowship; a common life in which members and ministries are mutually recognized and reconciled; and a common mission witnessing to all people to the Gospel of God's grace and serving the whole of creation. The goal of the search for full communion is realized when all the churches are able to recognize in one another the one, holy, catholic and apostolic church in its fullness. This full communion will be expressed on the local and the universal levels through conciliar forms of life and action. In such communion churches are bound in all aspects of their life together at all levels in confessing the one faith and engaging in worship and witness, deliberation and action.

2.2. Diversities which are rooted in theological traditions, various cultural, ethnic or historical contexts are integral to the nature of communion; yet there are limits to diversity. Diversity is illegitimate when, for instance, it makes impossible the common confession of Jesus Christ as God and Saviour the same yesterday, today and forever (Heb. 13:8); salvation and the final destiny of humanity as proclaimed in Holy Scripture and preached by the apostolic community. In communion diversities are brought together in harmony as gifts of the Holy Spirit, contributing to the richness and fullness of the Church of God.

3.1. Many things have been done and many remain to be done on the way towards the realization of full communion. Churches have reached agreements in bilateral and multilateral dialogues which are already bearing fruit, renewing their liturgical and spiritual life and their theology. In taking specific steps together the churches express and encourage the enrichment and renewal of Christian life, as they learn from one another, work together for justice and peace and care together for God's creation.

3.2. The challenge at this moment in the ecumenical movement as a reconciling and renewing moment towards full visible unity is for the Seventh Assembly of the WCC to call all churches:
— to recognize each other's baptism on the basis of the BEM document;
— to move towards the recognition of the apostolic faith as expressed through the Nicene-Constantinopolitan Creed in the life and witness of one another;
— on the basis of convergence in faith in baptism, eucharist and ministry to consider, wherever appropriate, forms of eucharistic hospitality; we gladly acknowledge that some who do not observe these rites share in the spiritual experience of life in Christ;
— to move towards a mutual recognition of ministries;
— to endeavour in word and deed to give common witness to the Gospel as a whole;
— to recommit themselves to work for justice, peace and the integrity of creation, linking more closely the search for sacramental communion of the Church with the struggles for justice and peace;
— to help parishes and communities express in appropriate ways locally the degree of communion that already exists.

4.1. The Holy Spirit as the promoter of koinonia (2 Cor. 13:13) gives to those who are still divided the thirst and hunger for full communion. We remain restless until we grow together according to the wish and prayer of Christ that those who believe in him may be one (John 17:21). In the process of praying, working and struggling for unity, the Holy Spirit comforts us in pain, disturbs us when we are satisfied to remain in our division, leads us to repentance and grants us joy when our communion flourishes.

19. This picture of visible unity in the Canberra Statement needs to be drawn out and developed. It will then be seen more clearly what steps can be taken on the way to

visible unity and what obstacles remain to be overcome. This is the task of the World Conference on Faith and Order in 1993. The Discussion Paper is to enable the Conference to fulfil its task.

20. The Discussion Paper begins in chapter I with the notion of koinonia in its biblical and theological understanding and then relates this understanding to humanity and creation. Chapters II, III and IV correspond to the three elements in the theme of the World Conference "Towards Koinonia in Faith, Life and Witness". Chapter V seeks to develop some conclusions for the churches which should challenge and encourage them to pursue their ecumenical commitment for the sake of God's purpose for creation and humanity. It is planned that the four Sections of the World Conference will each deal with the theme and content of one of the first four chapters while all Sections will be asked to deal also with chapter V in order to focus on what steps need to be taken now.

A number of questions are offered at the end of each chapter which relate to the sub-themes of that chapter. These questions are intended to facilitate discussion, but not to limit it.

I. THE UNDERSTANDING OF KOINONIA
AND ITS SIGNIFICANCE FOR HUMANITY AND CREATION

I.1. The biblical and theological understanding of koinonia

21. In many bilateral and multilateral dialogues, as well as within the understanding of certain world communions, there is a striking, emerging agreement on the use of the notion of koinonia to describe the understanding of the Church. The reason for this growing convergence is the conviction that in Christ Jesus God united with himself and with one another those dispersed by human sin and set against each other. In 1 John 1:3,6,7 this is expressed as an interrelationship in koinonia which reconciles us with God and Jesus Christ and with each other. It seems that insights coming from theological and ecumenical conviction find confirmation in experience in life. The notion of "communion" also helps us to understand the relationships of Christians with those of other faiths and of none, as well as our relationship with creation. The word *koinos* in common parlance of the New Testament times signified that which was "common" and not only a mark of religious belonging (Acts 2:44ff., 4:32). The idea expressed by the word *koinonia* — e. g. Acts 2:42; Rom. 15:26; 1 Cor. 1:9, 10:16; 2 Cor. 6:14, 8:4, 9:13, 13:13; Gal. 2:9; Phil. 1:5, 2:1, 3:10; Philemon 6; Heb. 13:16; 1 John 1:3,6,7 — is also expressed by other words: participation, partaking, sharing, fellowship, community. The sense of all these words is gathered in the word communion, the word most frequently used.

The concept of koinonia/communion offers the biblical framework and theological foundation for different models of unity, such as "conciliar fellowship", "reconciled diversity", "organic unity", etc. It is not a new model added to them.

Note on terminology: The terms "koinonia" and (its translation) "communion" are used in this Discussion Paper as synonyms. Biblical quotations are taken from the *New Revised Standard Version* (1989).

22. The reality of the Church as koinonia is intimately linked, indeed it is correlative with faith. For faith in the biblical sense does not only mean a certain content as is entailed in the Creed, but it means an existential act of the human person: living in communion with God. Thus the biblical understanding of faith presupposes that human persons in their innermost being are relational, "koinonia-shaped" beings — in relation to God and also in all other dimensions of life.

23. In putting this emphasis on koinonia, we have not chosen a new notion or concept. Communion between God and humanity is a fundamental theme of Holy Scripture. By creating human beings in God's image, God has created them to live in communion with him, in communion with each other, and as responsible stewards of creation. In the Bible this communion found its first expression in the story between God the Creator and Adam and Eve; it was followed in the covenant with Noah and the relationship with Abraham, before finding expression in the covenant between God and the chosen people, through Moses and King David. Based upon God's gracious act of freeing from slavery and oppression, the people of Israel were welded together and given inspiration in the law for living.

24. The Hebrew Scriptures show that living in relationship with God entails putting trusting faith in him, confessing the gracious acts of God in creation and salvation; resisting idolatry; keeping the sabbath and the festivals; and living a life of devotion built on adoration, petition and forgiveness. Characteristic of the life of *shalom* was living as a people committed to defending the weak, the orphan, the widow and the alien; loving the neighbour; and extending refuge and hospitality to the persecuted. It was the duty of the King (the Messiah) to see that these acts of justice (mi*sh*pat) and righteousness (*tsedh*aqah) and mercy (hese*dh*) (Mic. 6:8) were upheld in Israel by the whole community. Serving and preserving the earth (Gen. 1:26-31), practising restraint in the exploitation of the land (Lev. 25) and standing in wonder and praise before the mysteries of creation were all part of the maintenance of harmony (Ps. 8, 104; Job 28, etc.). This harmony was expressed and nurtured by living together in the community of God *(qahal yisrael)* with a common mind, rooted in faith and expressed in liturgy and in life.

25. God's teaching to Israel contained in the Hebrew Scriptures tells us that God not only intends communion for the people of Israel, but for all humankind. In the canon of Scripture the story about Israel is preceded by the story of creation thus emphasizing the unity of humankind. It continues in the story of the covenant with Noah which God made with humanity as a whole and with all living creatures. This universal dimension is further expressed in God's promise that in Abraham all nations will be blessed (Gen. 12:3, 18:18, etc.). The prophets of the exile draw out in a startling way the worldwide significance of God's relationship with Israel (Isa. 40ff.; Zech. 8:20-21, 14:9) and Israel's vocation to be "a light to the nations" (Isa. 49:6).

26. God remained faithful to the people, when they were faithful and when they turned away. Again and again the prophets called the people back. In the prophecies of Jeremiah God promises to the people a new covenant written on the hearts of the people and not on tablets of stone. Christians, in accord with the Scriptures, believe this covenant to be fulfilled through the life, death and resurrection of Jesus. This does not exclude the belief that God's gracious promises to Israel are still valid.

27. In the light of the ministry, teaching and above all the death and resurrection of Jesus, the Christian community was led to believe that God sent his Son to bring the possibility of communion for each person, for all peoples and in relation to all creation. Jesus proclaimed the Gospel from God saying: "The time is fulfilled, and the Kingdom of God has come near; repent, and believe in the good news" (Mark 1:14-15). This passage sums up the ministry of Jesus. Jesus proclaims this Good News by words, which include the parables, some of them using as examples realities of creation, and also by his actions, attitudes and options. Indeed, his whole life and finally his death and resurrection proclaim the Good News. His parables, his miracles, the exorcisms he works, all are related to the rule of God which he announces. When he incorporated into the people of God those who were shunned and excluded (e. g. Luke 5:27-32, 19:1-10), offering koinonia to all people, this action caused conflict and koinonia became a reality only through struggle and pain. The Kingdom moreover is not something just to be preached as such, and unrelated to his own person, for Jesus makes it clear that it is through him and in him that the coming age is breaking into the world (cf. Luke 17:20-22), that in him it has already come upon us. Through communion with God in him we already enjoy what is the heart of the Kingdom still to come in fullness and glory.

28. In his own life and ministry, nowhere more clearly than in the obedience to his death, Jesus revealed something of the intimate relationship between himself and his Father in whom he abides (John 15:10), and the power of the Holy Spirit working in him. The mysterious life of divine communion between Jesus and his Father and the Spirit is personal and relational — a life of giving and receiving love flowing between them. It is a life of communion at the heart of which is a cross; and a communion which is always stretching out beyond itself to embrace and enfold all within its own life. Reflecting upon Christ's own relationship with the Father and the Spirit Christians came to understand that in the divine trinitarian life (which is communion) plurality is so held together that there is no separation and the unity never degenerates into mere uniformity.

29. Through the power of the Holy Spirit those who are baptized die with Christ and rise to new life in him, and are thus joined to the Father (cf. Rom. 6:4-5). Koinonia signifies this relationship based on participation in the reality of God's own eternal life: "the grace of the Lord Jesus Christ, the love of God and the koinonia of the Holy Spirit be with all of you" (2 Cor. 13:13).

30. Expressions, words and images like "holy nation" and "God's people" (1 Pet. 2:9-10), "God's temple" (1 Cor. 3:16-17), "vine and branches" (John 15:5), "body of Christ" (1 Cor. 12:27; Rom. 12:4-5; Eph. 1:22-23), and others express a relationship with God, and/or with Christ and thus refer to a participation in the trinitarian life of God. They also express the relationship in space and time among members of the community. Their shared life, in which unity and diversity are inseparable, is grounded in the trinitarian life and reflects it. This divine-human koinonia is a gift of God, not the result of a gathering of like-minded people.

31. The relation between God and believers and among the believers expressed by the word koinonia is also described with other words as being "in Christ" (2 Cor. 5:17; Col. 1:27-28; cf. also John 15:1-11) and of Christ being in the believers through the indwelling of the Holy Spirit (Rom. 8:1-11; Gal. 2:20). This is closely linked with the

image of the "body of Christ". Those who are **baptized** into Christ become one with him and with one another (Rom. 6:4-11; 1 Cor. 12:13). Hearing the **word** of God together in faith and partaking in the ***Lord's Supper*** (1 Cor. 11:17-26), they share in him and receive the gift of koinonia; they become one body in him (1 Cor. 10:16-17).

32. In Acts 2:42 koinonia is mentioned as one expression of how the community is nurtured and lives together. The community receives and shares the apostolic teaching, they break the bread and persevere in prayer and communion. By having all things in common, a redistribution of resources ensures that each member of the community has his/her basic need covered. The koinonia is the sharing for the survival of all.

33. This communion with Christ and with one another entails:
— being rooted together in faith which is complete trust in the trinitarian God, changing life from within (e. g. Rom. 4);
— receiving and sharing the apostolic teaching, communion in prayer and in the breaking of the bread and in koinonia (Acts 2:42);
— authentic discipleship partaking in the sufferings of Christ (Phil. 3:10; 2 Cor. 4:7-11; 1 Pet. 4:13, 5:1) and modelled upon his example, which never forgets the self-giving of Christ;
— a sense of justice and compassion; a sharing in one another's joys, sorrows and sufferings (2 Cor. 1:6-7; Heb. 10:33; et al.);
— the courage to struggle for truth when necessary even at the expense of comfort and peaceful unanimity (Gal. 2:5);
— serving one another in love and mutual receiving and giving of material and spiritual gifts (Rom. 15:26-27; 2 Cor. 8:1-15; Gal. 5:13);
— the preaching of the Gospel to the whole of humanity (Matt. 28:19-20; Acts 2:14ff.;) which is inextricably linked with the glorification of God (Rev. 7:9-17, 21:24-26);
— care for the harmony of God's creation which is always linked to the glorification of Christ and God's children (Col. 1:14-18; Rom. 8:19-21);
— looking forward towards sharing in a glory that will come (Rom. 8:17), when all things will be brought to ultimate unity (1 Cor. 15:27f.; Eph. 1:10; Col. 1:19-20), a glory already anticipated in the celebration of the liturgy where we are constantly united to the life, death and resurrection of Christ.

34. It is in the Church that the Holy Spirit realizes this communion (koinonia). The Church is a community of the disciples of Christ, living in continuity with the apostolic community established by a baptism inseparable from faith and *metanoia*, called to a common life in Christ, manifested and sustained by the eucharist under the care of a ministry at the same time personal and communal and having as its mission the proclamation of the Gospel of God. This does not exclude that Christ is present outside of the Church, although there are different opinions about how to understand this presence.

35. Those who share in the life of grace are brought into communion with all who share in the same life of grace in each place and every time. The variety of gifts everywhere, working together, builds up the common life. Moreover, gifts of grace are bestowed in such a way that no-one is self-sufficient. Thus the disciples are one, while being enriched by their differences. Diversity as well as unity is a gift of God. God calls the churches to be a koinonia that is empowered by the Holy Spirit to be at

the same time fully united and entirely respectful of the diversity of persons, population groups and cultures. The church is to be catholic, that is, one in faith and diverse in expressions of this common faith and life: indeed this is God's design for the whole of humanity. This diversity must be encompassed by unity so that it does not lead to ecclesial, racial and other divisions; and unity must be enriched by diversity so that it does not degenerate into uniformity. In this way the Church is catholic. Catholicity is expressed at the local as well as worldwide level since in each place the fullness of communion is offered and experienced.

36. Diversity is not the same as division. Within the Church divisions (heresies, schism, etc.) are overcome as Christ brings Christians into a reconciled and reconciling community with himself (Eph. 2:14) which is God's gift of communion. However, it is also "calling" because communion is not yet fully realized in this world and all too often distorted by human sin, division and discrimination. The "already" and the "not yet" are in creative tension. Christian communion is already caught up in the once-for-all of Christ's redemption while still remaining in suffering, weakness and failure on the way towards completion of God's design until the Lord comes. This is a communion which exists already in history for the glory of God and for the sake of the world that God so loves.

I.2. Koinonia for the reconciliation of humanity and creation

37. Christians believe that God wants the Church to be that part of humanity which already shares the love and communion of God in faith and in hope and in giving glory to God's name. The Church is called to be, in the realm of spiritual life as well as in its commitment to the service of humanity and creation, in harmony with the plan of the Triune God revealed in the Scriptures. It is called, in the power of the Holy Spirit, to manifest the divine life holding out to the world the possibility of being enfolded within that divine life. This entails discerning and affirming the presence of the Holy Spirit in the good deeds of humanity and in creation.

38. The Church as *koinonia* is called to share not only in the suffering of its own community but in the suffering of all; by advocacy and care for the poor, needy and marginalized; by joining in all efforts for justice and peace within human societies; by exercising and promoting responsible stewardship of creation and by keeping alive hope in the heart of humanity. *Diakonia* to the whole world and *koinonia* cannot be separated.

39. In exercising *diakonia*, Christians are called to join with all people of goodwill expressing the same moral aims. Nevertheless they believe they have something special to offer not only in helping humanity in its search for a better life, but also to know and to enjoy that perfect koinonia which, they believe, is God's final purpose for the whole of creation.

40. Faithfulness to this vocation of *diakonia* implies the constant need on the part of Christians for repentance and renewal because human sin is present; division and disorder within humanity are also present within the community of the disciples. The frailty Christians share with all is, in a strange way, a common bond, not without consequence for their commitment to the whole of humanity. Because at the heart of the life of the community is the relation to the cross of the risen Christ on which sin has

been defeated through the shedding of the blood of Christ, Christians live with the assurance of God's final victory over sin. Nevertheless, the powers of evil are still at work within the world, within the Christian community and in its members, until the last enemy is destroyed (1 Cor. 15:25). This makes even more urgent the need for the Christian community to be centred upon the death and resurrection of Christ while at the same time proclaiming the redeeming power of the cross and the message that through sharing in the death of Christ new life is offered to all.

41. Christians believe that the life and destiny of humanity and creation are insepar-ably bound together. Paul says that the whole creation is groaning waiting for the redemption of the children of God (Rom. 8:19-23). The end of all things is to be caught up in the glorification of the one God. Similarly, Christians believe that the sin of humanity is integrally bound up with the state of creation. In its pride humanity has so often reduced its relationship to the created world to a relationship of selfish exploitation instead of service. Human sin corrupts the whole creation. This is why communion with God is not to be considered simply as an affair of personal relation with God; it also involves the responsibility of humanity for creation. The Church of God cannot be separated from the destiny of the whole universe. Jesus Christ is not only the Saviour of human destiny; he is also the Lord of the cosmos.

42. The Church of God is unavoidably concerned with the breadth and depth of God's salvation. It is called to be in harmony with the integrity of God's plan at every level of its life and work. The use of the elements of creation, human voice, water, light, bread, wine, oil, etc. in the bestowing of divine grace show that God does not intend to isolate humanity from its belonging to the whole of creation. Moreover, it shows that when humanity wants to relate to God, it has to do so in its involvement with the whole of creation.

43. Work for the healing of creation is not an end in itself. Christians know that the life of this world as it is will cease. Nevertheless their lives and the life of the whole of creation are called to point here and now towards the summing up of all things in the perfection of the life and love of God. They may not escape their vocation to care for the gifts of God in creation. This caring belongs to their communion with God.

44. Care for creation and responsibility for humanity are for Christians an expression of their communion with God who creates, redeems and sustains. In so far as the Church lives an authentic koinonia, faithful to diakonia, it is a "prophetic sign" pointing beyond itself to the fullness of the Kingdom of God, the "mystery" of God and God's plan for all people. The deeper the communion with God, the stronger becomes the will of the community to be involved in the service of humanity and of the whole creation. The deeper the adopted children are drawn by the Spirit into communion with the Father, the stronger their intention to be associated with the work of the eternal Son.

I.3. The use of the terms koinonia and communion

45. In this Discussion Paper the terms koinonia and communion have a wide reference. Koinonia is used to refer to the life of the Trinity or to that gift God offers in all its fullness to the whole of humanity and creation. They refer to the Church of Jesus Christ (cf. para. 34) and to the way in which Christian communions understand their

own life experienced at a local, national or worldwide level (e.g. the Anglican Communion, the Lutheran Communion, etc.). The terms also refer to the growing realization of churches that, in spite of their separation, they in fact already share "an existing though imperfect communion": they are not "out of communion" but share a "degree of communion". No satisfactory language has been found to describe this growing conviction; some talk of "impaired communion", while others speak of "restricted communion". Nevertheless the experience of already sharing together in the one communion of God's own life is a reality that already binds Christians together. The growing awareness of communion "is a significant result of ecumenical efforts and a radically new element in twentieth-century church history. And it provides a basis for renewal, common witness and service of the churches for the sake of God's saving and reconciling activity for all humanity. And it provides a basis and encouragement for further efforts to overcome these barriers which still prevent the recognition and implementation of full communion between the churches" (*The Church: Local and Universal. A Study Commissioned and Received by the Joint Working Group between the Roman Catholic Church and the World Council of Churches*, Faith and Order paper no. 150, Geneva, WCC, 1990, p.10; cf. also para 12).

Questions for discussion which relate to the sub-themes of the chapter and which are intended to facilitate discussion, but not to limit it:
1. Does the biblical witness suggest that koinonia requires common understanding and practice, and when is diversity legitimate?
2. Are structures and institutions absolutely necessary for maintaining communion, and what are they?
3. How is communion with God a call to live responsibly with creation?

II. CONFESSING THE ONE FAITH TO GOD'S GLORY

46. The common confession of the one apostolic faith has been emphasized in all statements on the unity of the Church, e. g. by WCC Assemblies (cf. the Canberra Statement), as fundamental for Christian identity and as an essential condition and expression of the unity we seek to manifest. Accordingly the work of Faith and Order, since the Commission meeting in Bangalore in 1978, has concentrated upon "Towards the Common Expression of the Apostolic Faith Today". This study was developed within the framework of three interrelated aspects: common explication, mutual recognition, and common confession of the apostolic faith. There are already occasions when this faith is confessed together. These occasions should be lifted up, undergirded, and made a regular element of growing communion by efforts towards common explication and mutual recognition of the apostolic faith. Furthermore, this study has taken the Nicene-Constantinopolitan Creed as a focus of the faith grounded in Holy Scripture, a faith which the Church is called to confess afresh today. The study has considered both the challenges to that faith in the contemporary world and also the challenges posed by the faith of the Church to the contemporary world.

47. Ecumenical conversations have led to the agreement that the communion to which we are called to move is a communion in which all believers confess and celebrate the

apostolic faith in word and in life for the glory of God and for the sake of the world God so loves. We are called to confess and celebrate the one faith, rooted in the witness of the people of the Hebrew Scriptures and in the testimony of the faith and mission of those who proclaimed the Gospel of Jesus Christ. This faith is faith in the one God which binds us together — the one God who, in trinitarian communion, is the caring Father, the creator and sustainer of all that exists; who is the eternal Son, born of the Virgin Mary, announcing and initiating the reign of God, crucified, buried and raised by God for the salvation and redemption of the world; who is the Holy Spirit, in whose power all life is inspired, renewed and transformed. This faith in the Triune God is the heart of the received tradition of the apostles and the whole company of witnesses.

II.1. Apostolic faith confessed, celebrated, and lived

48. For the glory of God and for the sake of the world God so loves, we therefore rejoice in the ecumenical convergence on the interrelatedness of apostolic faith and of life in harmony with what is confessed. When, for example, we confess that God is creator of all this must mean a life attentive to the goodness and preservation of creation. When we confess the One, Holy, Catholic and Apostolic Church we must be dedicated to working for the visible unity of the Church. We confess belief in women and men created in the image of God we must live this out in appropriate ways in the community of women and men in the Church (cf. *Church and World*, pp.50ff.). These and other expressions of koinonia in apostolic life are for the glory of God and the healing and renewal of the brokenness of the human community, its struggle for survival and its search for meaning.

49. Communion in apostolic faith and life embraces both a personal and corporate dimension. God draws human beings into communion with Godself and with one another as co-responsible persons. Each individual member's faith and life is integral to the communion of all believers, brought together and sanctified by the Holy Spirit. The apostolic life of the communion of the disciples of Christ is initiated and sustained by God's forgiveness of human sin and failure, and by the Holy Spirit's calling and empowering of Christians to be vehicles of consolation for all who suffer and despair. In the footsteps of the apostles and the witnesses and martyrs of all ages, the apostolic life of the koinonia stretches out beyond the boundaries of the Church in ministry of reconciliation and announcing the Gospel to all human beings.

50. The churches are challenged in a world marked by uncertainties and fears to move forward in order to share with one another their apostolic life and faith. As they respond to this challenge, they are called to be agents of reconciliation and peace in the world instead of being indifferent to, or even promoters of, human division. In this task the churches are sustained by Christ's unmasking on the cross of the pretensions of principalities and powers. However, reconciliation is not based on being indifferent to what is contrary to the Gospel, but on living the truth in a prophetic ministry in continuity with the apostolic faith. Unless there is passion for truth and justice, peace will be false. The acceptance of this challenge will make the shared apostolic life in the communion of churches one of the deepest sources of love, perseverance and hope in our world.

II.2. Apostolicity and apostolic faith

51. The term ***apostolic faith*** refers to the dynamic, historical reality of the Christian faith; revealed in the person of Jesus Christ, grounded in the normative witness of Holy Scripture, interpreted, transmitted, and proclaimed in and by the Church through the power of the Holy Spirit (cf. *Confessing the One Faith*, pp.2-3; Montreal 1963, p.52). It does not refer to one fixed formula or to a specific phase in Christian history. We are called to come to a deeper understanding of how this apostolic faith is witnessed to and transmitted by Scripture, Tradition and traditions. We reaffirm the convergence which was achieved at the Fourth World Conference on Faith and Order at Montreal in 1963:

> We can speak of the Christian Tradition (with a capital T), whose content is God's revelation and self-giving in Christ, present in the life of the Church... this Tradition which is the work of the Holy Spirit is embodied in traditions (in the two senses of the word, both as referring to diversity in forms of expression and in the sense of separate communions). The traditions in Christian history are distinct from, and yet connected with, the Tradition (Montreal 1963, p.52).

52. In using the term ***apostolicity*** (and apostolic faith) our intention is to evoke the comprehensive process of the continuity of the Church with all its members, gifts and ministries. Such continuity in faith, life and witness is expressed in being faithful to and transmitting:

> the permanent characteristics of the Church of the apostles: witness to the apostolic faith, proclamation and fresh interpretation of the Gospel, celebration of baptism and the eucharist, the transmission of ministerial responsibilities, communion in prayer, love, joy and suffering, service to the sick and the needy, unity among the local churches and sharing the gifts which the Lord has given to each (*BEM*, ministry, para. 34).

53. Through our ecumenical dialogues we can all recognize the Ecumenical Creed of Nicea-Constantinople (381) as a central expression of the apostolic faith. We are aware that the language of this Creed is conditioned by time and context. But for many churches its use in confessing and in praising God is at the same time an expression of continuity in time and communion with fellow Christians. We have also learned to recognize that both in churches which use and which do not use the Ecumenical Creed the same faith is expressed in preaching, worship, sacraments, older and newer confessional statements, and in the life and mission of the Church in the different social and cultural contexts.

54. Now, at the end of this century, we urge all churches to find ways to recognize in each other the apostolic faith. Those churches which do not use the Ecumenical Creed are challenged to recognize it as a central expression of the apostolic faith and thus to use it on occasion. Those churches which use the Ecumenical Creed are challenged to recognize the apostolic faith as expressed by churches in other than credal forms. Steps towards such mutual recognition are intimately linked with the discussion and reception process on *Baptism, Eucharist and Ministry*, *Church and World*, and *Confessing the One Faith*. This process also implies that all churches, while participating in the divine mystery, have the task to examine their own life in the light of the apostolic faith. They are therefore to acknowledge, personally and corporately, the

interconnection of confession of sin and confession of faith by constant repentance
(metanoia) and renewal where they have not been faithful.

II.3. The diverse expressions of the one apostolic faith

55. For the glory of God and for the sake of the world God so loves, we are called to
become a confessing communion of the one faith in many and diverse social, cultural
and religious contexts. We rejoice in the ecumenical convergence that the One,
Apostolic Church is also catholic. The need to interpret, live, confess and celebrate
the one faith in many contexts and accordingly in diverse forms of expression is not
to be regarded as a threat to unity, but as the necessary consequence of the
incarnational character of the Christian faith. Such diversity is integral to the
emergence of true and full unity and has its deepest foundation in the diversity in
unity of the Triune God.

56. Yet what has the potential of manifesting the rich diversity of the expressions
of the apostolic faith often leads to conflicts which threaten existing unity. This
raises in each church and in the ecumenical context the question of the criteria and
ways of holding together diverse expressions of the apostolic faith in a faithful
interaction. In our separation we have developed different criteria for circumscrib-
ing diversity. Together we have begun to indicate means by which we can discern
if the one apostolic faith is confessed, celebrated and lived in each diverse
expression.

57. It is also a task of the ecumenical community to engage in a process of theological
dialogue in order to discern together whether certain understandings and uses of
diversity threaten koinonia. This would be the case, for example, where these
understandings and uses of diversity become divisive by:
— making impossible "the common confession of Jesus Christ as God and Saviour
  [basis of the WCC], who is the same yesterday, today and forever (Heb. 13:8)"
  (The Unity of the Church as Koinonia, p.173);
— justifying discrimination on the basis of race or gender;
— preventing appropriate acts of reconciliation;
— hindering the common mission of the Church;
— endangering the life in koinonia.

Other threats could be mentioned. How can the ecumenical community address the
wider dimension of this problem when the social, cultural, economic and political
components of diversity are related to koinonia in faith, life and witness? How can the
ecumenical community struggle with actual divisions in theological convictions and
ecclesial positions so that these do not become church-dividing?

58. The churches in the ecumenical movement are called to maintain and deepen the
degree of communion in apostolic faith and life which they have achieved so far by
considering together the scope and forms of diversity in expressing this faith. If they
fail to do this there is a risk that diversity will endanger what has already been
achieved. But if they are committed to do this common consideration, they will
experience that struggles with conflicting positions arising from diversity can lead to
deeper common respect and understanding and that diversity enriches their growing
communion in apostolic faith, life and witness.

II.4. Discerning our common faith

59. For the glory of God and for the sake of the world God so loves we need to discern in all our churches how the authentic Tradition (i.e. the witness to and transmission of "God's revelation and self-giving in Christ", Montreal 1963) may, by God's grace, be present; how that Tradition may be expressed in word and in life today, and be preserved and handed on for a new day. The churches today use different ways and instruments for discerning, appropriating and teaching the one faith, in deciding about what is, or is not, part of the "faith of the Church through the ages" and its significance for today. There are also differences within the churches. Without further discussion and agreement on this subject (cf. *Canberra Report*, p.38) no full agreement in ecumenical perspectives of ecclesiology and thus no full recognition of each other as churches will be possible.

60. Churches are challenged as they move towards mutual recognition to face frankly, discuss thoroughly and seek agreement on questions related to taking decisions and teaching authoritatively. Already important work has been done. For instance the multilateral dialogue's work *How Does the Church Teach Authoritatively Today?* (1974-78) and other studies of Faith and Order on authority and biblical hermeneutics (1964-78) initiated research into this area of ecclesiology. These studies have led to a dynamic understanding of the relationship of Scripture, Tradition and Church which contributes to a common understanding of koinonia and the discernment of the common faith. Some bilateral dialogues also have made contributions. In the responses of many churches to *Baptism, Eucharist and Ministry* it has been said that the visible unity of the Church needs also structures — personal, collegial, and communal — which will enable Christians together to confess, celebrate and live their life in front of the world (*Baptism, Eucharist and Ministry 1982-1990*, pp.82,101). The way the churches responded to the Lima text also says much about the various ways in which the churches seek to teach and speak.

61. The catholicity of the Church requires a communion of all local churches to be held together by faith, baptism, eucharist, ministry, and also by common bonds or structures. In this way the fullness of Christian faith and life is available in each and all places. Although there are churches which do not believe that common structures are necessary for visible unity, restrictive experience ought not lead us to believe that all structure stifles evangelical freedom. On the contrary, further work of Faith and Order should focus on right structures serving a conciliar communion (cf. *Canberra Statement*, para. 2.1) of churches under the guidance of the Holy Spirit (John 16:13) and an authentic exercise of authority. Decisions taken in such a conciliar communion will require reception by the whole Church. Such structures and forms of authority should be seen as gifts of God to keep the churches faithful to the apostolic faith and enable them to witness together in evangelical freedom.

62. The present ecumenical discussion of the criteria and forms of discerning the apostolic faith (Scripture, Tradition, traditions and the Church — "the Tradition of the Gospel testified in scripture, transmitted in and by the Church through the power of the Holy Spirit" [Montreal 1963]) is the context in which the churches can already now discuss and discern, under the guidance of the Holy Spirit, what patterns are in fact normative for a common faith and life. It is only when the churches are in communion

with one another that they will be able in conciliar deliberation and decision-making to teach together the one faith in ways that are acceptable to all.

> Questions for discussion which relate to the sub-themes of the chapter and which are intended to facilitate discussion, but not to limit it:
> 1. Where in our life as divided churches do our actions reflect our common faith (see e.g. para. 48)?
> 2. How do we recognize the apostolic faith in one another's churches?
> 3. In what ways can we affirm unity with diversity and diversity with unity?
> 4. What structures of authority for common decision-making and teaching are necessary for the visible unity of the Church?

III. SHARING A COMMON LIFE IN CHRIST

63. "Where two or three are gathered in my name, I am there among them" (Matt. 18:20). The common life of all who believe in Christ crucified and risen is rooted in the proclamation of the word and in the celebration of the sacraments. We are called to live this life for God's glory. Reflections in Faith and Order on the barriers which are still in the way of sharing this common life in Christ have been focused in recent decades on baptism, eucharist and ministry. A significant and widely affirmed ecumenical advance as well as a number of remaining difficulties concerning these issues are reflected in the 1982 Lima document on *Baptism, Eucharist and Ministry* (BEM) and the unprecedented discussion and response it has provoked. A first evaluation of the official responses of the churches, a consideration of the critical comments contained in the responses and suggestions for further work on major issues emerging from the responses, has been published in *Baptism, Eucharist and Ministry 1982-1990: Report on the Process and Responses* (Geneva, WCC, 1990). There are other studies of Faith and Order and areas of work within the World Council of Churches like worship and spirituality, Christian education and laity formation, women and youth in church and society, the relationship between koinonia and justice, peace and the integrity of the creation (cf. *Costly Unity*, Geneva, WCC, 1993), and sharing of resources which are of significance for this sub-theme.

III.1. The foundation of our common life

64. The foundation of our common life is the one God in whom we believe: that life itself is a gift from God. We share this foundation with all those who believe in this one God. As Christians we confess that the love of this one God is expressed supremely in the sending to us of God's only Son, Jesus Christ. It is this Jesus who through his life, passion and resurrection reveals to us God's loving purpose which is the salvation of the world (cf. John 3:6-18). At the heart of this salvation is communion with "the God of Abraham, Isaac and Jacob", a personal God, whose trinitarian life is the prototype and source of all koinonia. The Church has a unique calling to live out this koinonia in the proclamation of the word and in the celebration of the sacraments, in faith, in life and in witness. This should challenge us to take our responsibility for our own failures seriously and strive to put into practice the possibilities offered by this new common life in Christ.

65. In the various responses of the churches to BEM, as well as in bilateral dialogues, questions have arisen concerning the meaning of the terms "sacrament" (or "mystery") and "sacramentality", when used to describe essential characteristics of our common life in Christ. In some cases, these questions indicate different theological understandings. There is a general affirmation that Christ is the centre of the Church as word and sacrament of God in history by the power of the Holy Spirit. Converging views in ecumenical dialogues indicate that in a general sense, the term "sacramentality" refers to God's salvific action in history mediated through visible signs; and the term "sacrament" to God's salvific action through particular ecclesial actions which actualize the saving presence of Christ through the sanctifying presence of the Holy Spirit. When we speak of sacrament as sign, this is to be understood not merely as pointing to the reality of Christ's saving presence, but also as participation in the reality which is a transforming power for the journey of God's people (cf. also the considerations on "sacrament" and "sacramentality" in *Baptism, Eucharist and Ministry 1982-1990*, pp.143-147). In some theological perspectives, life itself and every activity can be considered "sacramental" in so far as they make present God's transforming love in our world. Certain Christian traditions understand and experience baptism and communion in individual and corporate ways that are non-liturgical and non-ritual. These traditions remind us not to reduce sacramentality to sacramental rites.

III.2. Sacramental life

66. Among the most positive elements in the movement towards koinonia is the convergence in our understanding of ***baptism***, and especially the common affirmation of baptism as incorporation into the common life in Christ, in koinonia. The move towards convergence in our understanding of the ***eucharist*** (Lord's Supper) is to be celebrated. There are many common agreements that the eucharist is an essential manifestation of the communion we seek. This leads us to emphasize that baptism and eucharist are in fact intimately connected with the life of the Church.

67. In spite of this growing convergence, some questions remain regarding baptism and the Lord's Supper. As regards baptism, these questions concern not only different understandings of baptism and its sacramental nature, but also different conceptions of the relationship of baptism to faith, the action of the Holy Spirit and membership of the Church (cf. *Baptism, Eucharist and Ministry 1982-1990*, p.55). In order to move towards koinonia it is urgent that the churches endeavour to solve these questions as they continue the process of mutual recognition of the one baptism.

68. In our ecumenical relations we also know great pain caused by the limited character of our eucharistic unity. While for some churches (e.g. the Roman Catholic and the Orthodox churches) there are still serious obstacles on the way to full eucharistic communion, between other churches (e.g. Anglicans and Lutherans) eucharistic sharing is growing. These obstacles have their basis in the firmly held conviction, on one side, that eucharistic communion is the ultimate expression of full agreement and communion in faith and life; while, on the other side, eucharistic sharing is considered a legitimate expression of the partial communion we already experience. Are there ways to move beyond these mutually exclusive positions? We cannot rest until we reach the deepest ecclesial expression of Christian koinonia, namely fully shared eucharistic communion.

69. It is acknowledged by all that in the Lord's Supper we celebrate the death and resurrection of Christ present in our midst, we are united to Christ, we proclaim the word, we offer thanksgiving to God for creation, redemption and sanctification, we pray for the gift of the Holy Spirit, we receive forgiveness of sins, invoke the Holy Spirit, are brought together as a reconciled and reconciling community and celebrate this meal in the expectation of a new heaven and a new earth. There has also been of late more convergence among the churches concerning the sacrificial character of the eucharist, although disagreement still remains. This disagreement centres principally on the question of how the sacrifice of Jesus Christ on Calvary is made present in the eucharistic act (see John 6:22-63). A great help in reconciling the different approaches to this question has been the use made of biblical and patristic scholarship to probe more deeply into the meaning of the biblical term *anamnesis* inseparable from the notion of *epiclesis* (cf. *Baptism, Eucharist and Ministry 1982-1990*, pp.114-116,118).

III.3. Ministerial life

70. There is important ecumenical convergence concerning the fact the ecclesial ministry should be approached in terms of our shared baptism which enables the whole people of God to share in Christ's ministry. All have received gifts of the Holy Spirit and, therefore, all are ministers. It is in this context that both the ordained ministry and the ministry of the laity must be envisaged. However, it should be emphasized that all ministry entrusted to Christians should be exercised in ways other than those of worldly categories of power. Rather, all ministries need to be understood as **service** (diakonia). In this respect, as in all others, it is the duty of the Church to live according to the standards of the Gospel (John 12:24-26, 13:13-16).

71. Although significant convergence regarding the institution, ordination, functions and exercise of ordained ministry in the context of all ministry in the Church (BEM, ministry 34-38) has been reached, some of the most serious disagreements still dividing the churches relate to understandings and practices of ordained ministry. These disagreements concern the questions whether, and in which way, ordination can be considered to be sacramental; presidency at the eucharistic celebration; the ordination of women; and episcopal succession.

72. There is general agreement among the churches that "it is Christ who invites to the meal and who presides at it" (BEM, eucharist 29). Disagreement sets in, however, when we seek to determine who can lead the eucharistic celebration. Most churches reserve this function to an ordained minister. Others agree with this principle in general, but suggest that, under special circumstances and conditions, a non-ordained person may act as presiding minister, since Christ is the one who invites. Still others are happy to extend the role of presidency to those who are not ordained ministers. A way to overcome these differences would be to explore at greater theological depth the relation between presidency of the eucharist and ordained ministry. It could also be of benefit to put more emphasis on the fact that those persons who act as president do so not in their own right but in the name of Christ and in full communion with the whole community. In relation to the question of presidency at the eucharist the controversial issues of who authorizes the presiding minister, of a personal ministry of oversight and of the ordination of women should be further discussed.

73. Different decisions concerning the ordination of women and respect for these decisions should not prevent us from struggling with this issue and setting it into the broader framework of the role and place of men and women in the ministries of the Church, including the ordained ministry. There are further aspects concerning the ordained ministry of women to be taken into account: the reduction in the history of the Church of the diversity of orders/ministries leading to an over-emphasis on the roles exercised by men (cf. the recent pan-Orthodox appeal at Rhodes for the restoration of the order of deaconesses); a study of early apostolic writings; a serious theological debate on underlying basic theological issues like God's self-revelation in creation, history and in the particularity of the incarnation; the nature of men and women created in the image of God; ministry in relation to the priesthood of Christ and the priesthood of the whole people of God; criteria of decision-making in the churches (cf. *Church and World*, 60-63; *Baptism, Eucharist and Ministry 1982-1990*, pp.123-125). The experience of the churches which ordain women should also be taken seriously into account. Then this issue might cease to remain a dividing issue and we would be enabled, in a Gospel perspective, to come to a full recognition of the place, responsibilities and dignity of women as ministers in the Church (cf. *Ordination of Women in Ecumenical Perspective*, Faith and Order paper no. 105).

74. As regards the question of episcopacy, there is growing consensus concerning the need for a ministry of oversight — exercised personally, collegially or communally — whether this ministry be called episcopacy or not. Some churches, however, which do not necessarily reject episcopacy in principle, especially if it is not understood in a negatively hierarchical sense, question the normative character of such an office (cf. *Baptism, Eucharist and Ministry 1982-1990*, p.81). The question concerning the precise connection between ministerial succession and apostolic continuity of the whole Church is not yet fully resolved. A thorough investigation — within an ecclesiological framework — of different forms of an orderly transmission and recognition of ministry would be beneficial. The question of a primatial ministry should also be addressed.

75. It is urgent that these questions relating to presidency at the eucharist, the ordination of women and episcopal succession and structure, receive serious theological consideration. Without their resolution no reconciliation and no mutual recognition of ordained ministries are possible. Consideration needs to be given as to whether there could be intermediate steps towards such recognition.

III.4. Practice of common life

76. One of the most important developments in the ecumenical movement is that those who once could not even say a prayer together can now celebrate their faith and join in significant acts of worship (e. g. sharing in the Week of Prayer for Christian Unity, in the World Day of Prayer, in the Week of Prayer for Peace, in joint Bible studies and using the common Ecumenical Prayer Cycle). Through such common prayer and a meeting of minds and hearts on a deeper spiritual level, many are experiencing an "ecumenical conversion", which strengthens at the same time their rootedness in their own tradition and opens them to the insights and riches of the wider Christian community. Moreover, our common life in Christ is shared not only when we pray

together, but in all areas of our existence, including our sharing pain because of our divisions. Christian spirituality, therefore, is not to be understood as representing merely one facet of our Christian life, but rather as permeating its every aspect.

77. Our common life in Christ is enriched whenever we share with one another justly our spiritual and material resources, recognizing that we are all both givers and receivers. This common life is enriched when we rejoice in the gifts of others and enable them to offer these gifts in service to the Church and to society. This common life becomes a model for others whenever it takes the form of a truly inclusive community of men and women, young and old, differently-abled, lay and ordained, belonging to different races, cultures and ecclesial traditions as well as different socio-economic situations. Christian education, the formation of the laity, the renewal of no longer appropriate patterns of church life are essential conditions for moving towards such a community in which all equally share according to their gifts and responsibilities. It is thus that we become what we are called to be.

78. In the common Christian life every believer and all the churches strive to express ever more adequately before the world the koinonia to which we are called, in order to give a credible witness "to all people to the Gospel of God's grace" (Canberra). This witness involves an obedience which may lead to suffering (cf. John 17:14). Here Jesus Christ is our model who "became obedient to the point of death, even death on a cross" (Phil. 2:8). The martyrs of all times should be an inspiration also for our witness in words, deeds and life, and for our solidarity with the poor and the suffering.

79. In our desire to share a common life in Christ fully, we are grateful for the many expressions of koinonia that already exist among us. These we need to strengthen. One such expression which deserves special consideration can be seen in interconfessional marriages. The churches should not consider such marriages primarily as problems, but as a chance to develop forms of joint pastoral care and as an impulse to remove all conditions which are a burden for their common Christian life. Another important expression of koinonia is joint theological education and ecumenical formation which should be encouraged. This promotes mutual understanding between members of different churches, and enables pastors to minister effectively in interconfessional situations. In all our efforts we are to be guided by the "Lund principle": "Should not our churches... act together in all matters except those in which deep differences of conviction compel them to act separately?" (Lund 1952, p.16). "The source and centre of Christian community is its life in the risen Christ. It is a community of renewal, a pilgrim people, women, men and children called out in faith, journeying by the light of a star, warmed by a pillar of fire and fed enough bread for each day of the journey" (*Church and World*, p.64).

Questions for discussion which relate to the sub-themes of the chapter and which are intended to facilitate discussion, but not to limit it:
1. How can we move towards a non-divisive understanding of sacraments and sacramentality?
2. What are the most crucial issues relating to baptism and eucharist which we need to address on the road to visible unity?

3. How can further reflection on ordination and on the relation between apostolic continuity and apostolic succession move us towards mutual recognition and reconciliation of ministries?
4. What are the obstacles and possibilities for becoming a truly inclusive community?

IV. CALLED TO COMMON WITNESS FOR A RENEWED WORLD

80. Koinonia in the apostolic faith and in sacramental life implies and presupposes a witnessing community: the living and always renewed network of local churches and their members within the Body of Christ. Witness to Jesus Christ is an integral part of authentic Christian living. Ever since Pentecost the Holy Spirit has empowered the disciples of Christ to manifest their koinonia with God in acts of loving witness. This empowerment for witness continues today. In this section we explore five aspects connected with witness: Church and humanity, mission and evangelism, dialogue, the values of the Kingdom, and the care of creation. These themes deal with the authentic life of Christians and the relationship to others, i.e. to non-Christians. When Christians live authentically, there is no form of domination.

81. From the beginning the ecumenical movement (Faith and Order, the International Missionary Council and Life and Work) has worked towards the unity of the Church, common witness and the renewal of human community. It has become more and more obvious that these commitments are inseparable (cf. the Faith and Order study document *Church and World*, Geneva, 1990, and the studies on renewal including *The Community of Women and Men in the Church: The Sheffield Report*, Geneva, 1983, the work in the WCC of Church and Society, JPIC and the Commission on World Mission and Evangelism). We have learned in the process of this work that all realizations of visible unity between churches entail the renewal of broken relationships between members of the Church as well as work for renewal, justice and peace in the world. Moreover, common witness and joint action in all such efforts further and deepen the communion of churches with one another.

IV.1. Church and humanity in the perspective of the Kingdom

82. Church, humanity and cosmos should be seen in the perspective of the Kingdom. "In the Kingdom of God both the Church and the whole of humanity have their goal" (*Church and World*, p.22). The Kingdom, i.e. God's reign with its promise of salvation, reconciliation and renewal of the whole humanity and creation has come into our midst in the life and ministry, death and resurrection of Jesus Christ (cf. para. 27). God's Kingdom will be manifested fully when Church and humanity are taken up in the final consummation of all things. In this eschatological perspective of the reign of God already present and still to be fulfilled the interrelation of Church and world in the struggle for renewal and unity is to be understood. The Church is that part of humanity which has been led to affirm ever more fully the liberating truth of the Kingdom for all people. At the same time the brokenness of human community and the conflicts and struggles within humanity affect and involve the Christian community in each and every place. The Christian community is constantly called to repent and to

renew its own life and witness. It is sent by God to witness to and embody the promises of the Kingdom for all people. Christians are called to participate faithfully, despite ambiguities and failures, in struggles within the human community for justice, peace, care of the creation, liberation and true partnership between men and women, which are all concerns not foreign to the one creation of God (cf. *Church and World*, p.33).

83. In describing the relationship between Kingdom, world, Church, the terms "mystery" and "prophetic sign" have been used. The *Church and World* study document (pp.25f.) applies the word "mystery" to the Church, a use not common in all Christian traditions. The term is used to refer to the Church as a reality which transcends its empirical, historical expression, without, however, negating its historical character. The mystery of God is revealed in Christ, and so the Church as the body of Christ participates in the divine mystery and enjoys in faith the saving communion with Christ. The Church lives this mystery by receiving and proclaiming the gospel, by celebrating the sacraments and by manifesting the newness of life in Christ. It thus announces and anticipates the Kingdom already present in Christ. The Church stands with creation in anticipation, as it groans in pangs, waiting for the final consummation (Rom. 8:21f.; cf. *Church and World*, p.27).

84. *Church and World* also develops the perspective of the Church as "prophetic sign" in order to make clear that the Church, by participating in the divine mystery, is called to share in Christ's mission to all people. As a "prophetic sign" the Church, moved by the Holy Spirit, points not to itself but beyond itself to the reign of God. The Church is called to be a "prophetic sign" of the purpose God has for humankind and all creatures. The Church is a "prophetic sign" in so far as it lives by the renewing power of God's grace. As a "prophetic sign" it both points to the renewal of the human community and the life of the world to come. The Church set in this eschatological framework points human communities, political systems and ideologies towards the Kingdom reminding them of their provisional character. All are judged by the values of the Kingdom, including the life of Christian communities themselves. Whenever they fail to reflect the community of love, justice, freedom and peace, they fail to be the sign of the Kingdom which is their vocation. Whenever they acknowledge failures and repent of them, they stand as a sign of the divine grace and hope for a broken world.

85. For the Church to be an authentic prophetic sign its historical and cultural dimension and its pastoral work must be constantly renewed by the Spirit (cf. the studies on the "Community of Women and Men", racism and the handicapped). Despite human sinfulness, the love of God in Christ is mediated to God's people in such a way that, being judged and justified, they are set free to receive grace that makes them acceptable before God and initiates the process of sanctification. The sanctification or renewal of human beings is always through openness to the direction of the Holy Spirit.

86. It is, however, not always clear what is meant by "the renewal of the human community" or "a renewed world". Sometimes there is a tendency to look back and mourn the loss of the perfection of the biblical Garden of Eden. Sometimes there is a looking towards the vision of the new heaven and the new earth (Rev. 21) in which the whole of creation is seen enjoying the perfection that belongs to God's purpose. According to the Christian faith renewal is rooted in the creator God who makes "all

things new", and who in Jesus Christ has already begun God's action of recreation. Renewal is a process which, in spite of human sinfulness, is oriented towards a radically renewed and fulfilled community in the Kingdom of God.

87. The Church is challenged to work for renewal of broken relations in its own life and to join with others to work towards a world in which the presence of God is experienced and acknowledged; a world in which there is the healing of divisions and where there is more justice and peace; a world in which international institutions work for effective peace keeping, just economic relationships and a corporate responsibility for the poor and the dispossessed. The hope and striving of men and women of goodwill in the wider human community often stand as judgment on a Church which is called by its Lord to be a "prophetic sign" of the reign of God and of that "mystery" which transcends its historical, empirical expression.

IV.2. Common witness in mission and evangelism

88. Mission belongs to the authentic life of the Church. As Christians, who acknowledge Jesus Christ as Lord and Saviour, we are called to proclaim in word and deed the Good News of the reign of God, to live its values and be a foretaste of that reign in the world. Evangelism, which is the overt preaching of the Good News of Jesus Christ to those who have not heard, as well as those who are no longer in living contact with the Gospel, is part of the mission of the Church. Mission includes service, characterized by caring, healing and working with non-Christians for a renewed world, as well as evangelism. The disunity of the churches continues to undermine the authenticity and effectiveness of the mission of the Church. Thus the churches are challenged to seek their unity in order to be able to engage in mission and evangelism together.

89. Most Christians would agree that the proclamation of the Gospel to a broken world must take into account the whole of human existence in its spiritual, moral, cultural, social, economic and political dimensions (Luke 4:18-19). However there are differences in practice between and within the churches over a common approach to mission and evangelism. There are those who see the task of mission in terms of transforming society so that it increasingly reflects the will of God for humanity. Those who take such a view are urged not to ignore the transformation of individuals through personal conversion. Others, however, see the primary task as the proclamation of God's love in Christ for the salvation of individuals. Those who take such a view are urged not to ignore inhuman conditions and unjust social structures.

90. When in the past the Church has attempted to be faithful to the command "go and make disciples of all nations" mistakes have sometimes been made, not least in the way divisions of the Church and cultural patterns have been perpetuated in missionary work. However, we cannot wait until God's gift of visible unity has been received and lived before mission and evangelism are undertaken. Nevertheless, the continuing divisions between the churches are a scandal which undermine the mission of the Church, a scandal which is exacerbated by those who, in receiving the Good News, tolerate and even wish to maintain those same divisions in their own context.

91. Women and men are created in God's image. An essential dimension of this reality is freedom of conscience, including religious freedom. The issue of proselytism has become a crucial test for the ecumenical commitment of the churches. This is so with the emergence of pluralistic societies in former totalitarian societies and in other

places. Are the churches prepared to reaffirm as part of their growing communion that proselytism in the sense of a conscious attempt to convert Christians to another Christian community by unfair methods which violate the freedom of conscience of the individual is always an illegitimate means of evangelism? (Cf. *Toronto Statement*, 1950; and Joint Working Group between the Roman Catholic Church and the World Council of Churches, *Common Witness and Proselytism* [1970], pp.25-28; *Common Witness* [1980], pp.24-25.) Evangelism in another country should be always be undertaken in collaboration with the local churches.

92. The common witness of the churches in evangelism needs to be undergirded by Christian education in order that the people of God may be able to give an account of their faith in ways appropriate to their context. Such education is intended to prepare Christians, wherever they live and whatever their occupation, to make an effective witness through the meaning and quality of their lives and so exhibit an authentic way of Christian living by which others may perceive the Good News of Jesus Christ.

IV.3. Common witness in dialogue with people of other living faiths

93. In many parts of the world religion is used as an element in situations of division and conflict. The examples of the Middle East, Europe, Africa and India are all too evident. Religious affiliation, language and symbols are used to exacerbate conflicts. Too frequently we are ignorant of one another, unwittingly caricature each other and are intolerant.

94. Wherever there is fear and mistrust, there is a need for mutual knowledge, understanding and healing. It is, therefore, a God-given task for the churches to contribute to peaceful solutions of social, racial/ethnic, and national conflicts in which different religious communities are involved. To enter into a dialogue with people of other faiths is a first and necessary step in this reconciling task. For many Christians dialogue with the Jewish people is of special significance because of the common roots in the faith tradition of the Hebrew Scriptures and also in view of the often painful history of Christian-Jewish relations.

95. Dialogue begins when people meet each other. Dialogue depends upon building mutual understanding and mutual trust. In receiving and being received, we experience and can rejoice in our common humanity. Christians and their partners in the dialogue are expected to listen and receive the perceptions of others in their own terms, to enter into the other's understanding, to take the other's faith and life-style seriously.

96. Dialogue should make it possible to share with people of other faiths and traditions in common service to the community. In standing alongside them, we can become allies in working towards a reconciled community. This is not always easy as the values of other world faiths may come into conflict with Christian values. But common action, where possible, is part of our common human responsibility and thus part of the mission of the Church.

97. Dialogue is also part of evangelism, for dialogue cannot stop with mutual understanding and common action but includes authentic witness. Witness never involves coercion but always respects the freedom of conscience and the religious observances of others. Where there is mutual understanding and trust, every person will want to make their own authentic witness to their own religious faith. Christians

out of concern and love for other people will wish to share their own experience of the love of God and their commitment to Jesus Christ as their Lord and Saviour.

98. There is, however, no agreement amongst Christians about the theological undergirding of dialogue with men and women of other world faiths. Some base dialogue on an approach which allows them to recognize through the Holy Spirit the presence and action of God in other religious communities. So there will always be the possibility that Christians will have their own understanding judged and will be challenged to renew their perception of the Gospel. Those who use this approach believe that dialogue is part of the Church's mission: to work for a community in which there is religious harmony and an active toleration. Others base dialogue on an approach which witnesses to the uniqueness of God's saving work in Jesus Christ: "There is no other name under heaven given among mortals, by which we must be saved" (Acts 4:12). Many of those who use this approach believe that dialogue is primarily pre-evangelism. Others however want to combine both these approaches, and so while claiming that God, either as creator or through the Holy Spirit, is not without witnesses in every age and culture would want to confess Jesus Christ exclusively as their Lord and Saviour. These basic theological and missiological differences within and between the churches need to be addressed.

IV.4. Common witness to the values of the Kingdom

99. The Church is that community of people who, united with Jesus Christ by the Holy Spirit, live in the grace of Jesus Christ and participate in his work for the reconciliation, healing, transformation and ultimately the unity of all creation in God. This is God's work with which Christians cooperate by virtue of their baptism and acceptance of the Christian Gospel. When they are united with God and participate in Christ's redemptive work, Christians become a unique community which expresses God's love for the whole of creation. Because the life of this community is inevitably marked by the cross and resurrection of Christ, it is a life both of suffering and hope.

100. The identity and life of the Christian community is shaped both by its relationship with God and its relationship with the world. We recognize therefore that in their efforts to be faithful to the Gospel, Christians live their faith in the midst of the ambiguities of a very complex world. This is particularly true in the matter of ethical decisions and behaviour. In different situations Christians sometimes have different ethical responses, depending both on their interpretation of the Gospel and their perception and experience of social, political, cultural and economic reality.

101. While Christians, both individually and as churches do not always reach the same solutions to some of the ethical problems facing human communities, they do have values, the values of the Kingdom, to guide them. These include for example: the sanctity of life; the dignity and equality of all human beings created in God's image and redeemed by Christ; the responsibility to create and develop patterns of life in which justice, peace and respect for all creation can flourish. These values have their origin in our understanding of God's love and express aspects of the authentic communion between God and humanity. Such values would be implemented for example: by the calling to obey God rather than human beings; to repent of our own actions and forgive others and to live sacrificially, serving others before ourselves.

102. Christian discipleship and witness in the world are guided by divine revelation, the use of reason and attentiveness to the workings of the Holy Spirit in the life of the world. In this way Christians and the churches may be led to new and surprising ways of doing God's will. In situations where Christians or churches do not agree on an ethical position, they need to continue to dialogue with one another in an effort to discover whether such differences can ultimately be overcome, and if not whether they are church-dividing issues. In this respect the discussions about ethical issues which are part of some bilateral dialogues and of the Joint Working Group between the World Council of Churches and the Roman Catholic Church, are encouraging, and are a hopeful development in discovering acceptable diversity.

103. Much ethical diversity is tolerable or even healthy in a church which is a concrete community of obedience. There is a cheap unity which avoids morally contested issues because they disturb the peace of the Church. Costly unity entails discovering the unity of the churches as a fruit of pursuing justice and peace. Occasionally ethical issues indicate such fundamental differences in behaviour and in understanding of the faith that they become confessional matters involving sin and "moral heresy" (Visser 't Hooft) which can lead to separation. Thus German Christians who saw Nazism as profoundly sinful and also idolatrous separated themselves from a Church which compromised with Hitler and formed the Confessing Church. In more recent times apartheid was declared to be sinful and its theological supporters to be heretical and excluded in consequence from ecclesial fellowship (*Costly Unity*, 1993, p.9).

104. In a world increasingly influenced by science and technology, it is necessary that Christians, rooted in the Gospel and informed of the advances of human knowledge, equip themselves to dialogue with those whose decisions are crucial for the future of humanity. They have this responsibility whether Christians find themselves among those who occupy positions of leadership or not, for in both cases they are called to witness to God's love of creation. Christians have an opportunity both to learn from and influence those who carry responsibilities in politics, science, industry and commerce. A ministry of sympathetic listening and subsequent understanding of the challenges that such community leaders face provides the Church with an opportunity of witnessing to the values of God's reign for the wellbeing of all people.

105. The churches are to embody in their lives the Christian Gospel in every context. They are to live by the values embodied in the promises of the Kingdom. These values both judge and challenge the cultures in which the Church lives. Sometimes the Spirit of God may work through the culture challenging the Church to become authentic to its calling. Thus, for example, the inferior status and the unjust treatment of women contradict the biblical message that women and men are created equally in God's image and that both possess the fullness of humanity. While there is a common agreement among Christians that this sinful situation is in need of healing, we recognize that in different cultures and ecclesial bodies this healing will take different forms [cf. Sheffield report]. Christ's Body, the Church, is to be a sign of healing and reconciliation for every division.

IV.5. Common witness in the care of creation

106. The Third Assembly of the World Council of Churches at New Delhi in 1961 said: "The love of the Father and Son in the unity of the Holy Spirit is the source and

goal of the unity which God wills for all human beings and creation." As Christians, we live in faith and hope. Hope is not a passive waiting, but an active expectation. Because of the redemptive work of Christ, Christians expect the final healing, liberation and restoration of the whole of creation from the destructive powers of evil and look forward to the day when Christ is to recapitulate and consummate the whole creation in the eternal Kingdom of God (*Confessing the One Faith*, para. 82). God calls Christians to participate in the healing and reconciling process, creating visible signs for the new heaven and the new earth. This caring for creation is inseparable from the Christians' communion with God (cf. para. 44).

107. The goodness and wholeness of creation is constantly threatened by natural catastrophes and by human sin. The human addiction to power and the selfish accumulation of wealth both degrade the earth and undermine our present existence and the lives of generations to come. In consequence the meeting of the churches at Baixada Fluminense in 1992 as part of the Rio Earth Summit asked for a renewed Christian anthropology. Often the inherited biblical witness is heard in terms of a distorted anthropocentric emphasis which leads to an alienation of human beings from each other, from nature and from God. Thus koinonia is impaired. However the biblical witness emphasizes that human beings are an integral part of the creation — they are of the earth, earthy (Gen. 2:7). Thus, instead of dominating nature, men and women have a responsibility to preserve, and tend the earth, and to work with God to sustain the creation of which human beings are part (Gen. 1:27f., 2:15).

108. With such an understanding of anthropology, Christians are called to act responsibly in their own lives and with others to care for the creation. A billion human beings live and die in abject poverty. A proportion of the rest of the human race in accumulating and using an increasing amount of goods is destroying the environment at an ever-increasing rate. Are richer Christians called to witness by consuming less and living simply in order that others may simply live? Such a modest form of asceticism would be a witness to others and continue and strengthen a pattern of responsible living for the sake of a just world in which the care of creation is actively pursued.

109. God calls Christians to witness to and to work with others to create a just and peaceful society. Such a society has been described as "just, participatory and sustainable". There have been good programmes initiated which were designed to help people to help themselves, but have had destructive ecological consequences. The relationship between a "just, sustainable and participatory" society and the preservation of creation is not easily accomplished. What then are the connections between "economic justice" and "ecological preservation"?

110. The Universal Declaration of Human Rights has been important in the pursuit of the recognition of the dignity and freedom of every human being. This declaration has been the standard by which governments have been judged in the way they treat their citizens. Some have suggested that there is a need for an earth charter which will provide a standard against which governments and industrial and commercial interests can be judged. The complexity of the world's economic life and the reality of the mutual interdependence of nations point to the need for a universal declaration on the care of the planet. Christians would have insights to bring to such an enterprise (and in

this connection the recent WCC study document *Christian Faith and the World Economy Today*, Geneva, WCC, 1992, is a helpful basis for further discussion).

111. Throughout the centuries Christians have stressed that through Christ the whole created order is brought into the scope of God's redeeming love, and humanity thereby has a distinct role of offering the creation back to God in thankfulness, respect and reverence. The Church in its worship offers the creation back to God on behalf of all human beings. Not only in the realm of worship and mystical experience but also in the most secular commitments in the care of creation Christians are called to be in harmony with the integrity of God's purpose for all creation.

Questions for discussion which relate to the sub-themes of the chapter and which are intended to facilitate discussion, but not to limit it:
1. How can the Church be a prophetic sign in your local context?
2. Why is the unity of the Church important to the proclamation of the Gospel for a renewed world?
3. How can we achieve a balance between integrity in witness and tolerance and openness in dialogue?
4. What are the distinctive contributions and the limitations of the churches' involvement in movements for liberation and social change?
5. How does our faith shape our understanding and action in relation to peace, justice and creation?

V. GROWING INTO KOINONIA: ACHIEVEMENTS AND EXPECTATIONS

112. Having now addressed koinonia in faith, life and witness, we need to concentrate on, "Where are we?" and "Where are we going in the ecumenical movement?" According to the Canberra Statement: "The calling of the Church is to proclaim reconciliation and provide healing, to overcome division based on race, gender, age, culture, colour and to bring all people into communion with God. Because of sin and the misunderstanding of the diverse gifts of the Spirit, the churches are painfully divided within themselves and among each other. The scandalous divisions damage the credibility of their witness to the world in worship and service. Moreover, they contradict not only the Church's witness but also its very nature" (cf. para. 18:1.2).

What can the churches do together in your context to heal these divisions?

113. The goal of Faith and Order has always been and is to assist the churches to make visible the unity given in Christ. In order to achieve this goal ecumenical reflection has concentrated on the main elements of this unity: common understandings leading to confessing together the apostolic faith, the mutual recognition of baptism, sharing in the same eucharist, mutual recognition and reconciliation of ministries, common witness in mission and service, and common conciliar structures of teaching and decision-making.

Where are we in relation to this goal?

What have we not achieved, and why?

114. The ecumenical movement has explored various models of unity: organic union, conciliar fellowship, unity in reconciled diversity, communion of communions, communion in solidarity. The world conference is focusing on the concept of koinonia.

> *How does the concept of koinonia affect the understanding of these various models of unity?*
>
> *Are there other expressions to describe the goal of unity more effectively?*

115. The churches through the ecumenical movement have made significant advances in mutual understanding, especially since the last world conference in Montreal in 1993. Through the multilateral and bilateral dialogues convergence in faith has been achieved. Through local ecumenism the development of patterns of shared life, witness and resources has taken place. Convergence in faith and convergence in life necessarily belong together. Hence the importance of *reception* which is a process involving all members of the churches in reflection and discernment. Reception is not only an official response of the churches to documents, but is concerned with the whole life of the churches.

> *What steps need to be taken to maintain and strengthen what has been gained?*
>
> *What are the next steps the ecumenical movement needs to take?*
>
> *How can we achieve them?*

116. Different methods and forms of ecumenical activity are undertaken to enable the churches to move towards the goal of visible unity. These include the promotion of multilateral and bilateral dialogues resulting in convergence texts, common prayer (an example of which is the Week of Prayer for Christian Unity), and solidarity in suffering, witness and service.

> *What methods and forms of ecumenical activity are appropriate for the next steps in the search for unity?*
>
> *How can these different forms of actvity mutually enrich each other on the way to unity?*

117. All churches have to face the challenge that they cannot be satisfied to proclaim the Gospel of reconciliation as long as they remain divided. How can they demonstrate that in Christ Jesus forgiveness is offered as long as our memories remain unhealed and our histories unreconciled?

> *What steps can the churches take to repent and to forgive each other?*
>
> *How can churches become authentic instruments of reconciliation in a divided world?*

> *O God, holy and eternal Trinity,*
> *we pray for your Church in all the world.*
> *Sanctify its life; renew its worship;*
> *empower its witness; heal its divisions;*
> *make visible its unity.*

C

Appendices

Appendix I

MESSAGES

□ Introduction

As indicated in the editorial introduction, this appendix includes several of the messages received by the world conference. We regret that it has not been possible to print here all of the messages received. Those included come from larger, worldwide Christian bodies. They are printed in the order in which they were presented in plenary.

THE MOST REVEREND AND RIGHT HONOURABLE GEORGE CAREY, ARCHBISHOP OF CANTERBURY

Lambeth Palace, London

Dear Dr Gassmann,

I recognise the great importance of the Fifth World Conference on Faith and Order to be held in Santiago de Compostela, Spain.

The Conference comes at a significant point in ecumenical history. The visible unity of the Church is of primary importance if Christians are to witness faithfully to the Gospel in a divided world. I assure you both of my prayers and of the prayers of the Church of England.

Yours sincerely

+ George Cantuar

HIS ALL HOLINESS THE ECUMENICAL PATRIARCH BARTHOLOMEW I

To the esteemed Dr Mary Tanner, Moderator of the Faith and Order Commission, and to the distinguished delegates and participants of the Fifth World Conference on Faith and Order of the World Council of Churches, held at Santiago de Compostela, Spain, from 3 to 14 August 1993, grace and blessing from God our Father and the Lord Jesus Christ our Saviour.

It is with a great sense of satisfaction and hope that we welcome this important World Conference on Faith and Order with its most significant theme: "Towards

Koinonia in Faith, Life and Witness". Our Church, the Church of Constantinople which has been involved in the ecumenical movement from the beginning and has served continuously the ecumenical goal and vision of Church unity, will not cease to be committed to the efforts of Faith and Order, through its prayers as well as through the contribution of its delegation which on the occasion of this Conference is headed by His Eminence Archbishop Stylianos of Australia.

This Fifth World Conference of Faith and Order takes place after an interval of thirty years at a crucial moment of our history. As it has been observed the ecumenical movement has been undergoing for some time now a critical transition concerning its vision and goal in the midst of dramatic and historic changes that have been taking place in the world.

Our faith and our experience of the ecumenical pilgrimage, however, do not permit us to be pessimistic; they rather prompt us to continue and intensify our efforts to find ways in support of the ecumenical activity because the unity of the Church is now more than ever necessary.

We acknowledge with satisfaction that since the last World Conference in Montreal (1963), after a series of World Conferences in Lausanne (1927), Edinburgh (1937) and Lund (1952), the Faith and Order Commission and the ecumenical movement have grown up steadily through a number of great ecumenical events which have contributed to an enrichment of Christian history and made us all aware of the wonderful opportunities that lie ahead.

We express to all of you, beloved brothers and sisters coming from different Christian Churches and various confessional denominations, our joy and appreciation for such an historic event.

It is our sincere hope that your common consideration of "Koinonia in Faith, Life and Witness", may add decisively to all our previous efforts to receive together the divine gift of Church unity so that diversity among us may cease to be divisive and become, as at Pentecost, a living witness to the same redemptive reality.

Koinonia with the Triune God and with one another in Christ and in the Spirit, in which we participate only if we are prepared to humble ourselves and to repent, is the basis of the unity of the Church which we trust will inspire your deliberations.

We greet with great satisfaction the fact that Faith and Order has acknowledged the Creed of Nicea-Constantinople (381 AD) in its original form as the basis of our expression of the Apostolic Faith. We take the opportunity to propose that in view of our entrance into the third millennium the main leaders of contemporary Christianity make a common solemn declaration calling all Christians to build their unity on this foundation.

Bestowing our paternal blessings and good wishes we pray that the grace of our Lord Jesus Christ and the love of God the Father and the koinonia of the Holy Spirit be with you all.

Phanar, 5th of August 1993   Fervent intercessor before God

Bartholomew, by the grace of God Archbishop of Constantinople, New Rome and Ecumenical Patriarch

POPE JOHN PAUL II

To Dr Mary Tanner
Moderator of the Commission on Faith and Order
of the World Council of Churches

On the occasion of the Fifth World Conference on Faith and Order, meeting on 3-14 August 1993 at Santiago de Compostela, I extend warm greetings to all the participants and offer the assurance of my prayers that the Holy Spirit will guide and direct your deliberations on the significant theme "Towards Koinonia in Faith, Life and Witness".

I take this opportunity to express once again my regard for the Commission's patient dedication to the work of overcoming the divisions among Christians, for this discord — as the Fathers of the Second Vatican Council pointed out — "openly contradicts the will of Christ, provides a stumbling block to the world, and inflicts damage on the most holy cause of proclaiming the Good News to every creature" (*Unitatis Redintegratio*, 1). I wish likewise to reaffirm the commitment of the Catholic Church to promoting Christian unity, so that the prayer of Jesus "that they may all be one" (Jn 17:20) may be realized in accordance with his providential design for his flock.

As a means for achieving this incomparably important aim, reflection on the nature of *koinonia* seems especially appropriate, for ecclesial communion is not simply a subject of increasing theological interest but is a notion which the Sacred Scriptures use as a key for understanding the efficacy of the Lord's grace in the lives of his disciples. As Saint Paul writes, our call from God is "into the fellowship of his Son, Jesus Christ our Lord" (1 Cor 1:9). Made "partakers of the divine nature" (2 Pet 1:4), we participate in the very life shared by the Triune God: the Son in us and the Father in the Son (cf. Jn 17:23).

A deepened awareness of the profound mystery of ecclesial communion moves Christians to confess that God and not man is the source of the Church's unity; it leads them to repent of their sins against fraternal charity; and it encourages them, under the inspiring grace of the Holy Spirit, to work through prayer, word and action to attain that fullness of unity which Jesus Christ desires (cf. *Unitatis Redintegratio*, 4).

Important Faith and Order studies, in which Catholic theologians have also taken part for many years, have been of great service to the cause of Christian unity by identifying points of convergence and even agreement on issues over which believers have long been divided. This is indeed a significant accomplishment, which confirms hope in all who have the unity of Christians at heart. I join with you in praying that the Fifth World Conference on Faith and Order will, with God's assistance, bear abundant fruit in helping to resolve the remaining issues required for reaching visible unity in one faith and one Eucharistic fellowship. I ask the Holy Spirit to inspire in all present that "change of heart and holiness of life" (*ibid.*, 8) essential for responding to God's continual call to seek unity.

May the abundant gifts of the Triune God sustain you all in your efforts on behalf of Ecumenism.

Joannes Paulus PP. II

From the Vatican, 21 July 1993

HIS HOLINESS PATRIARCH ALEXY II OF MOSCOW AND ALL RUSSIA

Beloved-in-the-Lord Madam Moderator,
Dear Brothers and Sisters:

"Grace to you and peace from God our Father and the Lord Jesus Christ" (Rom. 1:7). May He grant us to confess with one mouth and one heart the apostolic faith of the Early Undivided Church which is the One Holy Catholic and Apostolic Church.

With these prayerful good wishes I warmly greet you as you have gathered together in Santiago de Compostela for the 5th World Conference on Faith and Order. I do it with a special joy, for precisely 75 years ago, in 1917, my great predecessor, who is now canonized by the Church as a confessor and martyr, His Holiness Patriarch Tikhon, welcomed and blessed the Faith and Order movement on behalf of the Council of the Russian Orthodox Church.

Despite the tribulations which befell our Church in the post-revolutionary period, a delegation of our Church took an active part in the first preparatory conference of the Faith and Order movement in August 1920 in Geneva.

On the final day of the Conference its participants were invited to attend the worship service at the Russian Orthodox church in Geneva. This event took place on the Day of the Transfiguration of our Lord.

Seventy-three years have passed since that significant conference in Geneva. We believe that the participants in the present conference in Santiago will come out with a careful analysis of the past and present of the Faith and Order movement, pointing out clearly and courageously the difficulties and joys they have experienced on the way, noting their achievements and failures and hopes for the future. It will help us to overcome the crisis and stagnation in Christians' progress towards the cherished goal of the ecumenical movement.

The 7th assembly in Canberra called the churches to the visible unity as koinonia in faith, life and witness. We are sure that the movement towards koinonia calls for unity in confessing the apostolic faith, for the Eucharistic communion, as well as for recognition of ministry in apostolic succession, and for a common basis of canonical order. This is the original and ultimate goal of the World Council of Churches and of the ecumenical movement as a whole.

We beseech the Lord that He may grant us all the wisdom and courage to be faithful witnesses and servants promoting the restoration of all-Christian unity in the One Holy Catholic and Apostolic Church. We trust you and rely upon you.

Grace of our Lord Jesus Christ and the love of God the Father and the communion of the Holy Spirit be with you all in your work and prayers.

WORLD ALLIANCE OF REFORMED CHURCHES

August 12, 1993

Dear Dr. Tanner,

In the name of the World Alliance of Reformed Churches, I send warm greetings to the Fifth World Conference on Faith and Order, meeting in Santiago de Compostela August 3-14, 1993.

By now, your meeting is nearly completed. I trust that the theme of *koinonia* in faith, life and witness has been fruitful, not least in calling attention to the real, yet not complete, communion we share, as churches, in Jesus Christ, and to the possibilities of fuller common life that real communion should afford.

We live in an age of social fragmentation, violence, and destruction of the environment which threaten human life itself. Yet this world also manifests signs of hope. We should seek to discern those signs, and by adding our participation and testimony to the power of the gospel, help turn them into concrete achievements. The Reformed tradition has held that faith, life, and witness are acted out not only in proclamation and sacramental life, but also in a communion of moral solidarity with all who do good and resist evil in the world.

I recall that the initiative for ecumenical study and action focused on justice, peace, and the integrity of creation first arose at the 21st General Council of the World Alliance of Reformed Churches at Ottawa in 1982. I am glad that these concerns are now on the way to being included in the work of Faith and Order, in cooperation with other units and departments of the W.C.C.

Reformed Christians acknowledge that they themselves remain divided in many parts of the world. Yet the Alliance reaffirms its commitment to work for the visible unity of the Church and to participate faithfully in bilateral and multilateral dialogues with other churches, confessional bodies, and communions.

May the grace of our Lord Jesus Christ, the love of God, and the communion of the Holy Spirit be with you all.

Jane Dempsey Douglass
President
The World Alliance of Reformed Churches

SUMMARY OF PLENARY SESSIONS

Plenary I, 4 August, 9h.

    Opening act of worship

    Moderator's opening remarks

    Introduction and greetings (the deputy mayor of Santiago, the president of the Xunta of Galicia, the archbishop of Santiago, the bishop of the Spanish Reformed Episcopal Church, the president of the Spanish Evangelical Church)

    Director's presentation

    Roll call (continued over several plenaries)

Plenary II, 4 August, 11h.

    Moderator's presentation, complementary presentations (Callam and Garcia Bachmann)

Plenary III, 4 August, 16h.

    Biblical presentation (Reumann)

Plenary IV, 5 August, 9h.15

    Biblical presentations (Onayeikan, Lee, Chan)
    Discussion of moderator's and director's presentations

Plenary V, 5 August, 11h.

    Presentations on the theme (Tutu, Zizioulas)

Plenary VI, 5 August, 16h.

    Presentations on the sub-themes (Pannenberg, Templeton, Khodr)

Plenary VII, 5 August, 18h.

    Discussion

    Greetings (the Archbishop of Canterbury, the Conference of European Churches, the Ecumenical Women's Synod of the Netherlands)

Plenary VIII, 10 August, 9h.15

    Spain: presentations on its religion, life and culture (Pose on origins; Fernandez on "the Way of Santiago"; Sanchez on Christian pluralism; Asensio on Protestantism; Hernando on the ecumenical movement in Spain)

    Greeting (the Religious Society of Friends, London Yearly Meeting)

Plenary IX, 10 August, 11h.30

Greetings (the Ecumenical Patriarch, the Pope)

Bishop Matthew's statement (on the Iakovos Fund)

Presentations on the future of ecumenical movement (Aagaard, Cassidy, Iakovos)

Plenary X, 12 August, 9h.15

Greetings (the Moscow Patriarchate)

First draft of Message — discussion

Reading of letter of "Pastors for Peace" mission to Cuba

Plenary XI, 12 August, 11h.15

Presentations on the future of the ecumenical movement (Joshua, Karefa-Smart, younger theologians)

Plenary XII, 12 August, 16h.

Report of sections I and II — discussion

Plenary XIII, 12 August, 18h.

Report of sections III and IV — discussion

Commending of section reports

Plenary XIV, 13 August, 9h.15

Presentations on Faith and Order and the WCC (Raiser, Keshishian)

Plenary XV, 13 August, 11h.

Greetings (WARC)

Second draft of Message — discussion

Presentations on Faith and Order and the WCC (YEMBA, Tarasar)

Plenary XVI, 13 August, 16h.

Presentation on Faith and Order and the WCC (Tillard)

Adoption of Message

Moderator's closing statement

Thanks

Closing prayer

SUMMARY OF WORSHIP
AND BIBLE STUDY ELEMENTS

A. Official worship events (all texts in English, Spanish, German and French)

Opening act, the opening plenary, 4 August 9h., plenary hall

Opening service, 4 August, 20h., Cathedral of St. James

Morning worship, 4-7 and 9-12 August, 8h.15, chapel, Seminario Mayor

Evening worship, 6, 9, 11, 12 August, 21h.30, chapel, Seminario Mayor

Orthodox vespers, 5 August, 21h.30, chapel, Seminario Mayor

Roman Catholic vespers, 7 August, 21h.30, chapel, Seminario Mayor

Spanish Protestant churches eucharist, 10 August, 19h.30, Franciscan Church

Silent meal with readings, 11 August, 20h., dining hall, Seminario Mayor

Vigil for victims of injustice, 11 August, 22h.-24h., chapel, Seminario Mayor

Closing service and procession, 13 August, 18h.30, Franciscan Church

Special venues:

One morning worship concluded around the fountain in the central courtyard of the Seminario Mayor

At the end of the closing worship a procession moved from the Franciscan Church through the streets of Santiago to the fountain in the central courtyard of the Seminario Mayor

B. Additional worship events coordinated through the worship team

Lima liturgy, 5-7, 9-13 August, 6h.30, small chapel, Seminario Mayor and chapel, Colegio La Salle

Lima liturgy, 8 August, 8h.30, chapel, Seminario Mayor

Oriental Orthodox liturgy, 8 August, 7h.30, oratory, Seminario Mayor

C. Biblical plenaries (all texts in English, Spanish, German and French)

Plenary III: "Koinonia in Scripture: Survey of Biblical Texts" by Prof. John Reumann

Plenary IV: "The Blessing Promised to the Nations — The Call of Abraham, Genesis 12:1-9" by the Rt Rev. John Onayeikan, "The Anointing at Bethany, John 12:1-8" by the Rev. Dr Dorothy Lee, "Sharing the Trinitarian Life, John 17:20-26, 1 John 1:1-4" by Dr Simon Chan

D. Publications: see Appendix IV

Appendix IV

OFFICIAL MATERIALS
RELATED TO THE WORLD CONFERENCE

Most materials were produced in English, Spanish, German and French

A. Discussion paper

Towards Koinonia in Faith, Life and Witness: A Discussion Paper, April 1993, Faith and Order paper no. 161, Geneva, WCC Publications, 1993.

B. Other preparatory texts

"The Fifth World Conference on Faith and Order", special issue of *The Ecumenical Review*, vol. 45, no. 1, January 1993, ed. Thomas F. Best.

Documentary History of Faith and Order 1963-1993, ed. Günther Gassmann, Faith and Order paper no. 159, Geneva, WCC Publications, 1993.

Lausanne 1927 to Santiago de Compostela 1993: The Faith and Order World Conferences, and Issues and Results of the Working Period 1963-1993, Paul A. Crow & Günther Gassmann, Faith and Order paper no. 160, Geneva, WCC Publications, 1993 (two articles reprinted from the above-cited issue of *The Ecumenical Review*).

Regional Consultations in Preparation for the Fifth World Conference on Faith and Order, Santiago de Compostela, August 1993: Summary of Reports, eds Thomas F. Best & Günther Gassmann, Faith and Order paper no. 162, Commission on Faith and Order, Geneva, WCC Publications, 1993.

The Unity of the Church as Koinonia: Ecumenical Perspectives on the 1991 Canberra Statement on Unity, a study document requested by the Joint Working Group, eds Günther Gassmann & John A. Radano, Faith and Order paper no. 163, Geneva, WCC Publications, 1993.

C. Worship and Bible study texts

Frances M. Young, *All of You Are One in Christ Jesus: Bible Studies*, Geneva, Commission on Faith and Order, World Council of Churches, 1993.

Prayer card.

Worship Book, Commission on Faith and Order, World Council of Churches, 1993.

Celebrating Community: Songs and Prayers of Unity, compiled by Janet Crawford, Terry MacArthur & Thomas F. Best, Geneva, WCC Publications, 1993.

Partakers of the Promise: Biblical Visions of Koinonia, ed. Thomas F. Best in consultation with the United Bible Societies, Geneva. Produced for the Faith and Order Commission of the World Council of Churches by the United Bible Societies, 1993.

In addition, five *banners* bearing the names of the venues of the five Faith and Order world conferences (Lausanne 1927, Edinburgh 1937, Lund 1952, Montreal 1963, Santiago 1993) were produced and used to integrate the various services.

D. Conference information

Conference Handbook: Fifth World Conference on Faith and Order, Santiago de Compostela, 1993, Geneva, Faith and Order Commission, 1993.

"Towards a Communion in Faith, Life and Witness: Fifth World Conference", brochure, 1993.

E. Related texts: ecclesiology and ethics

Costly Unity: Koinonia and Justice, Peace and the Integrity of Creation, report of the consultation on koinonia and JPIC sponsored jointly by Faith and Order (Unit I) and Justice, Peace and the Integrity of Creation (Unit III) of the WCC. (For the full publication of the meeting see *Costly Unity: Koinonia and Justice, Peace and Creation. Presentations and Reports from the World Council of Churches Consultation in Rønde, Denmark, February 1993*, eds Thomas F. Best and Wesley Granberg-Michaelson, Geneva, World Council of Churches Unit III and Unit I, 1993.)

F. Reports from the world conference

Immediately after the world conference the resulting texts were published together with the discussion paper as *Fifth World Conference on Faith and Order, Santiago de Compostela 1993: Message, Section Reports, Discussion Paper*, Faith and Order paper no. 164, Geneva, WCC Publications, 1993.

On the Way to Fuller Koinonia: Official Report of the Fifth World Conference on Faith and Order, eds Thomas F. Best & Günther Gassmann, Faith and Order paper no. 166, Geneva, WCC Publications, 1994.

Appendix V

BY-LAWS OF THE
FAITH AND ORDER COMMISSION

1. Meaning

In these by-laws:

The Commission means the Commission on Faith and Order of the World Council of Churches and includes both the Plenary Commission and the Standing Commission.

The Officers of the Commission mean the Moderator and Vice-Moderators of the Plenary Commission and Standing Commission.

The Secretariat means the Secretariat of the Commission on Faith and Order.

The Council means the World Council of Churches.

The Assembly means the Assembly of the World Council of Churches.

The Central Committee means the Central Committee of the World Council of Churches.

2. Aim and functions

The aim of the Commission is to proclaim the oneness of the church of Jesus Christ and to call the churches to the goal of visible unity in one faith and one eucharistic fellowship, expressed in worship and in common life in Christ, in order that the world may believe.

The functions of the Commission are:
a) to study such questions of faith, order and worship as bear on this task and to examine such social, cultural, political, racial, and other factors as affect the unity of the church;
b) to study the theological implications of the existence and development of the ecumenical movement and to keep prominently before the Council the obligation to work towards unity;
c) to promote prayer for unity;
d) to study matters in the present relationship of the churches to one another which cause difficulties or which particularly require theological clarification;
e) to study the steps being taken by the churches towards closer unity with one another and to provide information concerning such steps;
f) to bring to the attention of the churches, by the best means available, reports of Faith and Order meetings and studies;
g) to provide opportunities for consultation among those whose churches are engaged in union negotiations or other specific efforts towards unity.

• In force at the time of the world conference.

The Commission, in pursuing its work, observes the following principles:

i)   It seeks to draw the churches into conversation and study but recognizes that only the churches themselves are competent to initiate steps towards union, by entering into negotiations with one another. The work of the Commission is to act, on their invitation, as helper and adviser.

ii) It will conduct its work in such a way that all are invited to share reciprocally in giving and receiving and no one is asked to be disloyal to his convictions nor to compromise them. Differences are to be clarified and recorded as honestly as agreements.

3. Organization

a)   The Faith and Order Commission is constitutionally responsible to the Central Committee. It is part of Programme Unit I on Faith and Witness together with the Sub-units on Church and Society, on World Mission and Evangelism, and on Dialogue with People of Living Faiths.

b)   The Faith and Order Commission shall consist of a Plenary Commission and a Standing Commission.

c)   The Plenary Commission will have as its primary task theological study, debate, and appraisal. It will initiate the programme of the Faith and Order Commission, lay down general guidelines for it, and share in its communication to the churches.

d)   The Standing Commission will have as its task to implement the programme, to guide the staff in the development of Faith and Order work, and to make administrative decisions on behalf of the Faith and Order Commission, to supervise the ongoing work and to act on behalf of the Commission in between meetings of the Plenary Commission. It shall represent the Commission in relation to the Programme Unit I Committee and Council generally.

e)   The Plenary Commission shall consist of not more than 120 members (including the Officers and the other members of the Standing Commission). The Standing Commission shall consist of a Moderator and not more than thirty other members.

f)   Both the Plenary Commission and the Standing Commission shall be appointed by the Central Committee, in the following manner:

i)   The Plenary Commission, at its last meeting before the Assembly, shall appoint a Nominations Committee to prepare a list of names for the election of a new Standing Commission by the Central Committee.

ii) The Central Committee shall appoint the Moderator and the members of the Standing Commission, who hold office until the following Assembly of the World Council of Churches. The Standing Commission shall elect not more than four Vice-Moderators from among its members. The Moderator and the Vice-Moderators shall be the officers of both the Standing Commission and the Plenary Commission.

iii) The Standing Commission shall submit to the Central Committee a list of candidates from which shall be chosen the members of the Plenary Commission, who will hold office until the next Assembly.

iv) Vacancies on the Plenary Commission and the Standing Commission shall be filled by the Central Committee on the nomination of the Standing Commission.

g) Since the size of the Commission precludes full representation of member churches of the Council, appointment shall be made on the basis of personal capacity to serve the purposes of the Commission. At the same time, care shall be taken to secure a reasonable geographical and confessional representation of churches on the Commission and among the Officers and Secretaries. The Plenary Commission should include in its membership a sufficient number of women, young and lay persons.

h) Persons who are members of churches which do not belong to the Council but which confess Jesus Christ as God and Saviour are eligible for membership of the Commission.

i) Before any candidate is nominated for appointment by the Central Committee, steps shall be taken to ensure that his name is acceptable to the church to which he belongs. A member should be willing to accept some responsibility for communication between the Faith and Order Commission and his church and ecumenical bodies in his country.

4. The Secretariat

a) The Standing Commission, after due consultation between the Officers of the Commission and the General Secretary of the Council, shall propose for nomination the members of the Secretariat for appointment and reappointment by the Central Committee or the Executive Committee of the Council.

b) A sufficient number of Secretaries shall be appointed for the adequate performance of the work of the Commission.

c) The Secretariat shall maintain full consultation and cooperation with the General Secretariat of the Council, with Programme Unit I, and as required with other Units of the Council.

d) The Secretariat shall be responsible for ensuring the continuation of the work of the Plenary Commission, in accordance with the policy agreed at meetings of the Plenary Commission or Standing Commission. To this end the Secretariat shall keep in regular contact with the Officers and other members of the Commission.

5. World Conferences

a) World Conferences on Faith and Order may be held when, on recommendations of the Standing Commission acting in the name of the Commission, the Central Committee so approves.

b) The invitation to take part in such Conferences shall be addressed to churches throughout the world which confess Jesus Christ as God and Saviour.

c) Such Conferences shall consist primarily of delegates appointed by the churches to represent them. Youth delegates, special advisers, and observers may also be invited.

d) Careful attention shall be given to the communication of the reports and recommendations of the World Conferences to the churches.

6. Meetings of the Commission

a) The Plenary Commission shall meet at least once between Assemblies, but may be convened at any time by the Standing Commission after clearance with the Executive Committee of the Council.

b) The Standing Commission shall normally meet every year but may be convened at any time by the Moderator in consultation with other Officers of the Commission or at the request of not less than one-third of the members of the Standing Commission.

c) The Secretariat will be responsible for giving due notice of meetings of both the Plenary Commission and the Standing Commission, for keeping its minutes and other records, and, in consultation with the Moderator, for preparing its agenda.

d) A member of the Plenary Commission, by advance notice to the Secretariat, may name a proxy acceptable to his church to represent him at any meeting at which he is unable to be present.

e) A member of the Standing Commission may name a person to represent him at any meeting at which he is unable to be present but such a person may not vote.

f) Other persons may be invited to be present and to speak, if the Moderator so rules, but not to vote. In particular, in order to secure representation of its study groups, members of these may be invited to attend either body as consultants.

g) The Moderator of the Commission or, in his absence, one of the Vice-Moderators, shall preside at such meetings. In the absence of these officers, the meeting shall elect its own Moderator. One-third of the total membership (including proxies) shall constitute a quorum.

h) The Commission shall normally conduct its business according to the rules of procedure of the Central Committee. Questions arising about procedure shall be decided by a majority vote of those present and voting.

i) If, at any time when it is inconvenient to hold a meeting of the Standing Commission, the Moderator and Secretariat shall decide that there is business needing immediate action by that Commission, it shall be permissible for them to obtain by post the opinions of its members, and the majority opinion thus ascertained shall be treated as equivalent to the decision of a duly convened meeting.

7. Faith and Order studies

a) The Standing Commission, giving due attention to the general guidelines laid down by the Plenary Commission (see 3c), shall formulate and carry through the study programme.

b) The Secretariat, as authorized by the Standing Commision, shall invite persons to serve on the study groups and consultations. They shall pay particular regard to the need to involve members of both the Plenary Commission and the Standing Commission in the study programme, whether by membership of study group, consultations, or by written consultation. Due regard shall be paid to special competence in the fields of study concerned, and to the need for the representation of a variety of ecclesiastical traditions and theological viewpoints.

c) Study groups shall normally include both those who are, and those who are not, members of the Commission. They may also include persons who do not belong to member churches of the Council.

d) In planning such studies, all possible contact shall be sought or maintained with allied work already in progress under such auspices as those of regional or national councils or of individual churches, or of ecumenical institutes and theological faculties or departments.

e) Study groups shall prepare reports, as requested, for discussion in the Commission, at World Conferences on Faith and Order, or at Assemblies. Any such report should bear a clear indication of its status.

f) The publication of such reports and of other Faith and Order papers shall be the responsibility of the Secretariat, provided that adequate financial resources are available.

8. Finance

a) The normal working expenses of the Commission and its Secretariat shall be borne by the general budget of the Council. The Secretariat and the Standing Commission shall be responsible for drawing up an annual budget in conformity with the financial procedures of the World Council of Churches, and for submitting it through normal Council procedures, to the Finance Committee of the Central Committee.

b) There shall be a financial report annually to the Standing Commission.

c) The Standing Commission shall be responsible for deciding the allocation of available funds to particular studies, and the Secretariat shall communicate such decisions to the officers of study groups.

9. Revision of by-laws

These by-laws may be amended by the Standing Commission subject to the approval of the Central Committee. Any proposed amendment must be circulated in writing to the members of the Plenary Commission not less than three months before the meeting at which it is to be considered for adoption and, for adoption, requires the approval of two-thirds of the members of the Standing Commission present and voting.

10. Communication with the churches

The Plenary Commission and the Standing Commission shall be concerned to facilitate communication with the churches. They shall make generally available results of studies where such studies are formally communicated to the churches through the Central Committee. In certain studies, the Commission may invite a formal response from the churches.

MEMBERSHIP OF THE FAITH AND ORDER PLENARY COMMISSION

Moderator

*Dr Mary TANNER (Church of England), Council of Christian Unity, Church House, Great Smith Street, London SW1P 3NZ, England

Vice-moderators

*The Very Rev. Prof. Emmanuel CLAPSIS (Greek Orthodox Archdiocese of North and South America/Ecumenical Patriarchate), Hellenic College, 50 Goddard Avenue, Brookline, MA 02146, USA

*The Rev. Dr Paul A. CROW Jr (Disciples of Christ), P.O. Box 1986, Indianapolis, IN 46206, USA

*The Rev. Araceli ROCCHIETTI (Methodist Church), Julio Cesar 1264, Apt. 702, Montevideo, Uruguay

*Mrs Veronia SWAI (Evangelical Lutheran Church in Tanzania), Women's Work, P.O. Box 195, Moshi, Tanzania

*The Rev. Fr Jean-Marie R. TILLARD (Roman Catholic Church), Couvent Dominicain, 96 Empress Road, Ottawa, Ontario K1R 7G3, Canada

Members

Deaconess Bella ADEMOLA (Methodist Church), 11 Ikoyi Crescent, Ikoyi, Lagos, Nigeria

Dr Charles AMJAD-ALI (United Church of Pakistan), Christian Study Centre, 126-B Muree Road, Rawalpindi Cant., Pakistan

Dr Kamol ARAYAPRATEEP (Church of Christ in Thailand), 14 Pramuan Road, 10500 Bangkok, Thailand

Archbishop Mesrob ASHJIAN (Armenian Apostolic Church, Cilicia), Eastern Prelacy, 138 East 38th Street, New York, NY 10016, USA

*The Rev. Christobella BAGH (Church of North India), Bishop's House, Christ Church Compound, Bhagalpur, Bihar 821 001, India

The Rev. Alyson BARNETT-COWAN (Anglican Church of Canada), Anglican Church of Canada, 600 Jarvis Street, Toronto, Ontario M4Y 2J6, Canada

The Rev. Eva BREBOVSZKY-GERÖFI (Lutheran Church in Hungary), Deak Ter 4, 1052 Budapest, Hungary

Prof. Dr Wolfgang BIENERT (Evangelical Church in Germany: United), Hahnbergstrasse 5, 35043 Marburg-Cappel, Germany

Metropolitan BISHOY of Damietta (Coptic Orthodox Church), Midan Sorour — Coptic Church, Damiette, Egypt

Prof. Dr Klauspeter BLASER (Swiss Protestant Church Federation), Université de Lausanne, Faculté de théologie, 2 Dorigny, 1015 Lausanne, Switzerland

---

* = Faith and Order Standing Commission member

The Rev. Canon Hugh Blessing BOE (Church of the Province of Melanesia, Anglican), P.O. Box 19, Honiara, Solomon Islands

Prof. Dr Roberta BONDI (United Methodist Church), Candler School of Theology, Emory University, Atlanta, GA 30322, USA

The Rev. Fr Frans BOUWEN (Roman Catholic Church), Sainte Anne, B P 19079, Jerusalem, Israel

The Rev. Dr Sven-Erik BRODD (Church of Sweden), Sysslomansgatan 4, Box 438, 751 06 Uppsala, Sweden

The Rt Rev. Dr Manas BUTHELEZI (Evangelical Lutheran Church in South Africa), ELCSA Central Diocese, P.O. Box 1210, Roodeport 1725, Republic of South Africa

*The Rev. Neville CALLAM (Jamaica Baptist Union), Tarrant Baptist Church, 51 Molynes Road, Kingston 10, Jamaica, West Indies

Metropolitan CHRYSANTHOS of Limassol (Church of Cyprus), P.O. Box 6091, Limassol, Cyprus

The Rev. Keith CLEMENTS (Baptist Union of Great Britain), 28 Halsbury Road, Westbury Park, Bristol BS6 7SR, England

*The Rev. Janet CRAWFORD (Anglican Church in Aotearoa, New Zealand and Polynesia), St John's College, 202 St John's Road, Auckland 5, New Zealand

*The Rev. Martin CRESSEY (United Reformed Church), Principal's Lodge, Westminster College, Madingley Road, Cambridge CB3 0AB, England

*Metropolitan DANIEL of Moldavia and Bukovina (Romanian Orthodox Church), 16, Bd Stefan cel Mare, 6600 Iasi, Romania

The Rev. Prof. Kortwright DAVIS (Episcopal Church), 11414 Woodson Avenue, Kensington, MD 20895, USA

*Dr Sophie DEICHA (Archdiocese of the Russian Orthodox Parishes in Western Europe/ Ecumenical Patriarchate), 50, rue de Mareil, 78100 St Germain-en-Laye, France

The Very Rev. Prof. Dr George DRAGAS (Greek Orthodox Archdiocese of Thyateira and Great Britain/Ecumenical Patriarchate), University of Durham, Department of Theology, Abbey House, Palace Green, Durham DH1 3RS, England

*The Right Rev. Sigqibo DWANE (Church of the Province of Southern Africa, Anglican), The Order of Ethiopia, 508a Landsdowne Road, Landsdowne 7780, Republic of South Africa

Ms Marguerite FASSINOU (Protestant Methodist Church), B P 571, Porto Novo, Republic of Benin

Prof. Dr Pavel FILIPI (Evangelical Church of the Czech Brethren), Belgicka 22, 120 00 Praha 2, Czech Republic

Prof. Dr Kyriaki FITZGERALD (Greek Orthodox Archdiocese of North and South America/ Ecumenical Patriarchate), P.O. Box 477, Sagamore Village, MA 02561, USA

*The Rev. Prof. Duncan FORRESTER (Church of Scotland), 25 Kingsburgh Road, Edinburgh EH12 6DZ, Scotland

Ms Olga GANABA (Russian Orthodox Church), Department of External Church Relations, St Daniel Monastery, 22 Danilovsky val, 113 191 Moscow, CIS

Prof. Dr Beverley GAVENTA (Disciples of Christ), Columbia Seminary, 701 Columbia Drive, Box 520, Decatur, GA 30032, USA

Sister Donna GEERNAERT, SC (Roman Catholic Church), 90 Parent Avenue, Ottawa, Ontario K1N 7B1, Canada

The Rev. Dr J.W. GLADSTONE (Church of South India), Principal, Kerala United Theological Seminary, Kanaammoola, Trivandrum 595 011, India

Dr Salesi T. HAVEA (Methodist Church of Tonga), P.O. Box 57, Nuku'alofa, Tonga

Prof. Dr Mark S. HEIM (American Baptist Churches), Andover Newton Theological School, Department of Christian Religion, 210 Herrick Road, Andover Centre, MA 02159, USA

Ms Justina HILUKILUAH (Church of the Province of Southern Africa, Anglican), P.O. Box 57, Windhoek 9000, Namibia

Prof. Dr L.A. HOEDEMAKER (Netherlands Reformed Church), Wassenberghstraat 58, 9718 LN Groningen, Netherlands

*Prof. Dr Thomas HOYT (Christian Methodist Episcopal Church), Hartford Seminary, Hartford, CT 06105, USA

Prof. Dr Hristov Stojanov HRISTOV (Bulgarian Orthodox Church), ul. Stefan Karadja 8, 1000 Sofia, Bulgaria

*Metropolitan Dr G. Yohanna IBRAHIM (Syrian Orthodox Patriarchate of Antioch), Syrian Orthodox Archbishopric, P.O. Box 4194, Aleppo, Syria

Sister Margaret JENKINS CSB (Roman Catholic Church), Brigidine Convent, 12 Mary Street, Clayton, Vic. 3168, Australia

Metropolitan Prof. Dr JOHN (Zizioulas) of Pergamon (Ecumenical Patriarchate), Harilaou Trikoupi 99, 145 63 Kefalari-Kifissia, Greece

The Rev. Prof. Dr Keiji KANDA (United Church of Christ in Japan), 5-1-36-301 Kamikotoen, Nishinomiya-shi, Hyogo-ken 662, Japan

Ms Najila Abou-Sawan KASSAB (National Evangelical Synod of Syria and Lebanon), P.O. Box 70890, Antelias, Lebanon

Mgr Prof. Dr Aloys KLEIN (Roman Catholic Church), Johann-Adam-Möhler-Institut, Leostrasse 13a, 33098 Paderborn, Germany

The Rev. Arthur KO LAY (Myanmar Baptist Convention), Myanmar Baptist Convention, 143, Minye Kyawswa Road, Lanmadaw, P.O. Box 506, Yangon, Myanmar

The Rev. Fr Johns Abraham KONAT (Malankara Orthodox Syrian Church), Pampakuda, (via) Muvattupuzha, Kerala 686 667, India

The Rev. Dr Abraham KURUVILLA (Mar Thoma Syrian Church), Holy Trinity Anglican Church, P.O. Box 115, Erskine Ville, NSW 2043, Australia

The Rev. Fr K. Joseph LABI (Greek Orthodox Patriarchate of Alexandria), Orthodox Church, P.O. Box 10, Larteh, Ghana

Dom Emmanuel LANNE OSB (Roman Catholic Church), Monastère Bénédictin, 5590 Chevetogne, Belgium

The Rev. Dr Dorothy LEE (Uniting Church of Australia), Theological Hall, Ormond College, College Crescent, Parkville, Vic, 3052, Australia

*Prof. Dr Kyung Sook LEE (Methodist Church of Korea), 9-201 Chungwha Apt., Itaewondong, Yongsan-ku, 140 200 Seoul, Korea

Dr Lars LINDBERG (Mission Covenant Church of Sweden), Kottlavägen 116, 181 41 Lidingö, Sweden

*Prof. Nicolas LOSSKY (Russian Orthodox Church), 66, rue d'Hautpoul, 75019 Paris, France

The Rev. Harald MALSCHITZKY (Evangelical Church of Lutheran Confession in Brazil), Caixa Postal 2876, 90001-970 Porto Alegre — RS, Brazil

The Rev. Fr Marcello MAMMARELLA (Roman Catholic Church), 1, via Raffaello, 65124 Pescara, Italy

The Rev. Dr Frank J. MATERA (Roman Catholic Church), Catholic University of America, School of Religious Studies, Department of Theology, Washington, DC 20064, USA

*The Rev. Dr Melanie MAY (Church of the Brethren), Colgate Rochester Divinity School, Bexley Hall, Crozer Theological Seminary, 1100 South Goodman Street, Rochester, NY 14620, USA

Bishop Dr MELCHEZEDEK (Ethiopian Orthodox Church), P.O. Box 1283, Addis Ababa, Ethiopia

Dr Nestor MIGUEZ (Methodist Church), ISEDET, Camacua 282, 1406 Buenos Aires, Argentina

The Rev. Dr Samuel MWANIKI (Presbyterian Church of East Africa), Presbyterian Church of East Africa, P.O. Box 48268, Nairobi, Kenya

The Rev. James NDYABAHIKA (Province of the Church of Uganda, Anglican), Uganda Joint Christian Council, P.O. Box 30154, Nakivubo-Kampala, Uganda

The Rev. Fr Felix NEEFJES OFM (Roman Catholic Church), Caixa Postal 17, Betim — MG 32501 — 970, Brazil

Dr Kirsten Busch NIELSEN (Evangelical Lutheran Church of Denmark), Avangen 86, 5750 Ringe, Denmark

The Rev. Dr Elizabeth NORDBECK (United Church of Christ), Dean, Andover Newton Theological School, 210 Herrick Road, Newton Centre, MA O2159, USA

*Sister Dr Mary O'DRISCOLL (Roman Catholic Church), Convitto San Tommaso, 20, via degli Ibernesi, 00184 Rome, Italy

*The Most Rev. John ONAIYEKAN (Roman Catholic Church), Bishop's House, P.O. Box 286, Garki, Abouja, Federal Capital Territory, Nigeria

Prof. Alexy OSIPOV (Russian Orthodox Church), Department of External Church Relations, St Daniel Monastery, 22 Danilovsky val, 113 191 Moscow, CIS

The Rev. Prof. Martin F.G. PARMENTIER (Old Catholic Church), Burg. Lammboylaan 19, 1217 LB Hilversum, Netherlands

Prof. Dr Vlassios PHEIDAS (Church of Greece), 500 Vouliagmenis Street, 174 56 Alimos, Athens, Greece

Dr Juha PIHKALA (Evangelical Lutheran Church of Finland), Sotkankatu 18 B 57, 33230 Tamperere, Finland

The Rev. Dr Cecil M. ROBECK (Assemblies of God), Dean, Fuller Theological Seminary, 135 N. Oakland Avenue, Pasadena, CA 91182, USA

*The Rev. Raquel RODRIGUEZ (Lutheran Church of El Salvador), c/o Division of Overseas Ministries, Christian Church (Disciples of Christ), P.O. Box 1986, Indianapolis, IN 46206, USA

*The Right Rev. Barry ROGERSON (Church of England), Bishop of Bristol, Bishop's House, Clifton Hill, Bristol BS8 1WB, England

*The Rev. Dr William G. RUSCH (Evangelical Lutheran Church in America), ELCA/OEA, 8765 West Higgins Rod, Chicago, IL 60631, USA

The Rev. Fr Jorge SCAMPINI OP (Roman Catholic Church), Convento Santo Domingo, Defensa 422, 1065 Buenos Aires, Argentina

*Prof. Dr Turid Karlsen SEIM (Church of Norway), Det Teologiske Fakultet, Universitet i Oslo, Postboks 1023 Blindern, 0315 Oslo 5, Norway

Dr Matthias SENS (Evangelical Church in Germany: Church Province of Saxony [United]), Evangelisches Konsistorium, Am Dom 2, Postfach 122, 39104 Magdeburg, Germany

Dr David T. SHANNON, President (National Baptist Convention), Andover Newton Theological School, 210 Herrick Road, Newton Centre, MA 02159, USA

The Rev. Dr Herman SHASTRI (Methodist Church in Malaysia), Wesley Methodist Church, No. 9, Lorong 6/2, 46000 Petaling Jaya, Selangor, Malaysia

The Rev. Einar SITOMPUL (Batak Christian Church [Lutheran]), STT Jakarta, Jl. Proklamasi 27, Jakarta, Indonesia

Dr Constance TARASAR (Orthodox Church in America), 40 Beaumont Circle, Apt. 4, Yonkers, NY 10710, USA

*Prof. Evangelos THEODOROU (Church of Greece), Agathoupoleos 44, 112 52 Athens, Greece

The Rev. Livingstone THOMPSON (Moravian Church in Jamaica), Trinity Moravian Manse, 35 Montgomery Avenue, Kingston 10, Jamaica, West Indies

The Rev. Lucretia VAN OMMEREN (Evangelical Lutheran Church in Surinam), Evangelisch Lutherse Kerk, Waterkant 102, P.O. Box 585, Paramaribo, Surinam

The Rev. Dr Wismoady WAHONO (East Java Christian Church [Reformed]), Gereja Kristen Jawi Wetan, Jln S. Supriadi 18, Malang 65147, East Java, Indonesia

*Prof. Dr Dorothea WENDEBOURG (Evangelical Church in Germany: Evangelical Lutheran Church of Hanover), Düstere-Eichen-Strasse 60, 37073 Göttingen, Germany

Prof. Dr Gunther WENZ (Evangelical Church in Germany: Evangelical Lutheran Church of Bavaria), Himmelreichstrasse 2/I, 80538 München, Germany

The Rev. Olivia WESLEY (Methodist Church), The Methodist Church, 4 George Street, P.O. Box 64, Freetown, Sierra Leone

Ms Catrin WILLIAMS (Presbyterian Church of Wales), University College of N. Wales, Department of Theology, Bangor, Wales, Great Britain

Prof. Dr Antoinette Clark WIRE (Presbyterian Church [USA]), San Francisco Theological Seminary, 2 Kensington Road, San Anselmo, CA 94960, USA

*The Rev. Dr YEMBA Kekumba (Church of Christ in Zaire — Methodist Community), Africa University, P.O. Box 1320, Mutare, Zimbabwe

*The Rev. Dr YEOW Choo Lak (Presbyterian Church in Singapore), ATESEA, 324 Onan Road, Singapore 1542, Republic of Singapore

Members of the Secretariat

Dr Silke-Petra BERGJAN (Evangelical Church in Germany: Reformed) (till 30 September 1993)

The Rev. Dr Thomas F. BEST (Disciples of Christ)

Ms Béatrice FLEURY (Roman Catholic Church), administrative assistant

The Rev. Dr Günther GASSMANN (Evangelical Church in Germany: Lutheran), director

The Rev. Dr Dagmar HELLER (Evangelical Church in Germany: United) (as from 1 October 1993)

The Very Rev. Prof. Dr Gennadios LIMOURIS (Ecumenical Patriarchate) (till 30 June 1993)

Mrs Renate SBEGHEN (Evangelical Church in Germany), administrative assistant

Vikarin Ute THRÄNE (Evangelical Church in Germany: Lutheran), intern (1 November 1992 — 31 March 1993)